D1569551

INSIDE
NUMBER
10

INSIDE NUMBER 10

Marcia Williams

Coward, McCann & Geoghegan, Inc.

New York

DA
592
W47
1972 b

First American Edition 1972

Copyright © 1972 by Marcia Williams

SBN: 698-10484-6
Library of Congress Catalog Card Number: 72-76686

Printed in the United States of America

To My Mother and Father

Foreword

When I was invited to write a book about my job, I wanted to do so in order that others might know a little of what it is like to work for a leading politician, and more important, what it is like working for a Prime Minister at 10 Downing Street. I hope what follows has in some small way achieved that objective.

First and foremost I must thank Harold Wilson for giving me permission to write the book while still in his employ. Secondly, I want to express my deep gratitude to Terence Lancaster for the role he played in making it possible, with his editorial assistance, professional expertise, and great good humour. The book was put together by tape-recordings I made of all the events I wanted to recall. Thereafter the typed drafts of those tapes were rewritten by myself, and then edited by Terry. All that has been expressed is completely personal and subjective. It is how I saw it all.

My thanks are due, too, to my sister; to Rosemary Dehavilland for her typing of tapes and redrafts, and to Doreen Andrew and Fay Meek for the help they gave so readily. I am indebted to all the staff in Mr Wilson's office. To Joe Haines who has since the Election defeat been Mr Wilson's constant companion, helper and adviser; to my brother, Tony Field, who has been organizing the working of the office, with help from John Scholefield Allen.

The 1970 Election defeat has wrought many changes, some curious, in the characters and the scenario within the Labour

Party. But that is another story. I have no doubt the principals I have been privileged to work with and for will before too long be returning to the unfinished business of that Labour Government.

Contents

Illustrations follow page 210

INSIDE
NUMBER
10

If, of all words of tongue and pen,
The saddest are, 'It might have been',
More sad are these we daily see:
'It is, but hadn't ought to be'.

Bret Harte

I

Prologue

That the sun shone right to the end of the 1970 election campaign was the most ironic thing of all. It was shining when the Prime Minister drove to Buckingham Palace on 18 May to ask for a Dissolution, and it was shining still when I followed him into No. 10 Downing Street just before 7.00 a.m. on the morning of 19 June, for his last few hours in office. We had wanted a sunshine election and we got it. All politicians pray for good weather; traditionally it is supposed to help the party in power. Certainly it is true that it helps the party with an inferior machine, and nobody in their right mind has ever pretended that Labour has the superior machine. We could, and did, blame many factors for our defeat, but not the weather. That at least was on Labour's side. Or was it?

I recall the weather breaking only once during the campaign – on 16 June, the day the Prime Minister left No. 10 for the last time as a Prime Minister with power. There was a great storm that afternoon, and as he walked the few feet from the front door to the car that was taking him to Euston Station for the journey north and the final phase of the campaign, he was spattered with rain. One member of our political staff remarked that this was not exactly a good sign, but no one paid any attention to that particular omen.

We relied on more modern superstitions. They were called opinion polls and they showed we could not lose.

Curiously enough, this was the first election I was persuaded we would win. In 1964 I was convinced we had lost. We had an office bet, initiated by George Wigg, and my forecast for the result was a Tory majority of twenty-five. Even in 1966, when we managed to achieve a majority of ninety-seven, I still had forebodings of defeat to such a degree that, when the Prime Minister made his election announcement, I insisted that the political office equipment not needed for the campaign itself should be packed ready to move out. But 1970 was different. The sun and the polls combined to deceive us all.

We were not alone in being misguided. Leading Conservatives have since admitted that they were equally convinced of our ultimate victory, though I suspect they must have had some inkling of the trends developing as they received reports from their constituency organizations and their private daily poll.

The general picture, however, was one of success. The book-makers made us twenty to one favourites. Week after week the polls showed us ahead, and on the Friday before polling day, there came what most believed to be the ultimate proof. That evening it was revealed that the National Opinion Poll, the poll on which we in the Labour Party placed most emphasis, was putting Labour 12·4 per cent ahead. When I heard this I took two hours off duty for what I thought was a justifiable reason. I believed I should look back and regard it as my first celebration.

In those days it was believed that the maximum margin of error in a poll was three per cent. That put Labour 9·4 per cent ahead on NOP if you allowed for the maximum error. But even if you doubled the previously accepted margin of error, then Labour, if NOP was right, would still have a 6·4 per cent lead.

By that time there were few people who believed that the Tories could catch up. It seemed certain that Harold Wilson would be the first Prime Minister since Lord Liverpool in the 1820s to win three General Elections in a row – to achieve the political hat trick.

But, of course, this did not happen. As soon as that first result from Guildford flashed on the television screen in the Prime Minister's suite at the Adelphi Hotel in Liverpool we knew it was all over. The result showed a 5·3 per cent swing to the Conservatives. The party given by the Prime Minister to the Press was over by then, and he was sitting by himself on a settee facing the screen. Mrs Wilson, his political staff and some close friends were with him. He caught my eye and made a slight grimace. We both knew that unless Guildford proved to be a wild and isolated aberration, which was clearly unlikely, then the only question which remained to be answered was the size of the Conservative majority we would face.

That was the unanswered political question. But now there were before us enormous personal problems to be faced and resolved. There were also future political tactics to be decided. I went and sat next to him and we very quietly exchanged our views and assessments of the position. As we sat there, Harold had, at that moment of time, a town house in Downing Street and a country house at Chequers. Soon he would have neither. The family had sold their home in Hampstead Garden Suburb some time before. The only place they could call their own was their modest bungalow in the Isles of Scilly. Good for their holidays but not exactly a practicable or ideal base for the Leader of the Opposition! They also had a nice fat overdraft at the bank. All prime ministers, I have been told, leave No. 10 having lost a lot of money during their period of office. This loss goes with the job.

Now the Prime Minister would get the salary of Leader of the Opposition but this was likely to be swallowed up by expenses, not least the heavy burden he would carry to maintain a Private Office of satisfactory proportions and quality.

Clearly there was a lot of urgent work to be done in the hours that lay ahead.

Immediately after the night's third result, a telephone call was made to the girls who had remained behind in the Political Office at No. 10. They were told to start packing. They hardly needed the instruction. They knew enough about the statistical arts of politics, of swings and percentages, to know what the call was for. Back at the Adelphi Hotel we had to prepare to leave for the declaration of the count in the Huyton constituency. There we had a magnificent result. The Prime Minister's vote was up from 41,132 to 45,583 – a personal tribute and some compensation for what was happening in the rest of the country. But this could not drown what was for us the tragic message of the other results streaming in.

Our thankyous and goodbyes said in Huyton, we had to get back to London as quickly as possible. Fortunately, we had already planned to do the journey by road. For those first few miles on the road from Huyton I travelled with Mary and Harold in the back of their car, which was driven by Bill Housden, whom we had borrowed from the Civil Service at our expense for that part of the campaign. The question of where Harold and Mary would live was urgent. They would, of course, spend the weekend at Chequers. This is a traditional courtesy extended to all outgoing Prime Ministers by incoming Prime Ministers. After that, they would have to rent somewhere quickly while they looked around for a permanent and suitable home.

By the time we reached the motorway south of Preston, we had decided as much as we could at that stage and what I would put in motion immediately I arrived in London. I then left their car, as we had arranged. That way we thought I could travel in comfort back to London in one of the Political Office cars, and the Prime Minister and Mary Wilson would be able to snatch some rest in their car without being cramped. So I waited for the car I was to ride in and which I took to be just behind in the cavalcade following us. However, it didn't arrive because it had taken another route.

I waited there in the darkness on the side of the motorway. I had not exactly expected this day to be full of joy, but I had expected even less to spend part of it as a potential hitch-hiker. One car containing a friendly journalist and his colleagues literally (as they say in all the best novels) screamed to a halt beside me. But just as they offered me a lift back to London, another car belonging to the staff drew up. I hopped in, thankful that at least I should see the sun rise on our last day from the comparative comfort of a car and not from the side of the road.

We sped along at an alarming rate so that we could move in immediately behind the Prime Minister's car. There we stayed, mile after mile, watching anxiously and with great concern the two heads resting together while they snatched a few hours' sleep as best they could before the ordeal ahead. For myself the journey was a struggle as I tried to keep awake and control the turmoil of thoughts going round and round in my head, as I attempted to answer all the questions I persisted in asking myself about how the reorganization of Harold Wilson's life would proceed. I had helped to organize him into No. 10

five and a half years before, and now I was left with the
responsibility of organizing him out.

It was a beautiful day again, with a lovely sunrise. Outside
No. 10 the street was deserted, except for two solitary workmen
clearing away the traces of what clearly had been a crowd the
night before, though what that crowd had gathered there for I
do not know, for there was nothing to see but the front door and
the television scaffolding. Now, in the bright early morning, the
workmen waved encouragingly and sympathetically to the
Prime Minister and his wife. It was almost the last greeting he
was to receive as Prime Minister.

In the inner hall of No. 10, the members of the political staff
were waiting. The PM had a few words with his Press Secretary,
Joe Haines, about the arrangements that would have to be
made later for Press and television interviews. He then joined
his own staff who gave him a sad and subdued cheer, and
gathered round him reassuringly. Some were crying. One of
the girls handed Mary a bouquet. Few words were exchanged.
We were too tired and no one can possibly have the right
formula ready for an occasion such as that.

The Prime Minister then walked quickly down the corridor
to the Private Office to see if there was any urgent business: his
automatic action on arriving back at No. 10 from an out-of-
London or other engagement. He was, after all, still Prime
Minister. Some crisis might have required action. The rest of
the world doesn't stop functioning and going about its business
just because the British are holding an election.

But everything was quiet except for the tape-machine tapping
out the last of the overnight results. There had been counts in
430 constituencies and we had finished the night with a net
loss of forty-two seats. It was now merely a matter of waiting
for the right moment to concede. At that early hour the Private
Office was deserted except for the Duty Clerk. At that time the
official machine was merely ticking over – the action was to
come later. For the civil servants it was to be a formidable day
too.

We withdrew and took the lift to the second floor where the
Prime Minister has his private flat. In recent years we had also
established the Political Office on the same floor. The scene
there was chaotic. Personal papers and Political Office files

were lying in bundles all over the floor as the staff cleared the filing cabinets ready for the move across to the Opposition Leader's room at the House of Commons. Packages ready for transportation were already labelled 'The Rt Hon Harold Wilson, HM Leader of the Opposition'.

Then I suddenly realized that stripping the cabinets was a bit unnecessary. They were, after all, government issue, and we were entitled to identical cabinets at the Commons from the same source. It was therefore easier to shift our papers and files intact within the cabinets, and this we eventually did; but there was a brief period when we were packing and unpacking both at the same time.

This was a minor incident, a small irritation. There was so much more to be done. Estate agents were mobilized at second remove to locate a suitable temporary home. Packing-cases had to be found and removal lorries organized. There may be some machinery for helping a defeated Prime Minister to leave, but if there is I was not told about it.

A journalist has written about the change-over that 'It gives to the workings of democracy the dramatic immediacy of a *coup d'état*, with removal vans in place of machine guns.'*

Fine words but are they necessary or helpful?

It is a curious thing that there appears to be no way in which this country's former leader, his family and personal staff can move out of No. 10 with dignity. There is not even a formal hand-over from a Prime Minister to his successor. Everything is left to the civil servants. I realize that the new Prime Minister and the old normally have opposing political philosophies. Indeed they may not even like each other. But it seems to me that the common office, the common problems and the common terrifying responsibilities might also provide a temporary common ground on which they could meet after the result to discuss the immediate situation and its implications for the nation.

Surely it is not beyond the capacity of a politically sophisticated nation to devise a formula which avoids the situation, more suitable for a film comedy than anything else, in which my brother had to spend hours scouring London for packing-cases for the effects of the Queen's former First Minister, and in

*Anthony Sampson: *The New Anatomy of Britain* (London 1971)

which the man who was running the Government one day was sped on his way the next, with just about as much ceremony as a shop assistant found with his hand in the till.

Another early priority that day was Grandpa, Mr Herbert Wilson, then eighty-seven years old. He had been staying in the flat at No. 10 at the end of the campaign so that he could celebrate with his son on 19 June. Hurried arrangements had to be made for this active old gentleman to travel back to his home in Cornwall. I exchanged only a few words, my last ever, with him as I went through the flat to check the details of the plans for him. He looked sad and tired.

Outside No. 10 the crowd had started gathering. The numbers were to increase as the temperature rose. Camera-men were photographing everybody who entered or left the building, and there were cheers and boos for every visitor, depending on how well known he was and how well liked.

By 8.00 a.m. Mrs Pollard, Mrs Wilson's housekeeper, was serving breakfast for us all in the Small State Dining Room on the first floor. Mrs Pollard had believed the opinion polls too, and had produced what she had intended as a celebration meal. She had taken great trouble over the arrangements and wanted it to be a welcome and pleasant surprise for the returning heroes. There were table decorations and flowers. Even the legendary HP Sauce was also available. About twenty people had been invited, members of the political staff and key helpers, as well as a few personal friends. The victory breakfast, of course, turned into a wake. It became a disorganized affair with people dropping in and out at odd times to snatch a quick snack and then going away to their tasks.

I had time to eat just one sausage and a piece of toast and to swallow a quick cup of coffee, before being called from the table to the PM. Two rooms away, on the same floor, he was busy in the study, planning his return to the role of Leader of the Opposition. We discussed what sort of staff he would need. We tried to recall the organization we had established before which had brought us victory in 1964. He also asked the Private Office to put out calls to as many members of the Cabinet as possible, to see if they had arrived back in London.

At the same time he decided on his short-term political tactics. 'We'll have to play things quietly during their honey-

7

moon period. Of course we don't know how long the honey-moon will last. Somehow I've got a feeling they're not going to enjoy their honeymoon as much as some people do. I'll make only two major speeches at first, one during the debate on the Queen's Speech, and then nothing until the Party Conference at Blackpool at the end of September.' That's exactly what he did.

During the morning the Chancellor, Roy Jenkins, came through from No. 11 to see him, and one or two personal friends, both in the Government and from outside, called to see him. In the afternoon there was a final meeting of the Inner Cabinet, the Management Committee (as it was officially named) in the Cabinet Room.

Lord Goodman, Harold's solicitor, was inevitably another visitor. Television crews and well-known interviewers David Dimbleby, David Frost and others, were also coming in and setting up their equipment in the State Rooms not only, we realized, for the last interviews with Harold, but hoping of course for their first interviews with Edward Heath later in the day.

On the second floor it got hotter and hotter. No. 10 is not the best place in the world to work in during summer and on that day, as the temperature rose outside, the pressure mounted inside. Tiredness and frayed tempers were kept at bay only by the overwhelming realization of what it was all about, and what had happened with such abruptness. We wished once again that the reconstruction of No. 10 during the Macmillan era had included efficient air-conditioning, particularly as the offices of the Political staff overlooked Downing Street and caught most of the sun and this discomfort was heightened by the noise and atmosphere of the crowd outside.

One person remained completely cool, the Prime Minister himself. As people packed feverishly around him, as they removed ashtrays and radios and packed them away in boxes under his nose, as he could hear the almost non-stop telephone calls being made in an effort to find him a place to live in after the weekend, and as he received the constant procession of visitors, he remained absolutely calm.

An occasional burst of irritation would have been under-standable. It was, after all, not his day. But he stayed through-out the most equable person in the building. Neither then, nor later, was he to express to anyone what it had meant to him in personal terms. One could only guess. Most people in the building tended, to use a Yorkshire expression, 'to walk round him'. Some of us just plodded on with what had to be done.

During the early afternoon Bill Housden packed a suitcase containing just enough clothes to see the Prime Minister through the weekend. In any case, he had left some clothes at Chequers, ones he usually wore while down there. On the first floor, in the Middle Drawing Room, the scene of the famous Wilson parties, the Prime Minister held his last party of all. That was to say goodbye to the Civil Service staff at No. 10. It was, to me, a rather embarrassing affair. We all shook hands rather solemnly with each other. In their impartial roles how were the civil servants to behave? I was to see this more clearly later.

There was another important meeting to fit in. Thinking ahead, while most of us were looking back, the Prime Minister called the officers of the Parliamentary Labour Party to No. 10 to discuss with them immediate tactics, his own position and a significant change in Party procedure.

The Parliamentary Labour Party Chairman, Douglas Houghton, arrived with the Secretary of the Parliamentary Party, Frank Barlow, and the Assistant Secretary, Harry Mitchell. The Prime Minister first outlined his plans for the Opposition, and then discussed the position of a Party Leader who has just been defeated at the polls. The meeting to confirm his position by the Parliamentary Party was set up for the following week, to take place at Church House. It was after this that the PM suggested that the offices of Party Leader and Chairman of the Parliamentary Party should be separated.

When the Labour Party is in government the Party Leader is elected for the period of the Parliament by the back-benchers. The Parliamentary Party also elects a Chairman from their ranks as a post separate from that of the Leader. But in Opposition the Leader had always automatically been Chairman as well. This seemed wrong to Harold. The Leader, he believed, should not be the manager of the Parliamentary Party. Besides, the Chairman, whoever he may be, has considerable powers to 'organize' the way in which a Party meeting goes, and the Prime Minister felt that these powers would reside better with an independent Chairman. When he had been Opposition

Leader previously it had not been convenient to make the suggestion since his own election as Leader in 1963 took place during the run-up period to a General Election. Now he put forward his proposal and got immediate backing for it.

One important engagement remained to be carried out that day: to go to Transport House, the Party headquarters, to thank the staff and other workers for all they had done during the election. It presented us with a difficult decision. Should the Prime Minister use the Downing Street entrance for this visit? He still had to go to Buckingham Palace to submit his resignation. If he used the front door each time this would mean three appearances in Downing Street in quick succession. It would almost look as if he couldn't bring himself to leave the place.

We decided that such ludicrous bobbing in and out would just confuse the crowd outside as well as the television audiences. In the event he used the garden entrance at the back of No. 10. Inevitably, however, there were camera-men positioned there too, and next day the photographs and captions made it look as if he had left for the last time trying to escape the Press. In fact he left for his audience with the Queen quite properly from the front door.

There had been some confusion about when he should actually go to the Palace. He had already conceded defeat in a television interview inside No. 10 at midday. But it was not until after 2.00 p.m. that the 316th Conservative seat formally put Mr Heath's victory beyond doubt. At that point, the one at which Sir Alec had also conceded in 1964, the Principal Private Secretary, then Sandy Isserlis, made the usual inquiries of the Queen's Private Secretary as to when it would be convenient for the Prime Minister to see her.

The Queen, however, had already decided to spend Friday, the day after the General Election, at Windsor, so that she could go racing at Ascot. We were told, therefore, that she could either come straight back to London then, or the official resignation could wait until the early evening. It was decided to wait until 6.30 p.m. since this gave us additional valuable time for our own planning.

The crowd outside grew larger and became more restive as

the afternoon wore on. I couldn't blame them. They were hoping for action and there wasn't any. They had seen members of the Inner Cabinet arrive and had booed them. Denis Healey responded typically by giving the V-sign, though it was generally believed that he was expressing his opinion of the boos rather than the size of the Tory victory. This gesture had an unexpected effect. He got a tremendous cheer for it.

From time to time we were drawn away from the packing to look at the scene outside. People were shouting, cheering and occasionally singing. But the crowd's peculiarity was the mixture of supporters and opponents. I had never seen such an even balance on such a big occasion. The scaffolding for the television cameras and the general atmosphere produced an impression that a public execution was about to take place. This one time in our national life must be the nearest we now get to the days when the executions of eminent figures were watched with relish by sixteenth- and seventeenth-century crowds.

I noticed several people in the crowd I recognized from previous crisis days at No. 10, friends and foes alike. Whenever there had been something bad for us and good for the camera, there had always been a small 'tightly knit group of politically motivated' boo leaders outside. Were they part of a Tory Central Office rent-a-crowd organization? I don't know and probably never shall. Still it seemed to me a good idea to produce a response from our side as well. Accordingly a few of our party workers and supporters joined the crowd and helped to encourage those already there, who might have been too timid to express their feelings at a time of defeat, against the very loud and vocal and over-exuberant Tory support.

The result was that when Harold left, to go to the Palace and then on to Chequers, honours were even, the cheers and boos being about equal. In view of how we felt and the previous atmosphere this seemed at the time to be almost a victory. His car drove down the Mall led by an enterprising vehicle full of young people, displaying in the back window the poster 'Come back Harold, all is forgiven'. Good going for the morning after the night before.

He left but we stayed. That was the worst moment, for us, of all. The packing went on. The area within No. 10 in which we felt at all comfortable had now been whittled down to just that covering the old Political Office. Elsewhere it now felt like foreign territory. The Civil Service had adjusted and were waiting only for the arrival of Mr Heath. I remember thinking at that time that it seemed as if I had never been doing anything else but packing.

There had been some rather odd exchanges on the telephone earlier with the people at Tory Central Office representing Mr Heath's Private Office in Opposition. I made it clear that we intended to move into the Opposition Leader's room at the House that night. Indeed, we had nowhere else to move to. This surprised them. They appeared to think that we needn't move in for a week or so. I don't know where they thought we should base ourselves until then. Our view was that if we had to move our things away from No. 10, they would have to move their things away from the Leader's room. Eventually they accepted the situation. I had a distinct impression that they had suffered the same degree of shell shock over there that we had at No. 10.

Just as the scene was moving rapidly now to its close, there was a minor hiccup. The Civil Service porters did not want to move Mr Heath's belongings from the rooms at the House. The porters' action was touching but not exactly helpful to us. At last they were persuaded to move Mr Heath's effects out to Tory Central Office – a few bottles of cold beer on that hot day helped them to accept the political realities of the situation.

But there was so much stuff that by the time they had finished with Mr Heath it was too late for them to help us at the No. 10 end. So we had to leave our large possessions in the basement, clearly labelled and organized for removal on the Saturday morning. The smaller things we took over personally.

I left No. 10 just after Mr Heath arrived. We heard the cheers in Downing Street and saw the Garden Girls, the Civil Service typists, rushing from the basement in high excitement to see him in the front hall, and we heard the staff clapping as he entered. As I finally went through the garden entrance, I could see him in the Cabinet Room. With him, giving him his first briefing as Prime Minister, were the same civil servants who had been serving Harold a few hours before. The King was dead, long live the King.

But the day's difficulties and irritations were not over. At the House of Commons in the Opposition room, there had developed in that dusty and confused atmosphere the most unnecessary and ridiculous scene I ever took part in. For some strange reason an argument was proceeding about Harold's television set which had been moved earlier, together with his other Parliamentary equipment, from the Prime Minister's rooms at the House, to the Opposition rooms.

There was protest at the removal of our set. We were told that it really should be left where it was for a number of reasons. It had to be left for the new Prime Minister while we kept Mr Heath's old set. As it was a very old set indeed that we were being given, in contrast to our own, for which we had paid and which was only one year old, I declared this was a lot of nonsense.

There may have been reasons for the ruling but they seemed unnecessary at such a time not only because they were routine, but because they were discourteous to the outgoing Prime Minister and unnecessarily impolite at a time of great strain for everyone.

It needed the help of Gerald Kaufman, Harold's former aide, who had just won a seat at Manchester, Ardwick, to use all the authority of a brand new MP in order to keep Harold's set, where it belonged, in his room. This was not in fact the end of the story. During the weekend the two sets were swapped over again. I finally had to enlist the personal intervention of a Senior official at No. 10 before we could get our own set and keep it.

Very late that night, with the room in the Commons beginning to look less chaotic and more like a proper office ready to work in, I felt it was time at last to go home. My working day, if you can call twenty-eight hours a day, had begun at 8.00 a.m. on Thursday 18 June. I had managed to snatch a full two hours' sleep at the Adelphi Hotel that evening because I had known that there was a long, hard night in front. What I had not realized then was that the day ahead would be even longer and much harder than I thought, nor that I would end it where I did.

When I walked into the Opposition Leader's office at the House of Commons on 19 June 1970, it was hard to believe

13

that I had not been inside it for more than five years. The room looked just the same. The furniture was arranged in the same way. Even the dust seemed familiar. It was hard, too, not to recall the old feeling of our office routine of five and a half years before. A long time ago, not just in years but even more so in events and experiences.

Yet I had not in fact seen the room since 16 October 1964, the day after polling in the '64 Election, when I had gone there in great haste to help organize the removal of Harold's things across to No. 10 to the house which he had said he would make a power house for the whole nation.

The fact that Harold did not succeed in making it the real power house he visualized was one of the failures of the Government and one of the victories for the Whitehall Establishment. Even on that first day in 1964 it was easy to see that there would be difficulties ahead. Difficulties for everyone, and, at a lower level and on a small scale, for myself too.

16 October 1964 had begun with Labour ahead on the overnight declarations. The early editions of the papers had headlines about Wilson 'Sweeping In', but we knew that the results were not good enough to make the final result certain for us. The last editions were more cautious. One headline was: 'It looks like Labour'. That was more like it but we feared even that might be overstating the case. There were too many Tory strongholds to be counted on the Friday morning.

We had gone to bed very late, getting barely four hour's sleep before we were to catch the breakfast train back to London from Liverpool. We hoped all was going to be well, but the erosion of the Labour lead looked extremely damaging to our chances and affected our confidence.

Although we had carried out a comprehensive and hectic Kennedy-type tour of the country during the campaign, we still found time to spend a good period of the time in Liverpool. It was one of the most exciting, exhilarating and exhausting elections I have ever been involved in. Everywhere there had been the same sense of something new happening. The 'time for a change' mood enveloped everything.

At that time Harold's office was staffed by only two secretaries, myself and Brenda Dew, and an assistant, Susan Lewis, who with her constant cheerfulness kept us all going at the most wearing times. Brenda was extremely efficient. She had worked previously for Hugh Gaitskell as an assistant to Mr Gaitskell's secretary, Beryl Skelly; and Beryl herself was one of the best secretaries I have ever seen in the House. This small set-up was backed by a powerful team of officers at Transport House, with Peter Shore, David Ennals, John Harris, Sara Barker, Percy Clark and of course the General Secretary, Len Williams. The years out of office had welded them together into a fiercely cohesive fighting unit. We felt invincible, and probably behaved as if we were, though I doubted at the time whether it was a fact. What was important was the feeling, and this carried us through.

During our time in Liverpool, Harold's party had been based as usual at the Adelphi Hotel, and it was from the Adelphi that we left to catch the early morning train back to London on 16 October. I was very much afraid that Harold would step into the train ahead and step out at Euston with Labour well behind.

For a good deal of the journey south we kept the blinds down in Harold's compartment so that both he and Mary could get the extra sleep they both desperately needed. We were anxious, too, of course that he should not be photographed looking tired and possibly nodding off. However, at several stopping points along the line enthusiastic Labour supporters had gathered to cheer the man they believed would be their next Prime Minister. Each time Harold roused himself quickly and eagerly to return their greetings. He was as pleased to see them as they were to see him.

I don't think in the event he got more than a few minutes' consecutive sleep during the trip. Thomas Balogh, now Lord Balogh, soon to become Economic Adviser to the Cabinet, and one of the famous 'Hungarian twins', had his transistor radio with him. This radio, which functioned erratically owing to tunnels and other impediments, became the centre of our lives during the trip. We crouched over it to get the results, and the results, as we had feared, were not good. As each mile passed, it was obvious that our majority was either passing, or that it would be right down, if indeed we got a majority at all.

Len Williams was waiting for us at Euston, not to mention hundreds of Press and television lights and cameras and a crowd of jostling, curious, excited people. We were driven across London by hire car to Transport House, Party headquarters, where Len and his staff had very thoughtfully provided food in his room, so that we could eat there watching the results as they came in. Nobody in fact ate much; they were too busy watching the television screen and making calculations. On the other side of Smith Square, at Conservative headquarters, I imagine the scene was much the same. George Brown joined us with Mrs Brown, and Harold and George went into a huddle with Len Williams, working out what could or could not happen in the following hours.

But then suddenly, in the early afternoon, it was all over. We had our majority after all. The Tories could not catch us up now, but they could get very near, and they did, uncomfortably near. In the end the over-all majority for Labour was just five. Harold said to reassure us (and to reassure himself as well, I imagine): 'Winston Churchill always believed that one was enough.'

Labour had won. The Party had managed to pull down Harold Macmillan's massive 1959 majority, yet curiously enough the allegedly ineffectual Sir Alec Douglas-Home had tenaciously and successfully succeeded in keeping the turnabout to a minimum. It was a victory for both men in view of all that had happened over those immediately preceding years.

The first sign of the transfer of power for us was the arrival at Transport House of two detectives. They had come straight from Sir Alec's side to guard the new Prime Minister. The Secretary of the Parliamentary Labour Party, Frank Barlow, came up to me to announce their arrival, and I went out to speak to them and to put them in a little waiting-room across the corridor from Len's room. I then took Harold over to introduce them to him and so that they could then go through the procedure of explaining to him their role in his new life.

The scene was not without its comic side, however, since while they were briefing him, he had to use the time and the place to change into the clothes he was to wear to the Palace. The room was an extremely small one, and the three men carrying out the drill insisted upon by our present form of democracy must have made a strange sight. It must have also been uncomfortable on the one side and embarrassing on the other.

Once changed and ready to leave for the Palace, Harold gave his first instruction as Prime Minister designate: namely, that an old friend, Bill Housden, was to drive him to the Palace and from then on to be his official driver again. Bill had been with Harold at the Board of Trade in 1951 and the two had remained friends since. Harold was godfather to Bill's daughter, Jill. Bill himself had led a distinguished driving career. He had driven Harold Macmillan throughout his years both as a Cabinet Minister and as Prime Minister. He had also driven Selwyn Lloyd thereafter. Bill was summoned to Transport House. He was delighted and excitedly rang his wife to say 'I'm back'. Today he is still driving Harold as Opposition Leader.

Harold wanted the visit to the Palace to be a little more human than these affairs usually are. He wanted, too, I think, to share the moment with those closest to him. His father, Mary and two sons, Robin and Giles, were to go, and earlier in the day he asked me if in the event of winning, I would like to be included in the party. That is how his official car came to be followed by a second car. Certainly it must have been the most unusual and unorthodox swearing in of a Prime Minister for many a year, if indeed anything like it had ever happened before.

We waited in the Equerry's room at the Palace while Harold saw the Queen. A number of anonymous Palace individuals were there. To me they all looked exactly alike. They chatted to us while the audience took place. As I recall it, the conversation centred on horses. Perhaps it was assumed that everybody was interested in horses, though my knowledge of them is minimal and the Wilson family's less. It struck me at the time as an ironic beginning to the white-hot technological revolution and the Government that was to mastermind it.

From Buckingham Palace Harold took the family back to Transport House. The crowd there was by this time enormous and clearly carried away by the excitement of last-minute success and the razor-edge nature of the victory and of the Government it was to create. The life of 'The Perils of Pauline' Government had begun.

Harold drove straight to No. 10. By an arrangement we had both agreed upon, I left Transport House in a separate car with Herbert Bowden, then our Chief Whip but soon to become Labour's Lord President and Leader of the House. The two of us were driven to Downing Street and arrived a few minutes after Harold. I can recall the crowds but only the sight and not the sound. What impressed itself most upon me was the closing of the door of No. 10 behind me, and the quiet cloister-like atmosphere inside, impervious to and protected from the crowd outside – the crowd representing those who theoretically have the power to alter what goes on within.

Inside the civil servants were already with Harold in the Cabinet Room, waiting to brief him. It was almost a replica of the scene, without the staff applause, that I was to witness as I left Downing Street in June 1970. That morning they had been briefing Sir Alec and now they belonged to the new Prime Minister. Apparently only very substantial majorities ensure a staff greeting with applause. For us in 1966, and for Mr Heath in 1970, the staff at No. 10 lined up in the hall and clapped in the newly-elected Prime Minister. Not so in 1964. There were just the members of the Private Office, the four Private Secretaries, and the housekeeper, Mr May.

But there was the enormous difference too, between 1970 and 1964. When we left office in 1970, the briefing of the Prime Minister that had to take place immediately could not have been quite so tense. True, there was the Ulster situation, but we had already taken the decision to send extra troops immediately after the election, and all Mr Heath had to do was to rubber-stamp the decision. Despite all the talk of economic and financial crisis and difficulty by the Tories during the election campaign, Mr Heath found himself with a trade surplus running at more than £600 million a year. That night he was able to leave Downing Street and celebrate at a birthday party given in the Queen Mother's honour at Windsor Castle, in the company of the heir to Franco's Spain, Don Juan Carlos and his wife. Harold would have found it politically difficult indeed to go out to a similar party on that comparable night in 1964 apart from his economic crisis preoccupations, even if he had been invited, which would have been unlikely.

One of the presents, therefore, which Labour left behind at No. 10 for Mr Heath was the best present any Prime Minister can be given – time. The new Prime Minister inherited a situation in which he could plan his tactics, consult with his friends and sail his yacht in the weeks immediately following the Election. He did not need to show his hand until October when the Tories held their Conference at Blackpool, and later when Mr Barber presented his mini-Budget to the House of Commons. Action on such a leisurely scale was a luxury the Tories had certainly denied to us. In 1964 they had played it very close indeed and run the economy and the country to danger point.

On 16 October 1964 the problems came tumbling into Harold's lap that first night. Not only in this country but elsewhere there had been dramatic events in the twenty-four hours before. On polling day itself we had been shocked and surprised by the news from Russia of Khrushchev's fall from power, and hushed by what we were told of Chinese nuclear developments.

But overshadowing everything was the £800 million deficit which was the present left by the Tories for Harold Wilson, for the Labour Government – our notorious 'inheritance'.

Just as we had forced the pace Kennedy-fashion throughout the run-up to the election and through the campaign itself, we now had to face a Kennedy-type hundred days of urgent and instant action.

The new men in Government were very new indeed. Politicians, tacticians, strategists yes, some the best there were, but administrators and governors, not yet. The hard realities of being in power came with a deadening effect to all who had been carried along on that sea of electoral euphoria in 1964.

Harold was having to move very quickly indeed. The Press were apprised of how he saw the situation. They were told that though the Government might have a majority of only five, and that it would therefore be frequently at risk, it would still govern. There would be no compromise on that or about fundamentals. It would not be harried out of office as the Tories tried to harry the Attlee Government in 1950–1. There would be no attempt to make a deal with the Liberals in order to obtain the support of their nine Members. As long as the Labour Government survived it would act on the 'one is enough' philosophy.

A lot was happening, though not to me. While all this was

going on I sat alone in the waiting-room next to the Cabinet Room, where all the action was. I saw the people I knew so well, like George Brown, Jim Callaghan and Denis Healey coming and going, but as regards what was being decided and what was being announced I could have discovered more if I had been able to listen to the radio. But at that time I didn't even have access to a transistor. I had to wait until later to hear.

Still, it was my decision that I was in the waiting-room. I had decided previously that that was where I wanted my office to be, and Harold had agreed. I did in fact already know something about the layout of No. 10.

Some considerable time before the 1964 election, I had been taken to dinner and lunch several times by the late Sir Timothy Bligh, who was Principal Private Secretary to Sir Alec Douglas-Home, as he had been previously to Harold Macmillan. (Harold Macmillan had conferred a knighthood on Tim Bligh in his Dissolution Honours List in 1963.) These meetings were arranged so that I should learn something about the Downing Street set-up in case Labour won.

Tim Bligh made it clear during these meetings that the Civil Service considered that there was no place for me, or my office colleagues, at No. 10. I reported these views back faithfully to Harold, and there was a joint decision to disagree with Sir Timothy. My own view is that these dinners, pleasant though they were, represented a significant move by the civil servants in their predictable game. They knew I had been running Harold's Private Office in Opposition, and if he succeeded in capturing power in 1964, they wanted to make certain that they captured him.

One singularly odd invitation was extended to me during those pre-election months. Tim Bligh asked me if I would like to see over No. 10 on a Friday when Sir Alec was likely to be away with his family in Scotland. Naturally I agreed as the temptation was too great to resist. Actually to see inside this historic building, the centre of so many politicians' aspirations and hopes, was a significant and intriguing occasion. With great trepidation indeed, I walked up to that imposing front door one bright afternoon. I picked up the heavy knocker and knocked, rather too loudly I thought. I remember feeling very nervous and extremely ill at ease.

On the day of my first visit, I gave my name and said I had come to see Sir Timothy Bligh. He was told of my arrival and I was then taken along to the waiting-room until he was ready to see me. He came in and briefly described that room to me, explaining how it communicated directly with the Cabinet Room on one side, while the Private Office communicated with the Cabinet Room directly on the other side. A useful piece of information which I stored away.

Sir Timothy was a most elegant, charming and amusing man who had been a war hero and was, I am told, a powerful Principal Private Secretary. He asked if I would like some tea. Though I did not want any, he said he thought it would be an excellent idea for us to go through to the Private Office together, where tea was being taken at exactly that time by the Private Secretaries. They were all gathered there! This was seemingly a 4.00 p.m. ritual.

I had the chance to see them, and they had their first opportunity of finding out about me face to face. It was a rather curious meeting. They were not the sort of men I had envisaged as serving Harold Wilson in action. After my tea, served in the most beautiful china cups (which incidentally, I never saw again in that office), I was taken on a tour of the building. My reception everywhere was coldly polite, but I did not mind the understandable absence of warmth, since the tour gave me some idea of the layout of the building, and how it functioned. Apart from the private flat, Sir Timothy took me on a complete circuit, even through the famous 'Garden Rooms', in which he was something of a hero.

I left after about an hour and a half, knowing a good deal more about them and their set-up, but wondering to myself whether they really knew and understood as much about me.

Later Sir Timothy was to be succeeded by Derek Mitchell, an extremely clever and able man, perhaps one of the most brilliant civil servants I encountered. I received approaches from him too, for a meeting to discuss matters 'of mutual interest'. I was never able to respond because of the pressure of work in the election run-up.

All these recollections went through my mind as I sat in the 'waiting-room' on 16 October. When I had walked in with Herbert Bowden earlier, Harold had introduced me to Derek

Mitchell, and to the other Private Secretaries, whom I had of course met over tea. When Harold then sat down to get on with the work at hand, he said 'Let Marcia have the waiting-room for her Office.' So I went there and took possession – and waited.

At some point I received a message that Derek Mitchell would like to see me. We tried to come to some understanding that day, both about my role and my future life, as he saw it, in No. 10.

Much later there was a discussion with Harold as to what my exact title was to be. Private Secretary would have been perfectly correct, but this was objected to, though I was qualified academically by Private Office No. 10 standards. Derek therefore, together with Harold, thought up the title of Personal and Political Secretary to the Prime Minister. That having been decided, I was then left with it and to work out my own role.

I was too tired that particular day to consider all the implications of what had happened to me. I still had to go again to the House of Commons to work in the room there on the clearing up. I eventually left No. 10 at 10.00 p.m. to return to my home in Golders Green, having been up a very long time, and not having had a proper meal for twenty-four hours. As the day ended, I said to myself: 'I have an office and I have a title. But have I any work to do now?'

Ruinous Inheritance

This then was 16 October 1964, our first day in office. During that afternoon and evening I just sat it out in that room and looked out of the window into the garden of No. 10. And there was little to see except removal men coming to the Maudlings' home next door at No. 11 to take away some of their furniture.

There was complete silence and a sense of total isolation. Of course, I guessed exactly what was happening in the famous room next door, the Cabinet Room, but it was not until I saw Harold – briefly on that same evening, and then for more lengthy talks during the weekend – that I realized the overwhelming task in hand. The fact was that we had to fight a war on two fronts. We had this tiny majority and this enormous economic problem, much worse than anyone had anticipated – two problems which seemed incompatible with an effective Socialist Government. How could a Socialist Government hope to carry out the policies to which it was committed with an economic problem of this size and a majority in Parliament that hardly existed?

Harold was hit immediately by the magnitude of it all. It was devastating for him. There he had been twenty-four hours before, campaigning on a policy of getting Britain moving again, putting enthusiasm into everyone's hearts, only to be presented on the Friday afternoon with those small pieces of paper civil servants carry around with them, and which this time indicated the magnitude of the problems he now had to deal with.

Most people, I am sure, visualize civil servants armed with

neat notebooks and beautifully typed memoranda. Instead, they usually clutch a mass of papers and letters and notes on which they have scribbled comments in their own hand.

During the campaign Harold had realized there was a serious situation, but I don't think even he knew it was as big as it was. If you look at all his speeches throughout the campaign, you will notice that he underestimated the size of the deficit. It was not until he got to No. 10, and they actually brought him the figures, that he realized just how shocking the problem was.

Harold had never put such a high figure on it. But the Tories had known it was so bad, and had left behind their own preparations for dealing with it. Mr Maudling, as Chancellor of the Exchequer, had been considering a number of ways to stop the influx of imports – a plan at least to stabilize that side of the accounts. Obviously Mr Maudling had considered the alternatives that Harold was to be faced with; of devaluation, of quantitative restrictions on imports which are known as import quotas, and a surcharge on imports.

Looking back on those first days now, one's mind tends only to register the economic problems because they were so dominating. The actual formation of the Government, the innovation, and the excitement over the novelty of Labour in office again, are almost forgotten.

But there was, naturally, major news coverage as the top politicians like Jim Callaghan, George Brown, Gerald Gardiner, Denis Healey, Roy Jenkins, Patrick Gordon Walker, Dick Crossman, Michael Stewart, Ray Gunter, Barbara Castle, Tony Benn, received their appointments and had their photographs taken on the doorstep of No. 10. They were all well-known names and their appointments were widely welcomed by the Labour Party.

Harold's creation of the Ministry of Technology was accompanied by the appointment as its Minister of Frank Cousins. This was very controversial. Not only controversial in the country, but in the Party as well. During the preceding years Frank Cousins had become very well-known within the Labour Party as the left-winger who took on Mr Gaitskell and fought the campaign on unilateral nuclear disarmament, a campaign which caused great strife in the Party. He did not gain a popular image in the country, despite the solid majority for him in the Labour Party and in the increasingly left-wing dominated unions. Harold thought he had abilities and qualities, and wanted to have a major trade unionist in his Government. He felt that the new Ministry of Technology was the best possible place in which to put a trade unionist, particularly one who had, in his union work, been forced to come to terms with many of the developments and modernization schemes with which British industry must now be increasingly involved.

Then we had a new Ministry of Land and Planning, which Labour saw as an answer to the more vicious sides of the housing problem, exposed in the early 1960s. The Ministry of Land and Planning was going to be the department that would stop land racketeering. How easily some sections of public opinion have forgotten the Tory days of Rachmanism before October 1964. Then we were all deeply conscious of such social evils and exploitation. But in the event the new Ministry failed to do what we had hoped for, and the fact that land prices continued to rise was a major concern for us.

Also in those first few days of 1964 there was the creation of the Ministry for Overseas Development, which had Barbara Castle as its Minister and which was to do so much to reassure developing countries that this new Government had a deep interest in what was happening overseas, particularly in Commonwealth countries.

There was also the appointment of Jennie Lee as Minister responsible for the arts. This was part of our philosophy of bringing to the mass of our people a new quality of life. No longer was 'culture' in its widest sense to be the prerogative of those who had a lot of money. As a Labour Government we were committed to doing all we could to make sure the arts were fostered and that people had the opportunity to enjoy the arts as much as those who had the money and could indulge in private patronage.

There were the usual appointments with which some of us agreed and some disagreed. A curious one was that of Alun Gwynne Jones as Minister for Disarmament and his elevation to the Lords as Lord Chalfont. Labour Members found this difficult to accept at first, because he was not a member of the Labour Party and had always been a Liberal. Then again there was Hugh Foot, who as Lord Caradon became Minister of State at the Foreign Office and Britain's permanent representative at the United Nations.

Another appointment was George Wigg, as the Paymaster General, but responsible for security. For those of us who worked closely with Harold this was an important appointment, because George Wigg had been very much part of our lives over the preceding years. We had become used to him, too, as part of our office.

He had helped enormously in the personal organization of the election campaign. He had run things like a military operation, but his devotion and loyalty to Harold were great and indisputable and Harold had great confidence and trust in him.

Of course, Harold couldn't possibly have appointed the whole Government on the Friday, Saturday and Sunday before the Cabinet was to hold its first meeting on Monday. He made as many appointments as he could, and certainly had the Cabinet appointed by the time it was to meet on the Monday following the General Election.

That beginning was for all of us a nightmare, though I doubt very much if Harold would ever admit it. He has described how conscious he was, as he walked down the corridor of No. 10 on 16 October, that he had such a tiny majority to support him. But he doesn't go on to explain all the feelings he had during those first weeks after he discovered just what he had let himself in for. It is typical of him that he mentions it only in passing, and then goes on in his book *A Personal Record* with the accounts of what he then proceeded to do.

Everybody was extremely self-conscious during those first days because, although we had won the election, the majority was so tiny that our Government as a permanent feature was in doubt. Life was going to be precarious.

There was the problem that while we for our part felt insecure, those who were opposed to us were obviously not prepared to accept us as wholeheartedly as they would have done if we had walked into No. 10 with a majority of one hundred. And what few people now remember is that the

Tory Party had been defeated after thirteen years in power. The Tory Party has a very strong conviction that it alone is entitled to form the Government of this country. The 'born to rule' philosophy is no myth. It is subscribed to by a substantial part of the Conservative Party and totally subscribed to by the Tory Establishment in metropolitan London.

There was, therefore, no warm reception for us at No. 10. The Civil Service Establishment there was clearly not going to be relaxed and uninhibited in its behaviour when it feared that overnight this Government would disappear and its old masters would once again be back in power and wanting to know why these servants had behaved so badly in their absence. Few people will admit this to be the case, and most leading Labour politicians are unwilling to answer the question as to whether the Civil Service was hostile. The atmosphere at No. 10 was ice cold and very restrained. We were treated as ships passing in the night.

The Principal Private Secretary was meticulous in the following weeks and months in maintaining a gap between members of the political staff and civil servants and to preach the gospel of impartiality as practised by the Civil Service. But all he succeeded in proving to me personally was that he was totally devoted to preserving the *status quo* as left by the last Conservative Government.

The result of all this feeling was that the people who were personally attached to Harold's staff were made to feel like intruders and squatters, and they consequently behaved in a slightly aggressive way.

But not Harold. He plodded on with what he had to do. And I admire all of the members of the new Labour Government too for the way they behaved.

Many of them had never in their lives been in a Ministry and they had no idea at all of how a department worked. Most members of the Cabinet had never been in a Cabinet before. They must have felt extremely self-conscious as they set about their new tasks. They were still full of their electioneering, and still unaware of the shock they were due to encounter when the Prime Minister told them exactly what was in store for them. In those first weeks and months they were going to have to learn how to do their jobs the painful way.

None of this helped to break in the new Labour Government. When it has been out of power for many years, this is one of the great problems a political party faces. Edward Heath's Government elected in 1970 had only five and a half years separating it from the last Conservative administration, and many of the people he appointed had already had experience in Government departments. The social intercourse between the Civil Service Establishment and the Tory Party, which continues whichever Government is in office, also keeps them in touch, and to that degree readjustment is never such a problem for them.

But you can imagine the scenario in those first days, with the new boys coming in, very green, very inexperienced about the way government works, terribly enthusiastic, terribly excited, but conscious of the precariousness of their situation. And then the economic crisis that was to explode around their ears the following week.

As I sat in that room on 16 October, I had my problems too. Small individual problems, possibly, but problems which I knew that I would have to resolve myself, because the situation being what it was, I could not possibly hope to have the time to sit down with Harold and to ask him how he felt the political and routine side of his life could now be organized. On this I had to make decisions myself in negotiation with the Private Office, and confirm them with Harold later.

When Harold was sending for Ministers whom he wanted to appoint to his Government, and Private Secretaries were in doubt as to whom he meant, they might have come into my room and asked me for my advice, since clearly I knew every member of the Parliamentary Labour Party well.

On one occasion I discovered a certain Labour MP sitting all by himself at the table in the hall outside the Cabinet Room. I wondered what he was doing there. I knew that Harold was in the middle of Government appointments and this MP certainly wasn't on Harold's list. Later that night Harold told me that he had asked a Private Secretary to produce an MP. The Private Secretary had produced the MP's brother, who was also in the House. If he had known Harold or the Party well, he would have got the right man. Of course, the man originally selected by Harold got the job for which he was intended. But the brother was then made a Church Commissioner.

The Saturday and Sunday of that first weekend proceeded with no work for me, but with regular and brief meetings with Harold to find out what was happening. No. 10 does not really operate at the weekend. The normal functioning of the office, when the routine work is done, is from Monday to Friday, as in most government departments. It was consequently not until the first Monday morning that I felt the real impact of my own problem and saw that I had to take action.

We had been given a minuscule room upstairs which had previously been used by the Parliamentary Private Secretaries to the Prime Minister. It was so tiny that when Harold's files were brought over from the House of Commons and placed in the room, together with the filing cabinets and the filing boxes, the typewriters and the other equipment, there was virtually no room left in which to sit down. All you could do was to stand up and try as best you could to move around and sort the stuff out. Nobody in that building thought of putting us into the picture about what other accommodation there was which the Prime Minister could use and which had nothing at all to do with the Civil Service.

Only later did I discover that there was a whole section of rooms near the private flat usually used as bedrooms for domestic staff and for the housekeeper. Clearly Harold was not going to have domestic staff and was only going to have one housekeeper, so the other rooms, which were there for his personal use, could be taken over for his personal and political offices. This we were to do, but in those first few days we were left in this very tiny room with a great muddle of material and equipment. How pathetic it looked with the posters and election leaflets strewn around. 'Let's go with Labour' was the slogan on the posters but for us it required a certain gymnastic ability to go on using that room. These were not the only relics of the election at No. 10. In the private flat we were amused to discover the dining-room walls covered with Tory posters, mainly of Sir Alec.

When I took up the question with the Principal Private Secretary as to what correspondence would now be sent to myself to handle on Harold's behalf, I was informed quite firmly that I should deal only with personal correspondence in the very strictly personal sense, correspondence from Labour parties and correspondence from Mr Wilson's constituents. This, I was told, would be automatic. But to my mind it was not at all satisfactory and one of the first basic requirements, as I saw it, was that my colleagues and I should handle all correspondence with the Parliamentary Labour Party, and also all correspondence that came in from members of the Labour Party in the country and from all Trade Unions who were affiliated to the Labour Party.

After a great deal of argument, particularly about the Parliamentary Labour Party correspondence, I was able to get an agreement that we should deal with this particular batch of correspondence. But the Principal Private Secretary was very reluctant about Labour Members of Parliament, since previously letters from Members of Parliament of either party had always been dealt with in the Private Office, and I think he wanted to keep them under its control.

The system we were to adopt later on was that we handled this correspondence, but they always saw it downstairs anyway before it came to me, so that they were aware of what was being said. This was in fact true of all correspondence since it was opened by civil servants in the General Office in No. 10 and allocated afterwards.

Of course, the General Office at No. 10, the Garden Rooms, were baffled by the correspondence that started to come in. They were not used to getting so many letters from Trade Unions and they didn't seem to know one Trade Union from another. Thirteen years of Tory government had conditioned them to a very different sort of post, and it took us many months to get them to understand about our own sort of correspondence and also which Trade Unions were Trade Unions affiliated to the Labour Party.

By the middle of the first week, we had established a sort of basis for working. I was also left to organize the Prime Minister's political engagements, his constituency engagements, and to handle all the personal and private engagements and commitments he had. It was a fairly substantial and solid base from which to work. But we had a much bigger problem than this to tackle as well.

Although we were finding the change very difficult after so many years in the House of Commons, Transport House was even more disorganized about it all. They had lost some of their very senior people. The Director of Publicity, John Harris, had left to join Patrick Gordon Walker at the Foreign Office. There was an even more dangerous point when the Deputy Director, Percy Clark, almost decided to go too. That would have meant losing both senior people on the Press side. The Research Secretary, Peter Shore, had become an MP and was replaced by a member of his staff who was not well known to us at that time. The International Department had lost its Head, David Ennals, as he had also become a Member of Parliament. So there were now several important changes at Transport House. The staff there were still enthusiastic and delighted we had won, but there was a feeling of 'the morning after the night before'. I think they imagined that those who worked personally for leading members of the Party had now gone off to lead a more glamorous existence. They did not have any idea how upset we all were, how uncomfortable we felt and what a struggle it was to keep up our morale and to survive.

What had not been talked about and planned for before the election was what sort of links and liaison there was to be between the Party at Transport House, the Party in Parliament, and the Government. This was to prove one of the greatest problems we had, and one which we never properly solved throughout the whole five and a half years. There were no official lines of communication. Transport House had no direct way of being told what was happening and what the Government was doing.

What they did not realize was that the Ministers were having problems of adjustment too. As for the rest of us, the 'in-between staff', we were neither one thing nor the other. We felt we were remote from our friends in the Parliamentary Party and at Transport House and we had no new friends in the official set-up.

It was a great mistake not to set up some sort of machinery right away to make sure Transport House was kept in touch with us. Of course, when we had the first disastrous by-elections, action was taken to put it right.

But one could not expect Ministers or the Prime Minister to

31

take notice of this situation. Here they were, up to their eyes in an enormous economic crisis, their lives dominated by emergency Budgets, visits to America, Defence Conferences at Chequers, reappraisals, speeches in Parliament and all the rest. They could not at that stage have thought of this problem that was going to cause so much difficulty.

Those first months must have been extremely rewarding for civil servants. The situation provided a goldmine for them. Here were new Ministers who were inexperienced and would have to learn their jobs – and only the civil servants could teach them. This would, of course, sort the sheep from the goats and decide which Ministers would prove able to control their officials and which would not. If there had not been the thirteen-year gap I imagine that some people who succumbed to Civil Service domination might not have done this quite so easily.

The first Cabinet meeting was a brave one. Ministers were told the facts, they took it all on the chin, and talked hopefully of sticking to the Manifesto and the pledges they had made in the campaign. They shook their tiny fists – which were tiny indeed with a five majority, and said that we would stick to our main strategy despite every handicap. Within a short time after they had met and considered the situation, we had an economic statement and were told of the surcharge scheme. Strong advice was given that the best possible course of action was to devalue at once and blame it rightly and with justification on the Tories.

And, of course, this was what most people wanted to do, and would like to have done. Their number included Harold himself. But he realized only too well that if we had devalued, the subsequent run on the pound would have been enormous, that we would have become bankrupt during the following weeks, and would possibly have had to go to the country again for a bigger mandate. That we might then have had a landslide victory would have been insufficient reward for the measures we would have had to take afterwards.

As it was, the decision to impose surcharges on imports caused enough trouble, both before it was announced and later when the row broke out in EFTA. Transport House were totally baffled by the developments and scantily informed.

They had been warned that if there was a serious economic situation we would have to use Tory weapons, financial and monetary policies, to get the thing right, before we were able to use socialist methods of planning and economic management. Despite this it was still a shock to them when they realized just how much Tory weapons were going to have to be used, and this became increasingly clear to them with the first economic statement, to be followed later by James Callaghan's first emergency Budget, and the later crises that were to occur even before Christmas.

We tried as best we could to explain to Transport House and to others in the Party what we thought was happening and why it was happening, but the communication necessary was not as good as it could have been. This meant that Transport House, which could have participated in putting out propaganda to explain to the nation what was happening, and the situation we found ourselves in because of the Tory Government's policies, were frustrated because they were inadequately involved. They didn't have nearly enough information to formulate propaganda and to get a campaign going which would have said: 'This is the deplorable state of Britain and this is what the Labour Government is going to do to put it right.'

Harold did as much as he could personally in television broadcasts, but one or two television appearances are not a propaganda campaign and the lack of co-ordination and planning on this front was a grave disability.

Intermingled with all this was the Rhodesian situation. None of us knew very much about the Rhodesian background except for the history of the Central African Federation and the fact that Malawi was independent and Zambia was just becoming so.

Southern Rhodesia was the only country in the former Federation still left as a British dependency. Here was a country which, of the three, had the most sophisticated and articulate white minority, and which had enjoyed for a very long time a measure of independence never accorded to any other Colonial territory with a white minority. They now had to decide their future against the pattern of independence gained by the countries to the north of them. Small wonder that they started

33

to proceed along the road towards a unilateral decision to take independence if it wasn't agreed to by the British Government. Small wonder too, that in Salisbury, Ian Smith was looking at the United Kingdom scene, realizing that the new Labour Government would severely limit his own room for manoeuvre. He himself was to be forced increasingly faster along the road to a UDI.

The curious thing is that this was one subject that was never talked about very much amongst ourselves until later in 1965. But at the end of 1964, and in the first months of 1965, there were developments which really should have been causing comment and making us ask questions. I can only put down this lack of interest to the fact that Rhodesia was such a long way away, while the economic problem was so big that it engrossed us all. But Harold was aware of the potential magnitude of the Rhodesian problem and the Commonwealth Office Ministers were clearly preoccupied with it.

And then Parliament met, and my goodness, the poor Parliamentary Labour Party arrived in Westminster confused and shell-shocked, despite the elation they felt at sitting on the opposite side of the Chamber as the governing party. To say that they were puzzled and worried about what they had been reading in the Press about the state of the nation, would, I think, be something of an understatement. When, therefore, they received the text of the White Paper in October and heard the Queen's Speech at the beginning of November, they were reassured that we were going ahead on all the things we had set out in our Manifesto, but I think they were also somewhat puzzled to know how it was going to be done against such an extraordinary background. However, there it was, and the Queen's Speech certainly gave them some heart, particularly the decision on old age pensions and other social legislation.

Harold made his first speech as Prime Minister during the debate, and it is now remembered because of one phrase which he inserted into it, referring to Patrick Gordon Walker's defeat at Smethwick as a squalid campaign and saying Peter Griffiths would be treated as a Parliamentary leper for the lifetime of that Parliament.

We were four weeks past the election and had a month to our credit in No. 10. But the integration of the political staff was still so slight that there was a small scene over this speech. On our return from the House the Principal Private Secretary came into my room and asked me in a very critical fashion why I had allowed Harold to get up and make such an irresponsible statement, and how I could have allowed him to be so foolish as to give such a hostage to fortune. I pointed out rather acidly that it would have been very difficult indeed for me to have done anything about it since I had not seen a copy of the speech before he delivered it. I was then told that it had been put on my desk and indeed it had, while I was out at lunch. Since I left No. 10 after 1 p.m. and Harold was to speak at 2.30 p.m. the chances of my returning to find the speech were small indeed. In any case, if I had seen it, I would not have removed those words. We all felt strongly both about the Smethwick campaign and Mr Griffiths.

But this business raised a problem which we always found it difficult to solve. It was Harold's habit to dictate a Parliamentary speech to a series of Garden Girls, who then typed it out for the whole thing to be looked at by Harold and his Private Office staff.

The procedure was that Harold would sit at the Cabinet Room table and at ten-minute intervals a new Garden Girl would arrive from downstairs to provide a chain system for dictation. Each girl would rush away after her ten-minute spell and type it back, and theoretically at the end of all the dictation a finished article was ready.

In the first Government members of the Political Office were rarely asked to attend the meetings to consider the Prime Minister's Parliamentary speeches. We received copies, as I say, which were often late, and consequently any strong views we had on anything in the speech would be very difficult to get across in time to get alterations made. Later in 1966 this changed and we were included in the groups which met after the speech had been drafted in order to consider amendments. This was an extremely helpful move, both for us, because we wanted to know what was in the speech, and, politically, for Harold.

To summarize the months up until Christmas and to recall the landmarks is difficult now. The legend of the breathless first hundred days has caught on and has become something of a joke. Writers and journalists tend to refer to it in an amused fashion. Do they ever stop now to ask themselves what would have been the situation if the Conservatives had been returned with a majority of five on 16 October? Or indeed, if they had been returned with a large majority on that date? What would they have done after that £800 million deficit to get the country back on the right road? We had already experienced thirteen years of their methods and we knew what it meant in terms of inequality and which section of the community always bore the major burden.

Between October and Christmas breathlessness certainly existed. The surcharge controversy (so maladroitly handled), the recurring economic crises, the economic statements and the mini-Budgets, the raising of Bank Rate to an extraordinary level, all became part of our lives. And Harold's confrontations with Lord Cromer at this time did not help to set us off on the right foot.

Lord Cromer, to me, seemed a typical Tory, very Establishment, alien in every way to Harold and not so brilliant. Harold for his part was equally alien to Lord Cromer. Harold was the City's 'bogyman' dating back to the Bank Rate Tribunal, a Socialist who though clever and able was totally unacceptable. And, of course, Cromer persisted in recommending Tory remedies to Harold – remedies which he had seen administered in the past and in which he was well versed. I think one might ask the question whether the Governor of the Bank of England doesn't have the duty as a public servant to adjust his philosophy to the government of the day, or resign. If there is a crisis, should he not try and present remedies in line with the government's approach? One had the feeling that Lord Cromer had never thought of this at all – and not of resignation either!

No wonder Harold and Lord Cromer didn't get on. Since the speculation continued and was so massive, one is entitled to wonder how far Conservative politicians who had strong connections with the City helped to build up the fires of rumour and speculation which made the situation increasingly difficult. It all resulted in the Labour Party, both in the country and in Westminster and at Transport House, seeing a situation developing which they had learned over the years as part of their political history lessons. This was the situation of the

1929–31 Labour Government when they had been at the mercy of the City and of international financiers, and had eventually been forced into total collapse.

Looking back, I think we underestimated the rancour the Tories felt when they lost that 1964 election. They still controlled all the other levers of power in the country. They were the masters of industry; they were the masters of the City; they controlled the Civil Service, more or less; but now they had had snatched from them the one lever needed to make the others operate together efficiently, namely government itself. For the government gives the go-ahead and rubber-stamps the actions taken elsewhere. The Tories must have felt very sore indeed. It is naïve to suppose that they did not help to stir it up for the new Labour Government in City circles and that this in its turn reverberated across the Channel and sparked off further speculation by the 'gnomes of Zurich' who throughout the early period had continued to press upon Harold the need for freeze and squeeze measures.

Harold became increasingly angry about Lord Cromer. His inner dislike of City speculators and everything the City stands for in terms of making money instead of earning it came out very violently during this period, when night after night he would come into my room for a drink, and report on the exchanges he had had to endure and the situation as he saw it.

I think that basically he would have loved to have had an election on the issue of whether we were going to be a country unable to practise democracy because we were dictated to by overseas financiers. Thomas Balogh would have ridden in on the biggest charger he could have found to fight a battle on this front. And what a campaign it would have been, and what a landslide victory we would have had. But as Lord Cromer was clever enough to point out, what a disastrous result it would have had financially – indeed, the same result as immediate devaluation in that the consequent situation of bankruptcy would have meant measures much more stringent than he was then pressing upon us, and the idea was never seriously on.

One of the biggest events before the first Christmas at No. 10 was the Defence Conference at Chequers on 21 and 22 November, when the Chiefs of Staff and Ministers assembled to discuss defence policy in the light of the Labour Government's philosophy. For me it was my first encounter with another side of the Establishment, the Defence Chiefs themselves, including Lord Mountbatten. I don't think, with the best will in the world, I could describe any of them as superior intellectual beings. They seemed personable, as they say in America, but they ran absolutely true to type, and for those who do not take this side of life very seriously the whole thing has a comic air about it. As for Lord Mountbatten himself, he is a very nice man, and doubtless quite progressive with it. It is rather difficult to hold a conversation with him which does not quickly turn into a discussion about some matter personal to himself. This is rather endearing in a quaint sort of way.

The most ludicrous aspect of the conference was the security arrangements. Immense lengths were taken to protect Chequers. That the conference was held there at all was a little peculiar since Chequers is one of the least secure places at which you could hold one as it is extremely open. However, for that occasion the army moved in and patrolled the grounds, and thousands of extra police seemed to be milling about. Everyone who went to Chequers on that weekend was checked in and out meticulously, and their passes and 'names, ranks and numbers' were carefully monitored. It was a real field-day for those who delight in security although personally I couldn't take seriously the concept of Chequers with soldiers on horseback riding round the grounds.

I did not stay overnight but I was not in the least surprised to learn that a great state of alarm had occurred during the first night, when a white figure was seen running across the lawn. It was later discovered to be one of the ladies on duty at Chequers, who had discovered that Mary's cat, Nemo, was trapped up a tree and making a great deal of noise about his predicament. She had gone out very quickly to rescue it, not bothering to dress, and with just her dressing-gown over her night-dress.

During this pre-Christmas period we had the problem of the Wilsons moving into No. 10 as a family. Until then Harold had commuted between Hampstead Garden Suburb and No. 10. There was reluctance on Mary's part to move from her home where she had been for so many years, and she did not find the atmosphere at No. 10 particularly welcoming, so there was quite a period before the actual move took place. The operation took up a great deal of our time because moving home and putting furniture into storage can't be done overnight. It was also an extremely upsetting period emotionally, not only for Mary but for the whole family. To some degree this affected Harold as well. He had arrived at No. 10 to find great crises with which he had to cope, but he also had a family and a home and, like every family man, he was anxious that they should be happy. While much of the official work could be delegated, he still bore the final responsibility, yet during this testing time he was inevitably involved also with the upheaval in family life that comes with moving from somewhere you have lived for many years to an entirely new environment.

At last the move was completed, but not without a great deal of comment from the Press accompanied by photographs of Robin's harmonium being carried into No. 10, the cat arriving in a basket, and Mary's personal pieces of furniture being brought in through the front door.

Since there was no housekeeper in residence on moving day, and therefore no food, a friend came and with considerable aplomb produced a lunch of fish fingers and a home-baked pie.

Most of the furniture from Hampstead Garden Suburb was put into store and what is not widely known is that the Wilsons accepted the flat at No. 10 as it was. I don't think it ever occurred to them that they had the right to go to No. 10 and express criticisms of their accommodation and order changes. They accepted what was provided and made few, if any, demands upon the official housekeeper at No. 10.

Before Mary actually moved she did make an official visit at the invitation of Lady Douglas-Home. While Lady Douglas-Home was still there in residence during the first two weeks of the Labour Government, she rang Mary to ask whether she would like to come and have tea so that they could discuss details about the flat and how life was organized there. Mary was pleased to receive this invitation for two reasons – because of the nervousness she felt at having to move into this rather forbidding building, and also because of an old family connection. While Mary and Harold had been at Oxford, they had known Lady Douglas-Home's brother very well indeed, and Giles, their younger son, had been named after him. So this nice gesture on Lady Douglas-Home's part was genuinely appreciated.

This was not Mary's first visit to No. 10. She had come in on our first day, 16 October, together with 'Grandpa' Wilson and Giles. They were all shown over the building, apart from the private flat, by John Hewitt, now Sir John Hewitt. That earlier occasion had been a rather intimidating one and the impression they got was one they did not easily shake off in the months ahead.

Mary now started to attract considerable public attention, to receive a very heavy mail, and to get involved in commitments and engagements of her own. So we decided that one of the members of the Political Office should also be Mary's Secretary, in order to cope with her work. Brenda Dew, who had been with us at the House of Commons and had come across to No. 10, took over this job, and did the whole of her work as well as a great deal of personal and political work for Harold himself.

Almost before you could turn round at No. 10, the question was being raised of Harold's first overseas visit to meet the President of the United States. It is traditional more or less that a new British Prime Minister goes off to see the American President after an election. There was a great deal of flurry over this trip because of the multilateral nuclear force – a project which Harold managed to persuade Lyndon Johnson to give up in favour of Denis Healey's own suggestion of an Atlantic Nuclear Force.

A Prime Minister's overseas visits and the psychological effects they have are a fascinating subject in themselves. They affected not only all those within the building, but also Harold himself. The scale and number of overseas visits which he undertook were enormous. I had a strong view from the moment we took office that the real problems were at home and we needed to concentrate our attention there. I begrudged every moment spent overseas as I felt this was time taken away from concentration on the serious economic problems which we would have to conquer if we were to have any hope of survival. Thomas Balogh also felt particularly strongly on this, and on occasions was beside himself when too much time was taken up with foreign affairs. He felt Harold should be concentrating more on the home front. That first American visit started off the argument, though only in a small way. It was construed within the building as being sour grapes because we were not included in the entourage.

I had, in fact, been to America a number of times. The reason I was not taken on that first visit was mainly that the Principal Private Secretary had worries because never before had anybody political been taken abroad with the Prime Minister. It is difficult to tell if this view was accurate. But for another visit Derek Mitchell did helpfully suggest that I might have been able to go on the plane in the capacity of a 'maid' if Mrs Wilson was on the trip.

Of all the big visits Harold made to America the first was the most important and successful. The rejection of the MLF was the big gain here but I don't in fact think that the President would have agreed to this if he had not already been in a frame of mind where he wanted in some way to get out of the commitment at home. On the visit Harold made the discovery that the President and he had a great deal in common in their attitude to European countries, not least in regard to the German problem.

Back at No. 10, we were almost totally engaged in making arrangements with Transport House for the Prime Minister's visit to Brighton for the Party's first post-election conference. It was to be a weekend affair and to take the place of the annual conference which we had missed in October because of the election campaign.

It was an extraordinary experience for all of us. Before that year Harold's personal arrangements for the annual conference had been fairly easy because his requirements were limited. He took with him only a few members of staff and needed only a suite and possibly two or three other rooms.

But we were now presented by No. 10 with a list of requirements we should have to meet and told of the arrangements that had to be made for special communications, teleprinters and the like. The Security Officer trotted off to Brighton beforehand to 'case' the hotel. Harold had to take a fairly large entourage with him.

Our time at No. 10 was spent arguing both with Transport House and with the Downing Street machine about all that was required; whether we could manage with less accommodation, whether we could obtain more, and how it all should be done. It was a nightmare. Even the question of the PM's car was a major problem. We were told quite categorically we could not use the official one on any basis so an outside hire car had to be taken on.

For Transport House it was also a nightmare. An additional complication for them was the fact that Cabinet Ministers quite rightly all wanted to stay in the same hotel as the National Executive Committee. Before 1964 Transport House had only been responsible for arranging accommodation for members of the National Executive Committee and Party staff. But in the new situation there were many members of the Cabinet who were not members of the NEC, and who needed to be at the conference, and who in fact ought to appear there. These had to be fitted in and where they had detectives, as in the case of the Home Secretary and the Foreign Secretary, accommodation had to be provided for them too. Many Cabinet Ministers also wanted to take Private Secretaries with them which added to the confusion.

It was meant to be a great election victory celebration, but by the time we all arrived there, after the difficulties beforehand, we did not feel in the mood for celebrations.

Harold came back from America just before we were due to leave. His plane had had to be diverted to Manchester because of fog so he was delayed in getting to No. 10. This resulted in some rush over his speech. Brenda and I coped with it and not only got it all typed, but also did the stencilling of it, in order to get it ready for the Director of Publicity at Transport House.

Harold arrived back from America a trifle disembodied. He had been at the receiving end of the onslaught of economic problems, and then had been to America engaged in even more intricate ones on defence. Now he had the problem which face all Prime Ministers, of readjusting to the home scene after an overseas trip, particularly after the exposure to the grand VIP treatment one receives on these occasions.

As Harold's Political Secretary I was left in charge of him once again since the Principal Private Secretary had this very strict demarcation line between a political activity and an official one. This was always preserved throughout the years of the Labour Government.

There were other small irritations. Harold had to take with him to the Conference someone to look after the teleprinter and to take messages down from No. 10 as they came in. In later years a new Principal Private Secretary used to accompany Harold since the then Principal felt that it was his clear duty, as head of Harold's official office, to be present with him in case of difficulty so that he could advise direct. But in the first years the Prime Minister was only accompanied on any outside visit, except for overseas visits, by a young girl from the Garden Rooms, a shorthand-typist. A rather inadequate way to organize things, but it was accepted, since the advice given was that this was how things had been done before. Harold never queried it nor did he sit down and try to work out some new arrangement, clearer and more adequate, so that there was integration and exchange of information too. But then he really didn't have the time. The onus should have been on all of us to have found some way round it ourselves. But it is easier said than done for 'new boys'.

In the conference hall itself there was a feeling of success and happiness, but I am afraid it was muted by all the problems and difficulties that the Party knew we had to face.

One of the most important post-conference happenings was the success of Sidney Silverman's Bill to abolish capital punishment. It had gone through the House on a free vote, but when this happened the Tories proceeded to put on a Whip to stop it from proceeding faster, but in order too to stop the flow of Government business through the House. However, the Government stepped in to help sort it all out and by 1965 the Capital Punishment Bill became law. It was to be the first of a number of Bills setting a liberal pattern on social affairs for which that Labour Government will, in my view, become increasingly remembered as the history-books get written.

By 16 December, George Brown had got his famous 'Declaration of Intent'. He had been doing an enormous amount of work with the Trade Unions to try and get their full free and voluntary co-operation in moving towards some sort of incomes and prices policy, to help fight the inflation which was making the economic situation worse.

Everywhere we seemed to be getting to grips with the facts of life. At the same time we had the emergence of a very powerful

Opposition. They were well orchestrated and well organized. Their propaganda against us was particularly powerful. Their claim was that Labour was making the situation worse by talking about it so much, and that one of the reasons why we could not get the economic situation right was because people did not have confidence in us or our policies. Both of these were dangerous assertions in themselves, since they implied by logic that an electorate voting into power a party of a different political philosophy had no right to do this if overseas people do not like the policies they want to pursue.

One of the simple themes used for attacking us was criticism for delaying paying the increase in the old age pension, while increasing MPs' salaries immediately. This was to prove a particularly effective tactic in the New Year. We had increased Members' salaries as a result of a recommendation from the committee set up by Sir Alec Douglas-Home, well before the 1964 election. It was an all-Party committee and all Parties in the House of Commons were committed to accept its recommendations. That we were left with the implementation of the recommendations was our misfortune. But we kept our word and we went ahead and we never heard the last of it. Throughout the five and a half years, and even to this day, letters come in saying: 'Who are you to talk, you were the people who delayed the payment of old age pensions when you first took office, but increased Members' salaries at our expense.' If the staying power of a piece of propaganda is the final verdict on its success, then this was one of the most successful pieces of propaganda ever put across.

Christmas for Harold was spent in the Scillies that year. Afterwards it was to be spent at Chequers, with the family leaving for the Scillies on Boxing Day or the day afterwards. But that first year they wanted very much to go off to their bungalow as soon as possible, because of the experience of moving from Hampstead into No. 10 and not feeling at home. They wanted to go back to somewhere they knew, and to feel relaxed and at home, and away from it all.

Before they left, the Security Officer went to 'case' the Scillies, having consulted with me previously and armed himself with a map of the Islands, with the bungalow clearly marked.

The bungalow itself had to be equipped with special telephones and the Customs House on St Mary was taken over for the use of the No. 10 office. It was there that the teleprinter was installed which kept the Prime Minister constantly in touch with No. 10, and it was there too that one detective stayed and also, in the early days, the Garden Girl who used to accompany the Prime Minister. Later a Private Secretary or a Duty Clerk used to accompany the Prime Minister on all his visits to the Islands, but in that first year it was only a Garden Girl.

Christmas was a particular shock, in a personal sense, to us since we were suddenly presented with the task of sending Christmas cards to thousands of people, whereas before we had only sent them out in hundreds. The official office presented us with a list of Ambassadors, Heads of State, Heads of Government and other distinguished people, to whom cards had to be sent. The official office also took on the task of typing the envelopes for these cards. But anyone else who received a card from the Prime Minister had to be dealt with by the Political Office. These included any cards he wished to send to any members of the Press or television, to political friends, to any other VIPs and, of course, to personal friends. At the end of the day the list reached gigantic proportions. Literally days were spent just putting the cards into the envelopes and getting them ready for the post. There was also the question of choosing the card, ordering it, and paying for it – some five hundred pounds a year just on cards. Before then we had bought cards either from the House of Commons or ordinary ones available to the general public.

However, from now on it was clear that we would have to have a card specially designed for the Prime Minister. Later we decided on photographs, but the first card was a reproduction of a favourite Lowry painting.

All of this had to be fitted in with our other work. But we were making some progress in that we were expanding the space we had been given and we were managing to adjust ourselves in many other ways more easily.

There were also little tricks that we had to learn. When we first arrived at No. 10 we were firmly told that all letters to Transport House had to be sent through the post and paid for by us. This we accepted readily as the right course of action, and proceeded to act accordingly. We were also told that each Christmas card had to be stamped and paid for by the Prime Minister. It was only much later on that we discovered that in previous years it had been the custom for Christmas cards, except to political people and personal friends, to be paid for by the official machine. All this entailed a process of discovery since no information was volunteered to us.

On the question of deliveries of our letters and communications to Transport House, we also discovered by accident that in the days of the Tory Government there had been a regular letter delivery service by van from No. 10 to Tory Central Office. Once we discovered this, we insisted that the same rule should apply to us. But again it was all a matter of discovery and certainly not one where someone would appear and say this is what is possible for you to do and this is what is not possible. The rule was that everything in fact was impossible until you discovered by accident that it was possible and then proceeded to take action on it.

This all sounds trivial and most people might dismiss these things as unimportant. But taken in the context of life at No. 10, where small irritations of this kind can mount up, changing a whole atmosphere within an office and gradually spreading out to other areas as well, then it no longer remains trivial and petty, but takes on a different aspect. For this reason these small points were regarded with a feeling of anger by many. Anger that no one bothered to advise us on the possible and the impossible in order to smooth our path a little.

3

Walking the Tightrope

After Christmas there was the question of answering all the cards that had been sent to the Prime Minister. It is impossible to describe the magnitude of this task. Thousands of cards poured in from VIPs, from individuals, from organizations, and all of them received a reply.

I used to sit cross-legged on the floor in my room, surrounded by mountains of cards, sorting them into great piles and then putting them into boxes with labels on. Harold would come in to find me like this, and he would often get down to look at some of the cards. He was amused and touched by some of the very nice messages written on them. At bad times, when we were having our difficulties, they were encouraging and reassuring.

The New Year started with us in fairly good heart. First there was the big economic conference at Chequers. Harold had this fixation about holding all his major conferences there. He certainly liked it, and was perhaps influenced by the way in which Harold MacMillan had used Chequers for major conferences, particularly when he wanted them to get into the news. And this always happened with any gathering which took place at the country home.

There was also a great deal of excitement in the beginning of the year over George Brown's energetic activity on the regional development front and in his talks with the TUC about economic planning. George was very much in the public eye and very effective too. The triumvirate of Harold, George and Jim was indeed the dominating thing about these early months, despite the fact that Harold was the Prime Minister.

But the beginning of 1965 also saw the gathering of Vietnam clouds. I would hazard a guess that there was almost nobody either in the Government or in the Parliamentary Labour Party who genuinely felt a hundred per cent support for the line which the Americans pursued, and which we ourselves confirmed in the attitude we took up. Ernie Fernyhough, Peter Shore, Thomas Balogh, Dick Crossman, Tony Benn and all of Harold's close friends became increasingly perturbed by what was happening and increasingly fearful of where the escalation might lead. All felt a distaste that a Labour Government was having to go along with all this.

Another problem was also coming to the forefront at this time – immigration. Frank Soskice was at the Home Office and I don't think that anyone in the Party regarded him as a strongly liberal or radical fellow in these matters. The fact that we were moving away more and more from the old line we had taken on immigration was deeply disturbing to our colleagues on the Left.

It was a rather nasty atmosphere in which left-wingers had to live. The economic problem was preventing the things happening to which they had looked forward; there was no question of a liberal foreign policy with the Vietnam problem hanging over our heads; and the immigration question seemed to be another event in a series of not very acceptable policies. I think that people imagine that throughout this period Harold was somehow going his way rubber-stamping everything that happened without deep questioning and heart searching. If so they were mistaken. He was under considerable pressure and had continuing doubts and worries.

On 21 January came the first real major shock to everyone in the Government and the Party. This was the day of the two disastrous by-elections in Nuneaton and Leyton. In Nuneaton we retained our seat, but the majority was slashed, and in Leyton the seat was actually lost by Patrick Gordon Walker to the Tories.

We were shocked not only by the loss of a Labour seat, but also because of Patrick Gordon Walker's own personal position which had already taken a severe knock in the General Election.

Harold was also faced with a separate problem because he had lost his Foreign Secretary, since Patrick was not in the Lords, and was now not in the Commons either.

There was a deep realization that he could not allow the drift to go on, and something had to be done. It would be untrue to say that until then Harold had not realized how serious was the situation with regard to the political management of the Party. But because he was so busy and involved with everything, he did not have the time to sit down and work out some form of liaison with the Party, and some form of Party management, organizing the Government politically and co-ordinating their activities at Transport House.

The following morning a small group met in the dining-room in the Prime Minister's flat to discuss how to put things right. He put forward the suggestion that there should be a small liaison committee. Not an official committee, because that is not possible under the Constitution of the Labour Party, but a small unofficial committee which would consist of members of the Prime Minister's Political Office, of the Lord President's office (where legislation and Government business is arranged), and of the Heads of Departments in Transport House. Harold and George Wigg decided that this ought to be done and done quickly and George Wigg was made the chairman of the committee.

It started to meet almost immediately and George Wigg did an excellent job in the next few months in setting up machinery for co-ordination of information. We used to meet in his room at the House of Commons looking out on to New Palace Yard. It wasn't a very glamorous or very cheerful room. In fact it was very dark and gloomy, but it fitted in well with how we felt in those difficult days.

One of the most important tasks the committee set itself was to improve the communications between Transport House and Ministers, and to try to overcome the lack of co-operation from Private Offices. There was always a struggle for Transport House to obtain information about Ministers' whereabouts and what engagements they were involved in, though they felt that they had the right to know what they were doing, since they often received telephone queries from the Press, asking them why such and such a Minister was doing a particular engagement. With the help of the Chief Whip's Office, we eventually arrived at a system whereby each Private Office informed the Chief Whip's Office of all engagements the Minister was involved in, both political and official, and Transport House was then able to have all of them and to give full publicity to those engagements which came under a political heading. If a Minister had an engagement in his constituency this was useful for his constituency party which could be used for making an important Party statement, or some specific political point.

At No. 10 the atmosphere was not always downhearted. There was a certain excitement about it all and particularly the excitement of living dangerously. With Patrick Gordon Walker gone, Harold had to fill the gap and appointed Michael Stewart, but this left a vacancy in the Cabinet. He wanted Roy Jenkins to take this because Roy had already proved himself an extremely able Minister. The job of Education which Michael Stewart vacated was therefore offered to Roy, who then quite surprisingly turned it down on the grounds that he knew nothing about Education. This may well have been the fact, but if all Ministers were to turn down jobs on such a basis then Cabinets would be very small indeed. It was a very strong and powerful decision for anyone to make, and an extremely confident one. The result was that the job was then offered to someone who, an equal on the economic front and in ministerial quality, namely Tony Crosland, accepted happily and indeed turned out to be an excellent Secretary of State for Education.

While Harold got on with the many crises, the Liaison Committee worked hard at co-ordinating activities, and George Wigg started separately to collect material for preparing a record of the Government's achievements. He made them keep it up to date as the months passed by. The object of this formidable exercise was to collate all the material and make it available to every Cabinet Minister and every member of the Government; it was alarming and appalling to discover the ignorance of many Cabinet Ministers about the work of the Government as a whole. It was an exercise, not only in making a Minister himself sit and look at what he had achieved within his own Department (or in some cases, what he had not achieved), but also in making him realize that he was not really living on a small island, but had other colleagues who were also busy at work.

Those early months of 1965 saw the death of Winston Churchill. Once Churchill had died the speed with which we discovered how much of the preparation and arrangements for his State Funeral had already been made was extraordinary. It was totally catered for and all that had to be done was to set the wheels in motion. It was, I suppose, one of the last great state funerals of any politician we shall see in this country.

Immediately after the funeral, Harold had his first meeting with Ian Smith. It was the beginning of a curious relationship that was to develop over the years ahead.

Many people had come to the Winston Churchill funeral, politicians and statesmen from all over the world. In that sense it was one of the first 'working funerals'. We were later to get the Eisenhower working funeral, the Harold Holt working funeral, the Adenauer working funeral and even the de Gaulle working funeral.

Another development taking place was a bid to improve relations with Eire. Harold has a deep and genuine feeling about Ireland and a wish to see the troubles there solved – a desire which was in evidence long before the more recent troubles.

He began with the gesture of asking the Eire Government if they would like to receive the remains of Roger Casement, so that they could be buried in Ireland. This was the beginning of the pattern which was to go on until the end of 1965 with the completion of the Anglo-Irish Free Trade Agreement. Relations between Eire and the United Kingdom Government and with Harold personally were always good.

The extraordinary thing about 1965 was the number of his foreign visits. In March he went to West Germany to see Chancellor Erhard – always referred to in our office as 'Auntie Ettie', after one of Harold's aunts, to whom he bore a striking resemblance – and in April there was his first visit to Paris to meet General de Gaulle. Mary went on the trip too, and a new wardrobe was arranged, including a charming hat she wore to leave in, but which she detested and which made her feel uncomfortable. The Wilsons were becoming increasingly famous as a well-known couple and in publicity terms Mary was a growing bonus.

51

By 14 April Harold was off again on his second visit to the United States. He had now done three overseas visits in five months. Around this time Thomas Balogh and others began to get rather perturbed about it all, and vocal with it too. It was strongly felt that since Harold was the only senior member of the Government who had an economic training and background, he ought to be at home far more than he was in order to give more direction to economic policy. The curious contradiction about those years is that Harold was always accused of being a 'one-man band' and that his Ministers were just puppets. The opposite, of course, was true. He delegated to an enormous degree – far more, I guess, than does our present Prime Minister. Many felt he should not have done this so much on the economic front, since neither Jim nor George had Harold's expertise. In the old days there used to be a theory that if you were not a trained economist you made a better Chancellor than if you were. When Treasury work was far simpler than it is now and the economic and financial set-up much less complicated, this was probably true. But in the world of 1964, when everything had become complicated and sophisticated, and where the intricacies of economic theory were so involved, there should be either at the Treasury itself or at No. 10 a man who really did know exactly how things work.

It was curious that during this whole period the Government's economic adviser was never included in his party on overseas visits. This was partly due to the fact that the Press were particularly vicious about Thomas Balogh and Nicholas Kaldor, because they were Hungarians and also because they were new and different and Labour.

The story was that Thomas somehow dominated No. 10 and Harold's economic thinking in a sinister, Rasputin-like fashion. It is true that his contribution in economic thinking at No. 10 was invaluable and his analyses were extremely accurate. But what is equally true is that Thomas was never as fully integrated in the team surrounding the Prime Minister as people imagine he was. Quite the reverse.

Harold went off again at Easter to the Scillies for a week with the family to get away from it all and returned to hold a conference of the Socialist International leaders at Chequers.

The Socialist International which is largely unknown in this country is an international organization to which are affiliated democratic Socialist parties from all over the world. The leaders try to meet each year. The year for it to be held in the United Kingdom was 1965, and Harold as host thought it would be a nice gesture to invite them to assemble at Chequers. As it was a political occasion it was organized, together with Transport House, by the Political Office, a difficult operation, since while I was beginning to get used to No. 10 I had never had to organize anything for Chequers and didn't really know my way round very well. As Cabinet members were present, official staff from No. 10 were in the house, but took no part in advising on or arranging any of the details for the conference.

The situation of having a small parliamentary majority, with the inevitable political consequences, meant additional problems for us at No. 10 from a public relations point of view. The Press Officer at No. 10 was Trevor Lloyd-Hughes, an old friend from many years back and former Lobby correspondent for the *Liverpool Daily Post*. Trevor was extremely well liked by people who knew him well. His appointment to No. 10, however, had caused a good deal of criticism, not least from his old colleagues in the Lobby, just because he had been in the Lobby for a provincial paper. He started off not too well; he was nervous and tended to joke in a rather off-handed way with journalists and this they misinterpreted. A story circulated that at a Press conference on Harold's first American visit, Trevor took charge and his answers to questions were tape-recorded by the Foreign Office. Later, the story goes, the civil servants in the Foreign Office would jokingly play the tape at parties in order to provide amusement for themselves.

But Trevor did have his problems when he was appointed to the post. He had to live up to his predecessors in that job, not least Sir Harold Evans, who had been Harold Macmillan's Press Secretary and had functioned magnificently. Trevor tended to be too deferential, in my view, with civil servants. He wanted very much to be completely integrated and never realized until too late that this was not possible with them. It all meant that he practised an even greater degree of impartiality than the Private Office. He tended to shrink from any connection with any part of the work of the Government which could in any way be regarded as political. We were losers here since Trevor, in doing his job as he saw it, would often refuse to answer political questions. So consideration was given to the question of whether or not we could continue without having in No. 10 one person who was responsible for answering political queries from the Press. Someone who would direct Harold's Press relations from the political side. It became increasingly necessary as the parliamentary and political situation became more and more precarious and by May we had decided that we must take some action about the appointment of a separate Press Officer at No. 10 to deal with Harold's affairs. By August our search for a Political Press Officer ended with Thomas Balogh suggesting to us that a young man working on the *New Statesman,* and who had worked for Dick Crossman, might be the answer. Gerald Kaufman came along to see Harold. Thomas brought him through into my room to introduce him to me. He seemed to me a little distant and very shy and I wondered how my aggressive way of working would go down with him. But it turned out to be the beginning of a very long and close relationship which I greatly value, since of the very few friends I have, Gerald is one of my closest.

He could not join us straight away as our Press Officer, since he wanted to cover both our own conference at Blackpool and the Tory Party Conference for the *New Statesman.* This was agreed to.

At the beginning of June, we had our first Trooping the Colour ceremony, an antiquated occasion that is nevertheless enjoyed immensely by many people, particularly children. The Prime Minister has available to him a number of seats in the special stand just outside the back gate of No. 10 and in all there are about forty seats on this stand which he can use, apart from the seats which have already been allocated to members of the Commonwealth High Commission Offices. Harold always used the private seats he had for friends and others who had helped him over the years, not just since he had been at No. 10, but also previously. Inside No. 10 the place was always filled with the talk and laughter of children, because children from the High Commission Offices were allowed to watch the parade from the State Room windows.

When the parade itself was over, and almost invariably there was a heavy downpour of rain during our years, people came into the State Room, where they were served with refreshments. As it was June we usually had Pimms No. 1 to drink before everyone departed for lunch.

In the early years we tried to lay on a private buffet lunch for those of our friends whom we had invited along separately. Then we were able to exchange all sorts of stories and gossip about what had happened to us since we had been at No. 10. Later on we were to go out to lunch with a particularly close friend, who would take a private room at the Reform Club.

The end of June in 1965 saw the first of Harold's Commonwealth Prime Ministers' Conferences. I think few people realize the fascination the Commonwealth has for him and the delight he takes in it. This first one for him was particularly exciting. The Vietnam issue had been dominating affairs in Parliament, and inevitably in the Labour Party. Harold suddenly had the idea that of all the organizations in the world, perhaps the Commonwealth Conference might have the best possible chance of all of producing some sort of solution which they could present to the North Vietnamese, Chinese and Americans for consideration. It was for this reason that he hit on the idea of a Commonwealth Peace Mission, which could tour all the countries involved in the dispute to try and persuade them to sit down together at a conference table and talk the whole thing out.

The Commonwealth Prime Ministers' Conference took an enormous amount of time out of the diary. It traditionally meets for just over a week, with the two weekend social gatherings at Chequers. What one cannot adequately assess is the amount of time taken up both before and after the conference in preparations for it and discussions thereafter about what has happened. All in all, the Prime Minister became so deeply involved with it that it must have taken at least a month away from his time. Politically at home it seemed more time lost from attending to what we knew were those terribly urgent domestic questions. Yet the Commonwealth rightly is a high priority.

Already there was a worsening economic situation and because of this Harold decided at the end of June to make a political speech at Glasgow saying that there would be no election that year. This was a deliberate act to stabilize the situation, both on the political front and on the economic front. But it was a statement which caused all of us some anxieties as we sat and kept our fingers crossed that his judgement was going to prove right. It was.

He was in a sense disappointed to have to make the speech. He had been watching with some fascination the upheaval in the Conservative Party. They were already beginning to indulge in talk of changing their Leader, Sir Alec Douglas-Home, but they were frightened to make the change if they were going to find themselves presented almost at once with a General Election and a new Leader who had not made himself known to the general public. They were therefore dependent upon Harold for the timing of their own leadership election.

The speech in Glasgow gave them the green light and they were able to go ahead. But without that speech they would have remained in the same agitated situation, not knowing quite whether Sir Alec should be given the push or not. If there had been a September or early October election, they probably would have stayed where they were and allowed Sir Alec to lead them, but once they knew Harold had decided against an election that year, then they were all set to get rid of him.

In July Harold made his first visit as Prime Minister to Durham for the Durham Miners' Gala. What a difficult operation that was. In that first year it was classified as a political engagement, though later it qualified as an official visit since union engagements as a whole were classified in this way, along with the CBI. Later the arrangements were taken care of by the Private Office. But in that first year it was left to me to handle. I had great difficulty in the organization of it. The miners in Durham were certainly not prepared for the demands I had to make on them, not on behalf of the Political Office but on behalf of the officials who needed accommodation and equipment in the hotel.

The hotel was small and already filled to capacity by the time our arrangements were made. 'We didn't have all this trouble over Clem', was all I had said to me over the telephone. I really could not have been angry with anyone since I understood totally how they felt about it all.

For me it was a marvellous sight to see the Lodges marching past down through the City of Durham to the great parade ground, their banners waving aloft, marvellously embroidered after clearly painstaking effort. That year there was not one with Harold on it, but there was to be later.

I was amused, too, watching 'Grandpa' Wilson, who was so delighted with the whole occasion that he could not resist going out on to the balcony a number of times with Harold. When autograph books were thrown up to the balcony for Harold to sign, very often 'Grandpa' would catch them, sign them himself, and then throw them back into the crowd, forgetting to get Harold's signature!

It was curious that year to see one of the 'original' Garden Girls, clearly intrigued by it all, going out on to the balcony of the hotel to watch the colourful parades marching below her – a sight she was unlikely to have seen if there had not been the advent of this Labour Government. I am sure she did not realize how lucky she was. It gave her, no doubt, a store of good stories to tell when she returned to the Garden Rooms later. Did she, I wonder, talk of the extraordinary people she had set eyes upon, and what a peculiar Prime Minister they now had who indulged in such odd visits?

Because of our difficulties the Tories, with a brand new Leader who had certainly not yet found his feet, nor made any impression either in Parliament or in the country, decided to table a motion of censure in the House of Commons on the Government's handling of the economic situation. Harold decided to intervene himself on this. For the first time for many years, we saw the return of the old-style Harold Wilson of Shadow Chancellor days. All the ingredients were there: hard hitting against the Tory Party, setting out the record as it really stood and not as it had been distorted by Tory Members of Parliament and by the Tory Press, and the old humorous touches which people liked so much.

It was a great delight to the office. We were allowed to help with the preparation of the speech and some of the passages in it. We particularly welcomed it because it set out so clearly and so fully what the record was. In all our communications thereafter, either with people writing in with the general post, or in other ways, we were able to refer them to Harold's speech, to what we called the 'promises speech', so that they could see for themselves all that had in fact been achieved.

Before the House actually rose for the summer recess, there were those usual comings and goings to which we had already grown accustomed, between the Chancellor, the Governor of the Bank of England and the Prime Minister. Sometimes the Governor came in by the back gate, sometimes by the front door, depending on how serious the situation was. The Governor turned up just before Harold was due to leave for the Scillies, and before Jim Callaghan was going off to the Isle of Wight. Lord Cromer tried to persuade both of them to delay their holidays and to stay in London and he said that he himself had decided not to go to the Riviera, because of the seriousness of the situation. But these actions would, of course, in themselves have caused a great deal of trouble, because inevitably they would have started rumours and speculation off all over again.

So Harold quite rightly went off on his holiday. He knew it was the only way to stabilize the situation, and Jim went too. So there was nothing for it but the departure of Lord Cromer for his Riviera relaxation.

It was Harold's first summer holiday in the Scillies as Prime Minister. My brother was a close friend of Harold's and in later years he would often spend a great deal of the summer with him and also Easter and Christmas, but at the beginning Harold went off alone with his family, and a girl from the Garden Rooms to run the office in the Customs House and keep the link with No. 10.

One detective went but later an additional one was sent, because on that first summer holiday there was an assassination threat on the Islands. It was made by a rather curious Irish peer, who went to the Scillies carrying a gun and threatening to shoot Harold. He didn't do it, and failed quite miserably to rise to the occasion presented by the fact that he could have eliminated the Secretary of State for Foreign Affairs at the same time, since Michael Stewart was not only staying on the Scillies but was at one point in the same hotel as the would-be assassin.

The summer holiday was a good one, because the trade

figures for August were good. It was the first summer that the Press were invited to film and photograph this new Prime Minister on holiday with his family on the Islands. They found an ordinary man having an ordinary holiday with his family. No more departures for the 'Glorious 12th' for the shooting in August, or a dash for the Riviera sun, or an even longer journey to the West Indies. This was the extraordinary ordinary man on his ordinary holiday and the papers were full of it.

However, as was to become traditional, there was a crisis during the holiday period when Singapore seceded from the Malaysian Federation and Harold was forced to come back to the mainland to have urgent talks with Defence and Foreign Office officials. It was not only serious in a world sense but serious for Harold and for the Labour Government. Harry Lee was one of our closest friends. We had indeed known of him when his left-wing associations had been rather more left – in the days when Mr Marshall was Prime Minister of Singapore and the then hero in Labour Party circles.

But now Harry Lee had come closer to his Socialist International colleagues. He had a very good working relationship with Harold. He has a formidable wife, of very high intellectual calibre, who must be a tower of strength to him in many ways. We were to learn a year later, when Harry Lee came to stay at Chequers, the real reasons behind the secession of Singapore from the Federation. As he was to tell it to us, he had felt well set on the road, through careful political planning and I suppose a degree of 'infiltration', to have taken over democratically in due course the Malaysian Government himself and to have become in time the Prime Minister of the Federation. The Tunku Abdul Rahman must have realized the situation only too well, and decided to act and get rid of Harry Lee before he got rid of him. To avoid such a calamity Harry Lee had taken the only way out to him – secession. He set up the independent Singapore Government, and Harold and the Labour Government gave it their blessing. For this Harry Lee was always grateful.

On the economic front the situation slid backwards. We came under increasing pressures from America to take more positive and forceful action to curb the inflation that was doing increasing damage to the balance of payments position.

The old traditional pressures came for a freeze and squeeze period.

Just when things seemed to be progressing a little, we had the terrible shock of the death of the Speaker of the House of Commons. Here was the government of the day, formed by a different party than the one to which the Speaker belonged, with a three majority and faced with the loss of the Speaker. This was the first time for many years that the Speaker had actually died in office, and this increased the whole atmosphere of cliff-hanging which had been going on throughout the preceding months.

How much psychological study goes into this sort of political crises few people realize and the twists and turns in the development of the solution provide endless fascination and not a little amusement. It really is a sort of cat and mouse game with a bit of carrot and stick as well.

Everyone now imagines the choice of Speaker was automatic, but there were many representations to Harold that someone else should be chosen, and a particularly powerful one from George Wigg. Many felt that the main candidate might not have exactly the right qualifications for this office, which needs a special composure and balance whichever side of the House you come from. Many feared he might so lean over backwards to be impartial that he would give the advantage to the other side.

When the election should be was much discussed amongst ourselves within the Party, particularly on the Liaison Committee now under Dick Crossman's command. Fierce arguments took place about the timing of it all and whether it should be an autumn election. Despite Harold's June statement the discussions still went on and pressure was still put upon him to change his mind.

Peter Shore was a tower of strength politically, as Harold's Parliamentary Private Secretary. Together with Ernie Fernyhough, Peter was growing increasingly enthusiastic about the National Plan which George Brown had been working on.

George worked so hard on this. A great deal of the credit for the subsequent surge forward of Labour in the opinion polls is due to George for this work. There is no doubt that the National Plan at that time gave a pattern and coherence to what the

Labour Government was doing and what it wanted people to realize were its aims and objectives. As the National Plan emerged into the light of day people became more and more interested in it and its reception became increasingly good. It started to pave the way for the Queen's Speech later in the year.

We had been making the normal, or rather the abnormal, arrangements for our Party Conference, and at the end of September we went off to Blackpool to attend our second Conference in government.

It was a different Conference from the one we had the year before. It was confident, relaxed, balanced and, on the whole, good humoured. There was no doubt that the Labour Government had arrived. People had accepted it totally and Harold Wilson was the Prime Minister and the only one the British people wanted.

There was a rather odd argument with the officials about what the Garden Girls would be called – during the conference period. One could hardly call them 'Garden Girls' to our comrades. I asked the question in order to avoid any difficulties in communications within the Party once there. I hoped they would not, as they usually did when on outside visits, refer to themselves as the Prime Minister's Private Secretaries, since if they did it was likely that messages would get transmitted to them which were really meant for the Political Office.

There was great obstruction and an insistence that they could not be called anything other than Private Secretaries or Personal Assistants to the Prime Minister. All of these designations seemed quite grandiose for them. They are in fact first-class and most efficient shorthand-typists. All we wished then was for them to be called members of the Prime Minister's official office staff. We did not want our political friends to be confused. They could not know the set-up at No. 10, and this curious dichotomy between the Political and official offices. The time taken over this silly argument was extraordinary. Brenda Dew had to go up two days ahead of the rest of us in order to establish to everyone there that the office we had, as the Political Staff, was the office to contact, and not the room the Garden Girls were to occupy. A real storm in a teacup, and very tiring!

At the Party Conference we had, above and behind the

platform, a very tiny room for Harold with a desk and a telephone in it. Next to it there was a typing room for the staff to use while they were in the conference hall. It was to Harold's tiny room that the High Commissioner for Rhodesia came at the end of the week with a very serious message. Then began the real turn in the Rhodesian story. From then on the Rhodesian issue dominated foreign affairs and the work of the Labour Government, just as the position of sterling and the balance of payments dominated the economic and domestic scene.

It seemed at the time in the excited atmosphere of a Party Conference a lot of trouble about nothing. Our Overseas Secretary, Gwyn Morgan, was very much aware of its implications and the strong feelings it would arouse in the Party. But in the conference hall they had no idea of what was going on behind the scenes.

Then as soon as we got back to London we had a visit from Ian Smith. He was extremely popular. A handsome man, in a battered sort of way, with a great deal of charisma and attraction, he had been a fighter pilot during the war. We realized that politically it was going to be very hard going indeed to convince the general public that Ian Smith was a right-wing reactionary and that black Africans had the right to have a say in their own government in Rhodesia, and to convince them that the actions which Ian Smith was advocating could not be tolerated or accepted by the United Kingdom.

Back from Blackpool, the Political Office was greatly strengthened by the addition of Gerald Kaufman. He was given the room which the Parliamentary Private Secretary had used in the days of the last Tory Government, the very room which we had first moved into on our arrival on 16 October 1964. With Gerald there, our lives were happier, much more relaxed, much easier. He brought with him a great deal of political acumen and a very acute sense of humour, all of which were to be needed very much over the coming months. They were to be needed even more thereafter!

He was given the job of handling Harold's political press relations. He had to liaise both with Trevor Lloyd-Hughes and with Percy Clark at Transport House, two very different characters. It was a credit to Gerald that he was able to do so and to maintain a good working relationship with both throughout his period at No. 10. He shared, too, our kind of politics. He was left-wing, but a realist, and he also had a healthy disrespect for the System and for the Establishment which we as the 'foreigners' in the No. 10 building felt so strongly about.

Little wonder, therefore, that Gerald shared too the anxieties felt at Harold's suggested trip to Salisbury. George Wigg was also worried about it, though not, I think, on political grounds. Certainly he worried on grounds of security and became quite obsessed with the need for greater protection for Harold, not just in Rhodesia but on the plane out and back. A fantastically large entourage left London with Harold at the end of October for the visit. Also on the plane were a great number of Garden Girls who seem to have spent much of their time in the Governor's swimming pool, judging from the stories that were circulated in No. 10 afterwards. But there were no politicians, no Parliamentary Private Secretary, no political advisers at all. Harold not only went to Salisbury but called in at Zambia and Lagos on the way home for good measure.

The beginning of November and right through the period to the Queen's Speech was dominated by Rhodesia, culminating in the UDI on 11 November. The fact that the Queen's Speech in itself was an extremely good one and contained a great list of the Government's achievements together with what we hoped to do over the years ahead, almost providing a manifesto in itself for the next election, was overshadowed by the Rhodesian affair. Even Harold's visit to his niece's wedding in Cardiff was held under the shadow of what might happen in Rhodesia and whether UDI would be declared just as she was being married.

The wedding itself was very nice but slightly farcical. The bride was extremely pretty, very much like her aunt, Mary Wilson, and the bridegroom traditionally handsome – a picture-book pair in a picture-book wedding from that point of view. But the arrangements were a nightmare.

Since it was a personal engagement, the official office had nothing to do with it, and the arrangements fell on my shoulders at the No. 10 end. I was the only member of the staff there since it was a family affair and we forgot the Press would need looking after. So once there I had to take that job on too.

When we arrived at the tiny church, I discovered that the

minister had said the Press could take photographs inside and I had to tell the family that this had been agreed. They did not want the actual ceremony to be photographed, and so I then had to proceed to tell the Press that. There was a gallery running right round the church and the tramp of the feet of the Press on the uncarpeted boarded floors was absolutely deafening. Those below couldn't hear a word that was being said. In the end I was able to enlist the aid of a good friend, and distinguished photographer on the *Sunday Times*, Steve Brodie, who helped me to persuade everyone to leave – after they had taken a number of pictures, but before the actual marriage service was to take place.

A more sombre note for November was when the Member of Parliament for Hull North died. We were left with two by-elections, one in Erith and Crayford for Norman Dodds' seat, and now the one in Hull North. All this – and Rhodesia too.

The strong feeling in the country in favour of Smith, particularly when he visited the United Kingdom and when he appeared on television, was to swing back later in Harold's favour. The appearances that Harold made on television about UDI, though joked about by journalists in a good-humoured way, were in fact very effective. Particularly impressive was the one which he ended with the words 'Think again Prime Minister, think again.' It became a stock Lobby remark.

President Ayub Khan's visit provided the first occasion on which I attended any official engagements organized by Her Majesty's Government. I was appalled to see the sort of people who were invited along to such occasions. They were totally Establishment; stiff, formal and very 'British'. It was, however, a most enlightening experience from my point of view to see how stereotyped was the approach to each state engagement and official engagement, and how the guest lists were always the same, on a permutation basis.

Then on 15 December Harold went for his last overseas visit that year – to New York and then on to Washington. This was my first time accompanying him.

It was an unusual visit to New York in that we stayed not in the normal hotel, but in the private apartment of Senator William Benton, who was extremely nice and a very old friend of Harold's. He had offered the flat to him as a haven and an escape from everyone else. It was an extraordinarily opulent apartment, with a curious decor. Naked ladies in high black boots and large black hats, reminiscent of the Toulouse-Lautrec period, seemed to be everywhere. Even when we cooked our breakfast the following morning in the typically modern American kitchen, we were amazed to find that our breakfast china was also embellished with nubile ladies. Perhaps a delight for men, but there are few women who would want to have their bacon and eggs straight off such an unusual background.

It was on this visit that Harold addressed the United Nations for the first time. At that time he referred to the whole Rhodesian question. Beforehand there had been elaborate plans made by the African bloc to stage a walk-out during his speech. This happened, much to Harold's dismay and to ours. He still felt that the actions he was taking on Rhodesia were right, and that force and tough action of the kind the African bloc wanted could not be contemplated; that the moderate middle road of sanctions and persuasion, which he had chosen, was the only possible ones in the context of Southern Rhodesia and its own position within Africa and also within the context of United Kingdom politics. But Africans are not given to any easy understanding of British domestic politics and the walk-out which took place was very impressive but quiet. It had a devastating effect upon all of us.

We went from New York to Washington and it was there that I had my first meeting with President Lyndon Johnson and my first official tour of the White House. But it was only a brief visit and one did not have time enough to take it all in properly. But I did note – and like – the good-natured homely atmosphere about the Johnson family.

I had the misfortune to be placed in the Embassy with Mary and Harold, rather than in one of the hotels with some of the staff, where I would have preferred to be. I found the British Embassy stiff and stuffy.

Throughout the whole of that visit the Private Secretaries had gone to great pains to see I was included in all the functions which Mrs Wilson attended. But this meant unfortunately I was not included at all in any of the functions which Harold attended. Instead I found myself accompanying Mrs Wilson on a tour of ladies' tea parties and luncheons. I had to get reports of the serious business from Harold direct after the days' events had ended.

One enjoyable experience was lunch at the White House with a group of American ladies, all of them attractive, charming and delightful, but talking politics of a very different kind, often domestic and parochial. There were also included a number of American newspaper women, very formidable, very acute, with whom I must confess to have found myself at a loss, and not a little frightened. We left Washington for Philadelphia, to see Harold's elder son, who was at college there, before flying on to Canada and then back to London.

Only one thing remains to be said about that visit. That was the event in which we all had to take part – the switching on of the Christmas lights by the President and Mrs Johnson outside the White House. A lot has been said about the speech the President made then. My own view of it all, and this was shared, was that the speech, far from being complimentary to the British was meant critically, hitting out at us in an oblique way maybe but nevertheless an attack upon us for not participating in the Vietnam War. That is my view. And I was there.

By that Christmas we had taken over more accommodation at No. 10. Gerald was in the Parliamentary Private Secretary's old room. The Prime Minister's housekeeper had her own room with its own private bathroom. Immediately opposite was another room with a bathroom which Brenda Dew used so that she could be near Mrs Wilson. All three rooms were on the second floor on the same level as the private flat. Above Brenda's room and the housekeeper's room were two attic rooms, which more or less became the home of the Political Office. It was in one of these attic rooms that I did most of my work. In the room opposite was Peter Shore, together with his secretary. We were very close together and able happily to exchange views frequently on all that was happening, particularly when Harold came up to see us. I think that without the presence of Peter with us during those months, coming in every day and working in No. 10, we should never have had the feeling of confidence we did have which enabled us to get through the year, going confidently into the run-up period to the election.

But before Christmas came there was the excitement of Harold's first reshuffle. This was caused by the fact that Sir Frank Soskice, the Home Secretary, was not in good health. He had for some time wanted to leave his job and take life more quietly. But it was the beginning of a tremendous period for us. It opened the way to Roy Jenkins' appointment as Home Secretary, and of course it opened the way too to the liberal reforms for which I believe this Labour Government will be particularly remembered. The reforms, I believe, would have come anyway, but the actual management of it all owed much to Roy.

The other big appointment was that of Barbara Castle as Minister of Transport. Harold had a great deal of worry over whom he should appoint to such a job. After a very great deal of discussion he realized that of all the people in his Cabinet who had the right sort of mind to cope with the administrative intricacies of a Department like Transport, and to sell it politically and propaganda-wise, Barbara was the best qualified. The fact that she was a woman, which some thought would be a disadvantage, turned out to be an advantage, since it drew attention to her.

The Wilsons went off for their first Christmas at Chequers. This year, without the background of the upheaval of the removal from Hampstead Garden Suburb they felt more confident to celebrate Christmas Eve, Christmas Day and Boxing Day at Chequers. Then they went on to the Scilly Isles for a few days to celebrate their wedding anniversary, 1 January, as they traditionally do, on the Islands. Christmas at Chequers also gave them the opportunity of inviting members of their family there. It was also the first occasion on which they were able to hold a dinner party to which they could invite friends, of both recent and long standing, whom they wanted to thank in a special way for the help and support they had given.

4

A Very Public Place

Anybody who has ever worked at No. 10 never has to worry about a subject for conversation again. Whether you were there for years or merely for weeks, whether you were Prime Minister or messenger, there will always be somebody to ask: what goes on inside Downing Street? Is it as exciting as it seems from outside? What is the life of a Prime Minister really like?

The answers, of course, depend on what you did there – and on what you hoped to do. More than 130 people earn their livings inside the building. Some of them are very satisfied indeed. The permanents, the civil servants who are sometimes there for many years, become deeply attached to it. They think the system is splendid and they have an almost proprietorial attitude to what they come to believe is their building. To an extent that belief is right. In many ways No. 10 does belong to them.

But what of the temporaries, who include the Prime Ministers themselves? What of the people who come and go with them? These also succumb to the fascination of No. 10, but it is a different sort of fascination. For theirs is a unique role, operating as they do with the Prime Minister at the very heart of the Government. Sometimes they change No. 10, and when they go they leave behind their personal auras to mingle with those of their countless predecessors. They depart having both loved and hated No. 10, but inevitably they have been permanently affected by their experience there.

The truth is that No. 10 is both a dreadful place to live and work in and also an exciting place to live and work in. It is not beautiful but it is impressive. Its designers have not succeeded in making it either an efficient office or a comfortable home. It seems to exude an air of condescending contempt for both roles.

One trouble is its size. In fact it is much more spacious than its façade in Downing Street suggests. It is a big building constructed round a quadrangle and stretching far back towards Horse Guards Parade. But despite its area it is still hopelessly inadequate for the many people who have to work in it.

It is hot in summer and almost unbearable during a humid spell. Frequently it is noisy as well. There are cheering or cat-calling crowds in Downing Street in the front, and military bands rehearsing for hours on end at the back. Yet despite this the atmosphere inside usually is reminiscent of a cloister. There is a feeling that you have been cut off from the outside world. No. 10 is more of a monastery than a power house.

Certainly those who run the building seemed deliberately to ignore the most ordinary needs of those who worked there. It does not possess a canteen, or even a solitary vending machine. Senior civil servants can eat in the Cabinet Office Mess in Whitehall – a canteen for top mandarins – and the typists in the basement have their own kitchen where they can cook any food they need. In the attics, too, there is a kitchen for the telephonists. But for anybody who does not fit into these categories there is nothing. They have either to bring sandwiches or eat out. This is not the most helpful arrangement as many of those involved are precisely the people most needed for unexpected overtime or urgent consultations.

The messengers have provided their own solution. They have stoves on which they brew tea or cook rough and ready meals in their room on the ground floor. When we were at Downing Street their favourite dish seemed to be stew. We knew this because one could smell the stew over a large part of the building. Before we went to No. 10 people often used to refer to the sweet smell of success. I never realized that the predominant smell of political success would turn out to be the messengers' stew.

But many people who should know better say that this unique building is particularly suited for the needs of modern government and point out that one outstanding advantage is that the Prime Minister lives 'over the shop'. Personally I do not think this so-called advantage justifies all the other ana-chronisms. I am not sure that it is an advantage. The Prime Minister is too readily available just because he lives there. Often it is impossible for him to relax even when he closes the door of his private flat on the second floor. Future Prime Ministers might well consider whether it is not better to give up the flat and live in a private residence – near No. 10 but not inside it.

There is a back garden but it is rarely used. This is supposed to be shared with the Chancellor of the Exchequer, who lives next door at No. 11. Harold Macmillan tells an amusing story in his autobiography of how Gladstone, when he was Chancellor, prepared an elaborate minute arguing that the garden should be shared absolutely equally between the occupants of No. 10 and No. 11 and of how he prepared an equally elaborate minute when he was Prime Minister, arguing that the garden belonged primarily to No. 10.

What happens in practice today is that neither Prime Mini-ster nor Chancellor uses the garden much. Jim Callaghan went out there hardly at all, and I only remember seeing Roy Jenkins strolling there once or twice with an adviser when Budget time was approaching. I never saw the families from both houses relaxing there in the summer, enjoying the air and the flowers.

I always felt this was a great pity because the garden is charming. It has good lawns and trees, colourful borders of flowers and shrubs and high walls. On a few occasions Harold went into the garden to do his boxes. The staff tripped out periodically to ask questions and receive their instructions. There were some old wicker chairs and tables for his use, but they were so dated that he looked rather like a refugee from a Noel Coward play.

The trouble was that whenever one went there one had a feeling that people were watching – and of course they were. The garden is overlooked by the Whip's Office at No. 12, the typists working away in the basements of No. 10 and No. 11, and by anybody happening to glance from any of the windows of the dozens of buildings on that side of Downing Street. There is no sense of privacy – and yet there could be quite easily.

Simply by screening off a part of the lawns the families of the two houses could enjoy one of the few attractive private gardens in that part of London.

It is this garden that gives its name to the girl shorthand-typists employed by the government at No. 10. They are known throughout Whitehall as the 'Garden Girls'. There, at the bottom of the building, they live in a positive network of secretarial rooms, reference sections, filing areas, shredding machines and other devices. This is where a lot of the hard work of No. 10 is done – the regular daily round, often exciting, but usually monotonous, consisting of typing, filing, recording and drafting letters, speeches, cables, telegrams and other messages.

But, naturally, it is the ground floor that attracts most of the attention. This has the showpiece, the Cabinet Room, which is long, and in my opinion rather dreary-looking. Its table is coffin-shaped so that all members of the Cabinet can see the Prime Minister in his chair in the centre. He sits looking out over the Horse Guards Parade and directly behind him is the famous portrait of Sir Robert Walpole, the longest resident of No. 10, who was Prime Minister for twenty-one years. The curtains and carpets are green, the table is covered by green baize and the walls, painted cream, are just as unimaginative. Each member of the Cabinet has his own special seat, his own folder for his papers, and his own scribbling pad, pencil and ink-well. There are even candle-holders for emergencies. Everything is tidied, cleaned or replenished by messengers after each Cabinet meeting.

The door from the Cabinet Room to the corridor is covered in baize too – green on the inside to match the room but red on the outside to match the colour of the corridors. On one side of the Cabinet Room is the Private Office where the Private Secretaries work – two large intercommunicating rooms with great double doors connecting them with the Cabinet Room. On the other side is the smaller room which became my office. Then the long red-carpeted corridor stretches away from the Cabinet Room towards the front door. To the right of the front door is the elegant bow-windowed room used by the Press Secretary, with other adjoining press rooms. Just inside the front door are two rooms used by messengers, police, custodians and doormen.

Also on the ground floor are corridors which lead on one side to the Cabinet Offices in Whitehall and on the other to No. 11 and No. 12 Downing Street. It is possible to walk right along that side of Downing Street without going outside. There is a story that it used to be possible to tell whether there was a close relationship between Prime Minister and Chancellor by the state of the door between No. 10 and No. 11. If it was locked the conclusion was obvious. Of course the door was never locked while we were at Downing Street. I shudder to think of the sort of intra-party warfare that must have existed years ago when the door was actually locked.

The staircase near the Cabinet Room leads to the first floor and is famous for the pictures of former Prime Ministers hung along its wall, each looking down on his predecessor. When we were there Sir Alec Douglas-Home was at the top. Now no doubt he has moved down and Harold is in his place. Every new Prime Minister arriving at No. 10 must be affected as he sees these past Prime Ministers – and must also wonder how long it will be before he takes his place among them.

The first floor contains the study where Harold spent many of his evenings, and the formal State entertaining rooms. There is the White Boudoir, the Middle Drawing Room, the Pillared Room, the Small State Dining Room, and most impressive of all, the State Dining Room.

Across from the State rooms, on the other side of the quad-rangle, are the Church Appointment offices. The fact that they are there in No. 10, where space is so desperately needed, always struck me as amazing. I realize, of course, that the Established Church has to be administered and that, for the present at least, Prime Ministers have to take responsibility for the appointment of Bishops to dioceses and many clergymen to livings. But why should all this be done from No. 10? There can be arguments about possible disestablishment but surely none at all about the waste of office space on work that could be done perfectly well somewhere else. No wonder I was reminded of a monastery when I entered No. 10!

The second floor contained in our day the three rooms which we obtained for the Political Office and the Prime Minister's flat. The flat itself had a fair number of rooms but was dark and low-ceilinged. The decor and layout were hardly changed by the Wilsons. Since the building had, at great expense to the nation, been completely renovated just before the 1964 election, they did not feel they could ask for alterations so soon. It remained, therefore, largely as it was during the Douglas-Home tenancy.

Of course a Prime Minister and his wife can have a lot of changes made if they wish and if they insist. But nobody explained to the Wilsons what they could have had done. Mary Wilson did have modern Swedish furniture brought in for her bedroom, but the other bedrooms and the sitting-room remained just as Lady Dorothy Macmillan had arranged when she lived there briefly after the reconstruction.

If an estate agent had to describe it, I suppose he would say that the accommodation comprised five bedrooms, four bathrooms, one kitchen, a music room, dining-room and sitting-room. In the Wilson years the bedrooms were rarely used all at the same time. Mary had the large bedroom, with Harold sleeping in a smaller adjoining one, which was a sort of dressing-room. Giles, of course, had his own room, because he was a day boy at University College School when Harold became Prime Minister. Later, when he went to his teachers' training college near Brighton, he was at home for the holidays and many weekends.

What an estate agent's description would not provide would be the fact that, although it was supposed to be a private home, the flat was an almost public place. Whenever Harold was there the messengers were coming in and out, the telephone was ringing, the files and the red boxes were being delivered. It was a place in which you couldn't even enjoy a good family row because if you did the whole building would soon know. No. 10 is an inadequate seat of government and definitely not a home.

Above the flat is the third floor with the 'attic rooms'. On this floor are the numerous bedrooms provided for staff, senior and junior, who have to be on call during the night. Here, too, are the telephonists, with the famous No. 10 switchboard. I have never known such an efficient, expert telephone service anywhere else. It is superb at tracking down people in the remotest parts of the world, and finds usually unobtainable numbers. In times of crisis it is marvellous.

That then is the setting against which a Prime Minister lives and works. It is the setting against which Harold Wilson's days were organized with a number of small changes as time went by.

Some Prime Ministers start work early. Harold began comparatively late. He was normally on the go from 8.00 a.m. and usually worked a sixteen-hour day. He preferred to do a lot of his work at night. All of his life he had been an owl rather than a lark.

A typical day would begin with tea and the morning papers. With those morning papers would come a foolscap roneoed sheet giving a list of his engagements for the day. It had been prepared the night before.

Every evening a girl typed out the diary for the following day, with the engagements as they are entered in the book. I had always thought that Prime Ministers' diaries were enormously impressive books, probably leather bound and gold tooled. I found it was just a straightforward government-issue desk diary with a separate page for each day.

The diary was kept by a junior Private Secretary, who entered in pencil those engagements that would probably be accepted, in ink those which had definitely been accepted, and at the bottom of the page, in blue pencil, those engagements which had been refused. Once the girl had typed the sheet, stencilled and copied it, it was then circulated throughout No. 10 to all those who needed to know the Prime Minister's movements ahead of time.

Mrs Wilson, the housekeeper, the Private Office, the Press Office, the Political Office, the detectives, the front door, the policemen on duty, the messengers and the Security Officer all received a copy. As a day progressed engagements were inevitably added, and the sheet that was first seen early in the morning quickly bore no relation to all the commitments the PM was keeping.

But this first organizational task was the one that enabled everyone to co-ordinate the activities for the day. It was the skeleton around which everyone tended to work. Mrs Wilson's own private and public engagements fell into line with it, particularly where she was expected to keep an engagement with the Prime Minister. The Political Office naturally planned their day with it in mind, so that they could know when they might be needed, and when too they would be able to seek time with the PM.

Harold has a well-known interest in the Press, and enjoyed reading his morning papers, despite the continuing attacks that were later to be more frequent than complimentary pieces. He had read the first editions of three morning papers the night before. The proprietors of the *Daily Mirror*, the *Sun* and the *Daily Telegraph* sent them round to Downing Street by special messenger at about 11.00 p.m. His first job in the morning, then, was to check the final editions of these three papers, and of course to read all the others. He read them in bed while eating breakfast, usually bacon and eggs, sometimes haddock and poached egg. Once a year, he received from Hector Hughes, then the MP for Aberdeen North, a large box of Scottish kippers. Once they arrived he had kippers regularly until the supply was exhausted.

After his bath he went straight down to the Private Office. Some Prime Ministers deal with their red boxes before they leave the flat in the morning, but Harold always cleared his boxes before he went to sleep.

In the Private Office he checked the arrangements for the day and any developments during the night. He had a small card each day with the engagements typed on it since it was easy for him to carry this around. As the day wore on, the engagements would be amended, and more people would be slotted in as events justified: more meetings would be arranged, other changes made. These he would write in on the card himself, but the original foolscap might be re-duplicated if it became hopelessly out of date; and the long narrow sheet in the wooden stand which stood on the Cabinet table at the PM's place and on his desk in his study would also be retyped.

The key man in his Private Office, and indeed in the whole of No. 10, was the Principal Private Secretary, who was first Derek Mitchell, and then, from March 1966, Michael Halls.

The Principal Private Secretary is a man feared throughout Whitehall. He has constant access to the Prime Minister and, depending on his character and the character of the Prime Minister, he can be a very powerful person indeed. Different men interpret their roles according to their personalities and aims.

Another Private Secretary, the No. 2, is a Foreign Office man seconded at No. 10 and naturally he is the PM's foreign affairs expert. There is also a Home Affairs Private Secretary, who often came from the Home Office, though Harold was later to choose the Private Secretaries from a much wider trawl than the traditional big departments.

One Private Secretary has the sensitive job of looking after Questions to the PM in the House of Commons. The most junior Private Secretary usually keeps that all-important diary and deals with the correspondence arising from it. There is one rather separate Private Secretary, the one in charge of Church of England appointments, who acts also as a sort of curator for No. 10, and a liaison man between No. 10 and the Chequers Trust. He is the most permanent of them all, and tends therefore to receive rather special treatment.

Private Secretaries usually only serve a two- to three-year term of office before moving on to inevitable promotion and the beginning of an impressive Civil Service career.

Another separate Private Secretary, working apart from the others, handles the vast amount of correspondence pouring daily into No. 10 from all over the country, from individuals and organizations, all with queries, complaints or cases to be investigated. Then, out on a special limb is the Press Secretary, with his own unit of assistants and information officers.

These were the men who ran the No. 10 machine in our time. Yes, the men, for as far as I know there has never in fact been a woman Private Secretary in the Private Office.

These Secretaries arranged the Prime Minister's day, obtained the immediate tactical decisions from him, and hovered around him constantly, almost like vultures, whenever they spotted him alone, waving their pieces of paper hopefully as they pursued him from room to room. I don't think one of them ever actually invaded the bathroom, at least I'm not sure but the fact that nobody did was rather surprising. It was certainly the only place where he was safe, since they often accompanied him into the gentlemen's lavatory on the ground floor. My office was nearby, unfortunately, and I could often hear their voices in there, as they reported to him, argued a point, sought to persuade him on others. It was an advantage they had on me, since they could always give him their version of an incident before I could if he happened to pop in there before looking in on me in my office.

The first visitor of the day was usually produced at 9.30 a.m. but there could be a 9.00 a.m. visitor if the day was a busy one. Thursdays were always particularly active days because there was usually a Cabinet and, of course, Prime Minister's Questions in the afternoon. Harold saw a stream of Ministers whose subjects were coming up in Cabinet from 9.00 a.m. to 10.00 a.m. Then Cabinet met at 10.00 a.m. until about 12.30 p.m. or 1.00 p.m. A crisis was always quickly known about by the length of the Cabinet sitting.

Prime Minister's Questions between 3.15 p.m. and 3.30 p.m. each Tuesday and Thursday are the high spots of the Parliamentary week. Originally these periods were set aside so that the Prime Minister could actually provide information for the House at a high level, but it is a long time since Question Time has been regarded in just this way. It is now often turned into a totally political operation in which Opposition MPs take on the Prime Minister in a bid to discredit him or his Party. It is the nearest thing British politics has to gladiatorial combat. Sometimes it develops into a man-to-man affair, with the Prime Minister and the Leader of the Opposition facing each other across the Despatch Box like enraged bulls. At other times it is a carefully planned operation with MP after MP on the other side combining against the object of their hatred. There are very few parallels in other legislatures, and it is certainly one of the most dramatic set pieces in the Commons.

The demand for tickets for the Strangers' Galleries on Tuesdays and Thursdays is enormous and understandable. A Prime Minister realizes only too well that twice a week he has to prove that he is in charge of his Government and in control of his Party, and totally on top of his job. There is at least one instance of a Prime Minister who was physically sick before he entered the Chamber. Harold never even approached that condition, but he was certainly more tense than usual on the nights before Questions, and anxious to get away to the study, so that he might look through the Questions in peace.

All the staff, official and political, had an opportunity to discuss the Questions with him.

Of course the important thing was not his initial answer. That was invariably easy. What had to be done was to guess the idea behind the Question and to judge the supplementary questions that every questioner has a right to put, and the other supplementaries that would come from the Opposition side.

The essential thing was for the Prime Minister to be well briefed. Here he had all the resources of the Civil Service behind him. There was one Private Secretary who was particularly good at thinking up not just the political supplementaries that were bound to follow, but also the politically correct supplementary answers. He was responsible for the setting up at No. 10 of one of the best reference and indexing systems I have ever seen. In a matter of minutes he could trace a quotation attributable to the Prime Minister, however far back. Obtaining his services, however, was just the luck of the draw. We could have had somebody who was not half so good.

Both Gerald Kaufman and I went over to the House on Tuesdays and Thursdays in time to be present for the meeting of officials that gathered before the Prime Minister went into the Chamber. Everyone gathered at about 3.00 p.m. and from then until 3.15 p.m. the Questions were rehearsed, together with the possible supplementaries and answers. It was hoped that all contingencies were covered.

Why was all this so important and why do Prime Ministers put so much store on these occasions? Why, even more, do the Press make so much out of Prime Minister's Questions?

The answer really relates to Party morale. The Prime Minister, if he is to maintain his authority in his own Party, has to demonstrate his authority over the Opposition. If he does well it impresses first his Cabinet colleagues and also his back-bench supporters. Then it has its repercussions on television and in the newspapers. There is nothing like a good Press on the following morning for heartening a Party Leader. Afterwards it is possible to sense the reaction in the country as the effect of newspaper stories and the reports of MPs to their constituencies have their effect throughout the rest of Britain. Politicians are sometimes criticized for thinking too much of success or failure in the Chamber. The truth is, though, that what happens there does have a major influence.

These are normally the important exposures of the Prime Minister during the week. But sometimes he has to make other

major appearances in the House, either opening or winding up
an important debate. He will also have to be on the Front
Bench at times to support his colleagues, to form his own
judgement of their performances in the House, and to evaluate
other significant Parliamentary events.

Parliament is the Prime Minister's real lifeline with the
country. Here he is able to gauge what is really happening, and
how the Government's actions are being received, from the
reports he receives from MPs in his own Party. Here, too, are
welded the loyalties, the friendships, the alliances on which he
builds his own political life. He neglects it at his peril.

But, of course, a great deal of the Prime Minister's life takes
place outside Parliament. Engagements pile up – public and
private.

There would often be a luncheon for the Prime Minister to
attend. This could be some function away from Downing
Street, with another speech to deliver, or an official one at
No. 10. Sometimes wives were invited, sometimes it was an
all-male affair, often a 'working lunch'.

If there was a visit from a Head of State, there would be a
morning trip to Victoria Station, or, more rarely, to one of
London's airports. Sometimes the Prime Minister had to
greet an important visitor on the way in from an airport or
station, and at the beginning of the Government these occasions
often took place at the Tate Gallery. This always puzzled me.
Why the Tate? Was there at some time some protocol authority
hidden away in Whitehall with a passion for modern art?
Unfortunately the answer was less colourful: it related to
parking problems.

If the Prime Minister did not have an official engagement for
luncheon, he ate in the Downing Street flat. I should say he
ate there on three weekdays out of every five he spent at No. 10.
This was a family occasion with Mary, and with the boys if
they were at home. I usually ate with them too, and found
this a particularly valuable time. We discussed things throughout lunch and Harold brought me up to date on what was
happening, and we discussed the political implications.

Without these lunches, life would have been very difficult
since the Political Office was not particularly well-informed
about government business. Shortly after the Office had been

established I was put on the distribution list for receiving official home papers to read. However, my name was at the bottom of a long list of Private Secretaries and after those of the Press Secretary and his Assistant, which meant that by the time any paper reached me, the decision on it had been taken already, and often put into effect as well. Receiving papers so late meant that there was no point in even being on the list, so in the end I stopped reading them.

On some occasions Harold had a close colleague or friend to lunch, but on the whole he kept these a strictly family affair. In any case, the lunches were not exactly elaborate. He remained a Yorkshireman in his attitude to food all the time he was Prime Minister. Often the meal was a one-course affair, roast beef and Yorkshire pudding, or steak and kidney pudding. Occasionally there were soup and cheese as well. But he liked above all a steak, particularly a large one, with just a salad. He had a weakness for celery and a partiality to mince pies, even out of season.

There was never much to drink at lunch. We had water usually, but beer or a glass of wine if there was a guest. Afterwards we had tea. Harold likes coffee, but his first cook, a very nice Irish girl, Mary Wright, produced tea after lunch and that somehow became the custom.

In the afternoon we moved over to the House when Parliament was sitting. The officials established themselves in the ante-room to the Prime Minister's room and, after a battle, we in the Political Office also managed to get an office there.

In the beginning there was just one room for Secretaries and we were not allowed to use it, but I managed to persuade the Prime Minister and the Westminster authorities that the alcove in the Prime Minister's L-shaped room could be partitioned off to form another separate room. This was given to the Civil Service secretaries and we moved into their larger room.

All this was part of a significant change in the Prime Minister's routine, because at the same time it was established that the period after lunch until 6.00 p.m. on weekdays, except Fridays, should be allocated to the Political Office – apart from the period for Prime Minister's Questions.

That became the time when members of the Parliamentary

Labour Party were able to see him. The civil servants had gone and the political staff controlled his engagements and diary for four hours. A Prime Minister has also to be a Party leader, but it was difficult in the early days, when he was almost cocooned at Downing Street, for him to be in touch with his Party.

The new arrangement, we hoped, would alter this, and from the point of view of the back-benchers, it certainly did. However, the Civil Service did not relinquish their hold without a fight, and even when they had lost they put a good gloss on their defeat. For about this time I went to see Dick Crossman at the Ministry of Housing and he told me, laughing, that one of his officials had said to him that he had been told by a member of the Private Office at No. 10: 'At last we've got rid of them, they've been sent over to the House.' That somewhat understated the position. The fact was that we had got rid of them, from the House – at least, for four afternoons. And they had certainly not dislodged us from No. 10.

Once a week, on Tuesdays, the Prime Minister did not go back to No. 10 when he left the House. On that day he went to Buckingham Palace for his audience with the Queen. He was accompanied always by his Principal Private Secretary, for while the Prime Minister was briefing the Queen the Principal Secretary was briefing his opposite number at the Palace. Sometimes Harold was with the Queen for a long time. I often wondered what they found to talk about. Harold Macmillan only spent about half an hour with her each week, and I understand that Edward Heath rarely exceeds that time.

Harold, when questioned, as he often was by all of us, would always say that he was telling her what was going on. However, on one occasion he did come back with details of a new riding habit she had ordered for Trooping the Colour, so I assumed that they did not spend their entire time together discussing affairs of state. I think she found this Labour Prime Minister an odd phenomenon in her life.

Throughout the Prime Minister's day, Ministers and civil servants would be fitted into his diary as events made their visits necessary. In the early days, with the constant atmosphere of crisis, the economic Ministers naturally were his most frequent visitors. Thomas Balogh, on whose advice he depended a great deal, saw him by appointment at least three times a

81

week, and often met him informally in my room for a drink.

It was the position of Thomas which produced a change in the Prime Minister's working habits. For the first eighteen months Harold was at No. 10 he worked in the Cabinet Room. He decided he would like to work in there, as Clem Attlee had done. But he always seemed a very lonely figure, sitting at the middle of the table, working away in the huge room with nothing except the melancholy portrait of Sir Robert to keep him company. It was intimidating, and uncomfortable, too, for his visitors to be received there. But after 1966 Thomas, who had been working in the Cabinet Office in Whitehall and was physically isolated from No. 10, wanted to come into the building itself. He was found an office and in the general turnaround the Private Secretary who dealt with ecclesiastical matters was shifted from the study, in which he had been allowed to work after 1964, to a large room on the first floor, which we called The Museum. It overlooked Downing Street and had originally been the staff sitting-room for the private apartments. We had used it to house gifts sent to the Prime Minister and his wife from people all over the country.

This move left the study free, and it was decided to make it the Prime Minister's working room again. This was a great improvement. The Prime Minister liked it and so did all his visitors. It was furnished with modern light furniture, and the walls were hung with examples of the work of good modern English painters.

It was here that the Prime Minister worked chiefly in the evenings, which meant that it was here that he did his most productive work. He worked hard and he worked late. Sometimes there were official dinners, state dinners, often glittering affairs. We were always amused by the diary entries for these engagements, first the details, time and place and then in brackets (black tie and Mrs Wilson).

But as far as possible the Prime Minister kept his evenings free to study papers, to think out particular problems and to dictate speeches and sometimes his private diary. There was the occasional working dinner with trade unionists, leaders of industry and university representatives; and he enjoyed being able to concentrate on one area of policy, arguing it out over a meal. But these occasions were not his favourite ones. He likes to work in a concentrated way and he preferred getting in a group of people for a discussion, and giving them light refreshments to keep them going.

If there was not an official engagement he would rarely have a cooked dinner. His eating habits were not changed by his office. His practice was to go to the flat for a cold supper, sometimes a meat pie with salad, or at others a plate of sandwiches and a glass of milk. The sandwiches were frequently tinned salmon. It was quite a genuine statement of his taste when he was reported as saying that he preferred tinned salmon to smoked salmon. The fact is that although he likes fresh salmon and tinned salmon, he just can't bear smoked salmon at all.

He drank an occasional Scotch or brandy during the evening. And, of course, had to pay for it. The idea that the British government is run on a flood of taxpayers' alcohol is not well founded. If you want a bottle of anything in Downing Street, whether for your guests or yourself, you just send down for it, but you still have it debited to your private account. It was the same for his room at the House of Commons. Guests had to be offered drinks but the bill always went to Harold Wilson.

While he worked visitors still had to be fitted in. In the early years George Wigg saw him every evening. The Prime Minister also met financial figures, one distinguished merchant banker being a fairly regular visitor, in order to get the City's view of the situation.

This was consistent night work, every night for five days each week. The red boxes never stopped coming. These are the boxes that contain Cabinet Committee papers, Foreign Office telegrams, minutes and memoranda from Ministers, important letters from leading figures here and abroad, and files of letters for the Prime Minister's signature. The Political Office submitted a black box every evening containing similar documentation but relating to the Party and political matters and containing, of course, its own letters to be signed.

The Prime Minister had arguments with his civil servants about the amount of work that was loaded into the boxes. Many of the matters, he felt, could have been agreed with him during the day. By the last year I think he had got them to understand this, and to get the boxes to him as early in the evening as possible. The numbers dropped dramatically, and instead of having five or six, which was normal at one time, they eventually levelled out at two or three an evening.

A typical sight would be the Prime Minister sitting in an armchair near the window, one box on the floor by his side, and papers spread out over his knee, the radio playing pop music quietly in the background, and too often the inevitable Private Secretary or Duty Clerk hovering for an instruction or to pass on a message to him. Always there was the need for yet another decision.

It sounds a hard life, and it was, but the fact is that he seemed to enjoy these evenings. Some people break up their work; he preferred to clear it away in one major session so that every day was self-contained, with nothing left over when the round began again next morning.

There was, in the latter part of the Government, an enjoyable point in the evening, too, when Private Office staff and Political Office staff were leaving for home and called in to see if he wanted anything further. This often resulted in an animated conversation between us all, going over the day's events and looking ahead. Sometimes there was gloom at crisis times, but more often than not we managed to release the tensions of the day with a joke; and Harold's sense of humour in describing what had often been the harrowing experiences of the previous twenty-four hours would send us all off home feeling it was worth while, that we had made our contribution, and, more important, that he was good to work for.

I had been with him for many years and had often heard discussions about his personality by those who did not know him and thought him dull and difficult to understand. I watched with fascination those who came to work closely for him and with him, and was intrigued to see how attached personally they became to him over a period of months and then years. The secret was the sense of humour, the dedication to work and the high standards he wanted from everyone, together with his understanding of all our personality failings.

He was never in bed until 12.30 a.m. and he had very little outside entertainment. Sometimes he went to the theatre or the cinema, but he had to be prodded into going. He always went out, however, for family birthdays and anniversaries. When he did go out though, he enjoyed it immensely, whether it was football, the theatre, a cinema or a meal in a restaurant.

There was also his constituency work. In Huyton he had a cast-iron Labour seat with one of the best majorities in the country. There was no doubt who would be the Huyton MP at each election, and he could well have pleaded his Prime Ministerial responsibilities and left it to tick over without him, since he had the ever-watchful, loyal and hard-working Arthur Smith for his Agent. Many Prime Ministers have taken this attitude, and it is certainly a valid one.

Harold has, however, a deep sense of responsibility and attachment towards Huyton. Many of his constituents were the people who sustained him over many years during the vicissitudes of his political career, and he felt he owed them a great deal. In addition, he did not want them to feel that they had lost out, that because he had become Prime Minister they had been left with a first-class political figure but a second-class Member. Possibly they did lose something because he never exerted his influence to obtain special treatment for Huyton, as American politicians do for the areas they represent.

Still, what the constituents did get was a man who remained a strong Huyton MP even if his address was No. 10. He went up there at least once a month, sometimes staying overnight in a Kirkby hotel but more often returning by night sleeper.

When he took his monthly surgery at Huyton he sat behind a table with nobody else present, and wrote in his own hand the details of the people's problems. At one point I sat with him to take a note, but it proved unsuccessful and we abandoned this procedure. It wasn't that the atmosphere was awkward, but just that the constituents were a little more reticent when there was somebody else – a 'foreigner' – in the room. Obviously they wanted to see their MP alone, in a completely confidential way, and if this was what they wanted, and as he was their representative, this was what they got. They still get this. Unless there was some special reason, he signed personally every letter sent to his constituents.

No. 10 and Huyton were two parts of the Prime Minister's life. A third was Chequers. Harold loved the place but Mary did not. She thought, and I agreed with her, that it was gloomy and isolated. It had no real atmosphere, certainly not a family atmosphere, for too many purely temporary residents

85

have lived there. Chequers is a cold and negative place.

The first visits were not exactly welcoming ones for Mary, or indeed for Harold, but as Prime Minister he felt it less. Perhaps it was because the wives of the last four Prime Ministers had all had titles, Lady Douglas-Home, Lady Dorothy Macmillan, Lady Eden and Lady Churchill, Chequers did not seem to react favourably to the daughter of a Congregational minister. Everything had to be discovered by accident or by probing, nothing was volunteered in those early years.

Mary was told that under the terms of the Chequers Trust she could not be in the house when the Prime Minister was not in residence. Eventually the rules were studied and she was allowed to arrive in advance of the Prime Minister if he had an engagement elsewhere and would be late. Similarly, she was allowed to stay overnight if Harold happened to be summoned back to London on official business.

It was at Chequers, though, that Harold himself really relaxed. True, the red boxes still came, there was the No. 10 civil servant from the Garden Room on duty, and a teleprinter link with No. 10 was ticking away in the background. But Harold could work in his bedroom or the study, in the more family-like atmosphere of the white parlour, or on the terrace in the summer. And, above all, he could play golf, usually on Saturdays as well as Sundays, whatever the weather.

There were a few big conferences held there over weekends, notably on defence and economic policy, with one on the Common Market and several Socialist International Conferences, and joint Cabinet and Labour National Executive Committee meetings. But the Wilsons used it for personal and political entertaining much less than the present Prime Minister. Mr Heath seems to have at least one luncheon party for his colleagues or friends each weekend, but for the Wilsons it was essentially a family place, with simple meals, and a few Ministers or political friends being summoned or dropping in.

The fourth facet of the Prime Minister's life – and its most personal – was his bungalow in the Isles of Scilly. This was where he had spent his holidays for much of his married life. He liked the Islands and they suited him, and he saw no reason to change just because he had become Prime Minister. He went to Chequers for two or three days at Christmas, but as soon as

they were over the Wilsons left for the Islands. They had
another week there at Easter and three weeks in the summer.
But these holidays were always interrupted and it was very rare
indeed that the Prime Minister got the full five weeks away from
the Downing Street–Chequers network in the course of a year.

He often cooked breakfast himself in the Scillies, just as he
had done before he was Prime Minister, at home in Hampstead.
One concession to his new office was that the groceries were
delivered to the bungalow. Previously he or Mary had collected
them from the shops. And other changes were the special
telephones to No. 10 installed both in the bungalow and in
the Customs House which was used to house the No. 10 staff
who had to accompany him when he was there. One detective
often stayed in the Customs House too, while another was
lodged nearer the bungalow in a guest house.

The detectives were eventually equipped with walkie-talkie
communications in case Harold was wanted urgently, since the
Islands are spread out and a day's expedition to one of them
could prove embarrassing if the Prime Minister was needed for
a conversation, with no method of communicating with him.

But even with all these modern aids he would often go into
the nearest telephone box and ring direct, if he wanted to
speak to someone in a hurry.

I don't quite know what Harold got from the Scillies during
those years. It was not a holiday which would suit most men in
his position. Still, he never showed any interest in a holiday
anywhere else. There was plenty of golf, of course, and swimming. Mary and he would swim in the coldest weather and at the
end of the holiday would compare the number of times they
had each been in the water. There were the long walks round
the Islands too. Some days they would hire a boat and go on
trips to neighbouring islands.

They still do the same now. They take picnic meals and tea
and coffee in flasks, and Harold has his favourite books for re-
reading – detective stories, Carl Sandburg's *Life of Lincoln*,
and Kant's *Critique of Pure Reason*.

But always there would be some interruption and occasionally
a call away from the island back to the mainland, sometimes
even to London. One call was to the mainland in 1967 to
deal with the Government reshuffle. At the Queen's Hotel in

Penzance on the way home he told Peter Shore and Harold Lever of their promotions.

Obviously being Prime Minister must change a man. First of all there is the pressure on his character. He has great powers of patronage, which means that he is exposed to correspondingly great flattery from those, and there are many, to whom his favours can mean so much. This flattery occurred also to those who work closely with him.

But equally important, the burdens of office, the actual workload, seem to grow with each premiership, while the crises follow each other so regularly that it seems strange when there isn't one. Yet the crises and the hard work seem in fact to build a self-generating unit of ability to cope.

It is no coincidence that so many modern Prime Ministers have left No. 10 as sick men. Illness was the ostensible reason why two of them, Anthony Eden and Harold Macmillan, retired before the end of a Parliament. Even Lord Attlee, hardly an excitable type of man, suffered from an illness which was nervous in origin. Only Sir Alec Douglas-Home appeared to leave No. 10 in the same shape in which he entered it, and he was there for only a year. The burden which he shouldered during that period was also believed to be somewhat less than overwhelming.

The amazing thing about Harold Wilson was that he emerged comparatively unshattered. Few Prime Ministers in recent times have had such a gruelling period in office. At the end of his five and a half years there were some physical changes. He was a little heavier, though he would deny it, and his face certainly showed signs that No. 10 is no health farm. But to a large extent he was the same man who took on the post in 1964. Somebody has said that to be Prime Minister you need faith, hope and stamina, and the greatest of these is stamina. Certainly Harold had all three.

5

A Famous Victory

On his return from the Scillies Harold called in at my home in Golders Green, to see my family. Then we had a long talk about the political situation. It was for me a very memorable occasion. Our minds had been moving apparently along exactly the same lines. I thought the Government and the Party had received all the good propaganda we could expect from the Rhodesian operation: it could now only turn sour rather than get better. On all the signs we had, which included our lead in the opinion polls, my view was that an election at the earliest possible opportunity was desirable. Harold then said that this was exactly what he had decided, and that the end of March seemed to be the best possible time.

Political commentators were to make all sorts of judgements later about why Harold had the March election: most of them were wide of the mark. The plain fact is that immediately after Christmas he had already decided whatever happened that the election would be held in March and that this was the best and only possible time. The winning of Hull, though marvellous in itself and indicating that we stood a chance of doing extremely well, was irrelevant to the decision which had already been taken.

There was some apprehension at No. 10 about who would be chosen as the candidate for North Hull since the Vietnam situation was overshadowing internal events in the Labour Party; some were worried lest the Party got a very fervent anti-Vietnam War candidate, and this would do damage to our chances. After a talk with the National Agent, then Sara Barker, a person whom everyone respected very much, we were told by her that our candidate Kevin McNamara was, to use Sara's words, 'a lovely boy'. This was taken to mean that Kevin was, while possibly not right-wing on foreign affairs, definitely middle of the road, and not likely to cause any difficulties on the Vietnam front. Not many months later Kevin was to sign a Motion on the Order Paper in the House of Commons severely criticizing the Government's failure to dissociate itself from the United States on Vietnam. He was indeed 'a lovely boy', but I think he would not have come within that definition for Sara if she had known in advance. What was known was that the Hull North by-election was a magnificent victory. It gave tremendous heart to all of us, after all the difficulties of 1965.

It also meant that while Harold had always known we were working to a timetable for the end of March, everyone else thought that the Hull result gave the green light for this. They started in their own individual ways now of working towards it too. Terry Pitt at Transport House started work with Peter Shore and others to prepare the Manifesto for the election. The decision was also taken that the Budget was to be announced, though not as a Budget, but as a series of measures. If the Budget was not announced and did not take place before the election, we would be accused of holding back something sinister in order to get votes.

But there was also to be an outcry in the Party over the Vietnam situation, and the escalation which followed after the bombing pause over Christmas. Almost at the same time was the famous railway dispute. It is now legendary because of the lack of food in No. 10 to feed the hungry railwaymen. Both of these problems could have caused a serious deterioration in our electoral chances, but both of them were handled in such a way by Harold as to make sure that they did not get out of hand. On the Vietnam question the Parliamentary Labour Party was mollified to some extent by the fact that Harold decided to make a visit to the Soviet Union to talk to Soviet leaders who were co-Chairmen of the Geneva Conference. This held the ground for a little while.

I suppose the threatened rail strike in February 1965 was one of the more unusual and exciting events in our time at

No. 10. The Political Office greatly enjoyed it for the mere fact that we were involved in something that was actually happening downstairs.

The discussion with the railwaymen went on late into the night. It is, of course, true that railwaymen gathering together after being in conference all day do get extremely hungry. The Private Office, still to a large extent the old Macmillan/Alec Douglas-Home office, provided sandwiches made by Government Hospitality, small sandwich squares, very dainty and few in number, and certainly not enough to keep those hungry men in good spirits.

Brenda Dew and I with others in the building set off on a search for food. We were to produce by the end of the evening enough good solid stuff to make the men happier. We also took over the job of going into the Cabinet Room and serving them all with their glasses of beer, since every time an official went in the discussions tended to stop. They knew both Brenda and me by sight so when we went to help them to food and drink they seemed perfectly happy to continue with their deliberations. The end result was a successful one, and we, in an exhausted state, but very euphoric, happily saw them to their various forms of transport, from taxis and minicabs to official cars from their union offices, all speeding them on their weary way home in the early hours of the morning from their No. 10 talks.

Our first visit to Moscow took place before that election, and was a curious one too. We had with us Alun Chalfont and Frank Cousins. It was on that famous visit to Moscow that Mary and I had an extraordinary conversation with Frank Cousins on equal pay, when Frank was to denounce our views as quite unacceptable and to say that he totally disagreed with the whole principle, much to our amazement and surprise.

It was the first Russian visit we had spent in a dacha in the Lenin Hills outside Moscow rather than in a hotel in the centre of Moscow. At first everyone felt a little less comfortable than usual. There was a sense of isolation about it all and we were glad our party was large in numbers. The Russians, as always, were extremely friendly and kind.

There was now an imperceptible change between the Political and the Private Offices. We had ourselves learned a great deal about the workings of No. 10. We already felt less ignorant about how it was organized and also about the Civil Service set-up in general. We had established ourselves within the building and, with the approaching election, the Political Office was more and more in demand.

When the election was over, it was time for Derek Mitchell, the Principal Private Secretary, to leave No. 10 for a promotion.

When Michael Halls, Derek Mitchell's successor as Principal Private Secretary, came he worked within an easier atmosphere. The Government had a very large majority with all the security of knowing that Government was likely to last a considerable period. Derek Mitchell, however, had worked with Harold when the Government had a tiny majority and in a situation where he knew it was possible at any time that Harold Wilson might be Leader of the Opposition again and he would be working once more for a Conservative Prime Minister.

Derek was to go with us on the trip to Russia, as well as the officials still in the Private Office from the 'previous reign'. They were gradually realizing that Labour was likely to win the election whenever it was held. They were less condescending and a little more co-operative. Thomas Balogh wanted desperately to go with us, and we at last persuaded Harold to agree. But in the end it proved impossible because of Thomas's then serious heart condition.

Oliver Wright, who was still with us, was an outstanding figure on the foreign affairs front. He was the Private Secretary seconded to No. 10 from the Foreign Office. He is an enormously tall, well-built man full of *bonhomie*, exuding an Etonian air even though he went to Solihull Grammar. Perhaps that should have been apparent to us, but we were a little in awe of them all, testing our inferiority against them daily from those early months in 1965 onwards.

Our arrival in Moscow for that visit was Chaplinesque. For a start we landed at the wrong airport and the receiving party was sitting graciously at another airport at a different end of Moscow. On hearing what had happened they were rushed by car along the icy, snow-covered roads beneath us at breakneck speed in order to arrive in time to have the red carpet laid out in place, and as many soldiers and members of the reception committee as possible to greet us. But too few arrived to make it the grand affair that had been planned. I enjoyed this version far more!

Those of us who went in a personal capacity, and in my view most of the officials as well, had no real job to do on the trip. Brenda Dew went to look after Mary; Gerald Kaufman went, paid for by the Labour Party, in view of the fact that we were now so near an election and Harold felt that it might be necessary, if something blew up, for Gerald to handle any political statement that had to be put out from Moscow. I myself was paid for privately. I had now been to the Soviet Union a number of times with Harold, but this was my first visit there with Harold as Prime Minister.

The whole visit seemed to be taken up with visits to receptions, lunches, dinners and other functions, including a visit to the cinema, and of course to the Bolshoi Ballet. But the copious notes that were taken about the talks held, and that were locked away and kept so secretly, were, as far as I can remember, totally unnecessary. I cannot think of any single thing which was so secret or so urgent that it had to be recorded on the spot and rushed back to London as if it was going to change the course of history.

It was, therefore, something of a surprise to find that the visit to the Communist Party's Headquarters resembled an old-style visit to the Kremlin back in the early days. The windows of the building were heavily curtained and shuttered. A slightly sinister atmosphere touched one. The procedures for getting into the building and into Mr Brezhnev's office seemed much more complicated than any of the procedures we had to adopt in order to gain admittance to Mr Kosygin and other Ministers who received us in the Kremlin offices. That particular meeting with Mr Brezhnev was attended just by the Prime Minister, Oliver Wright and myself. No one else went with him.

Mr Brezhnev was a formidable and fascinating character, and one of the few Soviet Union politicians Harold had not as yet had the opportunity to get to know as well as he would have liked. The conversations which took place were polite and carried on in a friendly way. At the same time Mr Brezhnev expressed himself in an aggressive style. Many passages of what he had to say had an ominously threatening ring to them. The main gist of it all, as it always seemed to be on most visits, related to the question of Germany. Whoever visits Moscow from the Western world is usually subjected to the same lecture about Germany. It is Russia's main obsession. I personally don't condemn it. Perhaps we should count ourselves lucky the Soviet Union has this obsession. It seems to be the one safeguard we all of us enjoy in the Western world as far as the balance of power goes for future years. I cannot share the sanguineness of most people who tolerantly view the growth of power in Western Germany, and I find it far more alarmingly reminiscent of the inter-war years than one would like it to be. The two major problems of Japanese and German economic power recall too clearly old battles, old problems and old situations which have so far remained unresolved.

After we left Mr Brezhnev and drove back to the British Embassy we were a little subdued by the experience we had shared. We discussed what he had to say, and the warnings he had given about any question of a united Germany, of the dangers that Western Germany presented to the world, and also his remarks about the Common Market and the whole problem of political union within Western Europe. Harold always has had a very keen and deep understanding of how the Russians feel on this. It has been one of the influences on his own thinking about political integration within Western Europe.

We joked about Mr Brezhnev a little, saying that he was the George Brown of the Soviet Union. Mr Brezhnev is attractive: he is like George Brown too in a robust way. But he has a much sharper edge to him. He is clearly the dominating force in Soviet politics. But I don't think we realized his full strength within the Soviet Union until that visit in 1966, nor indeed fully at the time.

Going from Mr Brezhnev to the presence of Mr Kosygin is a quite extraordinary experience. He is the complete opposite. Mr Kosygin is a seemingly gentle, sensitive and intellectual character. For driving force, power and command there is Mr Brezhnev. Events after that visit and more recently seem to have proved this correct.

By the time our party returned to London, we were ready psychologically for the 1966 election. On 28 February Harold made the announcement, giving a four-week notice of the election date, 31 March 1966. As soon as the announcement was made the Political Office more or less took over the Prime Minister's life. The official machine ticked over doing the official work quietly in the background. The Political Office had grown in size; we had enlarged the secretarial staff, including amongst others Peter Shore's very efficient secretary, Mavis Blackwell, whom we shared part-time with him.

My first instruction to everyone was to pack everything ready to move at a moment's notice. All our box files within the office were tied together, our desks were emptied and cleared and our books were made ready to move. I expected defeat and hoped to meet it with dignity. There was, as I saw it, to be no hurried exit for any of us, and certainly not for the family. I even arranged with a close personal friend that furniture removal vans would be standing ready over the night of 31 March/1 April, in case they were needed to move the Wilsons out.

I had a bad election myself. I caught shingles early in the campaign. I had no idea it was such a painful complaint, nor so debilitating and depressing. But in any case, by comparison with 1964, it was a dead election.

The whole thing was run from No. 10 and we had little contact with our colleagues at Transport House. We made our separate arrangements and sorties into the countryside almost as totally separate organizations. There was daily liaison, but not the closely organized affair of 1964. Harold did not take the daily Press conference at Transport House and, therefore, his own involvement with headquarters in the general campaign was less than it usually is. For all of us there seemed to be two campaigns going on, our own personal one from No. 10 and the one being waged by the Party itself. It was not that it was a deliberate Presidential campaign; it was just that the very nature of running it from No. 10 made it separate.

We seemed to spend our lives on sleepers, which Harold loves and his staff usually hated. The important thing about sleepers is obviously that they enable you to travel during the night, and in our case to spend the early mornings at No. 10 every day throughout the campaign except for the weekends. On all our journeyings around the country we had to be accompanied by the inevitable two detectives and a girl from the Garden Rooms to look after the communications link with the official office at No. 10. Our own personal arrangements were therefore that much more elaborate because of the additional appendages we had. But we had George Caunt from the Parliamentary Labour Party, a tower of strength, to organize us on our tour.

The 1966 campaign was the one when a schoolboy threw a stink-bomb at Harold and hit him in the eye. It caused a great deal of concern at the office. It also caused upsets because the detectives who were with him had not been able to stop the incident. Even detectives are fallible. While it was a stink-bomb this time, it could easily have been something more serious the next. The boy who threw it was quite a nice little chap, and we were to hear from his family afterwards.

Although we had our ups and downs in that campaign personally, it was increasingly clear that we were going to win. We seemed to freewheel much of the time, and Harold took a number of liberties in speeches, which he might not otherwise have done, not least in his Common Market speech when he referred to Edward Heath as a 'spaniel' who was prepared to do anything in order to win European approval.

It was also the first election I could remember for which Mary had bought a whole new wardrobe of clothes. She purchased them from Digby Morton. They were very pretty and feminine and heralded the spring weather which we were to have on Polling Day itself and indeed through most of the election campaign. They were soft, pastel tweeds and suited her admirably. She and Harold made a very good picture together and were, I guess, to the average citizen watching the campaign, particularly on television, a very good example of what they expected in a Prime Minister and his wife.

There was a bad patch during the campain, when hostile audiences were encountered, in particular at Dunstable and later at Norwich. Everything seemed to be difficult and the result was that for three or four days a subdued atmosphere prevailed and even the principals seemed downcast. The Press seemed to think Harold was a little off colour at that time. They put it down to election fatigue, not knowing it was partly apprehension and fears about the way the campaign was going.

But the atmosphere had improved by the time we reached the part of the campaign in the Huyton constituency, and the reception we had there was tremendous. All the visits we made from the Adelphi Hotel in Liverpool to the constituency with Harold were an absolute joy. The cars were all decked out with red streamers and we drove in a long convoy accompanied by police on motorcycles. The interesting thing about the procession, particularly when it was in the Huyton area, was the enormous number of young children who wanted to come and look at him and cheer him. They gathered round him in enormous numbers when we passed school buildings. They would clamber up the railings and cheer and shout and clap as we went by. It was very much a children's election in that sense, and I remember it particularly for those young smiling faces, and the astonishment I felt that at such a young age they wanted to have a look at the Prime Minister as he passed by. Harold was also impressed by this.

We were on that election campaign accompanied as usual by a large entourage of Press and television people, since the polls indicated so clearly that we would win and they wanted to be there at the moment when the larger majority was achieved. By the time election day arrived Harold's friends had also gathered in the constituency, his personal friends like Beattie Plummer, Bill Davies and Joe Kagan, and a number of others from different parts of the country who wanted to be there when the results were declared. They all gathered in Harold's suite in the Adelphi Hotel and a very tightly packed atmosphere it was by the time the results were announced over the television.

Once the results started to come in the swing to us became clear, though we were not to realize until later that it was such a big one. In the early hours we thought it was still going to be a fairly modest one.

We then got the usual telephone call from Harold's Agent, Arthur Smith, that we ought to depart for the constituency for the count there. When we arrived outside the school where the count was to be held the .crowds were enormous. Inside the hall the excitement was even greater and the Party workers were cheering their heads off with delight at what had been achieved.

The count, however, was conducted with the usual dignity and a certain phlegm by the Clerk of the Huyton Council, Mr Willgoose, who on such occasions maintains the strictest impartiality and even manages to produce a deadpan voice. Then we set off for the Huyton Labour Club to thank the Party workers for what they had done to make the enormous result in Huyton itself possible. At that point quite inexplicably the election became depressing again. It had not been a very interesting or jolly one, but by that time it actually became more and more depressing as the success became greater and greater.

It was late when we all returned to the Adelphi Hotel and we were very tired. There were just a few hours' sleep to be snatched before we had to be up again to catch the breakfast train back to London which was, as usual, crowded out with Press photographers, television teams and journalists of all kinds.

At Euston Station the crowd was vast again and we had to push our way through to get into our cars to drive to No. 10. The General Secretary was there again to meet Harold and to congratulate him, and it was agreed that once Harold had been into No. 10, he would go over to Transport House and join everybody in the building for a celebration there.

Our arrival at No. 10 was extraordinary. Extraordinary because it was so totally different from the arrival there in 1964. For one thing in the entrance hall was Michael Halls, with his bright friendly smiling face, beaming his congratulations. The rest of the Private Office were all lined up in the entrance hall and Mr May, the housekeeper, had now lined up the other staff; they clapped Harold as he entered the front door and went down along the red-carpeted corridor to the Cabinet Room. It was, I suppose, what all Prime Ministers get with a proper majority, though I suppose theoretically it is what all Prime Ministers should get even with a majority of one.

We had arrived at last. We had the measure of it all now; so we thought. We had fought to establish ourselves and had succeeded. We knew the ropes and we felt at last we could relax a little and try to enjoy 'being in power', whatever that might really mean.

The main thing about the 1964 election and the months that followed is that while many people in the Party may have felt power as such, I don't think that within No. 10 itself there was this feeling that the Government really possessed it. Over those first months there was a feeling more of being squatters and usurpers. Then the trends became clear and it looked as if we would regain our place and with an increased majority. The 1966 election was the one when the Government really got the first feeling of control and power. It had not been there before. Now this particular feeling gave the inner confidence which had been so greatly needed and sadly lacking in 1964, and which the Government had needed so badly to help deal with the situation in which they found themselves.

In the months that were to lie ahead one could actually look around at one's surroundings and register them properly. For my part I had never looked at No. 10 and thought that here I was, in the corridors of power, in this historic building, working in a top job and having all these advantages. I had just got on with what I had to do, with very long hours of work, no relaxation and a seven-day week. I had never actually looked at the building properly, nor enjoyed any of the parties or functions that took place there that are part of the life of the building. I had never been in on any of those talks or activities that took place there, other than my own isolated world of politics shut off in the attic rooms, with the occasional meeting downstairs in my room next to the Cabinet Room.

Now there were bouquets and gifts to welcome us back; congratulations and smiling faces on all sides. It was a most peculiar feeling suddenly to realize what it all meant; this was No. 10, Labour was in power, the power which the Labour Party had wanted for so long.

True, the feeling was to be dissipated pretty soon and sharply by the events that were to follow; but even so, despite the ups and downs of the following years, throughout the second Government the feeling was there that Labour had the power; it had a right to be there and belonged as much in No. 10 as any Conservative or Liberal had ever done.

But we were so utterly tired and exhausted on that first morning, as one always is after an election. What I remember most of all despite the weariness was climbing into the lift with Harold to go up to the second floor; in answer to a query he looked at me most solemnly, saying in a very tired voice: 'Now we can have a rest from politics.' How wrong he was.

6

The Extraordinary
Ordinary Man

Harold Wilson's character has been analysed, mostly inaccurately, far too many times to count. But all those who have written about him, whether for newspapers or television, have done so as a result of what has emerged from his public personality. For my part I can only describe the Harold Wilson I have known and worked for over a period of fifteen years.

In my mind I always divided this period into distinct parts, each one helping to produce the public Harold Wilson, each one contributing, in the words of another book's title, to The Making of the Prime Minister.

Of course, I knew a great deal about him before I started to work for him. After I left London University in 1955 I was on the staff of the General Secretary of the Labour Party at Transport House. There were four in our office, two older girls who would be regarded as right of centre, and two younger girls, of whom I was one, who were both left-wing. Transport House at that time was generally right-wing, committed to the Leader, Clem Attlee. As a left-winger I was a great admirer of Nye Bevan. He was a hero figure to all of us, particularly the younger members of the Party. But Nye was always an enigma to us and I think he was probably an enigma even to himself. While we admired and idolized him we were never quite sure exactly what he would do. We knew the general lines of his policy and the ideals for which he stood. But, in a very curious way, there was a sense amongst many people who worked in the Party that Nye did not possess the particular quality that is needed to put ideals into practice. We doubted whether our objectives would be translated into practical politics if Nye became Leader. I think it was for this reason that we tended to look round for anyone else who could possibly fulfil such a role.

The post-1955 election period saw the emergence of that person when Harold Wilson took a leading role again in the Party's hierarchy. Previously he had been thought of as somebody who had been a very successful civil servant in wartime and who had later been a reasonably successful – and very young – Minister in the Attlee Government. Now he became notable as a very successful Party politician.

From the time of his resignation in 1951 until the election in 1955, he had not been out of the public eye. The resignation was hardly a minor event and it certainly ensured that, whatever happened afterwards, Harold Wilson would always be someone who would draw attention to himself. But during the 1951 to 1955 period he did not seem to involve himself as much with internal Labour politics as he could have done if he had wanted.

After the 1955 defeat, many people realized that there was a danger of Labour becoming out of date. The era of post-war recovery, of getting that pattern right, was over. The great achievement of Clem Attlee's Government was that it established a good economic base and a good pattern for the future. On this the Tories were able to build after 1951.

But the fifties saw the growing appeal of the consumer society. It was so great that any party based on idealistic principles, appealing to social values, found it hard going to get the message across to a public which was increasingly wanting the good things out of life, as they then saw them, in terms of television sets and washing machines.

The 1955 election was not a particularly bad one. The Tory majority was sixty. But the Party in that post-1955 period failed to come to terms with the problem of whether or not it was out of date. It looked around for a scapegoat and decided that it was all to be blamed on Party organization. Here Harold Wilson came into his own as the man who took charge of the small committee that toured the country carrying out a full-scale investigation into Labour's organization. It was a formidable job which in turn gave Harold Wilson a formidable base that later was to prove one of his most valuable assets.

In Transport House many of us watched him at work with fascination. He was becoming increasingly popular within the Party, and I think we realized that here was someone who did in fact share the ideals of the left-wingers, but who possessed the necessary streak of practicality needed to make those ideals a reality. This was, too, the one ingredient which other leading left-wing figures did not possess.

Harold Wilson had done things which irritated the left wing of the party, particularly when, after Nye resigned from the Shadow Cabinet and the Parliamentary Committee, in 1954, he agreed to take his place on the committee as the runner-up. He was never, therefore, totally embraced by them, though I think they probably regarded him as a safe ally when the crunch came. This was a justifiable assumption.

My time in Morgan Phillips' office was one of great value to me because I learnt a great deal about how the Labour Party works, both at Transport House and in the country. I learnt particularly that this is the real Labour Party, not the more glamorous section of it which operates in the Palace of Westminster.

Morgan was a staunch Gaitskellite. He was an extremely able and very clever man. There were one or two difficulties with him, but he was a first-class politician and tactician; he knew how to manage the Party and to keep it in line with what Gaitskell wanted. During my time there, when the organization inquiry was proceeding and the report was being prepared, there was a deliberate putsch against Harold Wilson to try and keep him out of the Chairmanship of the Organisation Sub-Committee. This was a key party post in view of the concentration on organizational questions. At the time the trends were not clear to me, but looking back I now believe that it was recognized that Harold was emerging as a formidable left-winger with ideals and also with practical ability and therefore someone to be feared, and carefully watched.

Certainly an attempt was made to cut Harold down but it was unsuccessful. I confess I played a role there. It was wrong for me to do so as a party official, but I wanted to see the Party's left successful. When I realised that there were plots going on I wrote anonymous notes to Harold, warning that certain things might be happening at certain times. Harold afterwards joked that he had wondered who it was and how this person came to be so well informed. But at least it was a small contribution towards that future career.

However, he knew nothing of this when he appointed me his Secretary in October 1956. He was then economic adviser to the timber firm of Montague L. Meyer. As his Secretary I worked with him in the Meyer office. I think that the period, from 1951 to 1956, when he was with Montague Meyer was one of the happiest in his life. He had a dual life, a business career which enabled him to operate within the political scene without becoming too totally involved in it. He was happy with the Meyer family and he enjoyed taking part in a business firm's life. I think he enjoyed it particularly because it was a firm that dealt with the timber industry, of which he had personal experience. He had a lot to do with this industry during his term as President of the Board of Trade, and the knowledge of the business world he gained then made him invaluable to the Meyer organization.

The Meyers liked him and he liked them. It was a small company run by a charming and capable family. I can remember particularly one occasion when they had an enormous problem facing them associated with some French tax case on which they had not been able to make any progress. Harold was able to pinpoint the one or two salient points in the case which were more important than all the others, which enabled the Meyers to win the case and to recover from a situation which would have been very difficult for them. He was very proud of that achievement. It was a financial technicality that was a challenge to his intellect and it was a challenge to him, as an 'outsider' in the business world, to prove that he was able to make an important contribution.

I think they were sorry when he finally decided to leave them. I certainly know that when he did go he was offered other jobs in industry. People recognized that he had a very acute mind, and that for any business firm he was a great asset.

He went overseas for the Meyer organization; he met other businessmen in the country; he helped to promote East–West trading relations. The fact that he had had a lot to do with fostering East–West trade during his period at the Board of

Trade was also an advantage to the Meyers. Of course, Harold now saw the difficulties of business firms and industry in general in their attempts to try to break into markets of this kind and the difficulties they experienced individually.

He came to understand a great deal about how industry works and about how business firms work – a knowledge from the inside rather than an academic knowledge from the outside. But now, looking back, I wonder whether this apparent advantage might not have been a disadvantage in the long run, for his specialized knowledge of the difficulties that business firms can encounter, and his sympathy with their problems, might well have made him less tough with some of them than he should have been when he became Prime Minister.

I have a theory that when he left the Board of Trade and joined the Meyer organization, he became a liberated person. He escaped the restrictions of ministerial life and also the confines of life at the top of a political party. He was less inhibited and was able to let himself go. He expanded and grew tremendously during this period.

Of course, a great deal has been written of Harold Wilson as a politician. It is widely agreed that he is a great Parliamentary speaker, that he dominated the House of Commons for many years, and that he is a great political tactician. But a great deal of the groundwork for all of this was done during this crucial period in his life.

The liberation from restrictions helped him, I am convinced, to become one of the most powerful debaters in the House of Commons. Soon there was no equal in the Party to him when it came to ripping the Tories apart and harrying the policies they were then pursuing. His speeches were a unique blend of political irony and satire combined with cool, calculated, destructive argument. He used to fill the House when he spoke. During this period, when he was Shadow Chancellor and led the Front Bench on economic and financial affairs, he developed the speaking style for which he became so famous.

Soon other leading members of the Party began to develop the respect and fear they were to have for him as a Parliamentary and political figure. Mr Gaitskell and those closest to him could not afford to ignore this man who so dominated the House of Commons and who rallied so much support in the Parliamentary Party around him, particularly since he spoke on the bread and butter issues which Labour MPs really had at heart, the vital issues of economic life.

He is an economist by training, he knows his facts, and so he knew what he was talking about. He had a wide range of business experience behind him, too, on which to draw. Together with this, he relished political knockabout; he was not afraid of wading in and lashing out at the Tories, and he had a gift for political jokes which made his speeches not only enjoyable but also occasions which rallied the Party to fight its real enemy, the Conservative Government.

Nobody can possibly understand how much enjoyment went into preparing the speeches he made in the House. There was an American comedian called Mort Sahl, who was one of the wittiest and funniest comedians of the 1950s, and it was a tribute to Harold's humour in the House of Commons when a *Daily Mail* cartoon showed Harold leaving the Chamber with a great pile of papers under his arm and an American tourist saying to a custodian: 'Who's that?' And the custodian replying: 'That's the Mort Sahl of the House of Commons.'

But life was enjoyable too because of the interesting work he did within the Party. This was fascinating for me because I am a committed political animal. I enjoyed the work that followed the Wilson Report, when he received hundreds of invitations from all over the country. It was a period when he spoke most weekends at big rallies, a period when he got to know even better the 'grass roots' – that terrible expression which has now become part of political jargon. But if anyone understands the 'grass roots' of the Labour Party, Harold Wilson certainly does, because in those years he put in more hours than one likes to recall touring the country, meeting the constituency parties, speaking at rallies and meetings.

The result was that he usually came top, or near to the top, of the voting in the constituency section of the National Executive Committee each year. He also came top, or near top, of the voting for the Parliamentary Committee of the Labour Party, once the initial difficulty of getting on to it had been passed.

In fact he became popular with the working part of the Party in Parliament and the country. I don't believe for one moment that they loved him then. Nor do I believe it now. But I think they have an immense affection for him and it is the sort of affection which is widely shared today throughout the population. They respect him enormously for his ability, they feel very affectionately towards him, they are not overawed by him. He was, or seemed to be, an ordinary sort of person, despite his great abilities and despite the unique nature of his character. He came from a background that they understood. He was comfortable in the presence of almost everyone in the Party, whether at the top or in the constituencies. He never talked down to anyone, and he had a great gift for conversation and for drawing people out. He was a very good listener and he learned a very great deal as a result.

He was naturally helped by his famous memory, which is certainly no myth. In fact it is fantastic. I often used to remark, when I was told he had looked in the files and not been able to find something because it was incorrectly filed away, that there wasn't really any need to have a filing system. He didn't really need the papers, he remembered almost exactly what was in them. Equally, he never forgot the smallest detail about a colleague or a friend, a constituent, or anyone he met in the course of his life. He frequently amazed people by recalling facts about them which they had sometimes forgotten themselves. He could remind them of when he had met them, where he had met them and sometimes of what their problems had been at that particular time. After he became Prime Minister, people suggested that this was done in a calculated way and that he cultivated this memory. This is not true. He does take a great pride in it, and I don't see why he shouldn't. I would too if I had been so fortunate.

In the House of Commons his memory became both a joke and a byword. He drew on it extensively during debates, and when people would quote speeches he had made and allege he had said something at a certain time, he would quickly rise to his feet and give them the correct quotation, with the Hansard or other reference, detailing the exact time, date or place of the particular quotation. When he was able to draw on this memory, and to combine it with his humour and economic expertise during a speech, it was formidable.

During this time, the only cloud on the scene for him was the Bank Rate Tribunal and all that led up to it. Harold was asked by Mr Gaitskell to see him in September at Frognal and later at the Labour Party Conference at Brighton in 1957. The whole thing was put to him then and he took it upon himself to handle it.

It was the watershed of one part of his career, since from that moment on he was 'at war' with the City. Of course, for anyone left of centre in the Party, this is no liability but an asset. But after being in a business firm Harold had learned to respect and accept the business world that earns money and works hard to get it, in the sense of working for exports or working to build up their own companies.

But the Bank Rate Tribunal affair, and the knowledge he gained during his years in business, the side of the business world that *makes* money instead of *earning* it, had a traumatic effect on him. He is by nature extremely puritanical on money matters. It's not that he couldn't make money if he wanted to. As a professional statistician with his background and economic knowledge, he is well equipped to play the market. I can remember that on one occasion he gave very good advice to a close friend of his, a man who is worth millions today. That friend has a lot of money to play around with. He made a decision based on advice which Harold gave him and the decision was to result in a very large financial gain. If Harold had thought that would have been the size of the result of his advice, he probably wouldn't have given it. He was just asked for an opinion without realizing that perhaps the end result was something of which ultimately he would not have approved. Because he does have a contempt for the makers of money though not for the earners of money.

The whole Bank Rate Tribunal situation revealed the seamy side of Britain's economic life which no left-winger, no Socialist, can ever really come to terms with or accept. But the tribunal marked another point in his life. Thereafter he became an embarrassment to what was then the Establishment of his own Party. This was to become very apparent after the 1959 election.

Once the tribunal was out of the way, and throughout the period in the run-up to the 1959 election, Harold gradually

started to realize that he would have to move more into the
entre of political affairs if he was to maintain his position; a
position dependent, as most positions still are, upon the
Leader of the Party, even for an elected member of the Parliamentary Committee.

So here the personality and the tactics of the Leader, Hugh
Gaitskell, were very important. Hugh Gaitskell's policy, ever
since he took over the leadership from Clem Attlee in 1955,
was to run the Party on a tight rein. This was his style, and we
are all entitled to have an opinion about whether this was the
right way to run a party. My strong view is that this style was
wrong for the Labour Party which, by its very nature, is such a
coalition of varying views on the left of politics that a tight
rein is the last thing that should be used.

However, Mr Gaitskell was the Leader then, and if you did
not agree with him or his policies, then you were assumed to be
hostile and unacceptable. If you decided to oppose him on
anything, it was therefore desirable to make sure that the
ground on which you fought was firm. It was Harold's good
fortune that from 1951 to 1959 he had acquired all the advantages of a solid party base. This enabled him to work with
the Establishment right-wingers.

The 1959 election saw another turning-point in his career. It
was then that he made the decision to leave the business world
and to move into the House of Commons permanently to
spend more time on party work. This was, in my view, one of
the crucial phases in the making of the Prime Minister of the
future. He initiated what I think was regarded by some as a
rather curious move. Not only did he decide to leave Montague
Meyer but he intimated that he would like to take on the work
of being Chairman of the Public Accounts Committee. There
are few committees in the House of Commons where you can
learn such an immense amount of detail about how government works and what is going on in government policy.
Harold approached Hugh Gaitskell about the possibility of
being nominated as the chairman and Hugh agreed to this.
Harold was still the Shadow Spokesman on Treasury matters,
and I think Hugh agreed with Harold that the experience of
being on this committee would be invaluable to him and the
Party.

What was obvious was that once the election was out of the way, there was a great deal of re-thinking going on at the top of the Party, and this included Harold Wilson's future. Dick Crossman shortly after the election said to Harold: 'What went wrong?' From this Harold was made to understand that Mr Gaitskell felt that Harold would find it very difficult ever to be Chancellor of the Exchequer because of his bad relations with the City which had resulted from the Bank Rate Tribunal. Whether this was in fact exactly what Mr Gaitskell had in mind, one can never know. I think it is probably true that he did feel there was an embarrassment here and that he had considered a Shadow reshuffle, moving Harold from where he was. Of course, this is what he did later on. I understand that at that time it was suggested that it might have been possible if we had won the 1959 election to have put Harold as Leader of the House instead of at the Treasury. That could well have been a fatal political error on Mr Gaitskell's part, because no position in the House of Commons gives one more power and authority than Leader of the House. However, that was not to be, and Harold continued after the 1959 election as Shadow Chancellor.

But he now started to lead another dual role. The earlier combination of businessman and politician gave way to the duality of semi-civil servant and politician. As Chairman of the Public Accounts Committee he re-emphasized and accentuated another part of his personality. In some ways he is a Civil Servant *manqué*.

The Public Accounts Committee enables one to look into the finances and the organization of almost every Government department on the home front. The Comptroller and Auditor-General was Sir Edmund Crompton, who was later to become the first Ombudsman, or Parliamentary Commissioner, under the Labour Government. Harold and he had a very friendly relationship. Sir Edmund is a delightful character, needle-bright, very witty, warm-hearted, and without the 'edge' so often found in top civil servants. Harold often referred to him as 'the Elf'. It was not meant in a derogatory sense, but because Sir Edmund is a small man, with this alert, darting, quicksilver way with him. It was a very good description of him.

Twice a week Harold met with Sir Edmund, to talk over what was to happen at the Public Accounts Committee meetings following. At these meetings they were able to assess all the facts the Committee was acquiring and review all the possibilities and lines of argument needing probing and inquiry within the Committee over the weeks ahead. Although the results of some of their work were not to be published until after Harold left the job, a great deal was achieved between them. One of the greatest, of course, was the Ferranti question, where an electronics firm had miscalculated their estimates to such an extent that a matter of millions of pounds had been paid out by the Treasury to them on faulty figures.

Equally important, throughout the period Harold was able to meet the officials of each department, to get to know them, to size them up; to understand them and to evaluate the work of their departments, and to know the general drift of policy and the way things were being handled. It was invaluable to him. I have no doubt, looking back, that it was invaluable to them, because while he got the measure of them, they also probably got the measure of him.

Most people know Harold's Civil Service background: that he was a civil servant during the war, and that at the Board of Trade as a Cabinet Minister, he was probably as much of a civil servant as he was a Minister. This PAC job gave him the opportunity to return to a world which he admires and which he likes working in, a world dominated by 'the System'.

I am not quite sure whether other leading colleagues of his realized during the 1959 to 1963 period the experience he was getting in this part of his life. Few of them knew much about the Public Accounts Committee, nor the work it did. Some probably didn't much care. But the fact that he was the Chairman also gave him a room in the House of Commons. This is one of the most valuable acquisitions an MP can have. A room in the House of Commons is something that even today is not given to every Member of Parliament. In those days it was not even given to every leading Member of the House. Only the Leader of the Party had a room to himself, and a minuscule outer office. Other Members, front- and backbenchers alike, had just lockers.

Since 1964 there have been enormous changes and modernizations, thanks mainly to work started by Charles Pannell and continued by Bob Mellish. Now MPs usually have somewhere to work; a room to themselves or a shared room with one or two or possibly as many as four other colleagues. But in those days if you had a room it was like gold.

After the 1959 election, Mr Gaitskell started on what was to be an enormous modernization programme within the Party. It was a programme which I have no doubt was right and which he was right to pursue, but the way in which he pursued it is open to criticism: Hugh Gaitskell never quite got the measure of the Party, about what it could accept at any one time, about how quickly or slowly you could persuade the Party to go along with you.

It was at this point that Harold came into conflict with him. The whole nationalization argument, the unilateral disarmament argument that followed, were large issues of policy and principles, on which Harold had views, and strong ones. But his strongest view of all, as a result of the work he had done with the Party in the country from 1951 to 1959, was his concern for what the Party wanted as a whole and how much it would accept at one time. That is still his primary concern. This is where he differed from Mr Gaitskell and this is the reason why we moved into the period when he had to go into opposition against Mr Gaitskell.

I think Mr Gaitskell's contribution to the Party was that he knew it had to come to terms with the modern world, and it had to be brought up to date. He acted as the catalyst in starting this re-thinking and re-shaping. Mr Gaitskell was right about the need to modernize the Party but maladroit in the way he tried to bring this about.

There was also the problem, as I have said, that if one did not agree with him all down the line it was taken as an act of personal hostility. Certainly in the run-up to the 1960 Conference and Mr Gaitskell's defeat there on foreign affairs, there was a change in the personal relationship between Harold and other leading members of the Party. The result was that after Harold stood against Mr Gaitskell for the Leadership a year later he was asked to move from the Treasury to Foreign Affairs.

This was meant, I believe, as a way of killing him off but it acted as an enormous challenge to him. I remember him coming up to the PAC room on the third floor of the House of Commons and telling me that Mr Gaitskell had offered him this, and that he felt that he probably ought to refuse because he suspected the motive behind it. But after a long talk he gradually realized it was a challenge that should be accepted.

If he was successful in it then he would have proved he was capable of a wider range of political activity, not limited just to domestic policies. No one usually becomes leader of his party unless he is both an able politician, has a good working knowledge of the domestic front and has *also* some experience in overseas affairs. Harold at that point in time had no direct experience of foreign affairs and this was his opportunity to gain it. This he took.

He did an enormous amount of homework on it: he read copiously, met ambassadors from every country, went on overseas visits; worked terribly hard to grasp the subject involved and to prove to the Party that he was capable of handling this side of politics. Certainly he was not as colourful or as interesting in that role as he had been in the Shadow Chancellorship. His speeches became more dull and he tended to become so 'statesmanlike' that compromise was inevitable. Left-wing politics in foreign affairs are far more difficult to adhere to by official spokesmen than domestic policies – and God knows, that's not saying much!

Indeed Nye Bevan had already adapted himself long before in 1957, with his famous 'naked into the conference chamber' speech. But Nye was now, after the 1959 election, Deputy Leader of the Party and he could speak on domestic or foreign questions as he desired.

Before Harold became foreign affairs spokesman, there had been his stand against Mr Gaitskell, which now has become shrouded in legend and a great deal of misguided over-analysis. All sorts of motives have been attributed to Harold for what he did. I can only speak as I recall the situation when I was working with him.

First, I must put one thing right. At no time in the period from 1956 until 1960 did I ever hear Harold Wilson speak in terms of becoming Leader of the Party. I don't think he ever thought he could ever become Prime Minister. He had always talked about his great ambition to introduce more Budgets in the House of Commons than Gladstone. I believe that this is what he wanted to do, and I know that he did not think in terms of the Leadership or No. 10. Since it was never mentioned or discussed in my hearing, I can only conclude that this fact does not accord with the attributions made later of his being a cold calculating politician and opportunist.

When he stood against Mr Gaitskell in 1960 he did so on the principle that you must seek to unite the Labour Party, rather than to divide it and drive it into a situation where argument developed into hostile clashes. He knew then that he could be involved in an act of political suicide. He himself was in no doubt about it, and spoke in those terms. It could mean the end of his career as a leading member of the Party. Sycophants have said that this was the bravest action of his life and defend him in this way. I don't personally think it was particularly brave. My definition of bravery is acting when the odds are unknown. Harold knew exactly what he was doing and what he was up against. He did it because he felt it to be right. Bold, perhaps; brave, no.

I think he always accepted that when you stand against leaders of the Party you don't beat them. Leaders are very difficult to move once they have been elected. The Parliamentary Labour Party always gives majority support to its Leader, however much criticism there may be against him. But I think he felt that someone had to fire a warning shot across Mr Gaitskell's bows to make him understand that you really cannot push the Party in the way he was doing. Harold wanted Mr Gaitskell to understand this. He tried to put it over in public speeches outside in the country and certainly within the Shadow Cabinet. But it was not then an acceptable view to the right-wing Establishment.

Harold went through a very difficult time then. He was very unhappy. His friends were on the left of the Party. His own inclinations were more towards their sort of policies. He had strong views on Party management. He knew from experience how the constituency parties worked and felt. For these reasons, therefore, he made the decision to stand against Mr Gaitskell and try to halt the drift, as he saw it, in the wrong direction, knowing that retribution would follow very quickly.

Often some of his friends would gather in his PAC room in the House of Commons to discuss what was happening. One of his very closest and most loyal friends, the late Sir Leslie ('Dick') Plummer, the MP for Deptford, would go over and over with him all the arguments for or against taking this particular stand. Trevor Lloyd-Hughes, who was later to become his Press Officer at No. 10, would often put his head round the door and say: 'Marcia, is he going to come out from behind his bush?' It was a very good way of describing Harold's inbuilt desire not to force an argument or to have a row.

At that time Mr Gaitskell was firmly entrenched. He was widely respected throughout the Party and while he may not have been loved, he had a firm hold on the movement.

Harold knew that, and everyone else who was involved in that particular episode knew it. So when Harold stood against him, he genuinely believed that this was the end. When the defeat was followed by his removal from the Exchequer to Foreign Affairs, he realized that this was the pay-off for what he had done.

In the Shadow Cabinet elections that year he came near the bottom of the poll, though in view of his stand against the Leader it was quite an achievement even to get back into it.

He worked tremendously hard during the year that followed, and by 1961 he had gone from near the bottom of the voting for the Shadow Cabinet to the top. That is the measure of his determination in the face of overwhelming odds. To fight back from a position where he had almost destroyed himself to a position where he could once again be accepted as a leading member of the Party, was a remarkable feat in just one year.

It is my strong feeling also that, whatever may be said by other people in other parts of the Party, Mr Gaitskell himself realized that there was a lot of truth in Harold's arguments. I think that gradually over the years, from 1959 until his death in 1963, he did start to become more flexible in his attitude to the Party, and this was demonstrated when he fell into line with mass opinion in the Parliamentary Party and in the Party at large, and came out against Britain's application to join the European Community.

There was one event at the 1962 Conference that indicated what sort of Prime Minister and Leader of the Party Harold Wilson might become. There was a motion during a constitutional amendment debate about 'guilt by association' – whether anybody associated with an organization with communist links was by definition to be regarded as a communist himself. Harold just could not accept this idea. He understands how the Party is made up. Unless you allow free expression within the framework of the Party, with a certain amount of direction from the top, then Harold felt you were on a disaster course. The motion was defeated. Harold was Chairman of the Party and he worked in the background to make sure that the Party realized what it was doing, and that the motion was not passed.

One of Harold Wilson's greatest contributions to the Labour Party has been his liberalization of it. I believe he could not have done this unless he had come from the Left himself. He did not agree with the totality of the arguments the Left propagated, since he believed you could only act in the circumstances which existed. This is an argument the Left can never come to terms with or accept and they are entitled to have this view. Harold doesn't share it. He sympathizes with them, he's more in tune with them, but he wants to see things done and, therefore, he is prepared to compromise to get those things done. But his liberal view that you should be allowed to believe what you want as a democratic socialist, across a very wide area, is one of his major contributions.

He doesn't care particularly what your position is within the Party so long as the views you hold are sincerely held and not for some ulterior motive. So long, too, as you are prepared to accept that those who don't share your opinions in the Party have a right to disagree, and should be allowed to develop their contrary opinions within the framework of the Party. It is the Leader's role as he sees it, to hold all these strands together and to guide them gently in a direction towards power. That is what political parties exist for – power. But by guiding them gently and correctly and holding them together you ensure that they are able to achieve the power they must have in order to put into effect all the things in which they believe.

In February 1963 the totally unpredictable tragic event happened that was to change the whole course of Harold's life. Hugh Gaitskell died. The leadership election that followed was a nasty one, and I for one would rather not recall the way in which the Labour Party conducted itself during that period. It was rough, tough and unpleasant, with no holds barred and many people deeply hurt.

The campaign was carried through in icy weather. There had been deep snow and it had never cleared away properly. Great frozen lumps of it were lying around on the streets for weeks. It was still there after 14 February – the night we waited with Mary in the Upper Committee corridor room belonging to the Public Accounts Committee Chairman, to hear the results.

The meeting at which the result would be announced was held on the floor below, and we could hear all the voices as members of the PLP assembled. We had already received an indication of the result from one of the officers of the Party. And then the result was finally telephoned through to us and confirmed, and it really was an extremely moving moment, because it seemed so incredible. We just could not believe that it had happened. It is not possible to say that it was beyond our wildest dreams, because in fact it had never really been part of our dreams. You really cannot legislate for some tragic event which will eliminate a leader, and so the assumption had always been that Mr Gaitskell would be there for very many years and would be at No. 10 eventually.

After the result we were a little paralysed by the magnitude of it all. We celebrated, a little nervously, at Ben Parkin's home. We didn't know quite what the leaders of the Party did, nor how their lives were organized, and yet the very next morning we were expected to be on duty downstairs in the Leader's room.

Harold, of course, dealt with this transformation in the way he does everything, relaxed and calm, giving the impression that he understood how it was done and was perfectly in control. For me it was a moment of confusion. I had little idea what was expected of me, though I knew that he wanted me to go on as his secretary. He had got used to the way I worked and I knew the way he worked. After seven years he was entitled to have around someone he was used to.

After his election, Harold kept on Hugh Gaitskell's Parliamentary Private Secretary, Joe Slater, now Lord Slater, who became one of our very closest friends and a staunch and comforting ally. He has written a fascinating autobiography and the passages in it about his time with Harold are well worth reading since here is a man who worked for two leaders, with Hugh Gaitskell as well as Harold Wilson. They are such entirely different characters that it must have been quite an experience to have seen them both at work. He was totally loyal to both.

Richard Marsh, who had been a firm supporter of Mr Gaitskell, has since written that once Harold Wilson became Leader there was 'the sudden outbreak of peace'. He continued: 'we all found it difficult to adapt.' It was a fact that until Harold became Leader, Labour had not known peace for a very long time. There had been all the arguments and there had been all the unfortunate confrontations on the way the Party should be handled.

But under Harold things changed.

His victory was so decisive that it meant that there could be no other challenger in the foreseable future. Peace continued and for this Harold was responsible. He deliberately included in his Shadow Government, and later his Government, many people who had been his violent enemies in earlier years. One outstandingly clever young right-winger was given a job in government immediately following a vicious personal attack on Harold. But he was the best man for the job at that time, so he got it.

At the time I was like everyone else in the famous 'stage-coach' to which Harold has often referred. I rattled along with the best of them, exhilarated by the speed and excitement, and I can remember looking at him and thinking to myself: 'Ah! This is the Leader of the Labour Party and I know exactly what sort of a Leader he is going to be, and when he becomes Prime Minister' – which he then felt confident he would be one day – 'I know what sort of Prime Minister he is going to make.'

I knew all the different sides of his character, but I had never actually pieced them all together and it was only the experience at No. 10 which enabled me to do so.

But what has been increasingly fascinating to me has been his emergence since that moment. His first television broadcast as Leader of the Party was a real riot and has often been satirized since. It was his first into-camera performance and he had been told not to sit in a wooden fashion, but to use his hands and his arms to express himself, as well as just his face. This resulted in hands suddenly coming up very sharply and a fist being pushed into the camera in a very threatening fashion. This was extremely funny. But because we thought it funny, we were also worried in case it had made a devastatingly bad first impression. We were amazed to learn afterwards that everybody thought it was marvellous and very real and genuine.

Later he became a master of the into-camera technique, and was completely relaxed whenever he had to appear on television. I don't think I know anyone who can do it so well and yet he is conscious of everything he is doing. He knows when he lights his pipe that he is lighting his pipe to make a relaxed break in the performance. He often rubs his nose to give himself a chance to think out the end of the sentence he has already begun. But the image which comes across is completely clear; it was and is the image of the extraordinary ordinary man: the first in this country people had seen reach the top in politics.

Over the years people had been used to having someone from a working-class background who had a memorable career while never actually reaching the top, with Lloyd George as the only exception. In the Labour Party there were many such characters. They received a lot of attention and held high positions, but the leadership usually went to Establishment people, from middle-class backgrounds. Harold Wilson provided a real break in that tradition, and people were, I think, fascinated by it.

He was a man with whom they could identify totally. His voice, with the slight Yorkshire accent, was immediately acceptable to them. He could easily represent what their son could be thirty or forty years from now. The Gannex raincoat which he popularized by accident became famous. It seemed to epitomize everything that he represented. It stood out because it was different from anything they had ever seen a leading politician ever wear. The usual regulation-wear for top politicians was the well-cut dark overcoat. No one had ever dashed around in a short, trendy raincoat. It was criticized very severely afterwards as being frumpish, old fashioned, and dreary. Yet the Gannex had been worn by Prince Philip for some time, and many other members of the Party and Tories also wore it. The fact that Harold wore it drew attention to it, and it also drew attention to him. He did look exactly like someone you could go up to and speak to, and this gave the impression that here was someone who understood you, understood your problems, knew what difficulties you had, knew what hopes, what aspirations you had.

Added to this was the fact that from the moment of his election, right through until the General Election in October 1964, he never let up for one minute. He was on tour in the country, he was on television broadcasts, he flew to America, he went on two visits to the Soviet Union, he travelled to different parts of Europe. He was continually in the public eye and continually being given publicity.

Then suddenly, slap bang on top of it all, Harold Macmillan gave up his job, and we were handed on a plate a perfect specimen of all the propaganda the Labour Party was using against the Tory Party: out of date, out of touch, and incapable of handling affairs efficiently at home. Alec Douglas-Home was tailor-made to go with such propaganda, a beautifully wrapped gift and the Tory Party couldn't have done us a bigger favour. The second half of the run-up to the election, therefore, was freewheeling until one hiccup right at the end.

I remember there was a distinct difference of opinion about this. It was in the July before the House went up and there had been a row in the House of Commons on the question of the sale of frigates to Fascist Spain. I felt Harold should play it fairly quietly and not too shrilly, particularly in the middle of the summer when people were going away on holiday and when Spain was the most popular holiday place. But Harold launched an all-out attack on Franco Spain; one result was that during August the Tories actually took the lead on the opinion polls. For one month they were ahead of us which naturally made us apprehensive.

I went down to the Scillies for a week to see Harold and we discussed the implications of the situation, doing calculations about how many people were on holiday and were Labour, how many were Tory and how accurately the holiday figures were represented in the polls. We realized we were now going to have a very tight fight indeed in October. It was hard going and touch-and-go throughout the whole of the campaign.

The election was one of the most exciting periods of my whole life. The people we had around us were good to work with – and good at their jobs. We all understood each other and we got on well together. Transport House was in tune with what we were doing because the years in Opposition had kept us tightly together. We went round that country like crusaders, we enjoyed every meeting, even though Harold repeated himself, as a politician does in every election, a thousand times. We enjoyed the jokes, even though we had heard them over and over again. It was the election when egg-throwing came back into vogue. Then it was Alec Douglas-Home who was the target. We were appalled by it and would have liked to stop it, but we didn't know quite how to do it. It was certainly counter-productive electorally.

We felt sorry for Sir Alec. He seemed a nice guy, but he obviously didn't know what it was all about. He didn't have the ordinary touch; he didn't know how to mix, nor take his share of knockabout politics. His whistle-stop tour of meeting the people was really more like a Royal tour. Harold had the advantage on him at every point along the line.

There was enormous excitement everywhere in the country, culminating in Huyton at the end of the campaign, with his own constituents, who had known him for years, greeting him as Leader of his Party and the probable next Prime Minister.

One of the amusing things about that campaign was the lack of deference shown to Harold by his own Party – a traditional Labour attitude to its Leader. When the campaign began we had to move out of the House of Commons and use Transport House as a base. We were graciously allowed to have the rooms of the Chief Woman Officer to work in. Harold had the use of the Chief Woman Officer's room, and her outer office was used by Harold's staff. Many might have thought that the Leader of the Party would have been given the best room in the building. He had the Press to receive and distinguished visitors. Harold never thought of making any comment on his surroundings. He was a little surprised when he saw what they had allocated him, but he accepted it and got on with the job.

And when 16 October arrived and we looked at Harold Wilson, who was now Prime Minister, I for one was extremely curious to see what sort of Prime Minister he was going to be.

I knew the different components in his character, and I knew exactly how they reacted and interacted on each other – the politician, the businessman, the civil servant and the Parliamentarian.

Some of us who were very close to him were worried it would be the civil servant who would dominate him, and I think it is fair to say that our fears were in fact justified to some great extent through the years of the two Labour Governments.

It is the fact that he does have such an admiration for and such a working knowledge of 'the System' that he tends to lean over backwards in his relationship towards it. He gives it the benefit of the doubt. He doesn't really want to argue with it. He admires the way it is organized and its methods of working. He admires its efficiency and he is often myopic about its failings and its short-comings and its inefficiencies, and this is a great drawback.

But to say that is not to give the whole picture. Throughout the years of the Labour Government the politician was always there ready at every point of time to take over and to steer events as needed. The only regret I have in my mind is that he spent so long allowing the civil servant to dominate him and that when the politician was called in to redress the balance he sometimes started just a bit too late to do the job properly.

It is interesting to pose the question, therefore, whether, if he had become Leader and then Prime Minister immediately after his years as Shadow Chancellor, the politician would have carried on dominating him. But there was the intervening phase that interrupted the flow in his career, when he was Chairman of the Public Accounts Committee and the sober spokesman on foreign affairs. So when he became Leader the immediate past influences were orientated towards the System. Only the fact that the election was so imminent gave the politician the opportunity to grab hold of the situation and control it. But once the door of No. 10 opened and he walked down that long corridor, then I think that the civil servant slowly took over again. This is purely a personal view and probably unacceptable to many who have more right to make judgement on this than I. But it is how I feel.

Those early days at No. 10 were like a silent movie where you know that things are happening but you can't remember the sounds and the feelings and the senses that accompany these happenings.

I hold the view very strongly that Ministers, and particularly Prime Ministers, should automatically suspect many of the activities of the Civil Service. I shall deal later with other aspects of the Civil Service, but here, because Harold's views differ so much from mine, I feel I must deal with his attitude to the people who control so much of Whitehall.

The important thing to remember about him is that his methodical and analytical mind, partly the product of his academic training at Oxford, together with his amazing capacity for work makes him an ideal civil servant and the model for a potential Whitehall 'mandarin'. No doubt if he had stayed on in the Civil Service after the war he would have reached the top.

When he went into Downing Street he regarded the civil servants as colleagues and friends. They did not control him throughout the time he was boss there, because he knows too much and his mind has such a wide range it would be impossible for anyone to run him in that sense. But they managed to handle him and they certainly had the measure of him and his personality.

Harold is a traditionalist, not only on this front but in other attitudes too. He is, I suppose, a typical Englishman. He is a staunch defender of most British institutions, with a great love for Parliament. He respects the monarchy and he enjoys much of the ceremonial in our lives, which I personally don't particularly like. But this is a small part of the man. He is a reformer too, and in many ways a very passionate one, but never a revolutionary.

Another of his features, and one that has been persistently derided, is his optimism. This was one of his great strengths and one of the reasons why he held the Government together during the period with the three majority. We couldn't have survived without it. When anything went wrong we would get very depressed and he alone kept us going.

Having seen Downing Street now from the inside, I see quite definitely that any Prime Minister who is not an optimist is as good as dead. The burdens are so tremendous, the crises so frequent and the decisions so frightening that if you ceased to be an optimist then you would have to give up the job. I don't believe for one moment that everyone who holds that office isn't an optimist.

Harold was criticized because he expressed that optimism so often in personal television broadcasts. I can't see why this was wrong. I would have thought that any leader, of either a party or a country, has a duty to make people feel optimistic about their future. Nobody criticized Harold Macmillan's optimism and he needed it in that first year when he took over the premiership. Only a supreme optimist could have snatched the Tory Party back from the brink of disaster after the Suez fiasco. It was his optimism that kept his administration going and made the Conservative victory of 1959 possible. In political terms it was justified, just as I feel Harold Wilson's optimism was justified.

The other great thing about Harold was that throughout his years at No. 10 he never lost his nerve. Even during the worst crises, the first shocks when he took over and found the situation as bad as it was, the dreadful recurring crises after the 1966 election and the eventual devaluation and post-devaluation days, he remained totally calm. Often he was reported in the Press to be sulking in his tent, or to have gone into purdah. In fact he had withdrawn a little from the public scene, but he was already planning how to win the next election and talking in those terms to all of us.

When we were twenty points behind in the public opinion polls he still maintained that the final result at the end of the day would be a close one. He always said that we should get the balance of payments right in the end, even though it would be a struggle. We did and he was right.

I can remember him looking troubled and doubtful on a number of occasions, either because of personal issues or small irritating events and more so at times of major set-backs like the D Notice affair. But these times never lasted long.

The Hamilton by-election was particularly bad, when a Labour majority of sixteen thousand was wiped out and resulted in a gain for the Scottish Nationalists. He was certainly affected by that result because of the long Labour tradition in Hamilton. But by the next morning he had bounced back, and was saying cheerfully that we would win the seat comfortably in the General Election, which, of course, we did.

One reason why he is in politics is because he really likes it. It's the life for him and he is good at it. It would be a waste of all his talents to be in any other job. If he had chosen another career he would have wasted so much, and this is one thing that he dislikes intensely – people being allowed to waste the talents they have. He wants people to have good homes, a fair chance to get on in life, better education for their children, and he sees the National Health Service as a shining monument to Labour and wants to improve upon it and make it even more of an example to the rest of the world. But above all he wants to see people use to the full the talents they have.

I know these are the aims of many politicians. He is not unique in any of this. But they are not bad ideals for a man to retain and feel so strongly about after having been a professional politician for so long.

He has been a professional politician for a long time, but there have been many influences in his life besides the ones in his professional career. What happened to him in Huddersfield during his young years after the First World War is still dominant in him. He hates poverty and he hates the idea of children or families being deprived. These things genuinely give him pain. He hates above all inequality between men for whatever reason. He can quote you examples of people he knew in Huddersfield during the years of the Depression, when unemployment figures were a total disgrace to a civilized nation, and when people who had genuine abilities, hardworking decent people, were deprived of the opportunity to work.

He is probably known most for his skills as a tactician, a talent acknowledged curiously and unnervingly by Enoch Powell. During the years at No. 10 one saw it most of all in the way in which he pre-empted issues. He saw a problem coming up long before other people and he studied it and planned a response to it. I think particularly of three large issues on which he did this – Rhodesia, Immigration and the Common Market.

There is nothing phoney about his feelings on racial equality, whether it is in Britain or Rhodesia. He certainly wanted to do a deal with Ian Smith but only if the six principles were observed. He wanted to get us into Europe if the terms were right, because he felt a Socialist Britain and a greater Socialism in Europe could create in time a social democratic Europe.

But the way he went about handling these issues, particularly his treatment of immigration, in his Birmingham speech, meant that to a large extent these issues were pre-empted as political controversies. He has a unique sense of what the general public want and of how far you can go with them and how far you can take them along with you. He instinctively knows how much the public can accept at one time on a particular subject, and I don't mean that in a derogatory way: he was the master of what many political writers scathingly dismiss as consensus politics and which they were so glad to see behind them on 18 June 1970. If you look back over the years of the Labour Government you will see that on the Common Market, on Rhodesia, on immigration and even to a large extent over the running sore of Vietnam, Harold was able to carry a majority of opinion in the open.

He also rather despised the cult that existed in the Party at one period when the expression of 'beliefs' took the place of the expression of policies. What may not be generally known is that he is a very warm person to work with and very easy to work with. He does make heavy demands on you and he tends to expect you to work at the same pace as he does himself, and to tax yourself to the full as he taxes himself. It's a little hard and a little difficult and sometimes one resists and wants to opt out. But nobody close to him ever does.

And this is the extraordinary thing about him: he can manage to persuade those who are near to him – not just political people but civil servants too – to work all the hours God gives and to work as hard as he works, and to live every minute of every crisis with him throughout all that period.

Of course, there are some parts of his character which one would like to criticize. Gerald Kaufman and I have a special private joke that he often deals more harshly with those who are closest to him than he does with those who aren't. One day when he was particularly rough with Gerald, I comforted Gerald with the thought that he had at last arrived, because Harold had been so awful to him that he must think highly of him, otherwise he would not have taken all that trouble to be so rude. Harold only takes the trouble to be rude and cutting to those for whom he does have a respect and affection and a high opinion.

There are no rewards in working for him – not if you expect to be praised regularly, thanked regularly, and generally made a fuss of. This you will miss. He may appear not to notice you, not to regard you and not even to involve you in the eventual celebration of something that has gone particularly well and something for which you have worked hard.

But this is small criticism compared with his other side when he will take the trouble to deal with the serious problems of those who are on his staff and who need help. He is capable of stopping in the middle of something of great importance to devote all his energies to helping somebody before he takes up again his other duties. This is the measure of him as a human being. I think there are few people of whom you can say that in any walk of life, and as far as I am concerned this is the greatest tribute you can pay him.

How can you go through a whole chapter of comments on Harold Wilson's character and personality, the chronicle of the 'extraordinary ordinary man' and end up by talking about the small parts of his personality which have become the subject of jokes and of derision, such as his love for HP Sauce and his liking for Yorkshire pudding? But it's true. He does like these things. He likes HP Sauce, though not as much as people would like to think. He likes roast beef and Yorkshire pudding and he does have very simple tastes in food.

As a boss he has great virtues as well as defects. For one thing he can take the mistakes you make and not make heavy weather of them. Some politicians can be very difficult if mistakes are made by their staff. Both Lord Attlee and Mr Gaitskell were very demanding.

I made an absolutely dreadful error of an engagement soon after I started to work for him. He had to go to a banquet, a white tie affair, at Guildhall, and I got the dates mixed up. He was sent off one evening in white tie and tails, which he hates, and he drove his own car there and went into Guildhall only to find that he didn't recognize any of the people gathering for the so-called banquet. After a number of inquiries he discovered that they were all hatters. He then returned promptly from the function and called in at my home. I wasn't there but he took great delight in telling my parents that he had been to a hatters' function in the City. But it was all done with amusement and without criticism.

When he was the Leader of the Opposition, Brenda Dew and I made an even greater mistake, when he had to go to a lunch which was in fact at the French Embassy. He dashed out of the office and as he left he shouted: 'Ring the Embassy and tell them I'm late.' We rang the German Embassy being convinced that this was where he was going and that was what he had said. He had been talking about the German Ambassador on his way out in conversation to someone else, and I think this was probably why we made the error.

But what we succeeded in doing was greatly disturbing the German Ambassador, who was giving a luncheon and hadn't invited Harold. When he got our message he had another place laid at the table and made his guests wait until Harold arrived. I think he said something to the effect that if Herr Wilson wanted to come to lunch then he was very welcome even though he hadn't in fact invited him for that occasion.

Meanwhile at the French Embassy they were all waiting for lunch too. When the Germans discovered the error, they laughed, and Harold laughed too when he heard about it, and took it all very well and wasn't a bit put out. I think that because he takes mistakes of this kind so well it makes you even more careful not to make any.

He is helpful in an office. At No. 10 Downing Street there was a strict demarcation line between civil servants and politicial staff, and since the political staff were small in numbers, particularly early on, we often found it very difficult just to cope with the mechanics of our job. When the mail got very heavy indeed and there were a lot of letters for him to sign, he would not only sign them, but would very often help with putting them into the envelopes, sealing them up, and getting them ready for the post. I don't think many people in his position would want to sit down with his political staff and do a tedious job of this kind. He had done this sort of thing before. When he first became Leader of the Opposition he was inundated with mail. It was so heavy that when the replies were ready he lined them all up along the table in his room – a table which is as large as the table in the Cabinet Room at No. 10 Downing Street – and he walked round signing them all. Then, because there were so many, literally hundreds lying there, he walked round with us sealing them up and getting them ready to be sent off.

He is meticulous about wanting to sign as many letters as possible to people who write in to him. It is not possible obviously for him to sign them all, because there are so many, but wherever he can do so, he will. He always tries to sign constituency letters, particularly when he has taken up a case, and his constituents always get very special treatment within his office. Letters coming in from Huyton are dealt with immediately and there is never any delay which we can in any way prevent.

He has an enormous sense of humour, and he can laugh about himself. We are allowed to imitate him. Not as expertly as Mike Yarwood does, but pretty good in a different way! We often make fun of the way in which we know he is going to react to a particular situation, drawing on all sorts of examples from the past. He will listen to it all and join in. He will even help out and give us additional ammunition, very unusual in a politician, because most tend not to have much of a sense of humour about themselves, and take themselves rather seriously. In particular they take themselves very seriously in front of their staff. Harold always amazes people by his relaxed and natural way of behaving.

So how do you sum him up? This is a difficult task indeed. It is a problem to define anybody in politics, even those who appear simple and uncomplicated. To sum up Harold Wilson is like trying to encapsulate *War and Peace*.

But if one had to refer to his most outstanding characteristic, for my part I would first want to talk about the curious contradiction there is between the public and private image. I think it would be true to say that most people have the idea that he is a very tough man, hard, determined, very ambitious and possibly a little arrogant. And, of course, there has been enough Tory propaganda around saying how devious, cunning and insincere he is.

However, Harold Wilson is in many ways a curiously soft individual. Soft in that he is incapable of showing that streak of hardness and toughness with colleagues that is really necessary.

Harold took the doctrine of 'turning the other cheek' to extraordinary lengths – and unnecessary ones. Very often people who were totally opposed to him personally would mortally offend him, but instead of meeting them and telling them exactly what he thought of them, he would be extraordinarily nice and polite to them. The point of conflict between them would soon be dismissed from his mind.

It is true that throughout the years of the Labour Government there were one or two occasions when there were definite moves within the Party to try to raise the question of the leadership and whether Harold should be made to go. These efforts were organized by particular individuals and Harold knew exactly who the organizers were on each occasion. They were usually the same ones. Indeed they still exist as a 'Wilson must go' group and continue their activities.

When he next met with them, after discovering what had been going on, he would merely be polite and charming to them as if nothing had happened. He might make some joke about the manoeuvres in which they had been indulging. This was particularly true of the 1968 manoeuvres, when Harold was abroad. One of the leading people involved in these manoeuvres went on a BBC *Panorama* programme when he was less than enthusiastic about Harold's leadership, and the only interpretation you could have put on what he then said in answer to questions by Robin Day was that he felt Harold was inadequate to the job. I myself sent telegrams off to Harold on this occasion which I drafted, to the amusement of the Private Office, for transmission through the Foreign Office secure line. I remember that the Foreign Office Private Secretary said on that occasion that he did not think he could remember ever having seen telegrams so colourfully drafted transmitted through the Foreign Office wires.

But when Harold returned he did not chastise any of the people concerned, and certainly not the principal. He treated him with the usual courtesy and politeness. He always prefers to let it go and to see how it develops and if it starts to get out of hand, he steps in fairly toughly, but always at the eleventh hour. I suppose there is something to be said for this particular way of handling things, but sometimes a lot of trouble could have been saved by an earlier operation.

With regard to Cabinet reshuffles he was particularly sensitive. He hated having to sack people, particularly those he liked and admired, and he even disliked sacking those he didn't like.

We had a joke about Harold and his decisions to tell his colleagues exactly what he thought about them and to put things right when they were going badly wrong. We always used to say: 'Ah! He has his feather duster out again.' I don't think that anyone who knows Harold Wilson well can visualize him wielding an axe, or raising a hatchet to anyone.

What this must never be confused with is any lack of courage to deal with a situation if he has to do so. He is not afraid of any of these people, and on rare occasions he will suddenly come out of his corner fighting in such a ferocious way that one can hardly recognize him.

Ray Gunter later became one of his greatest critics. Mr Gunter is an unusual character. He was at one time thought to be a latter-day Nye Bevan, so he must have sorely disappointed many people who saw him in this role. Harold was particularly kind to Ray Gunter when he was ill during the middle years of the Labour Government. On that occasion he sent him off to the Isles of Scilly to stay in his bungalow to recuperate and to return, when he was ready, to his job as the Minister of Labour. At all times throughout Ray Gunter's period in that job Harold was anxious not to displease him.

It was for these reasons that Harold, as I know, felt particularly upset by Ray Gunter's political attitude following his resignation.

In a curious way too, Harold was very gentle about George Brown. He likes and dislikes him at the same time, and I have a feeling that probably George Brown feels exactly the same way about Harold Wilson. They have had their differences, but whether they like it or not, there are certain things about them which are very similar. Although Harold has had the intellectual training which George Brown is always very vituperative about, Harold's background is similar enough to George's to enable him to find common ground with George. Harold's impulsive gesture of 1963 at Scarborough Conference, when he raised George's hand in the air, was really meant as a very warm gesture of affection to George, and a hope that the Labour Party could be united and that George would work with him. It proved to be somewhat of an error.

One of the greatest regrets Harold had was the sacking of Douglas Houghton. He did this because he had promised to bring Patrick Gordon Walker back into the Cabinet. But he recognized that Douglas Houghton had enormous abilities and it was a great loss to the Labour Cabinet and an action which Harold regretted very much afterwards. Ernie Fernyhough too, his PPS when he was Leader, was another difficult dismissal as he was very fond of him.

But he never sacked people in the way in which Earl Attlee sacked them. Apparently Clem Attlee would send for them and they would walk into the Cabinet Room and Clem would just shake their hand and say 'goodbye' with not more than one or two sentences to them. Certainly no explanation about why he was doing it, but possibly a few words to say they had done well, or some ambiguous phrase if they had not.

Harold went to enormous lengths when he sacked anyone to compliment him on all the work he had done and all the efforts he had put in for the Labour Government, and to express his own regret that this was what he felt he had to do. He would also explain at length why he had made the decision to do it. This often resulted in many of them arguing it out with him and saying that they did not feel that he should be sacking them.

The reshuffles at No. 10 were fascinating mixtures of agony and excitement. We loathed seeing the people sitting waiting to go in when we knew they were going to be sacked, but were excited when we recognized some colourful character who was about to be given a very good job.

During the last reshuffle I was amused to see Bert Oram waiting in the inner hall and Reg Prentice coming down the stairs from the Prime Minister's study. When he got to the bottom of the stairs Bert Oram looked up at him and Reg Prentice made a gesture as if to cut his throat, which I took as a signal to Bert Oram that he had been sacked. Of course, he had not been sacked but had gone up to tender his resignation. But he knew that Bert Oram had himself been called along to be sacked.

They did not know I was sitting there watching, but it was both extremely amusing and very sad because they are nice, genuine, able men who made a most enormous contribution in a quiet way to the work of the Government.

When these occasions were over, Harold would always come in and sink into an armchair and be given a drink and say jokingly: 'I'm covered in buckets of blood.' Part One of the Operation, the sackings, he was always glad to get out of the way, but of course Part Two, the appointments, he enjoyed very much – like all Prime Ministers, I guess.

On certain occasions people came along who would argue with him about their appointment, saying that it was not adequate for their abilities. One example of this was a well-known right-wing member of the Government, young, ambitious and consistently over the years passionately anti-Wilson. On every occasion he was called to see Harold when his job was changed he would argue about the question of his own abilities and how he deserved more than he had been given.

Then there was the sacking of Dick Marsh. It was afterwards attributed to matters which had no connection whatsoever with the decision that Harold had made. This angered Harold. His judgement of Dick Marsh's ability, and his liking for him, never altered at any point of time.

Harold had every intention of reappointing Dick to the Cabinet after a period out of office to reconsider things more seriously, and when he was then reappointed to the Cabinet, to a different job, he would increase in stature. In the event, of course, the election was lost and now the Labour movement has lost Dick Marsh. This leaves a serious gap in that particular generation, since he had all the makings of a leader of the Party.

I think the best example of Harold's total tolerance is one occasion late in the evening when Jim Callaghan came to see him. Jim was already at the Home Office and George Brown called in on the same evening. On that occasion the conversation rambled a little from the points that they had in fact come to discuss. It eventually wandered off in such a way that it ended up with Harold sitting in his armchair while George and Jim in front of him rehearsed the arguments about what would happen if Harold went under the legendary No. 11 bus. They continued this argument about who would succeed him for some considerable time until he had to interrupt to stop it continuing all evening.

Harold Wilson was far too kind as a Prime Minister. Far too kind to colleagues who did not deserve it and far too tolerant of some of the things they did. But the result of this kindness and this tolerance has been a unity within the Party and an ability on the part of the Party to survive even some of the worst differences of opinion it has had, not least the Industrial Relations Bill which one could hardly say was the most palatable offering with which the Labour movement has been presented.

I hope I see Harold Wilson 'warts and all'. I think he has made an enormous contribution to Labour politics for his tolerance, his good humour and – while being deeply offended, criticized and insulted – his ability not to take retribution for it thereafter.

His great strengths are his strong nerve, his ability to plod on despite all the difficulties, all the abuse, all the personal criticism and recrimination, having decided the course of action he is going to take and the long-term objectives towards which he is working.

7

Treacherous Tides, Troubles
and *Tiger*

Those words uttered by Harold in the lift at No. 10 on 1 April 1966, 'Now we can have a rest from politics', were still echoing in my ears when I left late that Friday night for home. It was the end of the campaign and he was tired when he spoke, but their implication still bothered me. I remember that I was desperately tired too. I wanted a rest that weekend, but I was pursued by the thought of all the debris left behind after the election and felt impelled to go back to No. 10 to sort things out.

There were books and boxes everywhere. Piles of stationery and copies of speeches and correspondence were stacked all over the place. The accumulation of weeks of campaigning had to be sorted out and put back in order. I had also to unpack and untie the files and boxes which I had made ready for moving out in case we lost. Here at least was one task that was really satisfying. It was the final proof that we had won.

That weekend I took the opportunity to stand back and have a searching look at my working accommodation at No. 10. The first months at No. 10 back in 1964 had been so crammed that I had accepted the new pattern of life without realizing all that it meant and whether it could be improved. Now oddly enough, I found myself impressed for the first time by the fact that I was working at No. 10. But I too found myself horrified by the general mess and the inadequate facilities that we had endured for so many months.

Even the filing system was the one I had taken into the Leader of the Opposition's room in 1963. It had not been pruned since 1956. All the correspondence from that year was in the cabinets, certainly in chronological order and clearly marked, but lodged in the same cabinets with correspondence right up to 1966. Here, all together and mixed up, was the record of ten years' work. Boxes of correspondence were inadequately labelled, and because of our lack of funds, we couldn't even afford alphabetical dividers in every filing cabinet. What a contrast to the efficient political machine which I wanted, and knew the Tories almost certainly provided for their Leader's office.

So, in the immediate weeks after the election, I set about sorting it all out, labelling it anew and putting it into some new and clearer order. Eventually things began to look better and even easier to operate. But the alterations involved a long, dirty job. Susan Lewis and I stayed night after night until 10.00 or 11.00, re-filing and labelling. We got extremely dusty and sometimes looked more like coal miners than office workers. It was additionally oppressive because our main rooms were still in the attic, and the tiny windows and sloping ceilings didn't improve the general atmosphere.

Among all this, life was made more interesting by hearing of the daily drama in the life of Harold's housekeeper, Mary Wright. She had met the man she was to marry and with whom she was very much in love. Like all romances it had its daily problems, Mary would come up to us each evening with cups of tea, to talk to us about everything else that was going on in the building.

During these early post-election days I equipped the large downstairs kitchen with frying pans, saucepans and kettles so that we could make ourselves a meal if we needed it at a late hour. Food was also kept in the large refrigerator there.

This, too, was when we got to know the new Principal Private Secretary, Michael Halls. I had heard a lot about him from Harold, who had sung his praises continually from the days when Michael had been his Private Secretary at the Board of Trade.

Michael threw himself into the job whole-heartedly, and his enthusiasm was infectious. We had happy times together there to balance the worrying and distressing ones. Throughout this time Michael's friendship and service to Harold and to those close to him was one of the most satisfying features.

As soon as he had begun to get used to No. 10 and its set-up we had a long discussion about the need for office changes and procedures on the official side. In contrast with so many civil servants he never said that something was impossible; he always explored the situation to see if changes were desirable and could be put into effect.

For a long time we had felt that the Garden Rooms, for a start, were not staffed in the way one should expect in the late 1960s.

The Garden Girls were predominantly middle class and often came from wealthy homes. They all had the same background, we were told, and certainly this is how it appeared. When the Prime Minister asked how they were selected he was told that they were recruited from a very select and expensive secretarial college in London. I knew the particular college well. Indeed, a girl from my own school had gone to it when she left school. She would often regale us all with stories about it, and when we asked about her shorthand and typing, she would laugh ironically and say: 'Oh, all right, but I fence divinely.'

Apart from this limited approach, and the unfairness of the selection from such a small field, there was surely a security risk too. The school could easily have been used, if anyone had thought about it carefully, as a way of getting somebody into No. 10. But more important to us was the fact that it meant that No. 10 was a closed building in the sense that there were no real opportunities for outside girls to get appointments there. The system was therefore slowly changed, and the selection of girls eventually took place as a result of advertisement within the Civil Service and by means of what was called 'a trawl' of each department.

By 1970 the girls with the twin-sets and pearls had largely gone.

One girl there in 1964 had worn a mink coat to work and driven a Mercedes Benz.

Gone, too, by 1970 were the traditional patterns of behaviour for the girls who accompanied the Prime Minister on tours. During the 1966 election I had made special requests that, just for this campaign at least, the Garden Girls with us should stop wearing fashionable hats, gloves, etc., and generally looking more elaborately turned out than anyone else around. Up until then one of the ludicrous sights at No. 10 was to watch an entourage leaving for an overseas visit, or indeed leaving for an United Kingdom engagement, dressed in beautiful hats, gloves, neat handbags, shoes, etc., the regulation wear for all well-bred girls from good schools. The headmistress of my own school, a direct grant church school, had always lectured us when we were in the sixth form on the mode of dress to adopt when going for interviews. Somehow those Garden Girls, uniformly yet elaborately geared, reminded me too much of those earlier instructions.

Mary was often hatless, but behind her would be a Garden Girl, impeccably turned out in beautiful headgear. For our people on political visits these girls were often a source of curiosity. They wondered exactly who they were, and we always had to explain that they were not personally selected by Harold and were not working for him politically, but were the official civil servants. They were all so formal and appeared so rigid. I realize that the accusation against me of inverted snobbery could be fair, and I accept it.

We wanted to see a new, democratic outlook in the building, with girls from all walks of life having the same opportunity to work there, and there was a gradual change. Possibly their politics became more mixed, though events on the last day at No. 10 proved they were probably still mainly Conservative. Still, at least their backgrounds were more varied. The closed shop was closed no longer in that quarter of No. 10.

As they changed, the attitude they had towards their opposite numbers in the Political Office changed too. They became more friendly and helpful. The increased majority could also have been a factor though.

'Mr Wilson's young ladies' as they were captioned in a 1965 *Daily Mail* photograph, showing a bevy of Garden Girls departing for Salisbury, Rhodesia in floppy summer hats, gave way to the more informal, but equally efficient and attractive cross-section of girls who worked there later. From then on hats lost their importance and girls looked more as if they were about to work than to attend a garden party.

Gradually, too, there were other changes under Michael Halls at a higher level. The Duty Clerks on duty in the Private

Office were given an increased status. They often accompanied the Prime Minister on an outside visit and particularly on his holidays, rather than a Garden Girl or a Private Secretary.

There were changes, too, in the Private Office itself, 'The trawl' became wider for these officials and Oxbridge gave way to other universities. One of the most brilliant secretaries at No. 10 while I was there was not an Oxbridge man, and neither was Michael Halls.

Between us, Michael and I also changed the whole system used in answering incoming mail at No. 10. As it grew in volume, we had been in increasing difficulties in the Political Office, since we were seriously short of staff and facilities. A similar development was happening in the Garden Rooms. It was clear our machinery for handling cases was clumsy, but everyone was deeply concerned that the whole manner of answering mail should alter, both in the Private and Political sections.

People writing in sometimes received a one-sentence reply, often printed, which merely acknowledged receipt of the letter. It was all rather impersonal and cold. The person who wrote in had often done so very enthusiastically or more often because of a desperate need for advice or comment. Of course, there were many letters from 'professional letter writers', and 'professional complainers', but one got used to identifying these anyway.

The question was: how seriously should you take the mail? There can be no real half-way house there. You either treat it all carefully, or you do the opposite and off-load it, or send a brief acknowledgement. It seemed wrong for a Socialist Prime Minister to do the latter. Extra staff were therefore recruited for the Garden Rooms, and a general correspondence section formed to handle the growing burden. There was also devised a method of speeding up the processing of cases through departments.

Harold reminded Michael that when they were both at the Board of Trade they had used the system of special files, and he suggested brightly coloured ones so as to be immediately recognizable as having come from No. 10, and headed in large heavy black type 'Prime Minister's Case'. Michael remembered the system immediately, and set in train a similar system for No. 10.

Vast quantities of garish orange folders were printed which both Political and Private Offices used, though with different numbering and reference systems. The cases brought to our attention in both upstairs and downstairs offices were sent to the appropriate department concerned for inquiry. They then drafted a reply based on the inquiries they had made and this was returned to us in the orange folders. Those returned to the Political Office were read through very carefully and the letter often rewritten not only to take into account Party policy, but also to humanize the officialese wording which so often bemused the ordinary citizen who had written in. Our new system worked, and worked very well.

Furthermore, the actual typing of the cases we handled was done downstairs after we had done our editing and rewriting. Michael pointed out that, even though someone had expressed in a letter the fact that he was a Labour voter, and this was why we upstairs were handling the correspondence, this didn't mean that the Civil Service secretarial staff should not shoulder the burden of typing them at government expense, since clearly everyone writing in should be treated equally. Otherwise the odd situation would have arisen where unequal treatment would have been given to those who were probably Conservative.

All of this produced an absolute revolution in our office. The heavy burden of mail was lifted from us and we were now able to sort out our own priorities and to get our office working in a much more efficient way than ever before.

We gradually began to take on extra secretarial staff as well. One of our first recruits was a person whom we came to know and like enormously, Doreen Andrew. She came from the Whips' Office in No. 12. She had gone there after the 1964 election, though prior to that she had been a secretary to the Co-operative Group of Labour Members of Parliament.

There were the alterations downstairs on the second floor, where part of the Church Appointments Offices were moved out and Thomas Balogh brought in. The suite of rooms involved included one large room, with a door opening directly into the corridor facing the Prime Minister's private flat. This room overlooked Downing Street, above the front door. Leading off that room were two other rooms, a small room for a private secretary, and a slightly larger room off that for secretarial staff and filing clerks.

Thomas was absolutely delighted and in his element. It was what he had wanted for so long, and had been patiently waiting for. He now felt he really was at the centre of things, and that his contribution could be so much greater. He recruited a very good team for his office. However since he did not have a proper secretary and needed someone who knew him and the Party as well, Brenda Dew was transferred from the Political Office to the Civil Service to work with Thomas. It proved to be an excellent arrangement.

On the political front, we also did an enormous amount of planning and work to bring Harold up to date with the new Parliamentary Labour Party. At every General Election there is a large turnover of Members. Some MPs retire from safe seats and new Members come in. Then there are new Members elected in marginal seats. In 1966 all this meant that there was a sizeable group of Labour Members who Harold did not know and who he now had to get to know.

They were a very unusual and different sort of MP from those we had been used to from 1945. In 1964 they had changed, but not quite so dramatically as in 1966. In 1966 they were much less political in the sense of understanding the machinery of politics, the Parliamentary system. They were consequently less ready to accept unquestioningly the Party rules and regulations. Some were Parliamentary iconoclasts. They did not necessarily come from the left of the Party, which might have been expected, but many came from the right as well.

Systematically, over a period of months, Harold met Labour MPs every Wednesday evening – not just the new Members, but also MPs in their Regional Groups. They would come, twenty-five or more at a time, to his room at the House of Commons. We would serve drinks and they would spend the evening asking Harold questions about policy and tactics. He would sit answering these questions solidly for sometimes up to three hours. In this way he grew to know the MPs individually, as well as to understand collectively how they all

worked, and also the effect which the new intake was having
on the older Members.

There were also the major Parliamentary innovations such
as the introduction of the new select committees. One reason
for this was that there was now such a large majority that the
Party really could not afford Members to sit around and not be
involved in the work in hand. One way of involving Members,
who clearly can't all be in the Government, is to get them
working on select committees, getting to know Parliament and
the work of government from that angle.

Other decisions were also taken about Harold's general
tactics. After each election there is always a period when
people are tired of politics in the sense of campaigning – not
just the politicians themselves, but the electorate at large.

Harold felt, therefore, that to continue to go around the
country, doing at least two political meetings a month, as he
always has done, was not right. Instead, he changed to attending large regionally organized receptions for Party workers.
They were arranged by the Regional Offices of the Party,
who invited all the surrounding constituencies, mostly the
active Party workers, to a reception. Harold would often be
asked to make a short speech towards the end, but more
important, he would go round shaking everyone's hand and
talking to them and answering their questions in a very informal
way.

The engagements he carried out where he made set speeches
now became usually the official visits when he toured housing
sites, opened new factories, and visited trade exhibitions,
hospitals, etc. These official engagements provided platforms
for putting over the work of the Government.

When Frank Cousins resigned as soon as the Queen's
Speech indicated that a Prices and Incomes Bill would be part
of our new legislation, a new Government began to emerge with
Tony Benn going to Technology and John Silkin becoming
Chief Whip. The Silkin appointment was one of the most
significant changes. While Ted Short, the former Chief Whip,
had been loyal and a good friend to Harold, he had never
been as close personally as John Silkin was to become. One
reason for this was that both of them, Harold and Ted, are
undemonstrative people. John Silkin is the reverse. He is

warm and outgoing, with a pretty thin skin for such a professional politician. Soon he had become a frequent visitor to No. 10 and not just in working hours. He started to drop in during the evenings as well to have a drink with us before we went home. And we, too, visited the Whips' Office at No. 12 on a fairly regular basis. This was something which had not happened while Ted Short was there, not because we did not like and respect him – which we certainly did – but because Ted was not the sort of person on whom one dropped in for an informal discussion. But with John there the liaison between the Whips' Office and No. 10 was widened to take in the Political Office as it never had before.

But life at No. 10 was not all cosy chats with like-minded friends. Far from it. Sometimes there were periods when nothing seemed to go right, when there was only bad news. As in July of that year.

It started off with a bang with the visit of Monsieur Pompidou, the French Prime Minister. This caused great trouble in Government circles. I am never happy about such visits. There is too much socializing, there are too many parties and, with wine and talk flowing, equally, there is always an opportunity for disaster. That particular July was an especially bad time for such a visit for too many sensitive subjects were being aired – and the French naturally did nothing to stop this airing.

France's curious economic and financial policies were given a fair hearing, and then the French in their turn talked loosely of a possible British devaluation. In this they were not discouraged by some who were closely associated with the Government and who should have known better. Obviously they thought this was an intellectual exercise and something which needed to be thrashed out so that its possible effects could be analyzed. But in the summer of the seamen's strike, with such a sensitive economic situation, this was dangerous talk, as the subsequent rumours and Press comment clearly demonstrated.

Devaluation, which was the dirty word of 1964, became news all over again, and everyone was joining in, even those enjoined specifically not to do so by the Prime Minister. It was infectious. Our opponents talked to make the situation worse, and many supporters and advisers could not hold themselves in because of the obsession they had about this particular subject. They just couldn't keep quiet and the talk kept breeding more talk.

George Brown, of course, became the great convert to devaluation and its great advocate. His Trade Union background no doubt prompted him to feel that the prices and incomes legislation and the increasing economic difficulties were so serious that there was no light at the end of the tunnel. He felt that devaluation would release us from the general darkness, from the legislative restraints upon which we were embarking and which would make us so unpopular with many friends in the movement. Devaluation would open the way to expansion. But, of course, the whole argument is all a chicken-and-egg affair and when it is indulged in it is always oversimplified in the context of the moment. There is no right time or wrong time for devaluation when it is such a bogy. Only when it stops being a bogy and becomes just another weapon in the economic armoury will it be possible to use it uninhibitedly.

I hated that summer. It all seemed so disillusioning after such a terrific election victory. We had won, yet we didn't seem to have won. The curious lack of elation I had felt on 31 March was symptomatic of the feelings that followed in the months afterwards.

We might be getting all sorts of things right organizationally, we might be feeling personally more at home in the general set-up, we might be convinced that at last we were the governing Party. But Government policy seemed to be going the other way. That was the whole contradiction of the two periods.

In the first one, from 1964 to 1966, we were badly organized, ill at ease and not at home; our liaison was non-existent, our facilities were poor, our arrangements for working pathetic and the atmosphere in the building all wrong. But Government actions were so swift and so exciting and our political tactics as a Government were so good, so quick and successful, that we thrived.

But then, just when we were starting to sort ourselves out on the administrative front, and were getting to know the system, to put the right people in the right place and to obtain the right sort of machinery within No. 10 for co-ordinating political work with official work, government policy ran into difficulties and with it came the loss of support in the country. The pattern reversed, and naturally it was all very depressing personally.

I went on two overseas visits that summer. Both, I think, can be described as extraordinary – and one as appalling.

The first was another trip to Russia, even though we had been there the previous February. The trouble was that I was ill throughout the visit. I left London feeling queasy, but not realizing I had the beginning of a bad cold. Because I was nervous that I might be sick I took with me cartons of Long-Life milk and packets of arrowroot biscuits as a possible protection against too much caviare and vodka and Russian cooking. I felt that even though I might have to refuse Russian meals, I wouldn't starve and my stomach wouldn't be in open protest. It was just as well because in fact I was to live on this emergency diet throughout the trip.

The main reason for the visit was Vietnam, that terrible shadow that hung over us and which we could never lose. Indeed, we did not seem to have the will to lose it. If only we had made a positive step there, some of the other pieces elsewhere might have fallen into place.

It was difficult, feeling so groggy, to register much on that visit. Harold's excitement at the serious and frank way in which Kosygin was talking to him, however, was infectious. Everyone seemed to become as excited about it as he was, since we felt that it was a breakthrough to know that Kosygin felt able to be so open and so frank with Harold about his own problems in Russia. It was fascinating, too, to look out at the rest of the world via Kosygin through Russian eyes. It is a cliché, but still valid, that if you are in Moscow then America and China look very different from the way they look when you are sitting in London.

Bill Housden took care of me beautifully during the visit. He was terribly concerned because I clearly was getting worse and worse. Finally, I had to give up going out of the dacha altogether and took to a chair, which was placed for me just outside in the garden. There I lay sleeping fitfully and half conscious of the fact that as I was in Russia perhaps I had better not drift off altogether in case anything odd happened. What I did not know was that Bill was even more nervous on that score than I was. He was sitting up on a balcony above me, also in a garden chair, refusing resolutely to move from there while I was outside. Bill had almost convinced himself that if he did not do this I would be taken off somewhere secretly and never seen again! But, of course, this was all fantasy, as the Russians were as thoughtful and kind as anyone could possibly be – and this was true of all the visits I have made to the Soviet Union.

Although I was not able to be present at any of the talks or go to any of the entertainments the Russians laid on, I did get another side of the picture which I had never seen before. Bill and I quite enjoyed ourselves being at the dacha, ostensibly alone. This calm, unhurried life was something I had never experienced in Russia before.

One thing that amused us was the bowl of fruit in the middle of the dining-room table, which was always seemingly miraculously refilled immediately after we had eaten an apple, even though nobody else was in the room with us and nobody would have known that we had taken one away. Either there was a particularly efficient housekeeper, who kept checking and re-checking the fruit bowls all over the dacha every two minutes, or else there was some other explanation. In the end Bill became quite obsessed with this and alternately wanted to take the fruit and then didn't want to take it. Just as his hand went out he became self-conscious at the thought of somebody watching him. There were, too, the hurried jobs Bill was given to do, which sometimes led him along curious paths. Dashing out to find someone he once went through double doors leading off the kitchen to find himself in a room where two gentlemen were sitting with headphones on. It was all very jolly and they smiled happily at him and Bill smiled happily back, but Bill and I afterwards were a little curious to work out what that was all about.

I did manage one outing, which was the dinner given by the British Ambassador at our Embassy for the Russians. I sat at a table with the former Ambassador to London, Mr Soldatov. He is extremely jolly, and a great conversationalist. However, it didn't matter which country you were in, the British Embassy always seemed to be the same everywhere, with the same sort of conversation, the same type of entertainment and the same stuffed-shirt atmosphere that stifled gestures of friendship which might have been made. I am sure the diplomats delude themselves that this is not so, and that times have moved on; that they are all being jolly progressive together. But to the outsider it doesn't look like that at all.

Although I loved being in Moscow again, I was so glad to get home and so glad to be able to recover from my bug and start eating normal food once more. Arrowroot biscuits begin to pall after a time.

Not long after the Russian visit, and when the dust had settled a little over the economic situation, we visited America. We had the usual dreary journey over, not lightened at all by the fact that our Ambassador was with us.

The British Ambassador had come over from Washington to accompany Harold back on the plane, so that he could brief him on the situation over there. I suppose it would have been more acceptable if the Ambassador had not raised recollections which many in the Party didn't like. He was the Foreign Office official who had been at the famous meeting Selwyn Lloyd had at Rambouillet before Suez. Whenever I saw the man it was the only thing I could think of.

This time we were taken from the Andrews Airbase direct to Blair House, the official hospitality house used by the President for distinguished visitors. This was the first occasion on which I had been there, since formerly we had always stayed at our own Embassy, or, before Harold became Prime Minister, at the Mayflower Hotel in Washington.

Blair House is opposite the White House and was used by President Truman when the White House was being renovated. It is a very beautiful house like so many old houses in Washington. While I can never take to the harsh air of constant activity, and the slightly dirty atmosphere in New York, I feel differently about Washington. It has a much more gracious atmosphere, even though it may be regarded as rather provincial. Blair House itself is magnificently furnished and the facilities there were fantastic. All the bedrooms were equipped with colour television as well as radio, the writing desks had pads, pencils and pens, all with the Blair House inscription on them. In each room's bathroom was a complete set of cosmetics and toiletries by a leading American manufacturer. It is amusing to remember how many senior civil servants could be caught popping these souvenirs into their pockets before they left. They were amongst the greatest memento collectors in the world.

There was a rather formidable American lady, who acted as the housekeeper and hostess, whom I found a little intimidating, gracious though she was. But American women are inclined to be formidable to British women, and American men more approachable. Certainly American career women seem a bit too brittle and efficient; their clothes are so immaculate, they make you feel as if you have just stepped out of a hedge.

This made it all the more terrible when I opened my cases and found something had gone disastrously wrong with my clothes. My dresses were so full of creases that they looked as if they had come straight from a washing machine. But Bill Housden came to my rescue once again. This time he found somebody in the building who transformed my dresses into something presentable.

I had hoped on this visit to America that I might be able to be of more assistance, to be more involved. There had been so much trouble over Vietnam, and we were now in the place where it had all started. Here we were meeting face to face the people who were primarily responsible for Vietnam.

But as with so many overseas visits, Harold was once more in the Civil Service's Intensive Care Unit. They threw up a screen around him to keep him 'clean' and only civil servants were allowed to brief him. Indeed, even some of the civil servants were 'booted out' and Michael Halls suffered almost as much as I did at the hands of the so-called 'experts'. These experts took it upon themselves to brief him on all questions, in other words to give him their advice on how they felt the Parliamentary Labour Party would react to all that was happening.

Of course, from time to time they had a word with me. No doubt some of the conversations filtered back to Harold in their own words, but they were such a solid phalanx that it was very difficult to break through them all. One had to whisper very quickly in Harold's ear as he passed by. This was appalling because the situation in Vietnam had been so awful and the feeling in progressive circles at home was so acute.

Gerald Kaufman, before he himself went on visits, never believed me when I used to tell him how awful it was and how difficult it was to get through to Harold; but when Gerald finally went on them himself he discovered only too well the difficulties and frustrations.

It meant, of course, that in the end one gave up. I opted for the task I had undertaken in Moscow – shopping.

Before I left Blair House, I asked everyone whether they wanted me to get things for them and my list was so long that it took hours to collect it all. Even now I can't remember all the things I got, except that I did seem to emerge from one store with an enormous number of boxes of chocolates.

There were other things about that hot, sticky visit that were also unpleasant. I didn't like the Churchillian references President Johnson made in his speech welcoming Harold. Perhaps President Johnson did really feel warmly towards him; but somehow it just didn't add up to me, not against that awful background of Vietnam. I had, too, to sit down in Blair House for private meals with a various assortment of people from the UK, who were strangers to me. Some were officials from the Foreign Office who had come across with us, and their views on Vietnam were so ghastly that it became almost impossible to sit in the same room. People who were supposed to be the experts were saying things which most sensible people back home, however ill-informed, would not have dreamed of saying. It is fortunate that I had committed myself to so much shopping because otherwise I might have broken up Blair House and been kept in America for the next twenty years serving a sentence for despoiling one of their historic buildings.

We left for Canada and I was glad to see the Canadian airfield even though we were not going on into Ottawa. Harold had just enough time on that visit to talk to Lester Pearson at the airport and to tell him what happened in Washington to put him in the picture and to get his views on the international scene, particularly on Vietnam. Lester Pearson and Harold always got on enormously well and were very much at ease with each other. It was an enjoyable meeting even though it was so rushed.

But the most interesting part of that short stop-over was my talks with a member of the Canadian Prime Minister's office. With time to kill while the two Prime Ministers talked, we sat and chatted in the refreshment lounge and drank many cups of coffee. The conversation inevitably came round to politics and I had to explain exactly my role at No. 10. After a time I could see that the man I was talking to really couldn't understand what I was talking about, and so I thought I would ask the one question I always like to put in other countries; whether or not when a Government changes, the personnel in the government offices also changes. The Canadian was surprised, and said that of course when the Prime Minister in Canada changed, then there was a complete change-over of staff in his office. The incoming Prime Minister automatically took in with him his own people who staff his office totally and became the civil servants for that Private Office. He seemed surprised to be told the system which we operate and thought it was rather complicated. He was right there.

That was my last American trip. I went on a few overseas visits afterwards, ones which were so clearly historic that it would have been criminal to have missed the opportunities they presented. But to go to America again as part of the system and be organized by the civil servants, that would have been unbearable. I couldn't endure again a situation where a screen was thrown round the Prime Minister and he was swamped with briefing documents and papers. They all related to problems which I am sure never arose on any occasion at any meeting at which he was present. What was appalling was the amount of work which must have gone into preparing just one folder for each journey. And his folder was duplicated in a less grand way for each of the civil servants in attendance. They were 'flagged' at all the so-called important parts, and the detail given was so fantastic that the mind boggled at such industry.

I can't help believing it might be better just to step on to an aircraft, go to Washington, see the President, have a long conversation with him informally, over lunch or dinner, with just the two top men present, and then return to London.

After a most rewarding ten-day holiday in Israel when the Israeli Government gave me a most friendly welcome and a concentrated tour of the country, I returned to London to an atmosphere still dominated by the argument about the Government's prices and incomes policy and the need for a pay stand-still and freeze to be added to the voluntary restraint we had already asked for earlier.

There had been a major reshuffle in the Government in which George Brown had gone to the Foreign Office. This was partly because of his announced desire to resign and partly because he felt he no longer carried any authority in the Department of Economic Affairs. Obviously if you are going to move a person of George's standing you have to move him to a post of the same standing or even greater – and one where you feel he can succeed. Harold genuinely felt that the Foreign Office might prove the one department in which George would expand, and this proved to be the case. Despite all the controversy that was raised then and continued afterwards with George at the Foreign Office, there is no doubt that he achieved a great deal.

Michael Stewart went to the Department of Economic Affairs, and while I admire the man for his own brand of socialism, and also for the way he conducts himself at all times in a fair and honourable way, I still feel he was not quite the dynamic character needed. Indeed, this seemed to be the beginning of the end for the DEA. It already had this enormous struggle on its hands to survive against the Treasury with all its power, and it needed particularly to have at the top a strong figure.

At the same time Dick Crossman was moved from Housing. This, too, raises doubts with the benefit of hindsight. He was by then in control of the department at last, and he had got the measure of his Permanent Secretary, though that had been quite a struggle and a separate story in itself. There might have been a chance of getting the housing programme moving with Dick. We had always placed an enormous emphasis on what we wanted to do in the housing field and this was, therefore, a major disappointment when we saw that Housing might lose out. However, Members of the Parliamentary Labour Party gained enormously from the move because Dick became Lord President and Leader of the House, and did this job with a style and panache it had never known before and which I dare say it will never know again.

The new Members got the full blast of the 'seminar technique' and whatever else happened from then on they never felt that they were out of touch or were not being kept as fully informed as they might of what the Government was doing – even though on occasions in some people's opinion Dick overstepped the limit and often gave them information it would have been better to keep to himself.

As a result of the other moves, Herbert Bowden went to the Commonwealth Relations Office and Arthur Bottomley, who was at that time Secretary of State for Commonwealth Relations, was moved to the Overseas Development Ministry, thus making it possible for Tony Greenwood to go to Housing.

Bert Bowden, now Lord Aylestone, was probably an ideal choice at that difficult time in our negotiations and relations with Ian Smith and the Rhodesian rebel regime. He had the appearance of the strong silent man, and was backed by Harold totally.

For Arthur Bottomley it was a sad day. On the other hand, at the Overseas Development Ministry he was able to keep his contacts with his African friends and with all those within the Commonwealth and the Colonial territories who depended on the British Government for survival.

Tony Greenwood, who is an extremely personable man, had, as Harold had often said, a very mollifying effect upon local authorities, particularly as they were becoming increasingly Tory-dominated at that time. But he was not quite as tough as, I guess, Dick might have been in getting a real housing drive going and bullying his own civil servants and the Treasury, as well as bullying the local Tory authorities into action at the same time.

Harold was now entering the beginning of the period of the battle with the unions. This was the beginning of the rift which widened over the years between the two wings of the Labour movement.

We really did have a job in the background to make sense of it all in propaganda terms. Our prices and incomes policy got little support from the Tory Press at any time, either then or later. In 1971 it was talked of with great liberality, particularly by the so-called serious newspapers. But at that time in 1966 their support was not quite as sturdy as they would

now make out. They were much more concerned with the
arguments within the Labour movement, reporting on their
significance instead of calling for a national effort to find a
workable prices and incomes policy to really get things moving
along the right lines. Though this is what they may seem now to
have advocated, at that time they were not converted and the
road to Damascus was a long way off.

In September 1966 the Commonwealth Conference which
gained for itself acres of newsprint took place. The Africans,
and particularly the black Africans, had ganged up on Harold.
Harold would rush back after each session with a dramatic
report of what had happened, reports that had to be qualified
later each day by either Michael Halls or Trevor Lloyd-
Hughes. I enjoyed the 'report back' parties just to see Harold
letting off steam. But as a Rhodesian 'bomber', I always was a
bit saddened by the whole thing and wished that the crisis
had been solved right at the beginning by tough action.

But the chief resentment felt was as always the enormous
amount of time that the Conference involved, in terms of
Prime Ministerial hours. Hours which were taken away from
what we regarded in the Political Office as the more important
domestic matters.

That autumn we had the pleasure of meeting for our Liaison
Committees in the Lord President's Office in Whitehall. Dick
had a marvellous office – a beautifully proportioned room with
windows overlooking Horse Guards Parade. It is not as
spectacular as the Scottish Office, but is none the less impressive for all that.

My first Liaison Committee meeting there was marked by
the fact that I got lost looking for the door to Dick's room and
found myself in the Old Cabinet Room used by George III,
with the throne at one end and the table in the centre.

Even so, to go to Dick then was less complicated than it had
been when he was at Housing. It had always been agony to
get to the meetings at the Ministry of Housing, because you
needed a security pass and a great deal of checking went on.
The security provisions at the Ministry of Housing were far
more rigorous than those at No. 10.

That autumn our discussions centred, of course, on prices
and incomes, and the implications of the loss of the National

Plan. We spent far more time in thought over this than we did on Rhodesia and overseas problems. We wanted to talk over together what it would all mean for the Party at conference at Brighton in October, and how it should be handled there. There were also suggestions for pre-publicity for speeches. Our only moan from the No. 10 side was that there didn't seem to be enough time because the Commonwealth Prime Ministers' Conference meant we would not be able to discuss the problems fully enough with Harold himself.

Conference at Brighton was much easier to manage, and the two sections of the Prime Minister's staff got on very well. Michael Halls went for half the week to make quite sure the proper liaison links were established with No. 10. He was then usually replaced, with an overlapping period, by another Private Secretary, a gentle, able man named Roger Dawe. So there was high-powered control over the arrangements at every point. The Garden Girl was usually chosen by Michael, who was always exactly right, on the basis of whom he thought would fit in with everyone.

At this particular conference we had a flat at the hotel next to the Prime Minister's suite which provided us with political and private offices side by side, as well as other rooms for Michael, Roger and myself. The Garden Girl was not far away, the detectives were on either side of the Prime Minister, and our girls from the Political Office were handy as well.

Unfortunately, my room was ludicrously small. George Brown, who occupied the flat above, had a detective who surely wore heavy hob-nailed boots instead of slippers. I was certain he used the room immediately above mine, but he always hotly denied it.

Michael was always meticulous in checking back the script of the Prime Minister's speech with No. 10 and the departments in Whitehall. That year Ella Wright, a new member of the staff with a considerable sense of humour, read the final text aloud so it could be checked for speaking and stencilling. As she gave her rendering of what Harold Wilson was going to say, her voice was deadpan and expressionless. As we worked into the small hours the intended rousing phrases with the encouraging rhetoric were reduced to something less, and we all ended up in my tiny room, my bed littered with papers, with Gerald, tears of laughter rolling down his cheeks, getting more and more convulsed as what were regarded as particularly impressive appeals to the Party were read out like income tax returns.

Above all 1966 was the conference when the Cabinet met away from London, a very rare event, and the car workers demonstrated about the state of their industry.

Our working relationships were now so close with the official office that in both events we became more involved than might otherwise have been the case. The hotel was, of course, delighted to be one of the only two places outside London where a Cabinet meeting had been held.

It did not seem particularly historic at the time as the Ministers were the same politicians we were there to help for conference. The meeting took place in the sitting-room of Harold's suite. But outside it caused excitement because it was so unusual and because here were politicians forced to hammer out further difficult policies on prices and incomes in the glare of their Party Conference, with all the consequential critical examination which would arise from a movement far from friendly on this sensitive subject.

When Harold succeeded in persuading the car demonstrators to send up a team into the hotel to talk to him, they all gathered in one of the hotel lounges. Roger Dawe came in to take official notes of everything said. I for my part sat quietly at the back in case I was needed for any messages. I became slightly hysterical at the sight of a well-known trade union leader and his wife sitting in chairs right next to the meeting, fast asleep and unaware of what was happening.

It was a conference enlivened by beautiful young ladies acting on behalf of Radio Caroline as well as unpleasant scenes with Lobby men about the stories of plots against Harold and about the Leadership of the Party, which were half true and half fiction.

Then the end of October brought Aberfan which can never be erased from any of our memories. I went down during the morning, when the news came, to see Michael Halls. We were in touch with Harold immediately, though there was no need as Henry James, the Press Officer with him, had already asked No. 10 for information. Harold was devastated. Both he and Mary have a genuine love for children and their reaction was spontaneous. They didn't know what to do, but wanted so much to do something, anything to help, to see if some of the pain could be alleviated for those who were suffering. We kept in constant touch all day, and well into the night, to see how everything was and what we could do. But we were all so helpless. Of course, all the right messages were passed to the right departments and all the right equipment and the right arrangements were made for whatever could be done. But in the end, set against the actual event, it seemed inadequate.

This was how Harold felt about it as well, and what was worse for him was that against the situation as it then stood, with the Press becoming increasingly more hostile, he knew that whatever he did would receive some critical comment. Yet it would have been impossible for him not to have acted as he did and gone to Aberfan. He had to be sure in his own mind that everything possible from the Government's point of view had been done, since he could not have forgiven himself if he had not gone to Aberfan and later on someone had told him that if only a message had been transmitted to him something could have been made easier and possible.

When I finally left No. 10 that night, very late, I remember going up to the Political Office to write in the Bring Forward folder we keep: 'Aberfan, 21 October 1966'. I don't know why I did it. But there it remained and each year it was a reminder of that dreadful tragedy.

That was the occasion when I took part in one of the joint telephone calls Prime Ministers are used to having with civil servants and advisers. When a Prime Minister makes a telephone call it is always usual practice for his Principal Private Secretary or the other Private Secretary on duty in his place, to listen in to what he says in case action has to be taken. But very often there are multiple phone calls when more than one person is linked in to the call, and that day four or five were linked in at a time in order to avoid delays. I was fascinated by the whole process, the sheer efficiency of the way in which it was done. I never ceased to admire the No. 10 switchboard.

Harold made up his mind that autumn that he would do a tour in the New Year of the Common Market countries, and at the traditional Guildhall dinner which Prime Ministers always have to attend Harold's speech was totally devoted to the theme of Europe. For people who dislike too much rigidity and formality, the Guildhall dinner is a trial and tribulation. It is the Establishment gathered together in the City of London to listen to the Prime Minister of the day and, if he is a socialist, it is assembled in a not very friendly fashion. Of course, it was a white tie affair and Harold detests wearing a white tie. It was therefore a difficult time for all of us on the staff because he grew increasingly irritable as the day went by at the thought of having to climb into the gear for the evening.

But in the end it was not the Common Market speech that became the most spectacular event of the autumn. For all this time Herbert Bowden was making frequent trips backwards and forwards to Rhodesia to see Ian Smith. On his final visit he was to raise the question of a meeting between Ian Smith and Harold on HMS *Tiger*.

The *Tiger* conference between Harold Wilson and Ian Smith was the most exciting event of my political life. It was also the most enjoyable. And, above all, there was the fact that the setting was almost unique. Not since Churchill and Roosevelt met on a warship in August 1941 to hammer out the Atlantic Charter had there been such a setting for an international confrontation. Other events, such as election victories, may have seemed more spectacular but they were always dominated by anxiety and overwork. But here in this ship sailing up and down the Mediterranean, watching two master politicians and their advisers at work, there was drama, tension and a fascinating setting.

I remember looking out of the aircraft window as we left London on 1 December 1966 and wondering how it had all happened. Sitting with me at the table on the RAF plane were the Prime Minister, the Attorney General and the Secretary of State for Commonwealth Relations – Harold Wilson, Elwyn Jones and Herbert Bowden. All were people I had known for a long time. Being with them was nothing unusual. But to be in a Service aircraft travelling to a secret meeting with a rebel leader in one of the Royal Navy's most impressive ships was really quite an occasion.

I didn't know what life would be like on one of Her Majesty's warships or what help I could get there, but I gained some slight satisfaction that my dresses wouldn't get creased through travelling in the low temperatures of the aircraft's hold. Bill Housden, who went on all these trips to look after the Prime Minister, had extended his thoughtfulness to me too, and had put my luggage in the compartment just behind us. One worry at least was removed; I wouldn't have to spend my first hours in the ship seeing whether I could get my clothes pressed.

Of course, there was the usual Civil Service entourage with us. The officials were headed by Sir Burke Trend and his Cabinet Office staff – for notes had to be taken of the meetings – and there was also a team from the Commonwealth Office headed by Sir Morrice James, a very nice man indeed, who was never very optimistic about a settlement. In addition we had Michael Halls, Michael Palliser and Trevor Lloyd-Hughes from No. 10. During the comparatively short flight there were the usual tactical meetings, the usual submission of complicated arguments and counter-arguments which were expected to arise during the talks. This time, in view of the unusual nature of the meeting, there was also an explanation of the mechanics of the conference.

And all this time another plane was flying towards Gibraltar with Ian Smith, a man who in constitutional terms was a traitor, a renegade, but also, as I was to discover, an attractive one. That made things more complicated and, therefore, more interesting. For if a traitor was unbearably ugly then one might be instantly repelled, which would make one instinctively conscious of one's own patriotism and higher principles. But this was certainly not the case with Mr Smith.

Yet a third aeroplane containing the Governor of Rhodesia, Sir Humphrey Gibbs, and the Chief Justice, Sir Hugh Beadle, the man I subsequently came to regard as 'the villain of the piece', was also making for the Rock. Sir Hugh, we had been led to believe, stood by the Queen and the United Kingdom during all these troubles. How far from the truth was that belief? Certainly nobody at that time realized the role he was probably playing.

As we came in to land at Gibraltar it was already dark so there was little for us to see. But the moment was enlivened for us all by a message from George Wigg over the radio just before landing. This instructed us to run to the safety of the airport building as soon as the aircraft doors were open and the steps in position. Back at home there had been rumours of attempts on people's lives and the usual scare stories which always circulate on such occasions. But George Wigg need not have worried. When the doors did open we were greeted by such a torrent of rain that we were more than prepared to run as fast as we could for cover. I had just had my hair done that very morning, only to find on reaching the protection of the nearest building that I was soaked to the skin and my hair was very wet indeed. Anyone who has had their hair permed knows what that means – nice crinkly waves, and a daily struggle thereafter to straighten them out.

I found it all very weird. There was the dark, the torrential rain, and the prospect of joining one of Her Majesty's ships we knew not where. But I expected the ship to be quite near to Gibraltar so I imagined that the next stage of our journey would be accomplished in a fairly comfortable fashion.

Cars suddenly appeared and we were bustled into them and taken to the dockside where we boarded a small launch. It certainly was small, with just two compartments below, one tiny one and one large one. The Prime Minister was ushered to the small cabin with the Secretary of State, the Attorney General, Michael Halls, Trevor Lloyd-Hughes, Dr Stone, the Prime Minister's doctor, and myself.

The other staff, the staff from the Cabinet Office and the Commonwealth Office, and the Garden Girls, went into the larger cabin. As we moved away from the dockside, I became aware that the naval officer I had seen on the plane out was the liaison officer between the Prime Minister's staff and HMS *Tiger*. He was now to be with us the whole time, looking after us.

Two years later he figured in our lives again when we met Ian Smith once more on HMS *Fearless*.

We moved away and were soon out of the harbour into the open sea. It was rough and a little daunting for most of us. As the small craft rolled heavily, I skidded in my unseaworthy shoes from one end of the cabin to the other, to be caught alternately by whichever distinguished gentleman happened to be in my way each time at the other end. Next door, in the other cabin, the situation was much worse. One highly stereotyped civil servant, from the Cabinet Office, was being violently sick in a most undignified way, as were two members of the secretarial team.

I am quite a good sailor, but after a while I began to wonder how long we would have to endure it all and whether we could manage to survive. I had very serious doubts about how much dignity we could all retain in these circumstances.

Then the liaison officer came to tell us that we were nearing *Tiger*. He said the sea was a bit choppy. No doubt this was how it was to him, but to me there were mountainous waves of frightening proportions rearing up all around me. He did admit that they were having some difficulties in bringing the launch alongside *Tiger* to be near the steps which had been lowered from the ship for us to board her. However, everyone was very jolly and joking and we left our small cabin and went on deck.

There we found *Tiger* towering above and moving up and down in a majestic way, while there were we bobbing about like a tiny cork. But at least the steps were in place down the side of *Tiger*, and on the bottom step a sailor was standing to give a helping hand to those who had to cross from the launch on to the steps.

Harold went ahead and I saw him disappear before me, and the next I knew he was running rapidly up the steps to be greeted at the top with all the usual courtesies extended by the Royal Navy to a visiting VIP. I came next, for some curious and then very unacceptable reason. I suppose it was because the gentlemen were giving way to a lady. The Captain said to me as I stood next to him in my unsuitable shoes, quite inadequate for jumping around in boats: 'Don't worry, Mrs Williams, it's all right. As soon as the launch comes level with the steps I shall shout out to you "Jump", and when I shout "Jump" then that's what you must do.'

This was splendid stuff except that I could see all around me nothing but violent water, steps that didn't seem to stay in the same place for more than one second flat, and a launch upon which I was already very precariously perched. I was also very conscious that I could not swim, so that when the command came to jump I was more than probably about to jump straight into the Mediterranean with no prior training for my survival. But what could I do? I could hardly hold up the queue behind consisting of Her Majesty's Secretary of State for Commonwealth Relations, the Attorney General, the Secretary of the Cabinet and a whole long list of other VIPs.

Suddenly the Captain's voice shouted in my ear 'Jump', and as if I had been possessed by an outside spirit I did exactly as I was bidden and landed, much to my amazement, on the bottom step. Only then did I realize that before I had made the jump I had thrown my handbag over to the waiting sailor. The poor young man had been standing there for some time holding it in his hand, awaiting the arrival of its owner. I then ran up the steps to join Harold.

We were taken as a very understanding priority to one of the officers' messes where they had laid out some drink and refreshments. A drink all round was very necessary! From then on, throughout the whole of the stay on that ship, I was to realize just how superb the Royal Navy is; their efficiency, courtesy and excellent management of the whole conference was a source of constant amazement to me. And the operation was all carried out at short notice in such a friendly, yet disciplined manner.

There were all the officers organizing the conference in the mess, and we were introduced to each of them in turn. I was told which cabin I would be occupying and introduced to the officer it belonged to, but who had now been transferred to other quarters. His only request to me was that I should not use too much perfume since it might remain after I had left, and if it got on to his clothes he would have some difficulty in explaining it away to his wife.

Meanwhile, what we did not know were the trials and tribulations being undergone by poor Bill Housden. When we left Gibraltar in our small launch we had done so with just our hand luggage. The bulk of the luggage and the red boxes were to follow on in a separate launch, even smaller than ours, with Bill aboard looking after it. Bill was absolutely terrified by the size of the seas around him as he rolled precariously along towards *Tiger*. He was even more dismayed when he finally arrived alongside, or at least as near as he could get. By that time the sea was even rougher, and it was even more difficult to bring a launch near the ship.

The Captain of the launch was reluctant to be too daring in case he damaged his vessel and had to answer for it back in Gibraltar, so there was a shouted argument between him and those aboard *Tiger* issuing him with instructions. Of course, Bill did not know that we had gone up by the steps and I suppose he imagined that what he was about to experience was something we had all in our turn managed to cope with. What happened was that they threw a rope over the side and suggested he tied it round him and then clambered up on to the fender over the side, and then on to *Tiger* that way. The rest of the luggage would then be hauled up similarly.

Bill took one look at the scene, considered it very carefully and decided it was not quite his style. The seamen in both vessels started asking him what on earth he was waiting for. He had to go up, one said, since otherwise what would happen to the Prime Minister's luggage and the boxes. Bill, who is rarely given to swearing, then looked very sternly at the young man in question and said: 'Bugger the Prime Minister's luggage.' He was quite determined to return at once to Gibraltar despite the choppy seas and his already queasy stomach, and stay there until the sea decided to subside.

After a great deal of persuasion they talked him into attempting it. He still hesitated so they shouted down to him that he was not to worry, they would pull him up. 'You must be bloody joking,' roared an angry Bill, 'I'm sixteen bloody stone.' He was eventually hauled over the side, and it was just after this that I met him again as he came into the wardroom where we were all having drinks. He announced that the luggage had now been brought aboard and reported to Michael Halls that the red boxes were in their place. I took one look at his face and made sure that the first priority was a stiff glass of brandy for him before he started distributing the luggage to the appropriate cabins.

Meanwhile, there had been another victim of the seas. We were talking about the arrangements for the arrival of the Rhodesian party, and when we came to details about Press briefing we discovered that Trevor Lloyd-Hughes was no longer with us. With the aid of one of the officers I found Trevor's cabin, which happened to be quite near to my own. I knocked gently on the door and went in to find Trevor lying on his bunk looking very green. The same rescue operation had to be put into effect with Trevor, and off I went to get a pill from Dr Stone, and a glass of brandy to revive him.

We were then taken on a tour of that part of the ship in which we were to live and operate for the following three days. Every route was signposted, every room was marked with the occupant's name and number, inside each cabin was a brochure containing details about the ship, postcards, and everything you could possibly want.

It was all more on the lines of an ocean-going liner than a warship. The main part of the party seemed to be on one level, and the secretaries looking after them on a level above. This caused some complications for me, since I was included on the lower level with the main body of the Prime Minister's party. It meant that while there were the usual facilities for gentlemen, there were no facilities for ladies there. I had quite a trek to find a bathroom, and was watched at every possible doorway or corner by a Marine on guard duty – as protection, I believe, though against what I was never quite sure.

The Prime Minister, of course, had the Admiral's quarters. His day cabin was used as a sitting-room in which to work and hold meetings, and there was an adjoining dining cabin. It was all very pleasant, and the dining cabin was quite spectacular with an enormous dining table.

I recall my horror on entering my cabin for the first time and finding that my ignorance of naval life was so total that I was unaware of how sailors got into their bunks at night. The bunk was somewhere near the ceiling without any visible means of getting up to it. When I inquired how this manoeuvre was achieved I was told that the strap hanging from the ceiling – this was rather like a strap in a tube train – should be grasped very firmly, one foot should be placed against the side of the bunk, and then with a good swing one should just haul oneself up into the bunk. All very fine for a sailor but in the end I got them to bring a small table on which I could stand and then launch myself from that into the bunk. But each going to bed and getting up in the morning was a nightmare of launching myself up and slithering back down.

That night we were shown to the Conference Room in which the talks were to take place. It was a large wardroom, very light, airy and spacious. I think that this was another mess room but I am not quite sure to which part of the establishment aboard the ship it belonged. But for that period it was called the Conference Room. Throughout our journeyings from our cabins to the Prime Minister's quarters and to the Conference Room, there were never-ending hurdles of gangways, narrow openings, plus the hazard of sea-going doors with high thresholds. There is no rushing at any of these because to do so and to stumble over the bottom part of the doorway means a headlong flight into the room you are entering – a dramatic but rather undignified way of making yourself known.

Later still we gathered in the Admiral's day cabin to recap on the exact timing of the arrival of the Governor with his Chief Justice. Once he was aboard Harold was to have talks with him. Then apart from a brief meeting with Ian Smith, Harold could go off to bed and await the opening of the conference the next day. It had already been agreed that Harold would not greet Ian Smith when he arrived, but that the Captain would meet him and escort him to his quarters. I suppose that a traitor is a traitor and Prime Ministers cannot go popping along to meet politicians who claim they are a legal Prime Minister when in fact they are not. So protocol was maintained, and Ian Smith was to arrive and to be taken care of without any formalities. But the Governor was an entirely different matter.

He was the symbol of our remaining authority in Rhodesia, and a man who was held in high esteem in both the United Kingdom and Rhodesia. His Chief Justice, however, was a curious gentleman who at that time had some spinal trouble. We discovered this when the Chief Justice had to be more or less hauled aboard *Tiger* because he was incapable of making the journey up in the way we had done.

As soon as the greetings were over, Harold took the two of them down to his cabin to give them a drink, to hear their first views of the whole situation and to brief them on the feelings of the British Government.

Being the Governor, and therefore Her Majesty's representative, Sir Humphrey Gibbs was accordingly treated with exceptional respect and deference by all aboard.

He did not seem to me to be entirely optimistic, though

clearly he hoped that something useful would emerge from the discussion. What was very clear was that he was a man who very much wanted a solution to the problem, but an honourable one. He was accompanied by an extremely pleasant Private Secretary who had served him loyally and whom we all liked very much. There was an instant rapport between Michael Halls and himself.

Sir Hugh Beadle, the Chief Justice, spoke up almost immediately. He used the most glowingly optimistic terms, hopeful that everything would be fairly easy to achieve. We should really have known from such over-optimism that the opposite would be the case. As I listened to him talking I had the feeling that what was being said in that cabin would be faithfully reported back word for word to the rebel Prime Minister so that, while Ian Smith would always remain up to date with our thinking, we would have to rely on Sir Hugh Beadle for the interpretation he would put on what Ian Smith was thinking. He always succeeded in keeping the real situation from us and it was always my view that this was deliberate.

At the end of the proceedings, when the thing had fallen apart and when Mr Smith was only agreeing to sign the final document as a record to take to his Cabinet rather than as a document which he himself fully supported, Hugh Beadle tried to sell this line to Harold as acceptable.

Clearly in constant communication with Mr Smith throughout the *Tiger* talks, Hugh Beadle knew the Smith situation and all that was happening back home in Salisbury and the pressures that were obviously building up there; he wasn't going to be caught out on the side of the Governor and against Mr Smith if he could possibly help it. But everyone gave him the benefit of the doubt beforehand, since it was thought that because he had stayed on as Chief Justice with the Governor after UDI he must in some way be on our side. Perhaps it was that he just liked being the Chief Justice.

Bill Housden had established himself by the time the Governor arrived in the early hours of the morning. We discovered that he had been quartered way down the ship, but after tactful explanations to the officers in charge that Bill was indispensable to the Prime Minister, he was eventually moved nearer to Harold and took over one of the cabins which had been allocated to the second detective. Everything on our side was therefore 'shipshape' and ready for the talks.

Although we had seen Ian Smith before, in London, there was still considerable interest that first night in witnessing the man who had taken such a deliberate and possibly irrevocable step in Commonwealth history. So as soon as Michael Halls had gone to invite him to Harold's cabin for a short talk before we went to bed, everyone seemed to gather in the dining cabin adjoining the day cabin through which Ian Smith had to pass.

As always he was charming and urbane. He made a deliberate point of saying 'hello' to each one of us, and smiling and asking how we were. He is in fact a politician who knows his art better than most United Kingdom politicians I have met.

While he was in the cabin with Harold, my role throughout that trip suddenly emerged. The seamen who served the Admiral's cabin were a little reluctant to walk into the talks and ask if those present would like a drink. I think they felt that if they did all conversation would cease. I therefore came to their rescue and offered to do the job partly myself. This was to become the pattern from then on. They prepared the trays and handed them to me at the entrance to carry in. In this way I had a unique opportunity of seeing Ian Smith not only at the talks in the Conference Room, but also more informally when he talked to Harold, sometimes just the two of them together and sometimes with the Commonwealth Secretary, the Attorney General and the Secretary to the Cabinet. It was a difficult job for me for the simple reason that I had to remember those curious doorways ships have. For the ordinary sailor this is something he takes for granted and never forgets, but I had consciously to remember them. As I balanced a heavy tray on one hand, I carefully lifted each leg slowly and purposefully to step over the threshold and into the day cabin. This caused a great deal of amusement from outside as the other staff watched me, and much more amusement from the seamen themselves. But there was even more curiosity in the day cabin as the more distinguished travellers within watched me come and go, wondering just when I would make the clearly unavoidable error and land a tray in their laps. I think that at times some of them might have welcomed the diversion.

Mr Smith's Private Secretary was less affable and much more of a tough guy than the Governor's, and his detective was exceptionally tough looking. Mr Howman, one of the Ministers who was with Mr Smith, seemed to be a jolly chap, though clearly one who knew what he was about and one who could cause difficulties. He seemed to me to be the sort of person who would seek information in a charming way, go off and digest it, and then do what he had to do, usually of a disruptive nature, behind the scenes.

Once Mr Smith had left Harold's day cabin we went off to our own cabins to get some rest before the talks started in the morning. I slept very little, not only because I found it strange to have the ceiling so close to my face and the floor so far away, but because the whole idea of being somewhere between Gibraltar and the coast of North Africa on a naval vessel had still not really registered properly. The bits that had registered were still filling me with a certain amount of disbelief and concern.

Nevertheless, I was up early in the morning. I dashed along to the Admiral's quarters where breakfast was laid out. Harold himself had breakfast in his cabin. He had a bathroom attached, and therefore there were no difficulties at all for him. He did not appear until it was almost time to go in for the talks, but gathered round the table were the top people from the Civil Service, the other Ministers, and the Private Office at No. 10. I suppose I moved instinctively towards Michael Halls and Elwyn Jones since these were the two I knew best of all. Indeed Elwyn, despite his serious misgivings, was jolly throughout the whole trip.

Everyone then went into Harold's day cabin to review once again the tactical line to be taken. I remained in the background with Dr Stone. Trevor Lloyd-Hughes, too, had a more limited role there than usual on overseas visits, since the Press who wanted to cover the talks were far away in Gibraltar and at that stage Trevor had no arrangements for contacting them except through the radio-telephone. The next day he was taken by helicopter to Gibraltar and back so that he could see the Press.

The Conference Room was most efficiently laid out. When we arrived Ian Smith was already present. When Harold came in

Mr Smith and his Ministers stood up, and Harold took his seat immediately facing Ian Smith and looking towards the portholes. Throughout those talks Ian Smith always referred to Harold as 'Prime Minister', and so did his colleagues. As you watched the two men, it was very clear that they were both taking careful stock of each other, though I think that Ian Smith was possibly taking more careful notice of Harold than the other way round. He clearly had taken a great deal of trouble in learning about Harold and his methods, and this was to stand him in very good stead indeed.

I would say that politically they were equally matched in their ability to handle talks. From our side the atmosphere was not a good one. It tended, I felt, to be over harsh. But we were still so near to the act of UDI and the shock it had caused, that people still felt strongly that Mr Smith, a man who came within the definition of 'traitor', should therefore be treated accordingly.

I feel, with hindsight, that perhaps the atmosphere could have been a little less censorious. I do not delude myself that this could possibly have led to a settlement, but it might at least have made some of the propaganda that later poured out of Salisbury less strong. People are so complex and the situation around them so involved that there seemed no value to be gained in refusing to attempt this approach in the first instance.

However, because of the nearness of UDI this was extremely difficult, and the scepticism felt by the Attorney General, by Herbert Bowden (who had already been at the receiving end of talks in Salisbury with Mr Smith), and by Sir Morrice James and other civil servants in his department, was so pronounced that it would have been difficult indeed for it not to have been infectious and for Harold to have taken a different sort of line himself.

The words Harold used in talking to Ian Smith were very rough, and those who imagine that this is just another of Harold Wilson's images of himself are mistaken. There was no question that he was extremely clear, precise and firm in all he said to Ian Smith about the views we held on UDI and the fact that the five principles, and in particular the first and the fifth, were ones on which we would not compromise in any circumstances.

The staff on *Tiger* had thoughtfully laid out coffee cups ready for a morning break, and pots of coffee were brought in. But again there was hesitancy on the part of the staff because they were not quite sure whether they should take it on themselves to walk round that table. Since no one gave them the order to do so, they stood back. Accordingly I volunteered once again to do the job, and I came forward and started to serve the coffee. I did this in what I took to be the right order. The first cup went obviously to the Prime Minister, and the second went to Ian Smith, and then I went down our side of the table and then down their side of the table. At some point during the break Mr Howman, Mr Smith's colleague, was the first gentleman to admit to not feeling quite himself. I was then dispatched to find Dr Stone, who was well equipped with seasickness pills. These were brought back and handed over to Mr Howman. I believe Ian Smith himself took one as well. What I do know is that Harold Wilson never took one and I was therefore more than a little amazed after the event to read that it was Harold Wilson who was seasick and for whom the tablets had to be sent.

When the talks were adjourned for lunch we went back to the dining cabin. We were all slightly euphoric since it appeared that a great deal of progress had been made. Certainly Harold and the Governor seemed optimistic. The Governor was not, of course, at the talks, and at each stage had to receive a report on them from officials.

After lunch we went up to the Quarter Deck for the first time to get some fresh air and to walk round and see exactly where we were. We really had very little idea of the position of *Tiger*. There was a fresh wind blowing but the sun was shining and it was a beautiful day. The sea was blue though still a little choppy; and, while we could not see Gibraltar, we could make out the coastline of North Africa. It seemed temptingly near.

Trevor Lloyd-Hughes and I did a brisk turnabout on the Quarter Deck, marching up and down, breathing in some good fresh air which we badly needed after being so long either in aircraft or below decks.·

A lot of official film was taken but Trevor and Bill Housden were able to take a number of private photographs. Ian Smith appeared on the Quarter Deck at the same time. He did not come over to speak to us as he clearly was not quite sure whether it was right or wrong to do so. But he smiled across at us all and exchanged jokes about being at sea!

The poor sailors on the ship were bewildered. As servicemen they clearly understood the situation about Ian Smith and his status, yet he was such a seemingly cheerful personality that it was very difficult for them to know how to handle him.

Our first afternoon session also seemed to go well, and I served tea just as I had served coffee earlier during the break. But Ian Smith did start to develop the unnerving habit of getting up in the middle of exchanges and looking out of the portholes as if he expected to see something quite strange. Perhaps he did. Or possibly, he was feeling queasy and hid it in that way.

Only later did we learn that *Tiger* went round and round in circles throughout that conference instead of riding at anchor. This may have been puzzling for him and it would surely have puzzled anybody observing us from the air.

Everyone wanted to go off early to bed that night, particularly the Rhodesians. They were obviously tired after having flown so far. We had only experienced the short trip from London but they had been forced to fly first to the island of Ascension, off the African coast, where they touched down before going on to Gibraltar. They were unable to cut the journey down because most African countries would not have allowed overflying rights.

The Rhodesians may have gone straight to bed, but we stayed up after dinner for talks. Most people seemed fairly happy except for the real sceptics who had arrived with a fixed view which they found required no modification because of subsequent events.

The Governor of Rhodesia had dinner with us, so it was a formal affair requiring dressing up. The dinner itself was beautifully done and very enjoyable.

The next day was far more hectic and heavy going. The atmosphere changed as the talks began to get bogged down. The previous day the ship's officers were all perky, but now our sense of growing disappointment was communicated to them too.

The large meeting in the Conference Room broke up

gradually into three a side, and the rest of those present adjourned. Again it became much more like some physical contest of strength between boxers or footballers.

Meanwhile a separate pantomime was being enacted elsewhere as Trevor prepared to go to Gibraltar by helicopter and Dr Stone agreed to accompany him. I was quite happy to go myself when the idea was first mooted, but I changed my mind suddenly when I realized that the helicopter didn't land on *Tiger*'s deck, but that passengers had to be winched up from the deck into the air! Today, when trouser-suits are ordinary day wear, all would be well, but for this sort of enterprise the regulation wear for secretaries in 1966 was not quite the thing. Joe Stone and Trevor later described their different feelings as they were lifted off and slowly pulled up to what looked to them an exceedingly small hole through which they were supposed to get into the hovering helicopter. Proximity proved it to be larger than it seemed and the operation in fact was performed with ease. But I gather it was pretty hair-raising for both of them.

The return was even more fascinating for those of us who were on deck to watch. Dr Stone returned as delicately as a ballet dancer. Trevor was a little more robust in his style. Neither took kindly to the jokes that Trevor's 'Mae West' was full of holes, and that the 'swimmer' had been standing there ready for any untoward happenings. Certainly the 'swimmer' was much in evidence. We were far more aware of him that afternoon than we had been when we arrived on that first dark stormy night.

As the talks turned sour the ship speeded up for Gibraltar. If at any point they suddenly seemed to look better the ship slowed down and turned round. Goodness knows how it was all managed but it happened, and the casualties on the seasick list grew as the day wore on. Ian Smith looked more frequently than ever out of the porthole that day.

At the tea break he brought his cup over for a refill and said to me: 'What a pity we aren't here longer so that we can get to know each other better.' I took it that the 'we' was collective, and there was no answer I could make. Perhaps if we had all been forced to stay there longer, and had not been on such a rigid timetable, there might have been a better result. The sheer speed and pressure of it all were ludicrous. Once the afternoon session ended the real in-play broke out.

Only the expert arithmetician could eventually keep up with all the twists and turns of the arguments about 'A' and 'B' rolls and cross-voting. The arguments about the process of the return to legality, though complicated, were more easily understood since here was a primarily political argument. But representation in a new constitution required good arithmetic as well as good politics. Clearly Harold and Ian Smith had both; but many lame ducks, if the expression can be used in this context, were rapidly left behind. The last full session with everyone present left a definite impression that the circumstances in which Ian Smith had been operating had changed – and changed dramatically. Some sudden influence, influence communicated from Salisbury, was the only explanation which could make his new behaviour explicable.

Dinner was to be given to the Admiral that evening but Ian Smith was not invited; in fact apartheid was total on that ship on that visit, except, of course, at the talks. The Admiral's staff prepared a magnificent table with full array of silver. But the food, beautifully prepared too, gradually got colder and colder. I went to my cabin and put on the essential little black dress, and then we all waited. At first we did so in the day cabin where we had a drink. But as the situation became more and more complicated, and different people came backwards and forwards for separate confidential and private talks, we ended up sitting in the dining cabin itself on chairs around the wall. We were waiting for Ian Smith to agree to sign the document which had been prepared by both sides on the basis that he would recommend it to his Cabinet in Salisbury. Harold was to recommend it similarly in London.

Just before dinner was due to be served Michael Halls was sent to ask Mr Smith if he had read the document and signed it. Not only had he not done so, but in fact he had been on a tour of *Tiger*. After the tour he called for his dinner, and agreed that he would read the document over the meal and let Harold have a reply as soon as he had done so.

The Admiral's dinner was postponed and postponed again as we waited on Mr Smith. I got hungrier and hungrier, and gradually, to the dismay of the staff, I began to eat my way steadily through the only bowl of After Eight mints. I discovered afterwards that the Admiral was addicted to them, and it was agonizing for his staff to watch me demolish them without wanting to explain to me the difficulties. In the end they whispered to Bill Housden, who told me to lay off, which I did.

Obviously Harold was misled by Ian Smith about the real powers he had to act independently. Anyone watching the shifts and changes at the end as he accepted one suggestion, only to put a block in the way of something else, would have realized it.

In the end the return to legality argument gradually began to take precedence over the actual terms relating to the five principles, on which the negotiations were supposed to rest.

Perhaps Ian Smith had come to *Tiger* as a gamble, nervous at leaving the shop, but prepared to try it on, knowing he would have to refer it back in any eventuality. When he had been asked in Salisbury by our people if he had full powers to settle, it is difficult to envisage any other answer he could have given without showing his entire hand. What advantage would there have been for him in this? To me, there seemed too little real understanding going around about the realities of the situation, or of the context in which both principals operated.

In addition I am not sure that many of the private talks we took to be on the record, when views were exchanged and often agreed on jointly, were seen in quite the same definite way by Ian Smith himself. Perhaps he thought the subject was just being aired to get his views of the possibilities. But even if one puts the lowest view on it, that he was deliberately misleading when he appeared to agree, I'm not sure what else he could have done in his own political context unless he was absolutely sure of his position at home in Salisbury. No one really has been able to evaluate the ups and downs in Mr Smith's internal position in Rhodesia, and how strong he has been, or weak, at any particular time. He has survived; that is true. But this has been taken as indicating that he is, and always has been, in a very strong position. The two do not necessarily go together. Behind the scenes may lie a whole story of manoeuvrings within his own party and in Rhodesia.

Perhaps that was exactly the right time for him to act firmly.

On the other hand it might have been political suicide. It could have seen the emergence of an even tougher racialist as Prime Minister and an escalation to apartheid in Rhodesia which would have been much faster than we have in fact seen.

Finally he caused everyone to lose their tempers by agreeing merely to sign the document as an exact record of what had happened and to take it back to his Cabinet for discussion. Then came the time for him to leave. Earlier he had made an abortive attempt to leave without giving Harold any final answer at all on the document. This was the action of a man, frightened not by what had happened on *Tiger*, but by messages coming through from Rhodesia. However, the efficiency of the Royal Navy made it impossible for him. The launch to take him ashore was briskly ordered away exactly one minute before he was due to set foot in it.

It was a grim departure. Everyone went up on deck to see him off, but the atmosphere was very unfriendly. Harold stood there, unsmiling and serious, and the staff tended to look the other way. Senior Ministers and advisers followed the line set by the Prime Minister.

It must have been a nasty experience for Ian Smith, and psychologically it must have had some effect on him for some time to come. He was someone who was used to being fêted, to being cheered and to being popular. There was nothing like that for him on *Tiger*.

After he had gone there was a deflated atmosphere aboard. The ship's crew were naturally bitterly disappointed since it seemed that their ship would not go down in history as the one which saw the signing of one of the most important historical documents between the head of the British Government and a Commonwealth country.

As for us, we went down to the Admiral's cabin and a party was laid on for the Admiral to make up to him for the dinner which he had not been given. Other officers joined in and despite everything it was not a completely sad occasion, as it gave us the opportunity of telling them all how impressed we had been by the way they had handled the administration of the talks, the speed and efficiency with which it had been laid on at such short notice, and the manner in which every single person, whatever his rank, had executed his tasks in such an efficient fashion. Harold told them that he hoped he would have the pleasure of seeing them at No. 10 on some occasion, and this he did.

Photographs were exchanged for the staff and for many of the crew as well, and, of course, special framed photographs were presented to the Admiral and the Captain.

On the Saturday morning Harold himself did a tour of the ship to meet everyone and to thank them for all they had done. We returned to Gibraltar in style, not in a launch but in *Tiger* herself. We were brought alongside the harbour and Harold was piped ashore in the way VIPs are, all very impressive and glamorous. We were then driven at high speed to meet Gibraltar's First Minister for short talks about Gibraltar's future and to reassure the Minister and the Gibraltarians that the Labour Party at least was determined that Gibraltar would never be handed over to General Franco and Spain. Then we joined our aircraft for home.

Monday was a waiting day. At No. 10 we did very little work all that day. We just sat around, mostly in the Private Office, waiting for the result of the Cabinet meeting taking place in Salisbury, tantalized on a wintry day by the stories of how hot it was there and how everyone in the meeting was sitting in shirt-sleeves.

We kept our fingers crossed, hoping that it would all come to a positive decision. Then came the let-down and Harold had to go to the House of Commons late that night to make a statement to say that the recommendations had been rejected by the Rhodesian Cabinet.

I think the Parliamentary Labour Party was in a sense relieved since feelings were so mixed. Harold, too, was half glad, half sorry. The Rhodesian two-day debate that followed in the House of Commons was a particularly nasty one, because of the racialist views that emerged during the debate – not only from Members on the Conservative side of the House, but from a few on the Labour Party side as well. Harold's own speech in the debate was enormously powerful and successful. It was the first occasion for a long time that I had been in the official box on the floor of the Chamber, beneath the Press Gallery, to listen to one of his speeches. I hate hearing him speak. It makes me too nervous. I loathe the shouting and exchanges in the House, particularly late at night. But he was superb because he felt strongly about it all, and he conveyed the frustration of having so nearly succeeded but yet having failed.

So passionate and successful was the speech that our people rose to their feet at the end in a great standing ovation, throwing their Order Papers in the air. I had never seen that happen before and I have never seen it happen since.

This was really the end of the Parliamentary year as there was no more important political news until the beginning of 1967.

There were still the usual Christmas parties at 10 Downing Street including one unusual one. We had continued the practice of giving a Christmas party for members of the Press, but on this occasion we also invited their wives as well. Since the numbers were so high two separate parties had to be given instead of the normal one. To one of these parties we invited all those members of *Tiger* who could get to London for the occasion. Not all were able to turn up, but a great many were and I think it was one of the most exciting parties we ever had. The crew were people we had grown to like, admire and respect in a very short time; it was a great pleasure to be able to entertain them in return for all they had done. They were intrigued in turn to see us on our home ground, so to speak, and in the setting against which we usually worked. We looked very different to them, just as they looked very different to us away from *Tiger*.

8

The Shadow of the Pound

By the beginning of 1967 we had established a certain work pattern in the Political Office. It was always difficult to see Harold for any long period of time before lunch, and the day had to be arranged to take this into account.

This meant that Gerald Kaufman and others, including myself, would arrive in No. 10 between 11.00 and 12.00 in the morning, so that by the time lunch came we had got our work organized for the rest of the day. Then from lunch onwards it was always possible to get time with Harold if it was needed.

It was usually a twelve-hour day, and very often, in times of crises, all too frequent in the years of the Labour Government, it was longer still, with the day's work going on into the small hours.

I was able to park my car in Horse Guards Parade, immediately behind No. 10, so I would usually come in through the back entrance, going past the Garden Girls' offices and the Cabinet Room to my room on the ground floor. Awaiting me on the desk would be special messages or letters that had been brought in during the morning and a more recent list of the Prime Minister's engagements than the one I had been handed when I left the building the night before. There would also be waiting for me, in the early years, a folder marked 'Mrs Williams'. This contained the letters that had been allocated to us by the lady in charge of the Garden Room, letters which she felt were within our province. Another folder would be sent up in the afternoon with post received and sorted later.

At first that folder would contain between fifty and sixty

letters, but as the years passed the numbers mounted and often they would be over the hundred mark and sometimes getting on for two hundred. They were so varied in nature that it took a considerable amount of time reading them through and deciding on what sort of reply they needed. Actually answering them was a further operation in itself.

When I had sorted the letters I would dictate answers to most of them to the girls in the office, leaving on one side those relating to engagements and also ones which had come in from Labour Members of Parliament about political questions. These I would take over with me to the House of Commons in the afternoon; and, once an answer had been decided upon and Harold had seen them and often dictated on them, I would type some of the replies myself and others I advised Doreen Andrew how to handle.

After lunch Gerald and I would spend our afternoons in the House of Commons. I returned fairly early in the evening to No. 10 but Gerald would stay at the House. It was his job to be in the Press Gallery and also to look in and out of the Whips' Offices regularly to see what help he could give to the Parliamentary Labour Party on Press questions. Gerald rarely returned to work in No. 10 in the evening when the House was sitting except when there were problems or crises.

Evenings at No. 10 were varied, but always included a great deal of typing. We always tried to make sure that at the end of each day all the letters we had received had been answered in some way, if only by an interim acknowledgement.

But each evening also saw a different visitor who would call in for a talk about the political situation and some of the problems that were arising.

Thomas Balogh was one of our more regular visitors, though he was a social creature and spent a good deal of his time attending outside dinners and parties. Peter Shore, although now a junior Minister, was also a frequent visitor, as were Dick Crossman in his new role as Lord President and John Silkin the Chief Whip.

During the course of the evening I would sometimes get word from a messenger that the Prime Minister was in the Cabinet Room and free if I wanted to see him, and on those rare occasions I would go and talk to him there. But very often, since he liked to roam around and to walk up and down a lot, he would come up to the third floor and suddenly appear in the doorway. The typing would stop and he would sit down on one of the typing chairs and we would have a discussion about the day's events there and then in rather less than comfortable circumstances.

Very often, too, if people called in downstairs to see if Harold was free for a talk they, too, would take the lift to the third floor and join us in our cramped quarters. I suppose for an outsider it would have looked very odd to see a Prime Minister and other Ministers and advisers, all sitting on typing chairs or perched on desks, crammed into a small attic room, talking seriously about some political problem, when there were all the rooms in the world below in which they could have spread themselves more comfortably.

Certainly the room I had on the ground floor was dignified and beautifully furnished. But most of my work was carried out either in the attic or on the second floor. The furniture in those offices was old, like the typing desks and the chairs. There were wash-basins in one corner of each room and we had a table nearby on which we made our pots of tea. There was no elegant chat over drinks in brocade and silken rooms except for the formal occasions when Harold asked people to come in for a talk in one of the larger rooms on the first floor or even sometimes in the White Boudoir.

I was usually very late leaving No. 10 during the week, but at least this meant that I could take with me a copy of the first editions of one of the morning papers delivered to the Prime Minister. I would have to go out of the front door at that late hour, because by then a security officer would have locked the door leading into the garden and I could not use the back gate. It meant a quick run down the steps from Downing Street to St James's Park, and then round to Horse Guards Parade to collect my car at the back of No. 10 and home through deserted streets.

This, then, was how I was living and working at the beginning of 1967 – the year of Harold's Grand Tour of Europe. It was also in many ways Michael Palliser's year too.

Michael Palliser had succeeded Oliver Wright as the Foreign Office man in the Private Office at No. 10. Oliver was such a colourful figure that everyone at No. 10 wondered exactly how Michael would compare with his predecessor. But at once we were aware that he was an extremely intelligent and articulate man with a forceful personality, a dedicated European.

Michael, married to the daughter of Paul Henri Spaak, had great influence within No. 10, particularly on problems connected with Europe. This was understandable in view of his background. He probably knew more about European Socialism than the Prime Minister himself. He was a superb French linguist.

Michael Palliser's position on the European question was infinitely strengthened by the support he got from Sir Burke Trend and William Nield, now Sir William Nield, who once worked at Transport House (without having its imprint left on him) and was at that time with the Cabinet Office.

Not all the civil servants were in favour of pressing so hard towards Europe. There was disagreement even inside the Private Office. It is not only politicians who fall out over policies.

Thomas Balogh played an interesting role at this time. He never disguised his personal dislike of the European project. Nobody could say, however, that he was ever uncooperative in providing briefings; he went out of his way to proffer whatever good advice he could on the intricacies involved in the Common Agricultural Policy and all the other financial and economic implications, such as the reserve role of sterling; his advice was invaluable.

Harold prepared for his Grand Tour of Europe when he was at Chequers during the weekend of 14 and 15 January. On the Saturday he played golf with my brother and gave a small dinner party for his friends, including Beattie Plummer and Commander O'Brien from HMS *Tiger*. But the main business of the day was the writing of the speech he was to deliver at Strasbourg on the Tour. The Sunday was devoted to a big briefing session on the Market. The Foreign Secretary, George Brown, came to lunch and everyone went to the study afterwards to discuss all the obstacles and hurdles.

The whole Grand Tour had the same effect as all overseas visits on the working of No. 10. Once again because of the man-hours taken up with travelling, jobs were continually frustrated, particularly when it was impossible to get more direct advice and instructions from the Prime Minister.

Harold's first European visit was to Rome since he had decided to go to the country where the Treaty had been signed. Rome appeared the appropriate starting-off point. However the major speech throughout the series of visits was to be at Strasbourg and one on which we in the Political Office were able to work along with the Private Office. The whole thing was, of course, processed by the Private Office, but both Gerald and I were able to make suggestions about the speech.

Clearly the visit to de Gaulle himself, coming after the visits to Strasbourg and Rome, was the vital one. Though the General was as enigmatic as ever, he was clearly dubious still about Britain's foreign policy and the Atlantic connection. It was Michael Palliser's show all along the line. His perfect knowledge of French made him an ideal interpreter for Harold, and consequently he played a major part in that visit. Being an exceedingly intelligent man, he had quickly grasped how Harold's mind worked. He knew the economic difficulties we had and therefore the policies the Labour Government had to follow. He knew too the policies which they would like to follow. Michael Palliser's influence over the enterprise was clear. This caused some tensions inside No. 10, though no one in the Political Office could help. It was refreshing anyway to see the operators of the System for once disagreeing among themselves.

Mr Kosygin arrived for a visit on 6 February – a Monday morning – in a fashion rather similar to the one we had experienced in 1966. Mr Kosygin was diverted from Gatwick to London Airport and the British had to do what the Russians had done in 1966 – rush a reception committee to the alternative airport in order to give Mr Kosygin the benefit of a so-called official reception. The Prime Minister had really to belt along the road to London Airport to make sure he was there in time to greet him.

The Kosygin visit had been much publicized because of the Vietnam initiative made by Harold. It seemed to be a never ending series of entertainments, punctuated by meetings which either broke up for secret consultations between the two, or were continued at places like Claridges Hotel rather than No. 10 itself.

Mary was pleased because Mr Kosygin brought with him his daughter, Madame Gvishiani, who proved to be a very attractive and likeable young woman. The two got on enormously well and for the first time it seemed that a visit from a Head of Government could be relaxed as well as important.

Few people recall that during Harold's two visits to Moscow in 1966 he was able to spend a long time alone with Kosygin going over the difficulties Russia had with China over Vietnam. Those talks then proved invaluable during Kosygin's visit to Britain in 1967. For in 1966 they had established a friendly relationship, and Mr Kosygin must have known when he came to London that Harold's understanding of the Russian position was very clear. There was a basis of mutual trust and confidence between them. It is, therefore, disingenuous of people to condemn Harold's optimistic version of the talks. They forget the background between the two men and the fact that they had already been over this ground a number of times before most realistically.

Kosygin was in Britain at the one time when it could have been possible to make progress. It was the New Year in Vietnam and there was an American bombing pause. It was ideal for a short, sharp stab at getting some sort of talks started between the participants in the struggle.

I don't believe Mr Kosygin was as optimistic as Harold because he understood only too well the nature of Chinese and North Vietnamese determination, and that both were prepared to wait a very long time to get what they wanted. All the Vietnam talks during Kosygin's visit were private and few people took part in them other than the Foreign Secretary, the principal civil servants, and possibly one or two others. In addition there were the comings and goings of the special adviser sent from Washington, Chet Cooper, and the American Ambassador, Mr Bruce.

One pessimist on it all at No. 10 was Michael Palliser. Afterwards I remember him coming into my room to tell me that the talks could not have succeeded. But what he did not know as well as Harold was Mr Kosygin's character; Harold would never have embarked on the initiative unless he had been convinced that it had at least a chance of success. Certainly Harold thought there was some prospect of movement, and it must be remembered that he was the one Western leader who had the benefit of having heard Mr Kosygin's thinking, alone and at length.

One pleasant aspect of the visit was meeting Victor Sukhodrev again. He was the principal English interpreter in the USSR, and many British people will have seen this good-looking, very charming man on television, always standing in the background, interpreting for Russian leaders at major international events, including Mr Khruschchev's famous meeting at the United Nations when he banged his desk with his shoe.

We remembered our first meeting with Victor because it was so funny. In 1963 Harold was in the Soviet Union meeting leading politicians and he asked if he could see his old friend, Mr Mikoyan, who had been ill. We were taken to Mr Mikoyan's dacha – an interesting event in itself, because I had never been in any Russian home before – and with us in the car were Mr Mikoyan's youngest son, Sergei, and a dark-haired young man. I noticed that Harold was being rather careful and choosing the topics of conversation, but I did not realize why he was doing this until he asked the young man how his newspaper was faring. The young man looked bewildered and then said: 'There must be some misunderstanding.' 'But you are from the *Daily Mail*,' Harold persisted. 'No,' said Victor, 'I'm from the Ministry of Foreign Affairs.'

I never found out why Harold thought we had a journalist with us, but I can understand why he thought Victor was British. Victor spoke English without a trace of an accent – he has a slight American accent now. This was explained when he told us that he had spent his childhood in London when his parents were working at the Soviet Trade Delegation in Highgate.

I sat next to Victor at a lunch at No. 10. Usually such luncheons for visiting politicians were all-male affairs, but in the Soviet Union they practise sex equality – or something very near it – and so for the first time I was invited along. And I didn't let Victor forget that the first time we had met we had been under the impression that he was working for a right-wing reactionary paper such as the *Daily Mail*.

If Mr Kosygin's visit did not become famous for ending the Vietnam war, it did attract a certain amount of attention for the fact that it marked a new phase in British Government entertaining. Until then there had been the stereotyped Establishment sort of entertainment with top civil servants, top businessmen and industrialists invited along to dinners and receptions for visiting statesmen. But we thought that perhaps the Russians might prefer to see something more representative of British life, and the reception for them was widened to include representatives from sport, commerce, entertainment, music and the arts. It was an enormous reception of almost two thousand people, held at Lancaster House since No. 10 was too small, and was as representative as it could be made of the new Britain. Despite this attempt the reception did not get a very sympathetic showing in the Press, even though the Press itself was more than well represented.

Now began the time when No. 10 was dominated by the D Notice affair. This was a story which was to be played out throughout the first six months of that year.

Again a lot has been written on this and Harold has been allocated the blame for initiating the first steps in the argument. He made a statement in the House commenting on a story about cables and security which had appeared in the *Daily Express*. He was acting on the information which was available to him. He had been told by the Foreign Office that the two newspapers intending to run a story of this kind – a rather old one, incidentally – were the *Daily Express* and the *Daily Mail*. Both had been warned by the representative of the Security Committee in charge of D Notices that such a story would be in contravention of the spirit of the D Notice system. The *Daily Mail* stuck honourably to the position as they understood it and did not go ahead with their story. But the *Daily Express*, whose guidance had been more loosely worded, printed it. They were unaware, they said, that they were being told categorically that the story was subject to a D Notice.

Harold was particularly angry that while one newspaper had held over the story, the other had gone ahead. Both newspapers were playing with something far bigger than they knew because there was much more to the story than could be revealed. No doubt thirty years from now the full story will be given and the whole thing set in its proper perspective.

However, as soon as the affair began a cloud of secrecy descended and the Prime Minister's discussions on it were limited to a few people. The Political Office was not involved. We were given briefings from time to time, but it was only just enough to enable queries to be evaded and not sufficient for a balanced view to be reached on whether the thing was being handled badly or well.

This was the only period when the door between my room and the Cabinet Room remained locked for very long stretches at a time. The door was always locked for security reasons, during Cabinet meetings or Defence meetings, but once these meetings were over the Private Secretaries or messengers would usually unlock my door. During the first half of 1967, when the D Notice affair hung over us, the meetings on it were so numerous that it was impossible for the Private Office to keep up with the locking and unlocking of the door, and it gradually became the case that the door remained locked. I would often have to pop round to the Private Office and through that way to unlock the door myself, in order to be able to go in and out later in the evening.

Members of the Political Office like Gerald and myself were expected to leave the room when discussions on the security aspects of the D Notice affair were taking place between the Prime Minister and advisers, and by the time the talks had moved to the political effects we had usually gone off to other engagements. The whole thing, therefore, became something in which we became less and less involved until the last stages. However, the depressing effect the affair had on the Prime Minister's morale was something we could not miss, and this in itself was infectious for those who worked closely with him. We all became obsessed with the matter and frustrated by the fact that we could not put right quickly what had been done in such haste.

The unfortunate thing about it was that it coincided with a year when there were controversial things going on within the Parliamentary Labour Party – not just controversy on major political events, but also the Parliamentary reforms of Dick Crossman and John Silkin.

The 1966 intake of MPs had come in very excited, only to be hammered by the July economic crisis and the political events that followed it. They were shattered by the severe economic measures of that summer and the whole prices and incomes policy argument that followed. The period of freeze and standstill and subsequent restraint certainly made a large section of the Parliamentary Labour Party truculent, and the truculence spread to other groups within the Party who would normally be more reasonable and understanding.

Until 1966/7 the strict discipline within the Party, dominated by the autocratic chairmanship of Emanuel Shinwell, had kept MPs very much in line in a rather military fashion. This tradition had the support of George Wigg, Chairman of our Liaison Committee at its inception, our first Lord President, Herbert Bowden, himself a fairly rigid Chief Whip when we had been in Opposition; and Ted Short, Chief Whip in the 1964/6 Parliament.

On the one hand the 'liberators', as they were regarded, were Dick Crossman, the new Lord President; John Silkin, our Chief Whip; and later Douglas Houghton, who succeeded Mr Shinwell as Chairman of the Parliamentary Labour Party. These were the men who opened up the Party in Government and ran it on a completely different line.

They were also responsible for experiments, experiments that were needed precisely because we had a big majority. On the other hand, these new tactics did not come at a happy time for the Government. Our policies were running into difficulties, and there was a great deal of heartsearching inside the Parliamentary Labour Party as the Government took actions which to many seemed opposed to their view of Socialism. Over the months the new style of discipline did produce fruitful results, but the change certainly did not go smoothly at the beginning, particularly as we were still smarting from what Harold described as 'the self-inflicted blow' of the D Notice affair.

When the Defence White Paper came up before the House in the spring, the Parliamentary Labour Party, seeing defence as an integral part of our whole economic policy and wanting great savings in order to provide money for our social policies, went into massive revolt.

At the vote on the Defence White Paper on 28 February, there were sixty-two abstentions. It was a very large figure and a shocking one for Harold. It was shocking too for the new team of Dick Crossman and John Silkin. Harold went to the Party meeting immediately following the vote to make the speech which was to become famous as his 'dog licences' speech. This was because of a phrase he used in which he suggested that perhaps MPs who persistently refused to support the Government might find themselves in difficulties in their constituencies.

The truth is, though, that this phrase was not in his original speech. Gerald and I went over as usual to the House that afternoon to go through the speech. Then it was typed out by Doreen Andrew in the Political Office. It was checked again by us, and we were all very pleased by the firm line he had taken. The version he took with him in his pocket had no reference at all to 'dog licences'. The first we heard about it was when Harold came back laughing. He was accompanied by Dick Crossman and John Silkin, and Gerald came in later. Then I got the full story of the famous insert. None of us realized how much it was to dominate the headlines the next day, though I think Harold had an inkling of this. But it was a phrase that certainly lived on, and even as late as 1971 it was being recalled when Harold made his Brighton conference speech on the Common Market, interpreted as meaning that every dog was allowed one bite.

What Harold was concerned to see then and over the coming years was that people who abstained, particularly on the Left, should not do so while being able to feel comfortable in the knowledge that the more orthodox members of the Party would tramp into the Lobby to keep the Government in office. Orthodox MPs themselves were to raise complaints later on this very score, asking why they should not be allowed to abstain too. Why should they have to keep the Party going so that other people could have pure consciences? But that was 1967 and by 1971 that argument had been, to use one of Mr Gaitskell's phrases, 'thrown out of the window'!

The new phase in the running of the Party produced a

clash, and one result of this was the resignation of Emanuel Shinwell as Chairman of the Parliamentary Labour Party, and the election of Douglas Houghton in his place.

Looking back, it is obvious that Manny Shinwell would never have approved the changes. He is an autocratic man with little time for other people's opinions. He disliked seeing what he undoubtedly regarded as the disarray in the Parliamentary Labour Party and wanted authority to be reasserted in the old rigid way.

Personalities were involved too. Manny Shinwell had a long-standing alliance with George Wigg, another great disciplinarian, who thought some of the new schemes hare-brained. In addition, Manny Shinwell and George Wigg were not cut out to get on well with Dick Crossman, the leading figure in the changes. George had the ear of the Prime Minister. Their opposition to Dick Crossman and John Silkin was responsible for a great deal of difficulty at this stage.

But then came the election of Douglas Houghton and a very different atmosphere. Douglas was able to become Chairman of the Parliamentary Labour Party because he had just lost a senior Cabinet post.

However, leaving the Cabinet gave him the opportunity to take over the Parliamentary Labour Party – and that is just what he did. His dominance did not become pronounced until the end of 1968 and 1969 but he laid the foundations for this in 1967 and early 1968. During this time he cemented another famous alliance – between himself and Jim Callaghan. They had been friends for many years but now it became a really active association. Douglas had a firm ally inside the Government while Jim had a superb associate at the head of the Parliamentary Labour Party. This was a two-way affair which was to prove more than satisfactory to both.

Harold, embroiled as he was with the Common Market, the D Notice affair and prices and incomes, had no time to be involved in what was happening inside the Party. This was a pity, but there is a limit to the number of horses that any Prime Minister can ride at any one time. Still, he never felt any regret about the Crossman/Silkin phase. He realized that this was one of the most imaginative periods in the history of the Parliamentary Labour Party. It was a liberal regime in the sense that Members were given much more say in what they did and they were consulted much more about events. At the same time I should like to dispel the idea, put about by John Silkin's opponents, that he was a weak Chief Whip. Quite the contrary. He was very firm, as people who abstained on three-line Whips or criticized the Government soon found out. What was immense was his knowledge of the Parliamentary Labour Party and each member of it. His great contribution was to keep the Party united during a time of major internal stresses.

On a personal note we in the Political Office found the change-over in the chairmanship of the Parliamentary Labour Party at least a minor release. There is no denying that we had been in awe, and even in fear, of Emanuel Shinwell when he was Chairman. When he came in for meetings or announced himself on the telephone his abrupt and severe manner was somewhat less than heartening for the rest of us.

On a political level we welcomed Dick's plans for presenting Parliament with new ideas and for involving members of our Party in Government. He held seminars for the 1966 arrivals, got Parliament working in the mornings, and produced Green Papers instead of White Papers so that policy could be discussed before it became the Government line.

But the year, bleak though it was in some ways, still contained plenty of happy and personal occasions. There was Harold's birthday party on 11 March for instance. This year his birthday fell at a weekend, the best possible time for a Prime Minister, so the celebration was held at Chequers and attended by members of his own family, some of mine as well, Beattie Plummer and Gerald Kaufman. And then soon afterwards, on 1 April, many of the party guests were assembled again at Westminster Cathedral for the marriage of his housekeeper, Mary Wright. It was a frosty day and as we sat in the stone-cold atmosphere we were absolutely frozen during the long ceremony. Harold and Mary sat on two chairs in the centre, almost as if they were getting married themselves rather than the real bride and groom.

Shortly before she was married, Mary Wright, who was employed privately by Harold, had been replaced at No. 10 by Mrs Pollard.

Mrs Pollard was someone I had known since I was a very small girl. My first memories of her were when she arrived in the Northamptonshire village in which I lived, after having escaped the German blitzing of Coventry. Like so many others, she had to leave her home and seek refuge in the countryside. When I was at primary school and high school, Mrs Pollard was a near neighbour and although I had not seen her for very many years, I thought of her when Mary Wright left. I knew Mrs Pollard's husband had died and she had taken up cookery both as a hobby and a job. She had gained high qualifications at a Technical College and had been a school meals organizer in a large Comprehensive School. Knowing that she had no home ties and could very easily give up what she was doing to come to London, we got in touch with her and she readily agreed to join the Wilsons at No. 10. She tells us now that she had the most terrible nerves when she envisaged having to spend her life serving elaborate meals, lunches and dinners, and carrying silver trays with delicate china backwards and forwards for afternoon teas. She had not then realized the simplicity of the Wilsons' tastes.

Two days after Mary Wright had married, a dinner was given at No. 10 for Vice-President Hubert Humphrey. Harold was delighted to have Mr Humphrey over and entertained him at Chequers the weekend before. But he also gave him a dinner at No. 10 because he was anxious that his colleagues and members of his staff should meet him.

He particularly wanted us to hear what Humphrey had to say about Vietnam, but some of us were appalled by the change we saw in the Vice-President. We had known him as the enthusiastic liberal reformer who had fought a lonely battle in 1960 to try to get the Presidential nomination away from Kennedy. But that evening he mouthed, almost like a record, a line on Vietnam which no liberal could possibly have accepted. The moment he was asked a question the answer came out absolutely pat before the last words of the question had been uttered. It became so disappointing that some of us moved away. The same line continued throughout the evening, and I heard very little else being talked about. I went away being able to repeat almost off by heart what we had heard Vice-President Humphrey say about Vietnam. He even had the casualty and death figures on a piece of paper in his pocket.

He left the impression of having degenerated from a leader into an ambassador. He knew the line thoroughly and put it over with great gusto and vigour. But though he may have seemed in total agreement one still had the feeling that it was too mechanical, it lacked real enthusiasm.

That Easter we had the Torrey Canyon incident – an interlude which, despite the serious and even frightening implications, was for me, I fear, a rather amusing one. I was spending Easter with Beattie Plummer, Harold's closest personal friend, the widow of Sir Leslie Plummer, the former Labour MP for Deptford, at her Essex home, and another guest was Sir Elwyn Jones, the Attorney General. We were all caught up in the business, for while I would be speaking about it to Harold on one telephone, Elwyn would be busy on another line in Beattie's study talking to his officials about the legal complications.

Indeed, it is still difficult to see how, with all the expert knowledge we had, and with Sir Solly Zuckerman, the man Anthony Sampson describes as the 'Court Scientist', behind us, that we could not get one ship destroyed efficiently and speedily. I wondered why we did not call in the Royal Air Force to bomb it instead of the Royal Navy. I got the impression of almost amusing ineptitude. It always remained a humorous episode to me because, among other things, of the attitude of Ministers, who were delighted to be involved in such an affair and at being able to discuss whether you should blow up the tanker or bomb it. They were absolutely riveted by the details. No small boy could have enjoyed it more.

Throughout this period the Government had been preparing the statement for the Cabinet on the Grand Tour. Everything was set out in enormous detail and masses of papers were circulated to all the members of the Cabinet for study. No one could say that there was not full briefing on what George Brown and Harold Wilson had done during their European Tour. The result was that when the time came to make a statement in the House, that Britain was proposing to make a formal application to join the European Community, the application was given one of the biggest majorities in history.

The Parliamentary Labour Party was quite happy that the European adventure should culminate in the application, made as it was against the background of a Labour Government. A Labour Government operating Socialist policies at home was considered an adequate setting for possible entry into the Common Market on the right terms.

It was a brave gesture. But it was followed, I am afraid, by the General's veto.

When the black-ball did come, most of the Parliamentary Labour Party I think breathed a sigh of relief – and this was despite its previous vote in favour. For what de Gaulle revealed in his speech of 16 May was that Britain could have no place in the Market unless Britain was willing to accept the European definition (which in 1967 meant the French definition) of how we should conduct our foreign policy and our economic and financial affairs. It was also apparent then how long and how difficult the negotiations would have been. Even if de Gaulle had been willing to let the discussions continue, they would have gone on only if Britain had been willing to sell the pass to the French and break away totally from the Atlantic alliance. And while some members of the Parliamentary Labour Party would not have been unhappy to see this happen in support of a genuinely independent British role, they certainly were not going to accept this in pursuit of a British role tied to de Gaulle's philosophy, a rogue elephant foreign policy and an economic and financial policy which at times stopped only just short of madness.

The Parliamentary Labour Party's attitude to de Gaulle was curiously ambivalent at this time. While many members were genuinely angry that de Gaulle should treat us in such a cavalier fashion, others had a sneaking admiration for his attitude. This is not to say that they supported what the French did, but they supported the technique the French used. They would have liked to see Britain also putting national interests first without any reference to the outside world. This attitude often affected people close to Harold.

Soon there was yet another overseas visit, this time to Canada and then on to the United States. The trip was dominated by the Middle Eastern situation for just as Harold was planning to leave for Ottawa the Egyptians closed the

Straits of Tiran and the situation in that part of the world started to come to pieces.

Back in Britain, Harold was caught up naturally with all the facets of the Six Day War in the Middle East. Inside No. 10 there were personal complications for some felt personally involved, through feelings and friendships with the Israelis. Gerald Kaufman, a Jew with strong Israeli ties, had an obvious interest in the outcome, and so did others who knew Israel and who numbered Israelis like Ygal Allon among their friends.

Certainly Gerald and I followed every act breathlessly while the Private Office quizzically and sceptically looked on. In the middle was the Prime Minister, realizing only too well the possible implications of the war for the country he was trying to put back on the road to economic recovery.

He had his private feelings too but his advisers were, I would say, about equally divided between those who supported Israel and those who supported Egypt. It was an agonizing period for him. He was able to see what was involved, not just for the countries immediately concerned, but also for his own country and his own Government. What he feared did indeed happen. The Six Day War scuppered the Labour Government. For what happened that summer in the Eastern Mediterranean produced inevitably the events that happened in Britain in November and December. This was the turning-point in the history of the Government and in the lives of all who worked for it.

Once the Israelis had won Gerald began proudly to sport a commemorative medal ribbon. This ribbon had been sent to him as a present and he had it mounted on a gold tie-clip.

But to Harold it was a constant reminder that everything we had hoped for might be slipping away. The harsh fact was that, though the Israelis had won, Britain had lost: now we had the overwhelming problem of getting our oil supplies through and facing at the same time a heavy cost to our balance of payments.

Only occasionally did Harold lose patience with Gerald when he was pressing hard on some specifically Israeli point. Then, looking at that ribbon, he would retort that but for the closure of the Canal Britain's position would have been better and our ability to help Israel might have been correspondingly greater: fair comment and fair criticism.

But the balance of payments was not the only thing that needed attention. So did the balance inside Europe.

As soon as the General had declared his veto on 16 May we were presented with a new situation. Until then we had made the running on Europe, even though we as a Party were not as dedicated to the Market as were the Conservatives, whose Leader was a loyal and long-term European. The aim now was to make certain that the European argument was kept within the Government's control and not allowed to pass to the Leader of the Opposition.

To counter any possible move by Mr Heath, Harold now took up the invitation he had received from President de Gaulle at the Adenauer funeral. In June he visited France with the express intention of reaching a separate understanding with the General and of producing an Anglo-French Entente distinct from the Common Market. The visit was a success and the potentially dangerous Market issue was neutralized by this initiative.

The visit was interesting not just for its political significance but for the way in which Harold was entertained. Mary went with him, and the General, still so uncompromising in public, proved a charming host at the Petit Trianon at Versailles. This was another occasion on which I preferred to stay at home. I realize now what a wrong decision that was and that I should have gone.

The only part I played in it all was very minor, giving my view on the choice of present the Prime Minister should take with him. On all these overseas visits a Private Secretary would ask me to express an opinion on the sort of gifts that should be taken. The usual procedure was for a well-known firm of goldsmiths, silversmiths and jewellers to send a selection of possible presents. These would be set out in the visitors' room next to my room on the ground floor. We would all then go in and decide which we thought the most appropriate. The drawback was, from my point of view, that the presents were always so traditional and often old fashioned. There was rarely anything exciting .or modern. They may have been appropriate, of course, for the people to whom they were given. But I often wished that they could be more imaginative and that some of our younger designers could be called in to give advice.

On the occasion of the Paris visit Harold received from the General a wonderful Sèvres tea-set in deep blue and gold. Harold and Mary have kept this very carefully, not only because of the donor of the gift, the General, an historic figure, but also because it symbolizes so much that is beautiful about France.

One other good thing happened in June. We saw the end of the D Notice affair. At last the Political Office was asked for its views. What amazed us, when we came to discuss it, was that nobody had thought of having the Government legally represented at the inquiry that had been set up. Whoever failed to advise Harold on this bears a heavy responsibility.

It was slightly comical too that almost everybody seemed to have welcomed the choice of Emanuel Shinwell as one of the Privy Councillors conducting the inquiry. The idea that he would inevitably be kind and understanding to the Government, and Harold, at a time when he had just lost the chairmanship of the Parliamentary Labour Party, embittered too by the events of the year, particularly by what he regarded as the growing indiscipline of Labour MPs, struck me as naïve.

So the committee reported after an inquiry in which the Government was not legally represented and the report itself was so unacceptable that it had to be rejected. And the consequent damage was even worse than the earlier events.

Gerald and others called in for advice at the eleventh hour could have done little to influence the handling of the affair, for it had been kept inside a very small circle indeed. At one point we were able to sustain the Prime Minister and this was when a suggestion was made that it would be a good idea to ask the Leader of the Opposition to see all the documentation so that he could have full knowledge of all the security aspects of the case.

But by then the real harm had been done. Very little action could be taken to put it right. No one could complain when the Opposition made as much out of it as they did.

The whole lamentable affair had hung like a heavy cloud over us for many months. It had sapped the energies of the

Prime Minister and his morale. We felt deeply concerned for him.

The cumulative effect of the affair on the Press, sensitive as they were from the Macmillan era about the Vassall Case and Government interference in Press matters, could almost be described as disastrous. Harold bore the full brunt of this at the time and for a long period afterwards.

That summer our lunch-hours at No. 10 were taken up with discussions about the real economic situation. After the Six Day War, Harold had been increasingly sensitive about what might be the repercussions for our balance of payments. When he was alone the dreaded word 'devaluation' was sometimes mentioned. The arguments for and against were rehearsed, particularly in the political context. Harold now feared devaluation might be forced upon us by the international events of that year.

Few in the Parliamentary Labour Party suspected Harold had given even house-room in his mind to such thoughts. But he was only too well aware that the situation could get out of hand. Although we were, as Jim Callaghan was to announce in an economic debate before the House rose, more or less in balance, and there were good hopes that this would get better as the year went on, there was always the danger that the effects of the closure of the Canal would be too great for us to sustain parity if there was any speculation at any time even on a small scale. With such a narrow margin he had to be watchful about any speculative periods.

Throughout July many of Harold's closest friends within the Government would ask me round for a drink or for tea. They wanted, yet often hesitated, to refer to the dreaded devaluation question. But they were anxious to transmit to Harold messages pressing him to take action on it. It was embarrassing. I could clearly not talk freely nor give away clues to his thoughts. But when people are passionate about a particular form of action they want taken, it would be difficult anyway to get over to them that while the person they are pressing might not agree with them in principle, he is nevertheless aware of what might have to happen and be prepared for action if it had to be taken.

No one could say that an opportunity of raising it with Harold had already occurred. Harold had got as near as he could to saying in a political context that if the moment arrived when the situation really did look impossible, then devaluation was something which would have to be considered. I can remember him during that period walking up and down in the dining-room at lunchtime. He would eat half his lunch and then get up from the table in a contemplative way. If the dreaded word was spoken, he got up and proceeded to walk up and down very quickly, rehearsing the arguments for and against with all the difficulties involved, setting out how he saw the position. He certainly did not have a closed mind about it, though he had a determination to stick to the parity under all circumstances unless the Government were overtaken by events. He did not want to see the Party experience the stringent measures which would have to accompany devaluation before any good effects could be felt. He knew it would break too many spirits.

The Parliamentary Labour Party was restless and increasingly unhappy about the whole prices and incomes policy, with the statutory legislation proposed, the standstill and freeze period we had experienced, and all the other ramifications. They were eager for any action which could get us out of the situation and help to move the country into a period of expansion again. Once more it was the chicken-and-egg argument. Whatever action they had in mind would inevitably be followed immediately by even more stringent and unacceptable measures, far more so than the ones they were so worried about at the time. What they all were unable to see, in perspective, was the enormous amount of work that had been done and the achievements the Labour Government had to its credit, on the social services front in particular, even after only two years in office.

Before we went off for our holiday that year Harold appointed Lord Hill Chairman of the BBC. This was greeted with some bewilderment, though Harold had gone to great pains to consider all the people who were qualified to take on the job from within the organization itself. If one was going to have a Conservative, he felt it was best to have the real thing and a man who had already presided over an organization where impartiality had to be observed because of the Act under which the ITA operates. He felt Lord Hill might even be able to educate the BBC in how to operate a broadcasting system on these terms, rather than in the spirit of the independent empire they had preserved for themselves.

We were certainly glad when the time came for Harold to go away for his summer holidays to the Scillies. That year I went there myself for a short time with Beattie Plummer.

Unfortunately, we had only just arrived when Harold had to return to London because of the incidents in Peking when our Legation was attacked by young Maoists. Our position in Hong Kong seemed involved, but events calmed down although Harold's stay in London coincided with angry scenes around the Chinese Legation.

During Harold's holiday he gave a lot of thought to a Government reshuffle so that he could bring in more new people and promote others within the Government. He had considered making the reshuffle before he went to the Isles of Scilly, but had rejected this because there was too much other work on hand. He wanted to give careful consideration to the qualifications of younger Members and to see how they could be slotted into a reorganized Government. He also hoped that any Press reaction to the reshuffle would be more balanced at the end of August than it would have been in July, immediately after the D Notice affair.

It was a curious reshuffle, though extremely successful in bringing in young people who were to prove very efficient and successful in their jobs. One Minister who had been asked to resign telephoned the Prime Minister the following day to say that he had thought it all over and decided that he really would like to continue. I suppose that the kindly way in which Harold had done the sacking left it so unclear, that the Minister had gone away with the impression that he had a choice. Harold was always sensitive about the feelings of those he talked to and careful not to hurt them in any way.

Many of those who were asked to resign were efficient, but young men were quite rightly eager and anxious to be given a chance. Every Prime Minister suffers from this problem that there are too many candidates for too few jobs. So inevitably there must be a residue of disgruntled ex-Ministers eventually in every Government, who feel they were retired before they should have been. The problem is insoluble. There is no easy way to reshuffle a Government.

But there were still many able young men who had to be left out because of the limited number of places. Some of these were to be the most active in the political intrigues that were to develop in the years ahead. Indeed, a number of them were to take the initiative almost immediately thereafter in rehearsing in public the devaluation argument, and to tie to it the question of whether the Prime Minister was up to his job.

Unquestionably the most important appointments in the newly re-formed Government were Tony Crosland to the Board of Trade, Patrick Gordon Walker to Education and George Thomson to the Commonwealth Office.

I was always amused after this reshuffle to hear stories about Gerry Fowler and his appointment. It was true my brother had been at the same school as Gerry. We knew him quite well. But the fact is I had not myself spoken to him since I was a small girl and do not believe my brother had seen him for about twenty years. What everybody ignored was that Gerry had a brilliant academic record and a political background that made him an obvious candidate for a post.

September saw our usual preparation for Party Conference. No one knew quite how it would go that year. There had been mutterings behind the scenes about economic policy, or lack of it. There were, too, political manoeuvrings about Harold's future, particularly among young right-wingers. They were organizing themselves extremely well – as always they are far more efficient in organizing a party within a party than the Bevanites ever were.

Conference was held at Scarborough, our favourite place. Harold liked it because it was in Yorkshire and he had known Scarborough since he was a child. Harold's father, too, was delighted, because he could tour Yorkshire and return to his early haunts on the way back to Cornwall.

We travelled up on the main line to York where we had to change to the branch line which would take us on to Scarborough. At York Harold got out, accompanied by his detectives, and was led along the platform by an enthusiastic Station Manager. Meanwhile, the staff had got out the luggage and the all-important red boxes but discovered that porters and even trolleys were in very short supply. Nothing daunted, we commandeered what appeared to be the only available trolley. After all, Harold was the Prime Minister and for security reasons we had to be pretty careful about the red boxes filled with Government papers.

At this point a member of the National Executive Committee, who was also a well-known MP, spotted our trolley and demanded with the full authority of his office that some of the luggage should be unloaded and replaced by luggage belonging to NEC members. This I refused to do. I was not a civil servant, but employed as I was by the Prime Minister, I was not going to see his red boxes or even his luggage spread all over York station. While we were waiting for a porter to take the trolley I stood my ground and physically defended the boxes and other cases.

Then another complication arose. Barbara Castle came up and asked if she could put her luggage on the trolley. She was a member of the NEC and I had already refused another member of the NEC. But I realized that she was also Minister of Transport. I could hardly give the brush-off to Barbara, who after all was travelling on her British Rail. So I made a quick policy decision. Ministers of Transport, yes; NEC members, no. Besides, Barbara was being, as always to our staff, particularly charming. At last we all moved off, Barbara and the rest of us happy, the other NEC member obviously less so, until we caught up with Harold's little procession.

This was followed by an even more amusing scene. The Station Manager, who was happily chatting to the Prime Minister, ventured a casual glance over his shoulder and became aware of the red hair and the unmistakable personality of the person who was his ultimate employer. He immediately turned round and attempted the impossible task of being polite and devoting his attention to his Prime Minister and his Minister simultaneously.

At Conference Michael Halls, Gerald and I worked together again to organize everything, together with Roger Dawe from the Private Office. It was a good working team, backing up the Prime Minister on both fronts, and keeping the two offices in line with each other. The arrangements were handled jointly, the burden was shared and the atmosphere congenial and happy.

It was strange to return to the Royal Hotel at Scarborough. As soon as we walked into the Prime Minister's suite our minds went back to 1963, the last time we had been there. In this same sitting-room had been written the famous 'technological revolution' speech that had caused such a stir when he first became Leader of the Party. We could hardly believe that in what seemed to be such a short space of time he had moved from Leader to Prime Minister and had already been in office three years.

There again, in the sitting-room, his friends gathered to help with reading and checking the speech for 1967 – people like Peter Shore and Tony Benn and Dick Crossman. This time it was written at leisure, not dictated at 3.00 a.m., as was the speech in 1963.

As I've already said, I hate to hear Harold speak either in the House or on public platforms; on the morning of his speech I was also very tired from staying up until about 4.00 a.m. to see that the mechanics of getting the speech out had been completed as efficiently as possible. So I went to bed to snatch a few hours' sleep before he came back at lunchtime. Unfortunately, Michael Halls was sitting in the Prime Minister's suite immediately below, and had turned on the television so that he could hear the speech delivered. It was so loud that it drifted up through into my bedroom. In the end I was forced to listen though I caught only the applause and the laughter without hearing the actual words. I could tell by the audience reaction that it was going well, and when I went down at lunchtime this was confirmed.

What the speech did was to present an outline, which was clear, effective and even dramatic, of what Labour had done and what Labour was trying to do, of what a Labour Government meant to the ordinary person in terms of increased security when unemployed, when sick, when widowed, when old, and of how the industrial reorganization we were trying to carry through would help to make up for the deficiencies of the past.

We knew there would be a hard time at Conference over the Government's economic policies, so it was decided to get this debate over at the beginning of the conference. With this out of the way Harold could concentrate on the positive side of our

policies. This meant that Jim Callaghan, who must be the man
to wind up the economic debate, spoke before Harold. His
speech was superb. I think it was the best speech I have ever
heard him make. It was clear, simple and confident. Everyone
in that hall understood perfectly what he was saying even when
he was talking about the most complicated financial and
economic points. He has this great art for popularizing the
difficult and intricate. He was an enormous success. Of course,
the speech would seem even more successful in retrospect if the
Government had not had to devalue the following month.

Most delegates went away feeling that it had been Jim's
conference. It was certainly not George Brown's conference.
George came under sustained attack from, of all quarters, the
Daily Mirror, the very people who had helped to get him where
he was and furthermore to keep him there. Whether or not it
was Cecil King or Hugh Cudlipp who put the knife in, remains
a secret. It certainly was buried deeply into George with a
black banner headline announcing: 'George Must Go'.

Everything was triggered off by George enjoying himself.
George, for a Labour politician, has an unusual feature: he
plays as hard as he works. I often used to thank God that at
least one member of the Government liked to do this and that
not everyone was stuck to the job for the whole twenty-four
hours of the day and night. Some leading Labour figures also
enjoy themselves, but in a more sophisticated jet-set way.
George at least is down to earth.

However, he had a bad time at Scarborough. Just before
Conference there were some unfortunate photographs when
George was pictured dancing at a party aboard a Cunarder in
New York. This was not a good beginning, and during the
conference there was a report from Europe about our economic
prospects that George, as a committed European, found
unfortunate. This made him very tense. One result was a
difference of opinion with photographers which got very bad
publicity for him and produced the anti-George article in the
Daily Mirror, the paper with which George had been associated
in the past.

For Harold and for Labour generally, Scarborough seemed a
good conference. I enjoyed it except for my experience at a
leading Scarborough store. I went there after a number of late

nights in the hope that I should emerge with a new, fresh look. I asked a sleepy-looking young lady to colour-rinse my hair and discovered when I emerged from the drier that I had changed from blonde to brown. It took weeks to put the colour right and almost as long for my morale to recover.

Back in London, a very sad event occurred. Clem Attlee died. Everybody was genuinely saddened. Most of the people working with the Prime Minister had known Lord Attlee only as a remote figure. I had come in contact with him at Transport House when I was working there and at Party Conferences. But he was always rather reserved and unapproachable.

He had been a father-figure to Harold, and Harold took him as the example of what he thought a Prime Minister should be. Whereas the pomp and ceremony surrounding Winston Churchill's going had been dramatic and impressive, the simple arrangements for Clem Attlee were more touching for those of us in the Labour Government. There were no grand speeches or elaborate ceremonies, but I think we felt more acutely because of it. Somehow it fitted in with the character, with the quiet, undemonstrative man who never pushed himself forward, but got on with his job in a brisk and efficient manner. Clem Attlee's going was typical of everything about him, clear, unassuming, and yet enormously dignified.

His death came as the Government moved into its most difficult period. The docks in Liverpool, London and elsewhere came out on strike. This had to be dealt with quickly, since the drain in economic terms was felt rapidly.

The demonstrations on Vietnam, too, became more disturbing and shrill. This was the internal manifestation of dissatisfaction with Labour foreign policy in general. Another unpleasant event in the foreign field was when the maverick French intervened again with comments on the British scene which, while rather old hat, became news each time they were uttered, and sparked off a consequential reaction in the City of London.

Some of the trouble stemmed from reports within the Common Market about the state of the British economy which the Government had known about during Party Conference. But an attack by the French Foreign Minister on our economic situation was a straight blow against Britain's economy and posed the direct question of whether devaluation must now be considered, since economic recovery was so slow. They were at it again!

The situation was not helped by the fact that one of our spokesmen in the Government, Lord Chalfont, a very relaxed and charming gentleman, became rather too relaxed, and retaliated against the French and de Gaulle by suggesting that the British might consider withdrawing their troops from Germany if the French insisted on behaving in such an irresponsible way. It was certainly 'bully' for Lord Chalfont as far as many were concerned, but how on earth could you say something like this without sparking off reaction even more dangerous?

The Queen's Speech came and went, with the most important part of it being the major Transport Bill which was carried through by Barbara Castle and Stephen Swingler and their junior Ministers, with great aplomb and efficiency. It was not the most exciting Queen's Speech anyone had seen, and the ghastly by-election results suffered in that month did not add to our jollity.

From then on events seemed to run away with the situation as bad omen followed bad omen and we moved irrevocably nearer and nearer to the thing we had imagined we could avoid, devaluation.

Once it was known that French comments had sparked off general discussion within Europe, particularly in banking and financial circles, on whether or not Britain should devalue, this meant in itself that Labour was now being pushed steadily on the road away from parity. Once this happened the whole atmosphere in No. 10 changed. Before, most people had walked around discussing most things quite openly in corridors, not worrying too much about being overheard. Now the atmosphere was quite different. Conversations had to be whispered, especially if they related even remotely to 'the subject' and the rumours. Meetings were held quietly behind closed doors. There was no relaxation about whether or not the door of a room was left ajar. It was firmly closed as you went in so that conversations could not be overheard from the corridors.

Everything was done by allusion, rather than by direct

reference. Sides were taken and the argument flowed first in one direction and then in the other. At one point of time everybody was saying it must not happen, and organizing systems of relief for the British Government to help to avoid it; and then the next minute the opposite happened, and we were being told that international financiers thought it was a good thing and, therefore, there was no need for any wide-scale relief operations to be launched on our behalf.

While the Prime Minister and the Chancellor clearly understood all these details, some of those around Harold were bewildered by all the comings and goings and the differing reports. First the Prime Minister was going to Washington to talk to the Americans direct, then he wasn't. Aircraft were standing by and then they weren't. Jim Callaghan's behaviour during the run-up to devaluation and during the week of devaluation was magnificent, and co-operation between Harold and himself total. This was the Labour Party at its best. There was no dissembling. The Government was in deep trouble and they were only too concerned for the Labour Party to get us out of it as fast as they could, so that the country could recover and the Party should not lose office.

During this time one might imagine Harold was devoting himself to devaluation to the exclusion of everything else. This, of course, is what could happen in an ideal world. But the threatened devaluation did not mean that Harold ceased to be the Head of a Government composed of widely differing characters, that he ceased to be a Party Leader, that he ceased to have problem after problem thrust at him that had nothing to do with the financial and economic situation.

I remember just a few of the complications of those months. There was a senior Minister who underwent a domestic crisis and came to pour his troubles out to Harold in the Cabinet Room, three hours which were invaluable to the Minister concerned but which were precious at the time. There was the other senior Minister, a right-wing member, who came back from America and started to express strong criticisms about LBJ and Washington's Vietnam policy. This was just another factor in the shifting Vietnam scene inside the Parliamentary Labour Party.

And there was George Brown, who was alternately confident

and depressed after Scarborough. One minute he was having his public after-dinner row with Lord Thomson, followed by remorse and threatened resignation; the next he was full of confidence and determination to put his critics down.

These were only part of the pressures on the Prime Minister. Both the Chancellor and George Brown were playing parts, not only in official Government talks, but behind the scenes as well with the senior outside people involved. George was trying to elicit information and views for himself on all that was developing, to make his own evaluation. While he had wanted devaluation in 1966, he was Foreign Secretary in 1967, and saw things somewhat differently and wanted to be briefed separately on it all.

I found it difficult to keep up with all the shifts and moves and to concentrate my mind on the economic crisis which was looming. As I typed the Prime Minister's diary late at night, I was often stopped and would have to go down to Michael Halls, who kept the diary locked away in one of the boxes in the Private Office, so that it could be put away for that night. I would then go to answer a distress signal from the Prime Minister on some point, possibly the need to contact a colleague privately.

Few can realize the difficulties Harold faced that October and November, with pressures coming in on so many fronts. And yet throughout it all he kept calm and strong and patient. He even extended friendship and personal help to those who at precisely that time were talking about his future in hostile terms.

There were political manoeuvrings going on about the occupancy of No. 10 – not only after devaluation but before it. In fact a senior colleague openly referred to it when talking to Harold one evening just before the devaluation agreement had been reached.

Gerald Kaufman was now called back each evening from the House and no day passed, even at the weekends, without a gathering to review political strategy and tactics. Michael Halls joined regularly in the review sessions. They were harrowing. Devaluation the Party could accept and stand up to, even the handling of it in the House and the country; but the accompanying package that we knew must follow still stuck in many throats.

It was a gloomy scene indeed. It was a minefield we were in: nationally, politically and personally. At No. 10 most people were only too conscious of all the implications as we talked together late at night. Harold would now have to draw very deeply on the support he had at the real heart of the Party in Westminster and the country.

The days edged nearer to 18 November and D-Day. Once the Cabinet had finally made the firm decision on 16 November, the load lifted a little. One became so involved in the action of it all that the worries surrounding it could be pushed a little away until it became time to deal with them too.

I had seen crowds outside No. 10 before, mostly cheering, happy crowds. They became increasingly silent, and then hostile.

On 18 November the atmosphere within the building was relatively subdued. The main work was now on the wording of the statement for that evening. Harold even had time for a social call from a group of Labour women from the country, and when he went to the front door to say goodbye to them, the questioning crowd gave him a subdued cheer.

I took time off before the announcement to do some shopping. It was a Saturday, but some stores remain open even on Saturday afternoons, particularly in the Strand and close to No. 10. I bought myself a present, as a conscious desire, I suppose, to comfort myself. It was one of the then trendy new outsize watches. It became known at No. 10 as my 'devaluation watch'.

Harold, Gerald and I watched the announcement of devaluation on the television set in my room downstairs. We were watching ITV but for some reason this channel failed to get it at the time it was put out. We were amazed and, indeed, put off by this. For one awful moment we thought perhaps something had gone wrong on the technical side, and the statement had not gone out. But then we switched on to BBC and we knew devaluation had gone ahead.

By the Sunday, when the country knew the facts, the crowd outside No. 10 was large and ugly. I believe there was a good sprinkling of Conservative crowd organizers. But even without these there was hostility.

Sunday morning was taken up with a major Press conference.

It was set up not in No. 12, as was usually the case for large Press conferences, but in the State Dining Room in No. 10. The Prime Minister and the Chancellor sat at a table with their backs to the window, overlooking Horse Guards Parade, with a phalanx of Pressmen facing them.

At least this occasion had its amusing side. Hardened Pressmen who for years had been watching crowds cheer and boo well-known political leaders, and had taken some satisfaction from their discomfiture, found a more unnerving situation facing them. When they walked up Downing Street, or crossed through the archway from the Foreign Office yard, a shortcut from the House of Commons. they were met with catcalls from the crowd. The people outside did not know who they were nor did they recognize them, of course, except for the television interviewers, but they clearly felt that these men had been involved in some way and had obviously to them had a hand in the devaluation decision. So they were given the bird – some rather more fiercely than others.

They shot through that front door faster than they had ever come through it before. Indeed, when it became time to leave later, many were reluctant to submit themselves to the ordeal once more, though some saw the amusing side. We certainly did.

The conference itself was fascinating. It should have been the Prime Minister's conference, since, as Head of the Government which had taken this enormous decision, he was obviously the spokesman. But it was gradually taken over by the Chancellor. Each question asked, and aimed at Harold, was quickly answered by Jim. It was some time before the penny dropped and Harold retrieved the situation.

When it was over Harold gave a buffet luncheon in the Small State Dining Room, for some of our 'White Commonwealth' Press friends.* For them it was particularly useful since they were able to question Harold separately and in greater detail. We at No. 10 were able to relax for the first time on this subject. No longer was there fear of mentioning the unmentionable. But so well schooled was everyone that even then it was difficult to use the dreaded word. Tongues just could not get round it.

Mrs Pollard had worked hard to arrange the cold buffet and

*See p. 227

afterwards I helped her clear away. Together we went to her room overlooking Downing Street and looked out to see the crowd outside. Mrs Pollard was, I think, a little shaken by the jeering and catcalls and shaken, too, by all the events that had happened so quickly and dramatically. She was comparatively new to it all and the fierceness of it shocked her. I tried to reassure her that those who were jeering today would be cheering tomorrow. And I was right. Tomorrow was a long time coming, but it came.

Then there was the Sunday night broadcast. From the start of the weekend there had been some disagreement with Harold about the actual timing of it. Some wanted it on Sunday since it was felt more people would see it than on Saturday. Saturday in any case would be caught up with the announcement itself and people would be trying to digest that. We had also to face the fact that if Harold did it on Saturday, then Mr Heath would have the right to reply on Sunday, and peak viewing then would give him a marvellous opportunity for putting across his criticisms. This view prevailed in the end, partly on its merits, partly because the announcement itself came so late on Saturday – for technical reasons – that it would have been impracticable to put the broadcast out.

Harold's draft of what he wanted to say, brought back from his visit to Liverpool and written on the train, was very serious and tough. After advice from colleagues and the guidance of the Treasury this draft was changed in both tone and context, and the famous 'pound in your pocket' phrase inserted.

I was present at most of the drafting sessions for the broadcast and I watched the changes in it. It would have been unnerving for a nation, after such a serious announcement, to see their Prime Minister appearing full of woe and foreboding, rather than reassuring them and giving them good reason to hope. He also had to ensure beyond doubt that there was no mad rush to draw out money once the banks were reopened. A leader had to speak frankly to his troops but he also had another duty at a time of crisis. He had to rally them.

His tactics were good and they would have been proved right but for one thing – the intense campaign waged by the Tories to get Harold out immediately after devaluation and particularly their unscrupulous manipulation of his 'pound in your pocket' phrase. It was the deliberate and provocative distortion of what had been said, and what had been done, that lowered confidence in the Government and in Harold. In all this the Tory politicians were more than helped by the largely Tory Press.

What began to emerge during the devaluation period was talk of the need for an Industrial Relations Bill. George Brown was one of the first to raise it. We had to make a demonstration to overseas financiers, and also to the general public in this country, that some of the strikes which had added enormously to the drain on our balance of payments could be stopped. People were very angry about industrial disputes, and opinion polls showed that they thought something ought to be done about them. The fact that many were unable to distinguish between the unofficial wildcat strike and the officially organized strike was never really recognized. The general public was then, and remains today, unclear about the distinction between the two. Labour politicians felt they should act in this area and show that from now on we would try to work out a solution to industrial stoppages through Government action. Of course the main events that forced Labour into devaluation were overseas, but it is true that the industrial disputes had helped to push us right over the brink.

The question had come up and from then on industrial relations became a growing topic of conversation.

But the most immediate political repercussion of devaluation was the future of Jim Callaghan. This was indeed a period for the connoisseur in politics. After the sharp act of 18 November there was mounted what I think one might call a 'Rescue Jim' campaign. His closest friends all played their parts. Even a relative who wrote for the Press assigned himself a minor role. The line was that Jim had been shut away in Harold Wilson's 'parity prison' and unable to change policy because of his master's fixation. If only Jim could have burst out with a resounding bang all would have been different. The whole drama was played to absolute perfection.

Jim Callaghan tendered his resignation the week after devaluation but only after he had, in a most forthright and courageous way, put before the House all that was needed to go with it.

My favourite picture

Inside the front door

The Cabinet Room

The 'New' Garden Girls
with Bill Housden

Some of the Political
Office staff

The Prime Minister
and some of the
Labour Party staff

Susan Lewis and myself
in my room next to the
Cabinet Room

My sister and me

The 'Hungarian Twins' at a *Time-Life* party

Preparing for 1966 election prior to Prorogation

Mrs. Wilson and Lady
(Beattie) Plummer at
a Christmas party

Sir Joseph and Lady
Kagan (Gannex) and
family at Chequers

A Christmas Joke: The Prime Minister with his son and
daughter-in-law at Chequers

Mr. Wilson with Mrs. Wilson and his sister in the Pillared Room

On board *Tiger*

On board *Fearless*

THE SHADOW OF THE POUND

While the Press briefing of some politicians slowly turned the blame towards Harold, nothing could be done except sit and watch. The operation needed little extra outside impetus since there were others not deeply concerned for Jim's welfare who were only too anxious to cash in on it if it caused a vacancy at the top.

Harold naturally refused to accept Jim's resignation. Devaluation, as he saw it, was a collective and not an individual decision, however much others might want to turn it. When Jim tendered his resignation he wanted Harold to appoint Tony Crosland to the Treasury. This was in a sense a pay-off for 1963 when he, together with Gaitskell's principal adviser, masterminded Callaghan's leadership campaign. It would also have been a putsch to put Mr Gaitskell's chosen heir in his rightful place. It was assumed by many in the early 1960s that in a Gaitskell Government, Tony Crosland would have ended up in the Treasury after a token period spent there by Jim Callaghan.

The situation after devaluation was not easy for Harold, nor was the choice of the new Chancellor.

Roy Jenkins has always been surrounded by a devoted group of supporters. His easy successes at the Home Office deservedly earned him an enormous reputation, and his skill in the House was well recognized. Yet the stories circulating were mainly to the effect that Harold would choose Tony, and that he dare not give the job to Roy since Roy would soon so outshine everyone that it would be too dangerous.

Jim allowed the 'will he won't he' situation to continue for a little time. It was to his advantage either way. During the arguments about his reasons for going and who would replace him, there would inevitably arise the question of Harold's own suitability for staying on too. It was also the case that if Jim decided to go he would still wield considerable influence since his splendid isolation behind the Treasury bench would appear like martyrdom.

Harold for his part wanted no resignations and the consequent stories about splits and arguments. He wanted the ranks closed and the best possible man put in the Treasury. He wanted Jim Callaghan given a new lease of life elsewhere. He had other candidates to consider besides Roy – not only Tony

Crosland but also Denis Healey. But the best and quickest reshuffle was clearly a straight swap.

The other candidates would have involved more than one move since Jim Callaghan was unlikely to accept a straight swap with Denis Healey to Defence, or with Tony Crosland to the Board of Trade. So Roy it was. This decision was made very early. Before it was put to Jim, however, contingency arrangements had to be made. There was the question of what would happen if Jim finally decided to go to the back benches. Then Harold would need a new Home Secretary. For this reason Dick Crossman was sounded out to see if he would agree to take on this job in such an eventuality. He agreed. He thought it exciting and was simultaneously both disappointed and pleased when the situation was finally resolved as it was.

But Jim's acute political antennae kept him in the Government. He accepted the new post. He was 'free' to express himself now in a new way.

Because of these prior contingency arrangements, it was believed afterwards that Dick Crossman suggested Roy to Harold. This is both true and false. Dick did not know when he came to Harold's room in the Commons to discuss the situation that Harold had in fact already made up his mind. Indeed all the possibilities had been examined and the decision taken at Chequers the week before. When Dick was told that Jim wanted to go and that Harold needed to replace him, Dick immediately suggested Roy. Harold quite naturally said he thought this right. Many were to be more sceptical around Harold and worried about what such a move might mean for Harold's personal future. They had deep forebodings about it all. They knew too well the intensity of Roy's followers and their dedication to getting Roy into No. 10.

Roy was appointed, not a little surprised, I think, after the heavy pro-Tony Crosland briefing which had gone out. He emerged slightly flushed and happy-looking from his talks with Harold.

After it was all over Harold sat down for a drink with a number of close friends to take stock of the situation. Everyone was at the House of Commons where the major part of the reshuffle of posts took place.

The Prime Minister's large room there, while dignified, does not in fact lend itself to cosy chats. It is a very high-ceilinged room, long with deep windows overlooking New Palace Yard. Down the centre of the room is a long green baize-covered table, surrounded by green leather chairs with the House of Commons crest on them. This table is used for emergency Cabinet meetings which have to be held at the House of Commons rather than No. 10.

At either end of the room there are old-fashioned, green hide horsehair sofas, but there is one comfortable armchair near the Prime Minister's chair in the centre of the table.

It is not a very inviting room for social occasions. It is a workmanlike room. At one end, near the doors leading to the Secretaries' rooms, is an enormous, ornately carved, wooden cupboard where stationery and drinks are kept. A huge glass mirror over the cupboard adds light to the room and acts as a constant reminder that there are others present as you sit there or walk around.

The heavy gold brocade curtains can be closed against the night and weather outside. Often we left them open, just to look out over New Palace Yard and the buildings lit up opposite in Parliament Square.

Despite its lack of comfort we liked it. I was once told that when Lord Attlee was Prime Minister his family used to climb from the windows on to a flat roof immediately below. Often, the story went, they used it to view official ceremonies like the Opening of Parliament or a function in Westminster Hall. They were eventually warned that the building was not constructed to stand people walking up and down on that part of it, and the Attlees had to give it up. How true the story is I don't know, but it was a nice one.

We all stopped there for a little while that night to have drinks and take stock of the new situation. A new era was clearly starting. The old triumvirate had gone. It was another turning-point. 'Sir Galahad' had arrived in the person of Roy.

Harold and he established quickly a close working relationship. And, let's face it, they needed to do this.

Labour had devalued, certainly, but a watchful eye had to be kept on how things would work out in both the short term and the long term. Roy's period at the Home Office, while it must have been thoroughly fascinating, had not conditioned him for the task ahead. If the situation had been a good one the transition might have been easy. But it was bad and the initial impact on Roy seemed considerable.

Yet his basic training as an economist, and his understanding and knowledge of finance, were to keep him in play until he had the measure of it all. The Parliamentary Party were on his side too, and wanting him to succeed in such difficult circumstances. This was half the battle won.

The Parliamentary Labour Party had rallied magnificently to Harold and Jim despite the shock. But the package hurt, as Harold knew it would; and when they also realized that there were significant back-up arrangements in case of any post-devaluation dangers to sterling, they were more than a little disillusioned. To them it seemed we had got out of the strait jacket without having escaped the tie-ups they had loathed so much in the previous years.

There was thus a happy hunting-ground for any faction wanting a new Leader, and some close to both new and old Chancellors were too hooked on these activities to let the opportunity go by. I have no doubt, too, that disappointments elsewhere within the Government helped to keep the scalp-hunters happy.

Dick Crossman, happy in his own knowledge that he had created Roy, formed a working alliance with him which included Barbara Castle from time to time. They were regarded by many as the new trio manipulating Harold.

We moved quickly and curiously then into a brief, sharp, nasty period when an issue of policy and principle was used for other reasons.

This was the possibility of renewing the sale of arms to South Africa, which for the Parliamentary Labour Party was the last straw. They had been assaulted quite enough on home affairs without having an overseas policy of principle wrecked for them too.

While the main drama relating to the change in Chancellors had been played out mostly in the Palace of Westminster, the South African arms story was played out in No. 10 mostly, it seemed to me, in my room downstairs. This was not really true but certainly there were comings and goings there on a grand scale throughout the whole day and late into the night. I seemed to be always replenishing the stock of drinks in there and getting the glasses washed as visitors came and went. Those who were close to Harold, who wanted to be informed of what was going on and to know what he was going to do, called in almost without stop.

Some Cabinet members felt, quite rightly, that the question of the sale of arms to South Africa had to be considered in the context of the realities of the economic situation. But nobody really dreamt a Labour Government would be so irresponsible or foolhardy as to revoke the decision they had taken in 1964 on taking office. Technically, however, before it went to Cabinet it had to be considered by the special Defence Committee who had the obligation of looking at all its implications, both for Defence and for economic reasons.

It was Jim Callaghan who set the fire burning by accidentally letting the Parliamentary Labour Party know that the matter was under review. Once reported as a fact there emerged a growing distortion of the whole thing, and eventually the issue itself was used as an instrument to question the Prime Minister's ultimate authority. It was an extremely sensitive situation for him. What was not realized by the Parliamentary Labour Party was that the Prime Minister was initially in a minority on the question. Many surprising characters who have since turned around were the principal advocates. Even those whose reputations had been built up on a liberal image were no better. Be it Rhodesia, Kenya Asians, arms to South Africa, or whatever, some escaped notice who should have been identified as supporters of reactionary right-wing policies.

Only after the small hunting parties of 'braves' had overreached themselves, and their briefings to the Press and to the Parliamentary Labour Party had got out of hand, did the situation resolve itself with Harold's final victory in Cabinet.

Dick Crossman unnerved everyone the weekend before the Cabinet decision by trying to work out one of his famous compromises which would have made things infinitely more dangerous. But it was purely a suggestion of mechanics and not one of principle.

Once those who were deeply involved within the Cabinet realized the sort of tide that was running inside the Parliamentary Labour Party, they quickly backed down; and when the Cabinet finally met, although Harold himself did not wish to press the issue to a vote, it was decided to take one, and many of those who before had taken one view now fell into line.

John Silkin was marvellous throughout and kept Harold fully informed of every development in the Parliamentary Labour Party. But he often had to be calmed down himself, so great was his anger at some of the stories reaching him.

Like the rest of us at No. 10 he felt Harold had gone through enough that year without this squalid episode being played out as well. John was deeply angry about it all and was as shocked as we were by some of those who were either genuinely prepared to sell arms to South Africa, or who were using this particular episode for other reasons. It was difficult to clarify even now to those outside how the two issues had been so cleverly intertwined.

Harold and those close to him were in a state of shock by the end of this episode. Everyone had soldiered on through devaluation and had watched mesmerized the technique used to switch the spotlight of responsibility totally to Harold. Then a breathing space was given with the reshuffle, the very novelty of which took some getting used to, only for all of us to be hit by a sledge-hammer on South Africa.

Then with Christmas only a few days away, Harold Holt, the Prime Minister of Australia, went swimming and never returned. So the No. 10 machinery ground to a halt while arrangements were made to fly to Canberra to what was to be the second 'working funeral' that year.

It was a tribute to Harold Holt's personality and status that he was honoured so widely at such a great gathering. From the United Kingdom the official plane took not only Prince Charles, but the Prime Minister and the Leader of the Opposition as well.

In Melbourne the scene was somewhat overwhelming, with President Johnson's entourage and the protection given him taking the Australians by surprise. It had never seen anything done on such an enormous scale before.

Our own security people who went out were highly amused by it all. Harold's chief detective, Inspector Gordon Fryer, scored game, set and match with his story of the visit and a conversation with American opposite numbers in the Cathedral at the Memorial Service. The Americans were curious to know why it was that Gordon and another detective were all that Harold had in the form of protection, and that Prince Charles had only one detective. 'Yes,' replied the Palace detective, we were told, 'but we have a fabulous radar system, as you know, back at HQ'. The Americans became silent, clearly wondering what speciality we had been able to devise. Obviously there must be something in it with the heir to the throne involved!

Back home we were in a bad state. I had prepared thousands of Christmas cards for Harold's signature. Now Mary was left to sign them all herself and we had hundreds of Christmas presents to hand out on Harold's behalf. It had been a depressing year and we felt it was an appropriately depressing beginning to Christmas.

Harold returned tired out after the long flight to Australia and back. Immediately he was off with Mary to Chequers for Christmas and to the Isles of Scilly for their wedding anniversary.

We staggered out of 1967 and into the New Year. That is the only way in which I can describe our feelings.

9

The Communicators

'Tis with our judgement as our watches, none
Go just alike, yet each believes his own.

ALEXANDER POPE

Harold Wilson's Government attracted controversy. That was natural. All Labour Governments should be controversial. But nothing has caused greater arguments in the media than his relations with Press and television. That again is natural, for the media, understandably, are obsessed with themselves and certainly nobody would describe Harold's interest in them as exactly superficial.

The Press version of relations with Harold is simple. It is suggested always that in his brief period as Leader, and during his first years as Prime Minister, they were not hostile to him and never vituperative. It is put forward that they were used as the instruments of his propaganda rather than acting as the independent people, with interests of their own, that they really are.

There is a good deal of truth in this. Harold did get huge coverage during the early years. He was a new face at the top. He was of use to them whether or not they were of use to him.

At the start of his period as Leader of the Party, Harold was the beneficiary of the journalists' main imperative, giving the public what it wants, today's news. He was the beneficiary because, being new, he was newsworthy in himself. Everything he did automatically attracted attention.

From the moment I first met him, he also had a particularly

strong resentment of the fact that the British Press is predominantly right-wing. This is something all good Labour
politicians resent and rightly. The vast power wielded by the
Press is hardly likely to commend itself to a Labour leader
when the Party's case so often fails to get across because of
insufficient reporting while the trivia, because they happen to
be newsworthy, are given the big coverage.

Despite this he felt an admiration for the working journalists
who had to live in the world of the Tory-dominated Press
while often being more inclined our way.

Because of the Tories' control over most of the Press, he
welcomed, as did most Labour people, the television revolution.
Television news started to give much more coverage immediately to political news. With the arrival of Independent
Television News, the Labour Party's advantages grew. Here
was a body that was controlled by rules demanding impartiality.
We were given a fairer crack of the whip. Another factor was
that the television camera cannot lie, inasmuch as the viewer
sees on his screen a man he either likes or dislikes on sight. He is
able then to make the sort of judgement he makes daily in his
ordinary life. He isn't being told by a newspaper writer that
'such and such' is ghastly. He is able to look at the figure
directly, hear him speak and make up his own mind about what
he thinks of him.

Now no doubt our pundits would like to wish this away, but
the plain fact remains that the high popularity rating of Harold
Wilson on all the opinion polls over very many years shows that
people liked and still like what they see on television. As for
Mr Heath, his record speaks for itself!

Harold started off with a number of other advantages with
the television and with the Press, but the deep misunderstanding which was to exist about their respective roles has
never been removed.

He still cannot accept that the journalist's and TV man's
role is limited to getting news, however unpleasant or however
pleasant, and to get it into the newspapers or on to the screen.
The journalist has no deep psychological interpretation of his
role. Frequently he couldn't make one if asked. He merely
passes on the stuff he gets and his editor views it in a similar
fashion. Only the final directive from the top, under which

they all work on the particular newspaper, decides the paper's policy and often how the journalist's story is treated.

Harold subconsciously accepts that this is the fact, yet daily resists the operation of it, as if he somehow feels he can influence the journalists' natural working pattern.

The journalists, for their part, never realized at the start how he felt, because the Wilson bandwagon was going along so rapidly that when they did eventually come to realize this basic misunderstanding about their role, it was too late to correct it.

By then there had been too much between them, both on the credit and debit sides.

What did the journalists gain from the Wilson years?

Harold did everything he could to give them greater status and respect, particularly to the Lobby journalists. Harold Wilson has always got on well with the Lobby system in the House of Commons where so much information can be exchanged and yet no attribution made, even if there are fingermarks everywhere. During his early years the Lobby consisted of senior people who had behind them years of political writing and a specialist knowledge of the political system. As the Lobby grew in numbers, however, the quality went down. Their own rules began often to be broken and the standards they originally imposed upon themselves were not always kept.

Now there can be two views of whether the Lobby system is a good or bad one or whether it should be preserved or abolished. An equally good argument can be made out for both. Harold could see both sides. He liked being able to talk off the cuff to a group of likeable chaps who were not involved in his own dramas in a personal sense, but were sufficiently *au fait* and friendly personally to be able to understand and to discuss all the ramifications with him on an informed but informal basis.

On the other hand, he did very much want to see the emergence of a Reston or Lippman. He would like, too, to have seen the establishment of the open, on-the-record, regular Press conference, so that there could be a dual system of Lobby-type meetings and open Press conferences operating together. We went into Downing Street after a period when our personal relations with the Press had been excellent.

The election campaign itself was run on a very cordial basis which culminated in an end-of-campaign presentation to Harold at the Adelphi Hotel, Liverpool, from the accompanying correspondents. They invited Harold to one of their suites where they thanked him for the co-operation and help he had given them. He was terribly pleased and valued the beautifully inscribed books they gave him more than most gifts.

The next period, immediately after the 1964 election, saw this cordial atmosphere partially retained, though the transfer to No. 10, with all the remoteness this involves, started to open up a gulf.

Although most of the men at the top in the Press world remained anti-Labour, outright hostility was veiled while the razor-edge situation remained. For one thing there was so much happening that news clearly had priority over views.

But once Labour was back the objectives of the Tory Press were clear and the battle lines drawn up.

There was an obvious determination to stop another Labour victory. There were to be no further Labour Governments and as a first means of ensuring this they had to get rid of Harold Wilson, whose popularity and political dexterity seemed likely to defeat them in their objectives. It was after the 1966 election, therefore, that their system came fully into operation again and they returned to normal business. And their normal business turned out to be not only a violent anti-Labour campaign, which was sustained throughout the years of the 1966 to 1970 Government, but an even more sustained and vicious personal campaign against Harold Wilson himself.

Yet to go back to late 1964 and 1965, throughout all that time we carried on much as we had before the 1964 election. Our Press relations were all done on an improvised basis with Harold taking regular Lobby meetings, and generally feeding out the daily tightrope sagas himself, backed up by the No. 10 Press Officer's conferences.

Harold's first Press act was to appoint Trevor Lloyd-Hughes, of the *Liverpool Daily Post*, as his Press Secretary.

He did this because he wanted a Lobby man who knew the Lobby world of Parliament and Whitehall. He needed this help particularly as all were so green in their jobs in Government. He felt that to appoint a senior daily or Sunday Lobby journalist would cause offence to those who felt they might have been chosen. He was both right and wrong again. Both at the same time, since of course appointing a major figure would have caused offence, but so did Trevor's appointment. Here was a provincial man, elevated above his nominal superiors, to whom they had to come for stories. This stuck in many gullets. One day he had been the Lobby's friend and liked by them all. The next they were doubtful about his whole character.

Harold liked Trevor. He got on well with him personally, and there should have been the basis for a strong and sound working relationship. The trouble was that no one listened to outside voices warning or criticism and no one took a closer look to see if anything needed to be done to put the Press set-up in better shape.

Trevor, I think, failed the first hurdle. He was not a forceful character, not pushing enough. He failed to analyse his personal role within No. 10 correctly, and failed to work out what sort of relationship he ought to have with the varied assortment of people there. He was told that he was a civil servant, and, therefore, the impartial dispenser of Government news. He turned therefore, totally and immediately to the Private Office for guidance and direction, and to Harold when he could make contact with him. In those early days this was not enough. The Private Office people were not sufficiently confident of our permanency to give the best advice to an outsider who might be even more temporary. They were unused, too, to acting as intermediaries.

Harold Macmillan's Press Secretary, Harold Evans, who has now become legendary as an example of a perfect No. 10 Press Secretary, had regular and intimate access to the Prime Minister. But because of the nature of our success in 1964 and the background to the victory we won, it was impossible for Trevor to have such regular and frequent access to Harold. He had, too, the problem of not being able to work out with Harold right from the start what role he should play, how his office should be organized, and what Harold personally expected of him and how Harold personally saw the work of his Press Secretary.

Civil servant or not, Trevor had the right to organize his office as he wished, but he sorely needed guidance on it.

Because he lacked this guidance he became as a consequence more of a civil servant than the civil servants, and so impartial as to make his news statements sometimes sound devoid of content.

In all this Trevor, immensely likeable, generous and kindly, a man of enormous charm and warmth, walked deeper and deeper into a sea of discontent on one side and intrigue elsewhere. He walked on unaware of what was happening, busily tailoring a new character which he felt was required of him in his new role.

The truth is, I am convinced, that Trevor was far too nice for that job at such a time in politics. Against the background of 1964 Trevor was too pleasant a person to succeed in pleasing his customers and employer both at the same time.

His cheerfulness and optimism nevertheless were a never-ending source of encouragement, particularly during the worst patches. When he went into No. 10 he wasn't even a Labour supporter. I suppose he was a 'don't know', with Liberal leanings. But his personal devotion and loyalty to Harold were total and Harold drew on it. He liked Trevor: he remembered their friendship over many years (not least during the 1960 'troubles') and he trusted him implicitly.

For many reasons then, we were forced by the summer of 1965 into the ever-increasing realization that we needed a political Press man in Downing Street, acting separately, independently and politically with the Press on Harold's behalf. An abortive attempt was made to obtain the services of John Harris, who was keen, but not only were there objections from the civil servants, but also from the National Executive Committee of the Party too. Indeed, the NEC objections came from one of Mr Gaitskell's closest friends who raised the strongest outcry possible at the thought of installing one of Hugh's closest confidants in Downing Street, working for Harold. What wounds there still appeared to be from 1960!

On the Civil Service side it was finally conceded that someone might be assigned, but he would have to sit in No. 12 so that the direct connection could be denied. What is so easy to achieve instantly today was so painful to establish then.

What would this man call himself? they asked. What then? Finally the elaborate title of Parliamentary Press Liaison

Officer was decided upon and Gerald Kaufman came, for better or worse, in October 1965. But the pettifogging criticism didn't end there. The battle continued, highlighted by a ludicrous and trivial scene when a most senior member of the Private Office was discovered physically snatching sheets of No. 10 notepaper out of Gerald's hands and telling him he could under no circumstances use it. There immediately followed further discussions and discussions, and discussions, about notepaper and when it could or could not be used by this outside gentleman.

Harold carried on, enormously overworked, but still generating his own news industry without realizing the day would soon arrive when rationalization and rethinking of the whole relationship would be needed. That day arrived soon after his triumphant 1966 return.

Harold has been accused of exploiting the Lobby system. Exploitation is a curious criticism to use about a system which feeds solely on the use made by one body of another. Perhaps mutual exploitation might be more valid but the word is still unacceptable. Harold genuinely felt that this was the vehicle he should use, and that as a democrat he should help to turn it into something better than it was. He is guilty indeed of trying, if one can pardon the expression, to create a new style of political journalism with the Lobby as a 'special court' base.

For that reason, whenever he went overseas consideration was given to whether the plane was large enough to hold the accompanying Press entourage. If not, could arrangements be altered to make it possible? If still impossible, could an extra Press plane be organized to fly out at the same time? Aboard the plane special treatment was again given to these gentlemen and at the destination special arrangements had to be made for the 'British contingent'.

Often this was not convenient to Harold, nor welcomed personally. He was not – although the myth says he was – continually anxious to be in communication with the Press. Quite the contrary, on occasions, when he was very tired or particularly worried, he would have preferred often to skip the odd Press conference or the talks on the plane. But he wanted the journalists to feel he accepted their wish that he should be accessible and he made himself so. He wanted them also to accept that he recognized and respected their role in Britain's political life.

Of course, I don't want to give the impression that he bravely staggered on, quipping and joking with Press men, even when it took its toll on his health and strength. It seemed politically worth while as well. It is no part of his character to ignore the reality or to be stand-offish or condescending. But nevertheless it is equally true that it was not always easy for him to be so accessible or so friendly for so much of the time.

One of the other difficulties about the day-to-day running of Press relations was that requests poured daily into No. 10 about every trivial detail relating to the personal life of the Wilson family, or of other little details affecting members of the Cabinet, in addition to the larger questions about major issues of government policy. This meant that the Press Office was always under excessive pressure, particularly because of the care taken in answering queries, no matter how small they were. I understand that this was not a practice that had been followed by previous administrations. Then the No. 10 Press Office limited itself to answering only the questions relating to government policy and leaving the little details to other sources. If this sort of approach has been re-established at No. 10 then it is a much needed one since no Press Office, particularly one with the number of staff at No. 10, should even attempt to answer some of the questions we received.

For instance, there would be the query about Harold's dog and why his paws were in a bad condition and, if they were, whether he had been to the vet recently. There would be questions about what make of pipe Harold smoked, his brand of tobacco or his favourite colour in ties. All of these, no doubt, are questions which go to make up the image which the Press wanted to write about, but for a key office of this kind to be inundated with this sort of telephone inquiry was ridiculous. But so meticulous were Harold and Trevor about accommodating the Press at every level that they allowed this situation to develop to the point where the Press Secretary was being rung up in the night about incredible trivia.

The turning-point in Harold's Press relations was the 1966 election.

The campaign was a very low-key one and inevitably this

meant that the close relationship we had with the Press in 1964 was not so much in evidence in 1966.

Then, once back at No. 10, the trouble began. A series of what Harold sees himself as political blunders brought with them bad Press coverage, and that in its turn saddened and angered him.

Outside events such as the seamen's strike and Harold's phrase about the 'tightly knit groups of politically motivated men' were followed by the 1966 'leadership plot' stories. Hard on the heels of this came the D Notices affair, the real watershed, reminiscent for the Press of the Vassall Tribunal and the six journalists who were then put on trial. The hostile and often inaccurate reporting of the first two events, and the understandable reaction of the Press to the third, produced a new and nasty turn in Press relations.

Soon the Prime Minister's regular meetings with the Lobby were discontinued and his meetings with them became rare. From then on their usual stories came either from unidentified sources within No. 10 or Whitehall or the House of Commons. Their reporting became increasingly hostile and even at times hysterical, and the personal vilification of Harold himself started to assert itself.

Side by side with this, however, grew a compensating good publicity given to Mary, almost like a subconscious inbuilt apology to Harold. Increasingly she became a political asset in publicity terms and extra thought had to be given to her projection, though she asked for little help and took the handling of it all confidently and very successfully upon herself.

Despite the personal attacks on Harold, his popularity in the country fell only marginally during that period. It always remained fairly high, and very high within his own Party. For this he could thank television and the visual first-hand assessment that each individual could make of him throughout the period.

Yet the Press campaign hurt, and hurt deeply. It became most onerous on those occasions when his family, especially Mary, were involved. One occasion particularly distressed him, when she came to him at breakfast in floods of tears after reading the papers, and asked if the attacks on him would never stop.

Yet serious thought had to be given to a way through to creating a new relationship with the Press, and a number of experiments were tried. One was a regular series of dinners at Chequers or lunches at No. 10 for each individual newspaper. Usually the owner, editor, managing director and chief political writer were invited, together with Harold and Trevor – inevitably all-male affairs. These were usually at Chequers and many guests stayed overnight. For the majority it was their very first visit to the Prime Minister's country home, and Harold had thought they would find this an interesting and enjoyable part of the invitation as well as giving them the opportunity to talk directly to the Prime Minister over dinner. It was surprising how many distinguished Tories had never been inside Chequers before.

Then he tried the experiment which became humorously known as the 'White Commonwealth Experiment'. As the Lobby had grown to enormous numbers, and since the regular meetings with all members were found impossible, it was decided to have fortnightly evening meetings at No. 10 with senior Lobby correspondents from a number of daily and Sunday papers. Unfortunately this leaked and caused great resentment to those not invited, and Trevor particularly disliked the idea, because it didn't include provincial papers. Consequently he rarely attended himself, though Gerald was usually present. I acted as the maid on these occasions, serving drinks and sandwiches, and Mary would call in to say 'hello' at some point in the evening.

Those evenings are particularly funny to me in retrospect, since some of the most sycophantic people present who each religiously recorded in their write-ups every word spoken by Harold are now amongst those who are most scathing about him. I never noticed such courage and independence of thought then, but perhaps in the case of one, whose mental acrobatics are becoming increasingly irritating, the new-style commercial journalism of the group for which he works lends itself more easily to such inconsistencies.

Those 'White Commonwealth' meetings were held in the White Boudoir – a very appropriate place! This was the small State sitting room on the first floor of the building. The sessions would often last three to four hours and were spent assessing not only the Government's position and its work, but the whole political scene as well as the fortunes and prospects of the Tory Party and of Mr Edward Heath.

By 1968 these meetings ended and, with the eventual re-organization of the official Press set-up at No. 10, the old Lobby meetings were reinstated.

The 'White Commonwealth' experiment was a failure because it was run like a seminar with Harold trying to make the journalists see the true light about our achievements and about our parliamentary and political set-backs and difficulties. He, therefore, became incensed when those same people proceeded later to write what seemed to him further trivial pieces based on a short-term, often sensational political event, rather than on the longer-term implications and background to which Harold had tried to direct them. The basic mis-understanding clearly still remained on both sides. They were there to report news and stories, and only a few to write informed long-term comments. 'Whither Labour' might be all right for some papers, but for the rest it was news that was wanted, news and not necessarily facts. Perhaps that's what galled most of all – it was news often based, as Harold saw it, on inaccurate facts.

Legend has it that Harold went into purdah at the time of the 1967 devaluation and remained there until Labour's fortunes revived. This is not so. On advice from many, long before devaluation, he decided to withdraw personally from direct Press contact and try a different approach.

This was because, as Labour's troubles developed, the Press attack and criticism were too great to be handled by the old method. Indeed the old method tended to exacerbate the difficulties.

Unfortunately the new methods also tended to do so as well in some cases. But he was never in purdah. There was no period of time when he had no communication with the Press at all. Indeed, quite the contrary, since a number of other methods were being tried out, though none obvious. The backstage method used almost totally by Edward Heath is described in the latter as 'open Government', while in Harold Wilson it was described as shrinking self-consciously and guiltily into purdah.

By the end of 1968 the nearness of the election run-up period demanded reappraisals again. Trevor was to move to the Cabinet Office to co-ordinate Government information and Joe Haines, the No. 2 political writer on the *Sun* newspaper, was brought in to No. 10 during 1969, first as Trevor's deputy and later as his replacement, as Press Secretary.

Joe Haines's arrival obviated the need for any further experiments and the old system was brought back. Joe Haines's style was rougher and more direct than Trevor's, and he had a honeymoon period in the Lobby that lasted out the Labour Government's life.

As we came nearer to the election, and as the polls slowly started to turn, Joe's job became easier as the news once again was generating itself within the building, both by the Government's actions and by Harold himself. The Press attacks, though still harsh, gradually lost some of their hysterical content. Still the vituperation of the past had left its mark on Harold. It was not the attack on his political views he resented, but the personalization of the attacks. The Press had turned everything into a denigration of his personal character, of his integrity and his honesty. He was, they had said, cunning, devious, a liar and a cheat. There was no word bad enough for him either by direct wording or by implication. Quite understandably, he deeply resented such a low level of attack.

No campaign was more sustained than the campaign against Harold on this personal level. His political views and attitudes were torn apart with his personal character. The two were put together and entwined so closely that it was impossible for people in time to judge them separately. This was the whole objective behind the campaign. The ordinary journalist involved in it was the unwitting instrument of that campaign, launched to destroy Harold Wilson's personal credibility in order eventually to destroy his political credibility as well.

The task for the Tories was to get rid of him at any cost and the cost was indeed a heavy one for him. This is really why such an enormous gulf opened up between Harold Wilson and the Press. He did not expect anything other than criticism from those who work for papers where a totally opposite political view is held. He expected the criticism to be harsh and often vicious, but he never expected it to be so brutally unkind. Clearly politicians should not be over sensitive, but there must also be limits to the kind of criticism to which they are subjected.

Yet, despite all this, and even during the worst periods, he continued to treat journalists as he felt they should be treated. They were invited to represent the British Press at most of the functions which were organized at No. 10. Not just the higher levels in the Press, but those at the more working political level.

But what of his relations with the real influence behind the newspapers – the owners and editors? On a personal basis I must say that in the main they were good.

The unique relationship for all Labour leaders is with the IPC Group, which includes the *Daily Mirror*, the *Sunday Mirror* and the *People*. For Harold it was more unique than for most.

Cecil King, the Chairman of IPC, did not get a job when the Government was formed because Harold felt he did not qualify for a Cabinet post, as many others had a better claim, and he felt the offer of anything less would be badly received. He was certainly right in that. They started off, therefore, at the beginning of the Labour Government clearly on the wrong foot. I doubt if Hugh Gaitskell, however, or any other Prime Minister of any other party would have been any more understanding. Perhaps Mr King wanted more consultation? But perhaps he didn't fully realize how difficult it was for the Labour Government just to keep going in those first few months, let alone remember to call in for consultation all those whose contribution could be valuable. Often the person is willing and anxious, but unable to act because of timetable difficulties.

As it was, the relationship deteriorated until the 1968 outburst, by Cecil King against Harold, on which we have preserved for posterity a box file of fascinating letters from all over the country commenting on the occasion. This occasion came only a few months after Mrs King had asked most anxiously and solicitously at a No. 10 party that we should all do our best to look after the Prime Minister since he was clearly tired. He was indeed.

For Harold the balance in his relationship with IPC was

preserved by his friendship with Hugh Cudlipp. Hugh Cudlipp is perhaps the only remaining outstanding old-style newspaper man in Fleet Street, extrovert, abrasive, forceful and dominating, yet utterly fascinating for all those reasons and more. He still towers over the present Fleet Street scene. There have, of course, been policy disagreements between them, yet they have retained throughout a close and friendly working relationship, no doubt because they both come from similar backgrounds where hard work has been the first criterion for success.

It is common knowledge that Harold gets on well with Lord Thomson. However, I believe he had been particularly naïve in his approach to the Thomson ambitions. *The Times* takeover was the classic example of Harold's too innocent acceptance of what for many other Labour members would have been open to suspicion. He believed quite genuinely that Lord Thomson would, as he said, ensure the political impartiality of *The Times* newspaper once he secured control over it. Indeed, assurances were given to the Monopolies Commission. Of course, evidence from other Thomson newspapers suggested that, while Lord Thomson is clearly a Tory, his papers often give good coverage to Labour and retain some air of holding the middle ground. However, to show his good faith to Harold, Lord Thomson immediately appointed as editor of *The Times* a former Tory Parliamentary candidate who in his turn selected a whole host of Conservative writers to support him in his impartial exercise.

Yet he continued in close relationship with Lord Thomson, on very friendly terms and dining with the organization regularly as with others.

His most unusual Press relationship was perhaps with the *Telegraph* owners, the Hartwells. Rigorously Tory, harshly anti-Labour, they managed nevertheless to carry out their role with more dignity than most of those they support and to carry on, too, some of the best old-style traditions in British journalism. Lady Hartwell is, of course, the more fascinating. Everywhere she goes she is the centre of a perpetually-mesmerized male audience. Vivacious, attractive, socially charming, she manages to fascinate leading Labour figures as much as Conservative. When Harold became Labour's Leader, she took on a wager that she would one day lure him along to one of her functions, since he said he did not go in for that sort of thing. She never succeeded, but a compromise was reached and Lord Hartwell and she dined at Chequers. Harold, like so many others, enjoys her company enormously. Indeed, we have often been amused at functions when rough-cut characters have deserted other company as soon as Lady Pamela arrived.

Her gentle husband is the perfect foil, quietly guiding his newspaper in the best tradition of journalism, even if in the worst tradition of politics. It was because of his respect for their independent contributions, however hostile politically, to the journalistic world, that Harold decided to make Lord Hartwell a life peer and therefore a real 'Press Baron' in his own right.

So much for Harold's relations with the Press. But what of his relations with television?

Because of the fact that Independent Television was organized in a very distinctive way and had a safeguard of impartiality imposed on it, Harold's relations with it were always entirely different from his relations with the BBC.

Certain sections of Independent Television were, of course, positively welcomed by him. For instance, the Granada Group in the North of England, with the immense influence it has, is well known to him through the Labour life peer, Lord Bernstein, who owns and controls it with his family. But other parts of Independent Television, even where owned by Conservatives, were more easy to get on with because they are subject to the rulings of the Authority. Often of course the interviews would be as rough and as difficult for Harold on Independent Television as on the BBC. No one would accuse George Ffitch for instance of treading more softly than Robin Day. Equally, while Alistair Burnet is the epitome of the middle-class gentleman, he nevertheless can be extremely acute and cutting in his interviews. So there was no escaping the toughness within an interview. What there was, that was missing elsewhere, was the implicit protection against untrue bias, and where bias occurred, machinery for appeal.

In the early days of the Labour Government, there was an asset in having as editor of ITN Sir Geoffrey Cox. Geoffrey Cox was a close friend of George Wigg's and consequently came to know Harold very well through George Wigg. Their relationship became a close one and added to the advantages we had in those early years. Then Geoffrey Cox left to go to Yorkshire Television, was knighted and was replaced at ITN by the elegant Nigel Ryan. The Authority is there and the Act is there, and Nigel Ryan, when appealed to, or approached, recognizes the duty he has and performs his job in a most efficient manner. There has been, therefore, a straightforward relationship between the Labour Party and Independent Television. We have known where we are. They have known where they are and we know the rules that are operated and have to be operated, and both sides understand them perfectly well and their limitations.

This is the real reason why there is a difficulty with the BBC.

It has been blown up now to such proportions that it has become ridiculous. There is no doubt that Harold has been extremely angry with the BBC on a number of occasions over the years of the Labour Government and since. Before 1964 his relations were very amicable with all levels within the BBC.

But anyone who watched the BBC coverage of the last election campaign with a fair eye can really be in little doubt over the selective editing of films, and the placing of coverage within a programme. The Tory case seemed to be put over clearly and successfully with Edward Heath's own personal coverage always of the highest quality.

Labour coverage was scrappy and uneven and often a programme would include a clear-cut extract in vision of a speech by Edward Heath. On the same programme there would merely be a shot of Harold leaving a train or getting on a train and what he had said at his meeting that evening read out by an announcer, no clip of Harold speaking himself. When complaints were made, the answer would be that they had not had time to get their crew down to where he was speaking, or some other excuse.

During the last election campaign the whole thing was summed up for me in one short telephone call I made on Harold's behalf. I was told to make sure that, when he reached the hall where he was speaking, the correct arrangements had been made for him to address a meeting indoors of our Party workers in the Committee Rooms. I telephoned through as directed only to find a very jolly Party member at the other end, cheerfully telling me: 'Everything is all right, the BBC have told me they are erecting a scaffold outside for Harold to use.' Of course he had used the wrong word, though the sentiment expressed was probably right. At least it caused amusement, even if we were irritated by the daily necessity of watching every newscast and keeping a continual eye on what the BBC was doing.

The trouble with the BBC is that it is a vast bureaucratic machine that is even more buried in its own bureaucracy than the Civil Service. It operates in a very similar way, with the same sort of hierarchical system. It unfortunately means, just as in the Civil Service, that there is always a top tier of special people who appoint the same sort of special people to follow them, while just below there is a second tier of extremely imaginative competent people, who if only they could break through would alter the whole complexion and character of the Corporation.

It is untrue to say that Harold has an obsessive dislike for the BBC as a whole. He is very much aware of the set-up there. He is exasperated by the bureaucracy. It is curious that what he finds acceptable within the Civil Service, he finds unacceptable in the BBC. Perhaps, however, to be fair, he feels that entertainment and flexibility should go together rather than rigidity and entertainment. He likes many of the personalities with whom we are told he is in greatest conflict, and enjoys enormously the interviews he has done with the BBC. What he has often objected to, and will no doubt continue to do so, is the way it has been administratively run and the fact that when he has spoken freely to them about some of his fears and criticisms, these have been fed out quite blatantly for Press consumption, or fed back to other top people in the outside world. That sort of relationship is bad in any organization.

The only occasion when Harold was extremely angry was after the 1970 election. It was the now famous David Dimbleby interview for a programme called *Yesterday's Men* which sparked it off. If the actual transcript of what was said could be read by all, they would be even more convinced than they eventually were that Harold was right in what he did. David Dimbleby is a very likeable character. Until that interview everyone had wrongly believed that we were able, despite our political differences, to have a good working relationship with him. Certainly the last day at No. 10 particularly, and even afterwards, led us to believe this to be true. For this reason alone Harold was tempted to agree to do that awful programme, legendary now, a programme which, according to the BBC's letter of invitation to take part in it, was intended to be a serious study of Her Majesty's Opposition at work.

One of the most publicized broadcasting and television relationships we had at No. 10 was with David Frost.

Our first real meeting with David Frost was when he came very early in 1965 to a summer tea-party in the garden at No. 10 which was held by the United Nations, as a fund-raising activity. He was extremely funny and amusing on that occasion and we all liked him.

I suppose one could say that at that particular time his career was not yet in full gear and he had not yet worked out the right style for himself.

Because of this, more than a little attention was given to the famous Frost 'breakfast' which Harold attended. Harold went because he thought David a likeable fellow and he had got on well with him. He really did not feel that there was anything particularly outrageous in going along to a breakfast function, rather than attending a lunch or a dinner or a reception in the evening. It is a very American habit and most politicians who have often visited America are used to it. In fact it is often more convenient to accept an invitation at that time in the day, when there is a heavily crowded diary of other commitments to fulfil later on. Perhaps in view of all the Press comment, it was foolish to accept. But Harold enjoyed it and the Press criticism, harsh and unnecessary as it was, had to be lived with.

Thereafter David Frost was in constant touch with the Press Office over the years, inviting Harold to do programmes with him. I am afraid that the experience of the 'breakfast' and the Press comments made Harold very wary afterwards about accepting further invitations. The situation became so peculiar that even leading members of the Government were also avoiding invitations from David Frost because of all the comment that might accompany not only the programme but the invitation itself.

Eventually it seemed that the whole situation could best be

handled by asking David to do an interview with Harold and Mary in No. 10 itself. We reversed the order of things. We ourselves put it to him that the invitation would come from No. 10 to him rather than the other way round.

This also gave the British people a chance to see for the first time a little of the building in which the Prime Minister works, since Mary acted as guide and took David and the cameras around the main public part of the building, pointing out the special points of interest. At the end of the programme there was a straight interview with Harold which, I think, everyone found successful, though it was not the usual abrasive interview politicians have with political interviewers. It was a much more personal occasion. It was hot too. Harold described it later as a Turkish bath because the day was so hot, the study so small, and the crowd and cameras and lights all produced a very warm atmosphere indeed.

The end result was good, and the wish then everyone had to re-establish good working relations with David succeeded too. Certainly I will not forget the very kind and courteous way in which he behaved to all of us on 18 June 1970. He seemed instinctively to understand how everyone was feeling, and, whatever his own views may have been, he made a point of being exceptionally considerate, saying exactly the right thing, not in a sycophantic way, but exactly right.

The Frost programme gave rise to the idea that perhaps it could be extended to Chequers too, the country home of the Prime Minister; an interview was eventually arranged for Harold with Alistair Burnet of ITV. He came down with a team to film a tour of the house and also to do a straight interview with Harold himself.

This, too, was a success. The general public saw not only the house but the Wilson family too, at home there, with Mary, Giles and Paddy the dog, all relaxing at a weekend, as well as the interview between Alistair Burnet and Harold in the Long Gallery.

There was a general desire that the public, the ordinary elector, should have as much a share as possible, and as great a knowledge as possible, of all the special places, functions and activities in which an elected Prime Minister is engaged. Harold wanted them to know about No. 10 and what it looked like and how it worked. He wanted them to know, too, about Chequers and how that came to be used as a country home for Prime Ministers. He wanted them to see every possible facet of a Prime Minister's life. This was part of his 'style' of government, and heavily criticized though it was, it nevertheless was a total break with the past. A little had been done with the occasional photograph before but not on the scale of the Wilson years. Whether, of course, it will continue will depend upon the new occupant and those, too, in the future.

The object of these two television programmes was to help break down the isolation of the past – the isolation between those who govern and those who are governed. Harold wanted the two to be brought closer together. This was possible certainly during those two special interviews. Harold had hoped to be able to build on this. It was not to prove possible, yet anyway.

Fort Knox to *Fearless*

The Party began 1968 with a hang-over. For both factions in the devaluation argument, there came the realization that a back-up policy was necessary, and that such a policy was going to be unpleasant.

After a lot of discussion the decision was made to throw prescription charges into the package in the hope that the general public would see it as a reasonable act; the 'gnomes' would give us their confidence, and the Government would be credited with a sense of balance during a time of great crisis.

It was unfortunate, and never worth what it cost us. The financial saving was ludicrously small in real terms and the exemptions were administratively costly. From a political viewpoint it proved folly and lost a great deal of sympathy and understanding from an already greatly overstrained Parliamentary Labour Party. Curiously, George Brown, right-wing in the earlier 1951 controversy over prescription charges, now took a leading role in opposing them.

All the good intentions and measures in the January and February of 1968 to help cushion the less well off against devaluation were not sufficient compensations in the mind of the Party. When the vote on the package came in Parliament twenty-six MPs abstained.

Everyone immediately got very excited. Gerald and I were going backwards and forwards between Nos 10 and 11 like shuttlecocks with messages. The Chief Whip sent a letter to the abstainers which, though constitutionally wrong, was a fair attempt to punish them by stopping them doing the one thing that meant much to them in Parliamentary terms, attending Party meetings and taking part in the Party's Parliamentary life. Of course, it also enabled them to lecture the Party on principles. Still at least they did this inside the Party rather than outside in the columns of the Tory Press, a later venue for dissidents.

Right in the middle of all of this Harold went off on another overseas visit. He visited the Soviet Union again.

By the end of February the Parliamentary Party, still suffering from the post-devaluation package plus growing indiscipline as left-wingers abstained on issues of principle, experienced yet more anguish from the decision to restrict entry into the United Kingdom of Kenya Asian refugees carrying British passports.

To many Labour MPs immigration had been totally a question of principle, with all decisions on it to be taken on principle alone. Others, while appreciating the principle, made themselves face the realities of life on a small and crowded island.

It was left to Jim Callaghan to tell the House and the Party of the Labour Government's decision on Kenyan Asians. It was not easy for him in the context of the growing concern felt about the jettisoning of so many things in which we believed.

In the Party, both in Parliament and at Transport House, there were divided counsels. The anti-Government minority was articulate and hostile. This decision was one more straw on the camel's back.

Harold had by this time lost George Wigg from No. 10. George Wigg had decided to resign his seat in the Commons to become Chairman of the Horserace Betting Levy Board and go to the House of Lords. There was a great deal of discussion at No. 10 about George Wigg leaving and strong views were expressed on it. What is fact and contrary to later stories, is that I myself tried very hard to get Harold to persuade George Wigg to stay on in his role as Paymaster General and principal adviser.

Despite all the arguments George Wigg could not be shifted. He felt, I think, that he wanted to do something different and something which had a special meaning for him. While his going meant that he was not permanently at No. 10, it did not mean that he could not call in to see Harold. This he did over a considerable period.

George Wigg's departure was not the only change in the Prime Minister's life at this time.

One new development was seeing junior Ministers from the Department of Economic Affairs for lunch at No. 10 since Harold had taken an overall responsibility for the DEA. These meetings took place in the private flat on most Tuesdays. At these lunches, Harold was able to discuss informally all the problems the DEA faced and to put questions to each of the junior Ministers to find out just how much progress was being made within the sections for which they were responsible. The Ministers involved seemed to enjoy the gatherings, though some of them were to prove dubious in their loyalties later on.

I attended the luncheons to help make sure the meal itself went smoothly. So much talk took place that the guests often forgot to serve themselves and frequently I had to move round the table to see that they got a proper meal rather than the absent-minded helpings they served themselves.

Harold's weekends were now mainly spent playing golf as regularly as he could with my brother. It was his only recreation and almost the only chance he had to escape from the red boxes and get fresh air and exercise. In Tony, Harold had the sort of friend with whom he could chat and talk, knowing that not one word would be transmitted under any circumstances to any outside person, not even his own family. Indeed, we were always fascinated to know exactly what they did talk about on the golf course, since we never got it out of them afterwards. It is a close though odd relationship, since my brother was until recently not a committed Labour supporter.

Then suddenly there emerged another financial crisis, this time about gold. Almost inevitably, of course, it was set off by the French, whose strong views on the price of gold had been widely canvassed and had been causing havoc and distress in monetary circles for a considerable time.

Thomas Balogh's antennae were as usual acute and tuned in to what was happening. He now became a regular evening visitor to put the Prime Minister in the picture.

Talk started around the building about speculative activity overseas. At first we all imagined it meant the pound alone again. But it was much more complicated. We were so conditioned, we never really felt safe with that pound of ours for long. What we had never envisaged was an attack on it of this kind, particularly so soon after devaluation.

Thomas's inbuilt suspicion of some of the machinations of the French was now helpful. He was always so fully briefed on all they did over there that he was acutely aware of what could develop as a result of their behaviour.

What amazes me now is that, on 12 March, only two days before the climax, Harold was even able to fit in the curious engagement he undertook to be present at the unveiling ceremony of the Ramsay MacDonald memorial. We had shuddered when this had first been suggested, but had decided that it was something that should not be avoided. But Ramsay MacDonald was soon forgotten as revaluation came into the vocabulary and everyone watched the reports of French gold buying. I had visions of vast vaults somewhere in Paris overflowing with gold and desperate Americans visiting Fort Knox in squadrons to review the situation and see if their supply was safe.

When on 14 March it became clear there was a crisis of monumental proportions, everyone at No. 10 came together very quickly from all quarters, official and political. Gerald and I were over at the House anyway that day, and the Private Office stayed on despite their usual practice of leaving after Questions. By the evening others had come over with Michael Halls in charge.

Unlike devaluation, there was more waiting than action. After all, it was not our scene despite its effects on our position.

The events of the day have become Labour folklore because they led up to George Brown's resignation, though at the time this was the last thing we contemplated. The Chancellor came and went looking very preoccupied and solemn and the phones were active, and George only entered our consciousness when some of us started in our different ways the 'search' for him.

What is a fact is that George was due to meet the Chancellor that night at ten o'clock to discuss the Budget. It seemed an odd time to me, but as a 'Deputy Prime Minister' George presumably felt that he must personally and separately be filled in on Budget details at an early stage. Still, this appointment in itself was incompatible with some of the allegations made the following day about the way the Prime Minister handled his Government.

When we returned to No. 10 Downing Street the homing point seemed once more to be my room. People didn't gather but they looked in and out. If Harold was there and a secret talk became necessary, then he went through to the Cabinet Room and returned later.

Much of the time was spent just waiting, and when Harold and I were alone he decided to dictate a note for the diary, since clearly we were again in an historic situation which was better recorded that day than later on. I typed this back as best I could when the room emptied at any point, on a Remington Rand noiseless typewriter I had bought so that my typing could not be heard in the Cabinet Room next door.

But frequently I had to down tools to take dictation, to hear the latest developments, or deal with other visitors who would appear for briefing and drinks.

The only light moment was a spontaneous burst of amusement when we heard that the Chancellor had experienced difficulty hearing Secretary Fowler's voice on the transatlantic telephone. In such a technological age, with a crisis of major proportions upon us all, it seemed highly ludicrous that the telephone link was so inadequate that two of the most important men in the Western world couldn't speak to each other without difficulty when our whole future might depend on the conversation. An indistinct line, while irritating for making luncheon engagements, is a bit ironic in an economic crisis.

It seemed a long night and then everything started to hot up suddenly. This began with a joint visitation from the Governor of the Bank of England and the Chancellor, who started to ask for weird things like the closing of the London 'Gold Pool' which I hardly knew existed.

Gerald was torn between the activity at No. 10 and the activity at the House. An all-night session was in progress in the Commons and that always got people excited in the hothouse atmosphere of Westminster. When, added to this, came the rumours of 'happenings' at No. 10 on finance, the situation in Parliament became electric. It was heightened when George

Brown came back to life and realized that there had been a 'lost evening', during which clearly a lot had happened.

While we were bemused by Privy Council meetings, Governors, Gold Pools and the lot, George was busy holding a special sort of 'Cabinet' meeting of his own. He ordered Harold to attend. Harold's instinctive reaction was to keep activity of this kind at the House and away from the Press while many instinctively reacted against the Deputy ordering his superior officer to attend upon him. Once this was resolved, the Ministers came to No. 10 instead.

Very tired and punch-drunk, we watched an assortment of Cabinet Ministers assemble at No. 10. They came to the building in groups, and although from the chatter as they came down the long corridor towards the Cabinet Room it was clear that they were puzzled by what was happening, they certainly did not seem to be in low spirits. Indeed, as is often the case at a time of crisis, there was a certain unreal exuberance and repartee. Some of us sat slightly dazed in my room, certainly too tired to do anything but raise our eyebrows at each other as the far from melodious sound of George's voice broke the silence.

It became increasingly clear, although we were not inside with them, that George was furious, and that we were in for repercussions the next day if he ran true to form.

There was a clue about what might happen later on, in George's actions in the House in the small hours when Roy Jenkins went across to make a statement in order to settle Members of Parliament, who had become over-excited and were creating a crisis themselves by questioning what was going on. George started buttonholing Tory and Labour MPs alike, telling them of his future plans.

I did not go over to the House for the statement. Not only was I too tired, but I also had to finish the diary off and put it away for the night. I waited after that until everyone came back to No. 10 and then drove home.

Friday 15 March was taken up with George Brown entirely. Enormous heartsearching went on. It was a great chess game too. George thought he knew Harold so well and that it would work out all right, while Harold for his part had no choice whatsoever but to sit it out and interpret the carefully-worded communication which he received in the afternoon as a resignation letter.

I spent the whole day downstairs in my room, which was unusual. I hardly moved except for lunch. We waited at No. 10 as everyone obviously was waiting also at the Foreign Office and at the official residence in Carlton Gardens. Indirect messages and emissaries were received but they were of no avail. Certainly most visitors throughout the day expressed the unanimous view that Harold should not weaken at the last moment.

Yet it was for me a very sad day. One got angry at the way George had behaved, but we knew too much about the man and his life not to feel extremely affected by the total inevitability of it all.

Harold actually sat for Ruskin Spear that afternoon in the Pillared Room on the first floor. It was not a long sitting but it gave an added piquancy to the event. Ruskin Spear was to show the portrait at the Royal Academy in due course, and to present it to Jesus College, Oxford, Harold's old college.

But by the evening George had gone and another milestone had been set up. All that remained was the intense speculation about what he would do next – the same speculation that had surrounded him for so long.

After he left, George's eye turned quite naturally to Transport House, where he could still operate. But the outstanding question was whether he would, or should, resign as Deputy Leader of the Party. In the end he managed to retain the title until 1970, mainly because he had been elected for a Parliament and not a Session and the onus was, therefore, on him to take any initiative. Since he did not do this, others had to decide whether to try to persuade him to go.

A few attempted this, but Harold, true to form, felt that it was possible to live with such a situation since clearly the Party and the country were genuinely deeply fond of George, though at the same time often critical of his behaviour. Since he was no longer in government then Harold felt they would accept, and would want to accept, a partially-integrated George.

George remained very much on the scene therefore and his self-chosen role was to prove as difficult to keep up with as his previous ones had been.

He felt deeply, and quite rightly, the abrupt change from the magnificence of office as Foreign Secretary. The room now allocated to him was not even in the House of Commons itself, but in the building used by Members in Bridge Street, across the road from the Palace of Westminster.

When I visited him there I was struck by the lack of consideration shown by those who really should have done better by him. Surely someone else could have been moved and a better place found for George to work?

He must have suffered more then than the Government as a whole did in June 1970, since at least theirs was collective misery and discomfiture, and his was self-chosen and solitary.

Over the coming months, of course, George took a closer interest in Transport House and the Party organization. He ranged outside his own special area as Chairman of the Home Policy Committee, and took in the General Secretary's office, the future of the General Secretaryship itself and the organization of the election of a successor.

He would occasionally press Harold very hard on all these questions, and from time to time there also arose the question of whether George should be taken back into the Government.

He never shrugged off 1963 even after all these events, since when he raised the question of his return he wanted it on his terms, as Deputy Prime Minister with a job and not just as a Minister with a government job. One can say one thing about him, he quite rightly had never underestimated his admittedly large potentialities and capabilities.

The early part of 1968 saw the beginning of the worst overseas situation which affected us directly – the civil war in Nigeria.

It was an abominable exploitation of people on both sides though I was never able to see why the Biafran case was less evil than the Nigerian one. No evidence produced then, or after, has proved that to have supported General Ojukwu's attempt to keep Biafra independent, would have solved any of the problems in that area. Harold's job was to do what he could to help produce the right long-term result even though in the short term he might be given a very rough time by the highly articulate Biafran lobby.

Side by side with Biafra he had the Rhodesian situation again too, simmering away and sometimes coming to the boil, particularly when the Party became deeply distressed about the vicious and retrogressive steps being taken there, including the hangings of people who had been held in jail for political reasons. Even Sir Hugh Beadle couldn't find a way round his part in all that, and was bundled out of Government House and out of legal recognition for the part he had played in it all.

Inside No. 10 it was about this time that it was decided that the Prime Minister should start to work in more comfortable surroundings. Labour could expect to stay in power the full term if it wanted, and therefore Harold felt more relaxed about reorganizing his way of life within the building.

I always thought the Cabinet Room a dreary and uncomfortable place for anyone to work in for long periods at a time. The stiff-backed chairs were certainly not made for comfort. There was also something impersonal about it all, however historic the room.

Obviously distinguished visitors like to see the Cabinet Room and to take part in talks there. But for the more intimate talks and meetings the Prime Minister at that point had nowhere to go except his private flat or some corner of the State Rooms.

So here was a problem and Michael Halls particularly, and myself too, tried to solve it. We had a look at all the accommodation that was available to us and the result of our survey was that one room held the key to everything – the so-called Museum Room.

This was on the first floor and overlooked Downing Street. Originally it had been a dining room, but it had been used by us partly as an office, partly as a store-room for the many gifts the Prime Minister received. These came mostly from supporters all over the country and ranged from paintings and sketches – many of them of great merit – to one box that was filled entirely with Bibles and crucifixes, all received from one very religious lady, who kindly sent Harold at least one Bible and crucifix every month.

It was in this Museum Room that Stuart Holland worked. He had been with us for only a short time – in which he proved his value – when he decided to accept a teaching and research post at the University of Sussex. His departure led us to have a good look at the room and decide that it would be just the place for John Hewitt, now Sir John, the Appointments

Secretary. For one thing it would enable his many visitors connected with Church appointments to reach him more easily. And for another it would enable his previous office to become the Prime Minister's study again.

This room, in which Harold was to spend so much time from then on, seemed a trifle gloomy, so Michael and I proceeded to set about it.

Harold himself particularly liked modern furniture, so we decided to try and lighten the room by choosing modern desks and bookcases, and by covering the chairs and settee in thick white tweed, and by having pale green curtains for the windows. For the walls Harold chose good examples of modern British paintings including a John Nash and a Lowry. We meant the room to be a comfortable work-room, but also one which distinguished visitors would find attractive and more relaxing than the more formal setting in the Cabinet Room below.

I had always thought it a little odd that Kings and Prime Ministers and Presidents had to sit on an upright chair by the side of the British Prime Minister at the Cabinet table and hold sometimes long conversations in uncomfortable physical conditions.

King Hussein always struck me as a good example of this discomfort since he is a very small man and I was never sure if his feet touched the ground when he sat on an upright chair in the Cabinet Room.

Michael's proudest contribution to the new study was a very modern clock for the Prime Minister's desk. It was almost spherical but looked rather like the shape of a lady's head. This type of clock has now become extremely popular, but when this particular one was obtained it was considered very modern and attractive. Many people who came to the study wanted to take it away with them.

The white carpet and the white coverings for the chairs and settee, together with the glass tables and the light oak furniture and pale green curtains, lifted the whole room and gave it a very light and pleasant aspect.

We had a looking-glass over the fireplace and below that on the mantelpiece was a present from Mr Kosygin, a ship carved from ivory. In one corner was a television set and a radio for the news and current affairs programmes. Harold usually preferred to listen to the news on sound radio rather than watch it on television.

The usual telephone system was installed, with the special link to the Private Office so that a button could be pressed to call for any Private Secretary he wanted or for a messenger or a Duty Clerk. Michael also had placed on the bookshelves in one corner a small stand to which was pinned the diary for the day, so that Harold could see his engagements at a glance. Off the study was a ludicrous lavatory. This was an enormous room, the size of a large bedroom in most ordinary houses. The lavatory and wash-basin were at the far end, and because they looked so absurd standing there in this long room a screen was placed round them, and the remaining area was filled with chairs, which could be brought into the study if needed.

What should have happened, of course, was that when the building was redesigned in the early 1960s this lavatory should have been converted into a small bathroom, and the whole room divided so that the second half could be a bedroom which the Prime Minister could use at times of crisis. Then he would not have to go up to the flat and disturb the family. It seems absurd that it was never done and such a lot of space was wasted.

The new study was only finished in August but it was used before all the right furniture had been put in and the right coverings and curtains obtained. The major speeches before the summer recess were worked out in there, and the Newtown speech in July was written in that room.

By the time the study was operational there had been changes in the staffing and running of the Political Office.

When Stuart left it caused problems because the volume of work was so heavy. Gerald and I were left with the entire correspondence, not just the specialized half which was supposed to be our responsibility. We had to find the right person to replace Stuart, and Gerald discovered him working at Transport House on the production of the Party newspaper, *This Week*. He was David Candler, one of the Transport House Press Officers, and Gerald was so impressed with David that he arranged for him to meet Harold and be appointed to Stuart's job.

We were lucky to get him. His Labour background was impeccable, and he was a trained journalist, able to write and draft well. His personality was kindly and quiet and he got on well with almost everyone with whom he came into contact. He was good at handling the general political correspondence, for which he now took responsibility, and at showing exactly the right degree of concern for the people who wrote in from within the Party for help, or for guidance on political matters. He was also to be of great help in the preparation of speeches and in getting them out to Transport House and the Press. David stayed with us right up until the end of 1970. But for the fact that Joe Haines came over from No. 10 after the election to act as Harold's Press Secretary, an obvious appointment, it is likely that David might have ended up after the election doing the job which Gerald had first started out to do in 1965, that of Press Liaison Officer to the Parliamentary Labour Party. When he left the staff it was a great pity, but the only job it was possible to offer him by then was that of Research Assistant and co-ordinator of Press information, cuttings and material. This did not, of course, have the same scope which the other job would have offered him. We also had serious financial difficulties and could not possibly offer the same salary as that of Press Secretary.

David Candler's accommodation problem at No. 10 was solved by another change when Thomas Balogh was given a life peerage. This meant the disbandment of the office Thomas had been given in 1966. The rooms he had occupied on the second floor near the private flat were now vacated and David Candler moved into one room, the political secretaries into a large room which Thomas had used, and Clare Dent, an able person who helped me on political engagements, moved into the Private Secretary's room in that suite. Gerald himself moved back from the room he had occupied opposite the housekeeper's room to the small room which had been our first room ever at No. 10, that one usually used by the Prime Minister's Parliamentary Private Secretary. It was back to square one in some respects.

Some of the furniture which Thomas had been using in his own room was divided amongst us. Gerald took an enormous sofa and a small occasional table, though he stuck to the old, rather worn desk he had always had in No. 10, since he had become quite attached to it. The room he had previously used, and which I had often shared with him, was now turned into a room for Mrs Wilson's own filing and work, which had grown enormously over the years.

From this room, used by her secretary, almost the whole of Harold's election campaign in 1970 was planned and executed.

So by the summer of 1968 the Political Office was now operating totally from the second floor in a much more integrated fashion. It was on the same floor as the private flat, with the Prime Minister working for most of the day in the study just one floor below, accessible equally to his official and his political staff. While the official staff naturally had first call, and first priority on his time, the political staff could also see him easily. If the messenger was not sitting outside to stop them going in, they could always knock and put their heads round the door to ask if they could have a quick word with him, which was almost always granted.

Harold became enormously attached to the study. It was very close to the private staircase which connects the first-floor State Rooms with the private flat, and therefore he could go very quickly up and down for meals or for anything he needed. If he wanted to change for an engagement, or needed to do something special with the family, it was now much easier for him. The family could also pop down to see him, a big contrast to the time when they had to go all the way down to the ground floor, and then often through the Private Office before getting into the Cabinet Room.

One of the results of the change was that the room I had on the ground floor was used less and less. The smoky atmosphere that used to prevail in the room at the end of the day no longer existed. The main focus of our work was transferred to the first and second floors and, because our operations were more compact, they became consequently far more efficient.

One of the other changes which took place within the building was the decision taken by Mrs Wilson about the corridors leading to the State Rooms and to the study. Along the main corridor she had a selection of good modern paintings hung to act as a contrast to the more formal and traditional paintings and prints which hung either in the waiting area outside the

State Rooms, or in the State Rooms themselves. The modern paintings were always enormously admired by those who came.

In the small area outside the study and leading to the State Rooms she had glass display cabinets placed with concealed lighting inside them. In these she set out all the gifts presented to the Prime Minister and herself by overseas Heads of States and Heads of Governments. They were an impressive selection, including the beautiful mother-of-pearl rosaries given to them by the Pope, the ornate enamel drinking glasses presented to them by the Russians, President Nixon's porcelain horses, an enormous gold and silver bowl and many other very gorgeous gifts.

Every Prime Minister during his years of office collects a very large number of gifts given to him when he visits overseas countries. I remember being told Mr Harold Macmillan's collection was so large that a special room was set aside at Birch Grove to house all the gifts. Whether or not this is true I do not know, but certainly the number of presents received by a Prime Minister does reach such proportions that it is difficult to find a place for them all. Mary felt that since they could hardly be put into everyday use, and could not even be set out adequately in the private flat, the best thing was to put them in display cabinets so that the visitors who came into the building could see them. She never suggested that they should be set out in the State Rooms, because she felt they were in a sense public areas and she had, therefore, no right to insist on the way they were decorated. Her only changes – which were very good ones – were to have the Middle Drawing Room refurnished with velvet chairs and settees in a dark chocolate colour, and a very beautiful Indian carpet in browns and muted greens and creams added. She felt even then she was using the taxpayers' money too freely, and although she was asked to choose and had not taken the initiative herself on it, she was nevertheless very conscious about the money involved.

At the end of March we had several by-elections, one resulting from the elevation of George Wigg to the House of Lords. At each by-election Labour was hammered very hard by the Conservative Party, and one of the biggest swings of all against us was in George Wigg's own constituency.

These by-elections, taken in conjunction with the bad local

elections, led to further 'Wilson Must Go' Press stories, and to manoeuvres within the Party. The hunting parties were out again looking for scalps and the Press was not reluctant to comment. The Budget was out of the way, Roy Jenkins was established as the Chancellor of the Exchequer, and some of his own group of personal followers seemed to feel themselves free to behave less circumspectly than when he was still on probation.

By this time the DEA was doomed. The argument which had begun so long before as to whether any economic department within Whitehall could ever challenge the power of the Treasury was to be finally settled with the abolition of the DEA.

It would only have been possible to challenge the Treasury if a department had behind it vast backing like the Ministry of Technology and the Board of Trade amalgamated together.

The Department of Economic Affairs, a completely new creature in Whitehall, had no chance from the beginning with the Treasury completely against it and determined that no other department would interfere in the economic management of the country's life.

This was one of the reasons why Thomas Balogh lost heart. The DEA to him was the one department which could have acted as an interventionist body within the government and could have made some sense out of economic planning and the co-ordination of departments involved in our industrial and economic life. As the DEA's authority was eroded, Thomas's enthusiasm weakened. It was a major pity that Thomas Balogh should now leave us at the very point when he was probably needed most. As we came into the period when the argument lay between industrial relations legislation and prices and incomes legislation, he was an outsider and not an intimate adviser. Harold was always more than happy to listen to what Thomas had to say, but Thomas was not inside the building and a part of the team, and so his judgement and warnings were not necessarily taken into account as much as they might have been in other circumstances. However, he remained and remains as close and loyal a friend as ever.

Peter Shore took over with great exuberance, hoping to make a success of it all, and indeed the part left to him, regional planning, was a field in which he was particularly expert. But it was just a small portion now of what the DEA had been when it was set up in 1964. Barbara Castle, who was now appointed Secretary of State for Employment and Economic Affairs, had handed over to her the whole operation of the prices and incomes policy as well as her other duties on the industrial front. Harold's appointment of Peter to the DEA was unfortunately a disservice as much to Peter as it was to Harold. Peter never had the full authority to do the job properly since Harold was the ultimate chief of the department.

Barbara Castle's appointment as the new Secretary of State caused major comment. Her previous assignment at Transport was a way-out job for a woman. But now, at Employment, she was invading the area regarded as an essentially male stronghold. No one doubted after her display of talent and ability at Transport that she would have the necessary spirit for the job. But there were fears that with the prices and incomes quarrel with the Trade Union movement on our hands and the question of industrial relations reform raised particularly by unofficial strikes, there would be headaches for someone with little past experience of labour relations.

Perhaps the most welcome of all the appointments in the Easter reshuffle was George Thomas as Secretary of State for Wales. Cledwyn Hughes, the former Welsh Secretary, became Minister of Agriculture, enabling Fred Peart to be transferred to the job of Leader of the House.

Fred Peart was a middle-of-the-road, dependable character, extremely popular with the rank and file in the Party. After all the excitements of the previous years under Dick Crossman, Harold felt that perhaps a quieter and less invigorating period might be welcomed. It also enabled him to let Dick Crossman concentrate on his speciality, the social services, and the co-ordinating work that had to be done there. Dick had worked on pensions and superannuation for very many years. It was the one thing he had wanted to achieve as a Minister, and his plans were only frustrated at the last moment by the 1970 election result.

One of the less happy developments in that reshuffle was the sacking of Patrick Gordon Walker. He went to the back benches and became less than friendly about Harold. As I have said, all

Prime Ministers face the problem of having too few jobs and far too many people to fill them. It is curious that few of those given jobs feel gratitude and very many feel positive resentment when they are asked to resign. Almost invariably those who are dropped feel that their particular contribution is far and away above that of their colleagues. Harold had been completely honourable with regard to Patrick Gordon Walker, not only when he gave him his first appointment at the beginning of the Labour Government, but also in keeping to his promise, made when Patrick Gordon Walker lost a second seat for us, and putting him back into the Cabinet at the earliest possible moment.

Tony Crosland went to the Board of Trade, and Ted Short went to Education. The latter appointment was to have very deep implications for Labour and for our policy on education. We managed to reduce defence spending below that on education, so perhaps that was the bonus we got in exchange for having a Secretary of State for Defence who was there throughout the six years, while the Ministers of Education came and went rather rapidly. We had continuity in priorities, but we didn't have continuity in Ministers.

April produced a memorable explosion – Enoch Powell's 'rivers of blood' speech on immigration. In this he vocalized much of the feeling that there was in the country about immigration, integration and the many physical difficulties of living with immigrants.

Although we realized only too well that to dissociate Labour from Powellism was not a winner in electoral terms, it was decided unhesitatingly that Harold should leave no doubt about where the Labour Party stood on matters of race. The only question was where and when he should do this, but luckily there was an early and obvious opportunity in the May Day speech he makes every year. By a coincidence the speech was to take place in Birmingham, the centre of racial unrest in this country and the very city where Mr Powell had made his speech. To seize this opportunity was quite a gamble since clearly the meeting could have ended up in a riot and Harold could have encountered ugly demonstrations outside the meeting as well.

But here was a challenge and there could be no question of

shirking it, for it was imperative that the Labour position should be put on record at once. In fact all the fears of disorder were groundless. The meeting was a success, Harold's speech was a triumph, and the whole affair had a great rallying effect on members of the Parliamentary Labour Party and our workers throughout the country. They had been provided with a genuine glimpse of the old spirit we had seen in 1964 and before. It was the sort of thing they needed to hear, a fighting speech about things in which they believed strongly.

But it did not halt the general feeling against the Government and Harold.

The Parliamentary Labour Party were smarting about the prices and incomes legislation. Even though they knew it had to come because of devaluation and the measures that went with devaluation, they were reluctant nevertheless to accept and swallow it. When it came to be voted on, even Harold's exhortation to all MPs at a Party meeting did not prevent thirty-five abstaining and one Labour maverick going into the Opposition Lobby.

Because of this situation, Harold decided to make another speech to the Party meeting and we were immediately engaged on helping with it. The speech became famous for Harold's reference to 'a silken trap' into which some Labour MPs were falling. What Harold was trying to warn was that the Conservatives and in particular *The Times* newspaper were saying Labour should have a new leader who would renounce socialism and break our traditional links with the Trade Unions. He tried to warn them that, if they were victims of such a trap, it would mean for them, to use words written by Peter Jenkins in another context, 'the replacement of the practical, down-to-earth, characteristically North country moral force of the historic Labour Movement by the moral imperative of Metropolitan liberalism'. (This struck me as being particularly apt then. I only wish he had used the same words in 1971 in other arguments.)

The 'silken trap' speech once made, there was some stability as the Parliamentary Labour Party accepted it and settled down. We were now at the Whitsun recess and unrealistically hoped we might escape for a little rest, only to be told that the Chief Whip had such a heavy timetable that a mere week would be given for the holiday. In the event Harold had so many big public meetings to attend during the period that we didn't really get a holiday at all.

The result of all the work and pressure upon Harold during the recess meant that when the House reassembled he was more tired than usual for the run-up period to the summer. Because of this he seemed unnecessarily rattled by the behaviour of the House of Lords when the Rhodesian sanctions order came before them. The Opposition staged a rather silly trick in getting all their hereditary peers – who rarely turned up at the House of Lords except when the Queen opened Parliament or on some other special occasion – to show up in force to vote the order down. They couldn't stop Rhodesian sanctions, but Harold was exceedingly irritated that a body constituted as this one was should have the power to hold up House of Commons business and cause so much irritation and worry at a time when concentration was needed on other fronts. For this reason he gave immediate consideration to the question of House of Lords reform. Many thought he should have decided on a straight curtailment of their powers or gone for abolition. He felt so too later. What he should not have done was to have embarked upon a compromise project of reform.

This was to become a most expensive diversion for a considerable time. It sapped not only Harold's energies but the energies of those who had to run the Parliamentary Party and members of the Parliamentary Party themselves who became increasingly irritated with the whole thing, as it took longer and longer to go through the House.

As the year progressed a pattern emerged containing the issues which were to combine together and lead to the defeat of 1970. There had been prior murmurings about the need for action on unofficial strikes and legislation on industrial affairs. This had been raised at the time of devaluation because of the effect strikes had upon sterling and the contribution they had made to the eventual devaluation itself. But now, in the summer of 1968, there came the publication of Lord Donovan's Royal Commission on Trade Unions and Employers' Associations. The Donovan Commission had been set up by Mr Gunter in 1965. It should really have done its work years before when the Tories were in power. The Tories in fact had continually refused to take action. Edward Heath, when Minister of Labour, had categorically refused even to consider the idea. Now the Donovan Report came out at a particularly sensitive time. The general public saw industrial relations solely in terms of strikes, rather than in the wider terms of the organization of labour. Unofficial strikes understandably exasperated people, but the Donovan Report itself, while referring to the problem of unofficial strikes, gave no recommendations about how to deal with them, confining its recommendations to improved collective bargaining procedures on a voluntary basis.

For Harold one question was how the Labour Party could keep the initiative on this so that Edward Heath and the Conservative Party could not make capital from it, and in so doing destroy some of the things which were most valuable in the broad industrial picture. He knew that this was a field in which the Tory Party would be only too glad to intervene. As with immigration and with crime and violence, they felt that industrial relations provided an area where they could stir up a great deal of feeling in the country.

Barbara Castle, as the new Secretary for Employment and Economic Affairs, was pushed right to the front of the fight. Donovan was now in her court, and she had to deal with it.

Behind the scenes there was a continuing argument amongst Harold's friends and advisers on the whole field of industrial relations legislation and prices and incomes legislation. Many felt that he could have one of these or neither of them, but we couldn't have both together, which was what we seemed now to be thinking of taking upon ourselves.

The Parliamentary Labour Party found it very difficult to accept the prices and incomes policy, but when the votes came the majority loyally voted for what was recommended. To suggest to them, therefore, that they should now also accept legislation on industrial relations, which would require them to vote on things they found equally unacceptable, seemed too much. Many wanted a clear-cut decision that the prices and incomes policy was the thing on which we would hope to survive and create the right basis for success in the future. To throw this away, or even to endanger it by imposing legislation on industrial relations as well, was thought to be foolhardy. Thomas Balogh argued, and continued to argue, that unless we got a prices and incomes policy hammered out in the Labour Government, with politicians and Trade Unions agreeing on what they would both give up in order to obtain the maximum number of things they both felt strongly were most needed, then we should never get the picture at home right.

Harold, on the other hand, realized that while this was only too true, the Tory Party would continue to vote and campaign against a prices and incomes policy. But they would also campaign very vigorously indeed on industrial relations, telling the nation daily that the only way its life could be regulated was by introducing legislation to bring people in the unions within the law. This would be very powerful propaganda.

At the end of June came the surprise resignation of Ray Gunter. Many felt sure that this was because he found life strange at the Ministry of Power, but the reason he gave for his resignation was that he wanted to go back to the 'grass roots' of the Party. He suggested that there was desperate disaffection because of the unpopular things we had been doing and he hinted strongly that there were questionings about the leadership. He was a sort of honorary member of the Cecil King Coalition Government group.

It was about this time that we received a number of telephone calls from Vic Feather about how the TUC would take the prices and incomes legislation – and about how it would be received at the summer conferences of the unions and the September conference of the TUC. And there was no doubt how it would be received there – badly.

But all this was behind the scenes. The big public event of that summer was Harold's great 'hit back' speech to which I have already referred, his address to the Welsh Labour Party rally at Newtown.

This had been arranged a long time before, through the usual Transport House machinery. At that time the National Agent was Sara Barker and the Meetings Officer was John Taylor. Every six months or so they would come across from Transport House to discuss Harold's Party appearances. They made a formidable team. We were all devoted to Sara, who had spent her whole life dedicated to the Labour movement, while John had spent years perfecting the technique of producing

Party leaders to the best possible advantage. They usually came to No. 10 in the afternoon and we would sit down with the Prime Minister in the Cabinet Room or in the study with the 'forward diary' in front of us.

They would then produce a file of requests from all over the country asking for Harold to attend this annual dinner or that regional rally or reception. The initial problem was to ensure that each region had a visit from him every year, but, of course, that was only the beginning of it. We had to make certain that exactly the right engagements were chosen for each area, and we had to look ahead and guess what would be the most appropriate occasion at that time.

Then we had to fit in things with the official programme and, therefore, the Private Secretary in charge of the official diary had to be brought in.

All this was brim-full of complications, and how John and Sara, and her successor, Ron Hayward, managed their juggling trick over the years with so few complaints always amazed me.

An additional factor was Mary Wilson. As the years went by she became increasingly a great political asset and eventually she emerged as a major figure in her own right. The Party wanted to see almost as much of her as they did of Harold, so John Taylor also had to take on the job of planning for Mary as well. Besides the many engagements which she fulfilled jointly with Harold there were others when she was requested separately, and then we had to make sure that these did not clash with anything she was expected to carry out with the Prime Minister.

For some time Harold had been concentrating his public appearances in the main on receptions for groups of constituency workers. These were on a regional basis, organized by the regional office concerned, and masterminded by Sara and John. The technique proved to be enormously successful. Harold and Mary both enjoyed them, and in the course of two or three years they met thousands upon thousands of Party workers, spoke to them, shook their hands, and left them all with heightened morale.

But, as I said, there were exceptions, and Newtown was the most memorable. Here Harold urged the Party to begin the great fight back to regain public support so that the Tories would not reap the benefits of the hard but necessary things that we had done. Looking back on that speech it seems a sad occasion, despite Harold's triumph at the time. For, despite his warning, what he feared did happen. Even while it was being written, and particularly when he included the quotation from Aneurin Bevan about the Tories reaping what Labour had sown, we had an uncanny feeling that this would happen once more, as it did.

Still, we enjoyed helping with the Newtown speech. It was an address of great spirit and boldness and the speech's rallying effect put a stop for a period to the ever-increasing calls for a change in the Party leadership. Above all, it gave us something to get our teeth into at a time when all of us in the Party badly wanted action. Harold knew that there would come a point when we should have to go on to the offensive again, and Newtown was designed to do just this. Newtown was our first important political operation mounted from the study, and it became the model for the production of party political speeches in the future.

The girls from the Political Office came down in rotation, just as the Garden Girls did for a government speech. Each took dictation for five or ten minutes at a time and then left to type out her particular section. Gerald and I assisted Harold in the processing and checking and David Candler was there as well, controlling the flow of girls and seeing that the drafted pages were collated properly.

The system could work, of course, only if there was sufficient staff. In our early days at No. 10 we had so few that we couldn't possibly have organized such a system. By 1968 we had more people and we could just cope. As time went on Harold got so used to all the manpower – and womanpower – available on the official side that he expected the same service from the political side as well. This placed an additional burden on us, but we always managed to meet his requirements.

Perhaps the most unusual incident that year was the official appointment of Len Williams, our General Secretary, as Governor General in Mauritius. Len Williams came to see Harold at the House at the time. Harold laughed about it afterwards. He was extremely fond of Len. Len was a very natural, unassuming person. When Harold said to him that he thought he would look absolutely splendid in the uniform of a Governor General, Len replied that it was in fact not the first time he had worn a uniform. When Harold asked him what that uniform had been, Len said it was the uniform of an attendant outside the Argyle Theatre, Birkenhead. Both Harold and he roared with laughter, but felt that democracy had taken one step forward, at least in Mauritius.

What is forgotten about the conflict that took place over the vacancy that Len Williams left was that no one really wanted the General Secretaryship. Those who were put forward as candidates accepted with reluctance, and the ones that people particularly wanted would not be drafted.

Harold started off by suggesting the very man who got the job in the end, Harry Nicholas, only to be told very firmly by George Brown that Harry could not possibly be a candidate because he was too old. Later, after a number of developments, George suddenly emerged as the champion of Harry Nicholas, which to say the least was rather a surprise for Harold when he recalled George's earlier statement.

Perhaps there was a misunderstanding. At any rate Harold didn't think so. But what happened now was that the Press suggested almost universally that Harry Nicholas was the nominee of the Right while Harold was sponsoring Tony Greenwood on behalf of the Left.

As usual, Harold went to the Scillies for his summer holiday. This year he took with him his Trinity House flag since he had now become an Elder Brother of Trinity House, something he had wanted to be for a long time. He even had a flagstaff set up at the end of the garden outside his bungalow on the Scillies where the flag flew when he was 'in residence'. The Captain of the *Scillonian*, on which he travelled from the mainland to the Scillies, also ran up the Trinity House flag as a compliment to him when he was aboard.

The holiday in the Scillies was once more an interrupted one, by the Czech crisis, and the House of Commons was recalled to debate the issue. The Cabinet was also called, and the opportunity was taken at the same time to discuss the secret meetings that had been going on in Rhodesia. But the two-day recall of the Commons, which proved to be too long to discuss just Czechoslovakia alone, was also taken up with a debate on the even more desperately agonizing situation in Biafra. There people were starving in their thousands, with the very necessities of life not available to them. There was no argument for them about whether they could or would live in a society in which they could not freely express their views, only about whether they could live.

I was with the Prime Minister in his study at No. 10 on 27 August going over some of the present problems and work when a messenger ran in to say there was a riot in the street outside. We rushed into the main office of the Political Office to see what was happening. Outside was the most frightening scene I have ever witnessed. There was an enormous crowd demonstrating about government policy in Biafra. They had an effigy of Harold which they covered with paraffin and set alight to make a full-scale bonfire. They then proceeded to do an African war-dance round it, crying out slogans. After this they made a rush on the front door in an attempt to get in, either with a view to wrecking the building, or getting to Harold himself.

What was extraordinary was that there were so few people on protection duty either outside the building or inside. Of course it was a recess, but the Prime Minister was back in residence, even if it was only temporarily. It seemed to me that the previous arrangement had not been changed to meet the new situation. In the end we ourselves were telephoning around giving the instructions for Security Officers to be found and for more police to be sent over from Cannon Row Police Station to subdue the scene, if they could. They arrived quickly, but not until after what seemed to us an extraordinarily long wait when we were quite convinced the crowd would break in. What they would have done to Harold if they had was anyone's guess. We were able to joke about this afterwards, but it all seemed rather real at the time.

Biafra was too complicated an affair for anyone knowing all the facts to be certain either way that one side was completely right or wrong, though many of us had strong reservations about whether, as a Government, Labour should have continued the sale of arms to Nigeria. However, what is true is that if we had not done so the Nigerians would have turned to the Russians for help. They had told Harold as much on many occasions.

Harold was always being told by the Nigerians that the situation in Biafra was just about to be brought under control. This was said over and over again and never proved correct until too much tragedy had overtaken the area. On the other hand Nigeria was an independent state within the Commonwealth, and Harold accepted the assessments they made. They had the men and the materials and by normal standards the assessments they made should have proved correct. That this did not occur was due to peculiar African factors, as well as the intervention of our French friends, who, pursuing once more their independent way in international affairs, proceeded to sell arms to the Biafrans and cruelly kept them going far longer than otherwise would have been the case.

The Nigerians never had a very good Lobby in their favour, nor any public relations backing. Biafra, on the other hand, had a highly efficient public relations organization putting their case.

Harold took infinite care over relief for Biafra, sitting for hours alone or with friends and advisers trying to work out ways of getting through relief which could not be blocked by Colonel Ojukwu. As Harold has said about this and many other problems: 'The Head of Government had to face these problems not singly, or single-mindedly, but simultaneously, against the background of a hundred other issues, economic, financial, diplomatic, and political. The headlines, however, sensationalized or selective, fail to measure even the tip of the iceberg in the sea of democratic government, where the heaviest and most lethal pressures are below the surface, sometimes concentrated within the heart of the individual.'*

After these events, extraordinary for a summer recess, Harold was able to return to the Scillies for a further few days before coming back to London for the beginning of the political year.

The first event in the 'Political Calendar' is always the Trade Union Congress. We were waiting for this to pronounce a view on the Government's prices and incomes policy. It did. By a massive vote it came out against the wages policy. This augured badly for our own Party Conference where we had to

*Harold Wilson: *The Labour Government 1964–70* (London 1971).

debate the prices and incomes policy as the central feature of
Conference It was clearly most unpopular in the movement
and party workers and activists thought it was causing too
much unpopularity in the country. Everyone was, therefore,
in no doubt that we would have a fairly rough ride at the
Party Conference at Blackpool.

We travelled up to the conference on the Sunday. Monday
itself had been purposely arranged so that the prices and
incomes debate could be taken then and got out of the way
before Harold himself spoke at Conference. This was the
second occasion on which he had been able to persuade the
organizers to have the most important subject of the year
debated early on, so that Conference could have full discussion on it before Harold himself spoke. This gave Harold
the opportunity of commenting on the topic in question and
pronouncing a benediction or otherwise.

The main line of Harold's speech was a rallying appeal to the
Party and our people to get them back into a fighting mood.
He was given an extremely good reception after the speech,
and the old rumours about his replacement were temporarily
buried once again when he showed himself firmly on top.

That same day Harold held a full-scale meeting in his suite
at the Imperial Hotel with all the Ministers connected with
the Rhodesian question. They discussed whether, on the basis
of the information brought back by Sir Max Aitken and Lord
Goodman from their secret visit to Rhodesia, Harold should
now go off again to see Mr Smith, and if so, where the meeting
would be held and the exact date.

The meeting was fixed for 8 October at Gibraltar. This time,
however, we were not to be forced out to sea, but the conference would be held in one of Her Majesty's warships
anchored firmly in the harbour alongside the quay so that
people could come and go easily.

Everyone seemed to want the talks conducted in a much
more friendly atmosphere than the 1966 talks. Special arrangements were made for Ian Smith so that not only did Harold
have a warship to himself, HMS *Fearless*, but Ian Smith had a
separate one for his own party, HMS *Kent*, moored alongside
Fearless.

This time we were going in October, not December, and the

weather conditions were much better. It was still hot in Gibraltar, and a summer wardrobe was really required.

This I carefully prepared but still managed to forget the one thing one should always take, a comfortable pair of sandals.

We arrived in Gibraltar on 8 October, accompanied by a large party including special people like Elwyn Jones and Michael Halls. And this time Gerald Kaufman came as well. We were then driven in hot sunshine with great ceremonial splendour from the airport to the quayside. Towering above us was an enormous ship, *Fearless*. It is impossible to describe how large it seemed, and the approach to the deck was correspondingly daunting. The gangway had been elaborately laid out in an 'L' shape, leading from the quay to the side of the ship, and then off at right-angles up to the deck.

At the foot of the steps on the quay was a sailor, who immediately saluted everyone on their arrival. At the first platform before the last approach there was another sailor, who also saluted as each person reached him. Then, at the top, lined up in full formal white uniforms, were all the officers of *Fearless* ready to receive the Prime Minister and his party. It was quite a physical effort to mount such a large number of steps at such high speed in order not to leave too long a gap between myself and the person in front. Then, feeling tired and dishevelled from the journey out, I had to go down a long line of officers who were waiting to be introduced. On *Tiger* I had been protected from this by the fact that we arrived in the dark and in a storm, so then I had no opportunity to worry about how I looked. But this time everyone on the ship looked so immaculate that I was immediately aware that my own appearance did not quite match up.

When we got aboard we experienced again the superb efficiency of the Royal Navy in organizing a function of this kind. The whole ship had been turned into a floating conference centre. The cabins had been changed round to accommodate the Prime Minister and his staff, and on the Seacat deck there was an enormous' awning, shading tables covered with glasses and refreshments. Chairs were dotted around to relax in, and there was a faintly colonial look about it all.

I was struck by the fact that almost all the ratings looking after us were Asians, in the main from Hong Kong. As with the staff on *Tiger* they did their job wonderfully.

For the first half-hour or so on arrival we chatted up the officers at the reception, generally getting to know all the people around. We were then shown the Conference Room and our cabins. We were also taken to Harold's quarters, so that we would know where to find him. His day cabin was slightly smaller than the one he had used on *Tiger*, though the dining cabin was larger, and his night cabin with its bathroom was also bigger.

We were all situated near him. Gerald Kaufman and I had cabins close to each other and just a few cabins away from Harold. This time I had no difficulties in getting in and out of my bunk. This one let down from the wall, and could be put away during the day if wanted. The whole cabin was much larger and the facilities for the ladies aboard nearer to me.

When we went back on deck we were able to notice for the first time *Kent*. This was the vessel Ian Smith was to use during the conference, and had been brought alongside *Fearless* so that he could have separate accommodation, and not feel a second-class citizen. We were delighted to find that the Captain of *Kent* was an old friend from the *Tiger* visit. We did not go over to *Kent* until after Mr Smith had left at the conclusion of the talks, though we frequently walked along our side of *Fearless* to look down and see what was going on aboard *Kent*. In order to get on to *Kent* one had to come up from the quayside to the deck of *Fearless*, cross over *Fearless* and then go down another gangway connecting the two vessels. We knew, therefore, that when Mr Smith arrived we should be aware of the fact, since he would have to cross *Fearless* before joining *Kent*.

The gentlemen aboard *Fearless* had a luxurious time. They received perfect service, better probably than in a first-class hotel. Whenever they changed a shirt or needed anything washing at any time of the day, it would be whisked from under their noses by the ratings looking after them to be taken away, laundered and brought back sparkling clean. All of them returned to the United Kingdom at the end of the conference in exactly the same condition as they left, with suitcases full of beautifully pressed clean clothes. The ladies, on the other hand, had to return as one does from a holiday with a lot of pressing and hard work ahead to get their wardrobe back into good condition, since the laundry service didn't extend to us.

The first evening in Gibraltar was spent acclimatizing ourselves to the ship itself. We discovered it was as much an army vessel as a naval one. It was very much a working vessel, modern and up to date in warfare terms. It was equipped with the Seacat missile. Instead of being commanded by an Admiral it was under a Commander-in-Chief of Troops, since it was an enormous troop carrier containing armoured cars, tanks, and other motorized vehicles.

The Seacat missile aspect of the ship's role was a little frightening. It also had its ludicrous side. In the quarters allocated to Harold, which belonged to the Commander-in-Chief of Troops, there was in the bathroom, right next to the lavatory, a large red button with red lettering saying 'Caution, Seacat Missile'. One had an almost irresistible urge to bend down and nonchalantly push the button and wait to see whether a Seacat missile speeded off into Franco Spain or, more likely, ripped straight into Gibraltar. Certainly it was a great temptation to all who went into that bathroom and saw the notice. What I don't understand is why it had to be there? Presumably the decision whether or not to launch an attack is not normally taken in somebody's bathroom? I suppose there was some mechanical or technical reason why it had to be there and not in a more obvious and formal setting.

The following morning all the Press who had descended upon Gibraltar for the talks came aboard. This time they came in large numbers, in.contrast to the *Tiger* talks when few had come because those talks, being at sea, were inaccessible. They were invited aboard for drinks and a tour of the ship. This was a welcome decision because for the *Tiger* talks few people had really known what it had been like or how the conference had been organized. Now the Executive Officer of *Fearless* took them on a tour which took in the main conference room, the Prime Minister's quarters, and all the staff facilities. Then they came out again to have drinks with us and to wander around and to look down at *Kent*, which was waiting for Ian Smith.

That afternoon the Governor of Rhodesia arrived with a

screaming police escort, followed shortly afterwards by Ian Smith and his party. This time he had with him Mr Lardner Burke. Everyone had heard a great deal about him and he was regarded as a bogyman. Mr Howman was there again too. Some of the Rhodesians seemed to recall some of our faces and gave us a greeting as they went aboard *Kent* to settle in before coming back aboard *Fearless* to join the Prime Minister in his cabin for the first talks of the conference.

The talks that evening were informal. Present were our Commonwealth Secretary, George Thomson; the Attorney General, Elwyn Jones; Ian Smith and Lardner Burke, together with Michael Halls and Michael Palliser. Present too, of course, were Sir Denis Greenhill, the head of the Foreign and Commonwealth Office, and the Cabinet Secretary, Sir Burke Trend. Gerald and I were also there.

It was a short day really. By 8.30 p.m. Mr Smith and his colleagues had returned to their own ship for the evening, to have dinner and to go to bed early. We had our meal in the Prime Minister's dining cabin and then, as we had done the previous evening, we had drinks out on the Seacat deck, before going off to bed ourselves.

Thursday was the real start of the *Fearless* talks. The pattern was similar to those on *Tiger* in that the Prime Minister and Mr Smith met in the Prime Minister's cabin before everyone went into the main conference room. Then, from 10.00 a.m. until 1.15 p.m. the first part of discussions with the Rhodesians took place. There was a lunch break with the Governor of Rhodesia, and the afternoon meeting lasted from 3.30 p.m. until 6.00 p.m. Once the main part of the afternoon conference was out of the way, the Prime Minister again had the Commonwealth Secretary, the Attorney General, Mr Smith, Mr Lardner Burke and Mr Howman on this occasion in his day cabin from 7.00 p.m. until about 8.30 p.m. They talked over what had happened during the day and discussed what progress they felt had been made.

The Prime Minister and Mr Smith did not meet until 11.00 a.m. the following day. Gradually as the conference proceeded it broke up into small groups where legal points were considered separately by those mainly responsible for these matters.

The Prime Minister that day gave a lunch for the Captains of both *Fearless* and *Kent*. Gerald and I were excused and spent most of our time in Gibraltar. Later the conference was clearly bogged down in detail. Until something was thrown out that clarified the difficulties it was little use for us to stay around at all.

Even on the Friday evening the conference went on with meetings with Mr Smith and his Ministers, not in the day cabin, but lined up around the Prime Minister's table in the dining cabin. It was not until midnight that night that Ian Smith left the meeting on *Fearless* to go back to *Kent*. He was urbane and charming as always as he passed us and he smiled as he went off.

Harold, for his part, remained extremely cheerful and relaxed, and the whole atmosphere was totally different from *Tiger*. This seemed a hopeful sign.

We had thought it might be possible for us to sneak off on the Saturday on one of the small aircraft flying across to North Africa, particularly if the conference stayed bogged down in small detailed meetings. But this never came off and the most we got out of that visit to Gibraltar was a journey to the top of the Rock to look across to Spain. And, of course, we saw the world-famous Gibraltar apes. They seemed in jolly good condition to me, and I was confident that Franco would have to wait for a long time if the legend was true that they would have to die off before British rule in Gibraltar came to an end.

The conference continued its tortuous path on Saturday with the fragmented meetings concentrating on specific points. The lunch the Prime Minister gave for the Governor of Rhodesia was preceded by a special cocktail party to which Mr Smith came with his colleagues. This was fascinating as we had the opportunity of talking to him informally, as we had always wanted, and striving to find out what sort of political animal he was. He was just as extraordinary as we had guessed.

He clearly held strong racialist views which we found unacceptable, but I'm bound to say that they would probably be regarded as fairly liberal in Rhodesia. The gulf between us on policy remained, and always would do. It was impossible for that to be bridged. But professionally we had a sneaking regard for him even if the rules of the game demanded that we should maintain a distance. We had more than a sneaking respect for his political acumen and debating powers We enjoyed that cocktail party more than anything we had enjoyed for a long time. At last we had been able to nobble him as a politician and to talk to him personally.

That day ended for me in a humiliatingly comical fashion. All the committee meetings had produced an assessment of how far or how little Mr Smith would go with regard to the five principles. So once the Rhodesians had left that Saturday evening to return to *Kent*, all the United Kingdom party gathered in the main conference room until 12.30 a.m. to discuss the implications of what had been happening. Gerald and I had been up in Gibraltar talking to the Press, and lack of taxis and constant security checks in the docks meant that we arrived back at *Fearless* very late – and with a lot to catch up on.

The paramount question was still about any possible Smith guarantees, and about this Gerald and I had the most enormous argument in my cabin later that night. He got very excited and walked up and down the cabin talking to me in a most concentrated fashion. Then he sat down very heavily on the end of my bed. I was extremely surprised and indeed somewhat battered, when the bed's mechanism reacted immediately and the bed shot up into the wall, leaving Gerald on the floor and me shut firmly up in the bed in the wall, with just my head sticking out.

We then had a hushed conversation as to whether we should seek the aid of one of the Marines or naval ratings outside to help get the bed down again. One thing we had to consider was what they would think about us having an argument in my cabin so late at night. We had to get the bed out some way, and succeeded eventually in a half-hearted fashion. It came down almost the whole way but not quite – and that was how I had to sleep for the rest of the night.

When I went out the next morning it was clear that the whole ship knew about the incident. I had the most solicitous inquiries from every officer and rating I met as to whether or not my cabin had been gone over by the engineers to make sure everything was in order. When I arrived back after breakfast I discovered that it all had been put right again and the bed had been well and truly mended. A postscript to this is that when Gerald returned to *Fearless* at Lagos in 1969 for the Biafran and Nigerian talks, he had a photograph taken specially for me of that cabin with its unmanageable bunk.

On the Sunday morning we all put on our best bibs and tuckers and went to the main deck of *Fearless* for a church service. Lined up on one side was the United Kingdom delegation and on the other side the Rhodesian delegation. The Prime Minister read the lesson. It was all very formal and beautifully carried out in what I would call more a British than a Christian way, but it is difficult and even impertinent for me to comment on which particular sentiment was being expressed in the organization of such an extraordinary tribute to the Almighty.

This meant a morning gone, because a church service of that kind on board a ship can't be done in just five minutes. When it was over everyone returned to the main conference room for very brief talks. After lunch we met again in the main conference room for two hours for a general meeting about all that had been discussed so far. The meeting was adjourned for twenty minutes and then carried on until 8.00 p.m. This was the meeting when the question of the guarantees dominated the talks. If an agreement was reached, could there be any guarantee that the Rhodesians would adhere to it? Later there were talks on the general package and on the system of guarantee, and these went on until 10.00 p.m.

But already, on the Sunday, Mr Smith's staff were making arrangements for his return to Rhodesia. We knew that we were not going to get any answer out of him then. He seemed to be satisfied with very many aspects of what had been put to him, but I think the one thing that was totally unacceptable this time was the system of guarantee. Whereas two years before it had been the question of the return to legality on which the talks had broken down, this time they were clearly going to break down on the question of how you could guarantee any agreement reached.

The Rhodesians were to leave on the Sunday evening.

After our morning meeting was over they went back to *Kent* to get their things together. Then they came back to *Fearless* to have a drink with us before finally going off. It was all done in a most friendly way and, as Mr Smith parted

271

company with us, he had something very nice to say to each in turn. He wished us all well and said he hoped that we would all meet again. We gathered together to see him leave the ship, with full honours accorded to him as he went down the gangway to be driven off to the airport with his colleagues.

Throughout that whole conference the sun had shone, and each day had been hot, warm and colourful. We had sweated it out in the conference room for many hours with additional separate meetings with Mr Smith in Harold's day cabin. In those meetings in the day cabin Ian Smith was fascinating. He was also much more circumspect about what he said when Mr Lardner Burke was present. On other occasions he went further than he had done on *Tiger* in expressing his own personal views about the situation. Throughout the whole confrontation between Harold and Ian Smith, I felt that they had rather more in common with each other than they would probably have liked to admit, particularly in their approach to politics, and certainly in their expertise and their efficiency in being able to keep their options open. In this I am sure it is far more necessary to keep one's options open in Rhodesia than it is in London.

On Monday we had a rushed Press conference in the oddly named HMS *Calpe*, which is really just a building in the docks. We then accompanied the Prime Minister on his tour of both *Fearless* and *Kent*. He was introduced to as many of the staff on both ships as possible, and tried to have a word with any seamen coming from Liverpool.

Unlike our return from *Tiger* there was little drama on our return from *Fearless*. There was no tightrope-walking in the sense of expecting an immediate answer; we had to wait now to see how everybody would react to what had been worked out.

In the autumn came the results of the American Presidential election.

There was some amusement for us, however, as we recalled rather uncomfortably a visit that the President-elect, Richard Nixon, had made to London earlier. At that time he was in eclipse and certainly didn't look like a winner. However, it was arranged for him to see Harold at the House of Commons, where we were working that afternoon. He arrived when the Prime Minister was having a small Press conference which had not yet finished and Mr Nixon was asked if he would mind taking a seat on the sofa outside the Prime Minister's room. The girl on duty went in to interrupt the Prime Minister's meeting to announce that his next appointment had arrived. The Prime Minister asked who it was and she said: 'It's only Mr Nixon.' That was some remark.

We recalled it with a little embarrassment but some hilarity afterwards, as I am sure the President would himself. The trouble with politics is one never knows where people are likely to turn up next, and in what capacity. The moral of it all, which Harold knew only too well, is that you must always make sure everyone is treated equally. He always went out of his way to do this. Whenever Mr Nixon had been in London, Harold had always taken great pleasure in seeing him and hearing his views of the political scene in the United States.

The main event in what remained of October was a Government reshuffle, the most important part of which was the amalgamation of the Foreign and Commonwealth Offices under Michael Stewart and the reorganization of the social services under Dick Crossman.

On 29 October the Queen's Speech was read out at No. 10 to the whole Government at the usual party held every year for these occasions. This traditional party is given at the Prime Minister's own personal expense from his own salary. Everyone gathers for drinks and the Prime Minister then calls for silence and proceeds to read out the Queen's Speech to them all. As soon as one gets to this point in the proceedings, all the doors are closed so that outsiders cannot hear.

The reception is usually held in the large Pillared Room on the first floor since this is the largest of the State Rooms. As soon as the reading starts the big double doors connecting the Pillared Room with the other State Rooms and the dining room are firmly locked to outsiders.

To some joking and 'hear hears' the Prime Minister then reads out what the Government intends to do over the coming year. That coming year of 1968/9 did not sound particularly exciting then, but it was to be one of the most important for the Labour Government because of the action we promised to take on the Donovan Report, action on industrial relations.

There were other emotive things in the Speech too, like the lowering of the voting age to eighteen.

Meanwhile there were the usual Christmas preparations to cope with in the office, the Prime Minister's Christmas cards, and all the other arrangements that had to be made.

We had never before taken it upon ourselves to make suggestions about decorating the State Rooms for Christmas time. Mary had felt it an impertinence to suggest that she should take it over herself, though we had often wanted to have a traditional Christmas tree somewhere in the building.

She decided in 1968, however, that she really ought to suggest it. After a lot of consultation it was decided that one could be obtained from the Chequers Estate and brought up to London. This was duly arranged. But it was not just as simple as that. When the tree arrived Mary had it placed in the Pillared Room since this was the main reception room for entertaining. It was an enormous tree, almost to the ceiling. We were very pleased with it, though it was a bit of a problem to find suitable decorations. Indeed I am afraid that the ones we had were quite inadequate as we were unprepared for the size of the tree. The over-all effect at the end of the day was quite good, but not as good as we would have liked.

What I had hoped to see at No. 10 one day was a Christmas tree like the one I had seen in a State Room at the White House in 1965. Mrs Lyndon Johnson had shown it to us with great pride and it really was a most beautiful Christmas tree. It was perfectly decorated; straight out of a glossy American film. It was decorated with ginger-bread men, and those beautiful long striped walking canes made of peppermint, and all sorts of other figures cut from marzipan and other sweet mixtures. The colours were beautiful, not too exaggerated. I always recall it and pictured such a tree standing in No. 10. We had a more traditional English Christmas tree with tinsel and lights and coloured bells and balls.

Harold wanted to make sure that year that there really was a staff party. On each occasion before the Prime Minister had been away from London, or some other event had happened which had meant we had to cancel any party. We had a double problem, however. We not only wanted to entertain the staff at No. 10 at Christmas, but also to entertain Transport House staff as well. We took an enormous risk and invited both groups to the same party on 18 December. It was in some ways a riot. When we said 'the staff', we meant just that and everyone who worked in No. 10 was invited. The lady cleaners were delighted to be there and did the most enormously enthusiastic 'knees-up' at the end of the evening. They were very lavish in their kisses and embraces for the Prime Minister, much to the amazement of the housekeeper and a little bit to the astonishment of the Prime Minister himself, who was rather overwhelmed by it all. But he loved them, and in the main they liked him.

It was surprising how well the Political staff from No. 10, their comrades from Transport House and the Parliamentary Labour Party staff got on with the No. 10 staff. They had never all come together before in this way, and it was interesting to see Transport House actually meeting the people with whom we had been working for so long. By then there had been changes and on the secretarial side the young ladies were rather different from those there in 1964. I think a lot of eyes were opened on both sides, since Transport House and the Labour Party did not appear to be such villains or so uncivilized as some had thought. On the other hand the civil servants were not as remote now as the Labour Party had thought they would be.

The policemen and custodians all came up on a rota basis with those on duty taking it in turns and then returning to their posts. It was enormously successful and we greatly enjoyed it, and hoped that everyone else had done so too.

Many photographs were taken, including a special one which Harold asked for in which the whole of his Political Office staff gathered together in front of the Christmas tree with him in the centre of the photograph. That is the one everyone wanted. It was the first time as a political office we had been photographed together.

On 20 December, the usual turkey presentation took place just before lunch. The Turkey Federation each year sent along a representative to present to the Prime Minister a gigantic turkey. Usually the turkeys were so big they could not be cooked in the oven at Chequers. It was quite a large oven, but the turkey was often too big and had to be taken over to

Halton RAF Camp to be cooked in the Service kitchen there and brought back to Chequers afterwards.

But before going to Chequers Harold gave a big party at Lancaster House for paraplegics from the Stoke Mandeville Hospital – particularly for those who had competed in the Paraplegic Olympic Games at Tokyo – and there was an unusual family treat for the Wilsons, they paid a visit to the cinema. Their choice was 'Till Death Us Do Part', the film of the much-discussed television series. They took Mrs Pollard the house-keeper with them, and all came back laughing.

Harold and Mary invited a small party of people close to them for dinner on Boxing Day. Beattie Plummer was naturally invited, but this year she had friends staying with her at her house in Essex and they came too. They included Gerald Gardiner, the Lord Chancellor, and Lord and Lady Shepherd. We had a traditional dinner, even down to the wearing of paper hats.

It had been a hard year but it had its compensations. After all, not everybody gets the chance to see the Lord Chancellor of Great Britain wearing a Christmas-cracker paper hat.

11

The Last Temptation

The New Year was completely overshadowed by the tragedy in Biafra. The situation there was deteriorating rapidly. Every attempt to get talks between Nigeria and Biafra broke down. The United Kingdom was responsible for several initiatives behind the scenes, including contacts with the Biafran regime, but the deadlock remained.

Lord Shepherd had been to Nigeria before Christmas and the report he brought back gave little ground for hope. One of the problems was that the troops on both sides did not seem efficient enough to conduct a war at all. However many arms were supplied, the forces were not capable of using them properly. And meanwhile the optimistic forecasts from Lagos about the end of the war still came to nothing.

There had been long talks for some time at No. 10 about whether Harold should go to Nigeria. He felt it necessary for several reasons. It was vital to see for himself exactly what was happening, and also to make a further bid to force General Gowon into speedy action. Above all, he wanted Gowon to be told that the continuing supply of British arms, and political support in all circumstances, would soon have to be seriously reconsidered.

Every effort was made to arrange a Christmas visit, but the difficulties proved insurmountable. From then on every consideration was given to the timing of a visit. When the announcement was finally made in March a great deal of work and time had already been spent on it.

The New Year opened with two major events: the Commonwealth Conference which was to be Harold's last Commonwealth Conference, acknowledged by even those who take little interest in these matters to have gone well, and the background talks about Barbara Castle's industrial relations document *In Place of Strife*.

By the time the Cabinet had already agreed the general lines of the industrial relations policy, sections of the Party were gravely disaffected and attitudes had been taken. Many seemed to base their reactions on newspaper reports.

The Industrial Relations White Paper came out on 17 January and then, on 28 January, Dick Crossman brought out his earnings-related superannuation scheme. Two major issues of home policy were now on the agenda for that year. Both were enormous in their ramifications and in the amount of controversy they were to cause the Party in different ways.

But it was the Lords Reform Bill that was to gum up the Parliamentary works for many months, cause great irritability, and seriously detract from the speed and force with which the other two major measures could be handled. The Parliamentary Labour Party just could not take an argument within themselves on a subject so major as industrial relations and the whole policy of free collective bargaining on which they had been brought up, the superannuation scheme for which they had waited for some twenty years, as well as a very sophisticated and slightly superficial argument about Lords reform.

All this meant that relations with the Parliamentary Labour Party became even more important than usual and here we were helped by the decision, taken late in 1968, to revert to the practice of the earlier days of the Government and appoint a second PPS for the Prime Minister. The choice fell on somebody serving in the Whips' Office, Eric Varley, who was given his own desk in the Political Office at the House of Commons. Harold Davies and he thereafter carried on the job jointly until Eric left for a Government appointment. They were a curiously assorted pair. Both were from socialist working-class backgrounds and had a great deal in common on that front. Yet there was an age gap, which meant that one typified the new Member as much as the other typified the older Member of the 1945 intake.

As soon as many members realized the Industrial Relations

Bill was going to cause trouble, the group who felt passionately and sincerely about the freedom of the Trade Union movement found themselves in an uneasy alliance with very many other people who were merely using the situation for their own different purposes. So many influential people were to take a positively anti-Government line on the whole subject that a minefield was created in which the plotters hoped the Prime Minister would stumble.

Before much of this could develop, however, Mr Nixon paid his first visit to Britain as President. Harold, considering how such a visit should be handled in this country, bore in mind that though the President was coming in a period which was the beginning of his term of office, it was for us the beginning of the run-up to the election, and he had to be careful about this, recalling how Harold Macmillan had blatantly used President Eisenhower in this respect. Anyway, was Mr Nixon a debit or credit as far as electoral approbation was concerned?

Harold decided that the last thing he wanted was too many scenes outside No. 10 Downing Street, or a drive from London Airport like the one undertaken by Mr Macmillan with President Eisenhower. The conclusion was reached that perhaps the one place the talks could be held was Chequers. It was out in the country and ideal for the purpose.

The visit was an enormous task for Trevor Lloyd-Hughes to organize and he did it superbly. There were many discussions about whether the Prime Minister should agree to be flown from London Airport to Chequers by the Presidential heli-copter. It had to be decided whether a British Prime Minister on United Kingdom territory should be conveyed from London Airport to the Prime Minister's country home by an American helicopter, and a Presidential one at that. The idea seemed to some unwelcome, incongruous and out of keeping with our status as an independent country. Harold agreed, but he was advised by his officials that it was impossible to provide any-thing else which would satisfy American security, and that it was easier to agree to let them use their own equipment than to argue it out with them.

So the decision was made but in the end much of the argument was pointless. Fog closed down, the helicopter was useless and everybody had to travel by car. Even then a hired Presidential car was used and not the Prime Minister's.

The day after President Nixon left London the Prime Minister attended a lunch organized by the Party to say a formal farewell to the National Agent, Sara Barker. She was being replaced by Ron Hayward, a very able, extremely likeable and frank person who had been the Party's Southern Regional Organizer for many years. He and I got on well, although during the 1966 election he did call me 'a bad-tempered old bitch'. This upset me at the time but I liked him for it. Few people would have said it, even if they had thought it. And I knew it was true – well two-thirds true perhaps. I hope Ron would agree 'old' was a trifle unfair.

Everyone was extremely sorry to see Sara go. We had worked well with her over the difficult years of the Labour Government and relied on her wisdom in so many ways. Harold hoped that when the time came, if it was possible, he would be able to send her to the House of Lords where she would be able to continue her work for the Party. But, of course, we lost the 1970 election and in the Dissolution Honours there were too many other claimants for the limited number of life peerages.

By the beginning of March the Biafran situation had become more critical than ever. Obviously the Prime Minister had now to visit the area himself and Harold and those close to him who were also going on the trip – such as Gerald Kaufman and Eric Varley – became engrossed in the preparations.

There were great security risks for a British Prime Minister to take on such a visit and, in view of Harold's previous experience with warships, it was inevitable that the Royal Navy would be called in. HMS *Fearless* was, therefore, ordered to Nigeria for use as a conference centre even though Harold and his party did not actually stay on the ship.

Unfortunately, the visit coincided with another internal Party crisis. On the day before Harold left, the National Executive considered the industrial relations document, and this was the occasion for the Home Secretary, Jim Callaghan, to fire a warning shot across the Prime Minister's bows and express open dissatisfaction with the Government's policy.

As always with Jim Callaghan, this was a brilliantly executed operation. Clearly the Trade Union movement was not going to accept what the Government was proposing. The whole

future of the Party could well be at risk, and obviously middle-
men were going to be needed to act as a bridge between the
Trade Unions plus the constituency parties (who were also
becoming disaffected), and the Government itself. Jim, by now
entrenched at the Home Office, was ready to take on this task.

Here was a role for which he was ideally equipped. He was
by now in full control of his department, with time too to
operate skilfully in the world of internal Labour politics, where
he is completely at home. He was also helped by the fact that
for some time he had been engaged, in his role as Party
Treasurer, in the quiet but methodical forging of links between
Transport House and himself. All in all it was a bad time for
Harold to be away from the country. The NEC meeting, with
its ambiguous votings on Barbara Castle's *In Place of Strife* and
the subsequent headlines about Jim Callaghan's role, took
place on 26 March. Harold left for Lagos on 27 March. He was
not to return to London until 2 April. By that time the Easter
holiday was beginning and he left almost at once for the Scillies.

It was a hectic time. I was in London and was sorry to miss
the visit to Ethiopia planned after the Nigerian talks were over.

But my job was to act as a messenger, to be with them all
until the last minute, to see them off at the airport, and to
keep them informed through the Private Office and the
Foreign Office of any political developments at home.

The drive out to London Airport on 27 March was very
quiet. Everybody was worried about what might happen
while Harold was away, and nobody knew the situation he
would encounter on his return.

All in all, in fact, there was a great deal for Harold to hear
and to deal with on his return, but the main thing was how
members of the Government and the Parliamentary Labour
Party felt about a Cabinet Minister like Jim striking a rather
original attitude about collective responsibility on a major
piece of Government legislation.

It was for this reason that in the Cabinet meeting immediately before Easter, Harold delivered a warning about
how he expected Ministers to behave. This amounted to an
open reprimand, though it was a trifle odd that the Prime
Minister even had to remind his colleagues that what they
decided in Cabinet was supposed to be a collective decision.

At least the Easter holiday was uninterrupted and Harold returned to London refreshed to start the real battle on industrial relations. The next three months were the most unpleasant, disastrous and dramatic of all the time at Downing Street.

The Chancellor introduced his Budget almost immediately on everybody's return and gained great popularity for the style in which he did it. However, he omitted to tell the House that one of the major money-raising efforts the Government was to indulge in that year, that of increasing Health Service charges, was not being announced by him at the time, but would be left for Dick Crossman to do later on. Though Dick never complained, many of us thought that he was carrying the can for something that was not going to be well received, while the Chancellor, introducing an outstandingly popular Budget, got the credit once again for its style and, to a certain extent, its content.

The Budget itself sparked off the reshuffle that lost us John Silkin as our Chief Whip and brought in Bob Mellish. This was because the increases in Selective Employment Tax caused a small riot among the Co-operative members of the Parliamentary Labour Party. They had to demonstrate loyalty to the other half of their organization, and they abstained on this issue. The regular abstainers had no hesitation, and some right-wingers did it just for the hell of it, to show left-wingers that they could abstain too. Even then the Government majority was still as big as Edward Heath's 1970 figure. It seems inconceivable now, looking back, that anybody could believe that by changing the Chief Whip, and apparently abandoning the liberal regime, we would somehow lessen the number of abstentions and make the discipline within the Parliamentary Labour Party keener.

Not everybody was sold, at the time, on the theory that John Silkin was less efficient in getting a vote than someone who was as down to earth and as blunt and outspoken as Bob Mellish would be, if called upon to perform the same task. It proved to be the case that someone who gave the appearance of being very tough, forthright and persuasive, was no more effective at getting the sheep safely into the fold at the end of the day.

Harold, however, had every confidence that the new Chief

Whip was extremely tough, and that the legislation he wanted would now go through because of this. What I do not think he ever bargained for, was that the same Chief Whip would eventually persuade him that he might not want the legislation as much as he thought he did. John Silkin would probably have told Harold all the difficulties: but having done so, he would have tried to get the vote organized. Many were sorry when the change-over took place, though they understood the reasons for it. It was more of a psychological move than anything else. Harold hoped that the sheer psychological impact would bring the Parliamentary Labour Party into line and create a new atmosphere.

Despite all the changes, the grumblings about Harold's own position still continued too. The left wing lost their nerve this time thinking the grumblings were indicative of a much more widespread feeling than they were. So agitated were some members of the Left that I was sent for on a number of occasions to be told of what seemed to them to be an imminent attack in the open on the Prime Minister's position. Nothing like this in fact emerged, though the demonstration of loyalty they showed during that period was enough to head off those who were playing a leading role in the campaign, including one very small group around one senior member of the Party.

Harold retaliated in his usual way, by telling the May Day Rally at the Festival Hall: 'I know what's going on; I'm going on.' The Political Office at No. 10 took great delight in preparing that particular speech, and watching Harold insert that particular statement.

Meanwhile the man who was emerging as the key figure of the year was the General Secretary of the TUC, Vic Feather. As events unfolded our assessment of him proved to be correct. Many felt that he was a more formidable figure than his predecessor as General Secretary, George Woodcock. George was more articulate and more sophisticated, essentially an intellectual, in contrast with the down-to-earth Vic, but Vic clearly would turn out to be the more skilful politician.

It is only an academic exercise, but I often wonder how George Woodcock would have reacted during the vital months of 1970. Could he have sold his colleagues the penal clauses, which after all only came to three, if he had wanted? Clearly this question did not arise with Vic because he never wanted to do so. There were several reasons for Vic's attitude. He was a new boy to the job, still on probation. He had to prove himself. He had no wish to run against the tide at this point. Instead he wanted to turn the tide in the direction that he wanted it to go. In this he was successful.

He understood Harold's make-up very well and realized that ultimately in any major dispute between the Trade Union movement and the Labour movement, Harold would be anxious to agree on a compromise. Vic Feather pushed the 'crunch' argument very hard indeed, and finally achieved a compromise situation. He even made everyone believe that something positive had been achieved. To be fair it had.

But what Harold did not obtain was a really detailed commitment fully spelt out. We got a 'binding agreement' in general terms, the first of the 'Downing Street agreements' of a year that was to see another Downing Street agreement.

It was a traumatic period for Harold. For very good reasons some of his closest friends came out against him. Some felt the subject was wrong and the choice of priorities wrong. Peter Shore in particular felt passionately for the prices and incomes policy, which was reflected in his attitude to industrial relations.

Roy Jenkins, powerfully supported and guided by Treasury thinking, wanted the industrial relations policy instead of prices and incomes. His alliance with Barbara Castle, curious though it was, clinched the argument. They were totally steadfast throughout on it and between them made the running at one point when Harold was in Nigeria and Ethiopia. The decision had been made then to include the announcement about Barbara's Bill in Roy's Budget statement.

There was a deep necessity to do something on this front, but clearly the way it was tackled was wrong. With hindsight, what should have come first was a full discussion with the movement as to what could be achieved, rather than stepping straight into the arena. If the other course had been chosen, Vic Feather would have found it much harder to have operated in the way he did. Instead he had the battleground all to himself and, expert as he had become in knowing the principles involved in the battle, on our side as well as his own, he was clearly destined to emerge the man who achieved most out of it.

Harold was able to go on one of his very few shopping expeditions on a visit to Liverpool. He managed to slip out from the Adelphi Hotel to Lewis's store opposite and buy himself a new suit. He loved these trips because, even though accompanied by a detective, he had the feeling of escape into the outside world. He also changed his style of coming back from Liverpool and the constituency. He had always travelled back to London on overnight sleepers, and then down from London to Chequers by road. But my brother, who worked just outside Wigan, started to pop over to Huyton after he had finished work, and join Harold at his engagements there. Then he drove him down from Liverpool to Chequers. He used to arrive there about 2.00 a.m., rather late, but still able to sleep in a proper bed and lie in the next morning.

Meanwhile Jim Callaghan's reputation grew as the year went by. He was one of the most talked-about politicians in the country. He was the man who had stood up for the Trade Union movement against the Government's proposed legislation and had become the champion of the unions. He was the statesman and man of common sense on Northern Ireland. He was the expert politician fending off Opposition arguments and countering with good political stuff on the battle over the Boundary Commission recommendations. Roy and he kept up a constant battle that year to prove which one was entitled to be regarded as the heir apparent – or was it the heir presumptive?

Labour's popularity within the country still took no dramatic turn upwards. We were to have bad by-elections still in the summer. Yet Harold was already deeply conscious at No. 10 that a lot of thinking was now necessary on election strategy. Once the summer holidays were out of the way we should have to give our thoughts more and more to this.

There were nevertheless light touches that summer. At the beginning of July the Prince of Wales was invested at Caernarvon Castle. However splendidly this was produced by Lord Snowdon, the sheer fantasy of the situation was inescapable – not to mention the cost. Mary and Harold enjoyed it very much. They were particularly pleased to be able to purchase the chairs they had sat on at the ceremony, and they have them now at Grange Farm.

In July Mary gave the first party in a series she was to have for active Labour women workers throughout the country. She started off with a large party for the main committee which runs Labour Women's Organizations. Later she had parties for each regional group at No. 10. They were very jolly affairs recalled by Mrs Pollard with great pleasure. She can tell you exactly what sort of cakes she prepared for each region. She took special care to try and bake the sort of cake which was probably best known and eaten in that area.

Before holiday time President Nixon came over again. This time it was only a fleeting visit and there were problems for him in coming down to London for such a short period. The decision was made that he would land at the US base at Mildenhall, in East Anglia, and that Harold would see him there.

As Mildenhall is close to Beattie Plummer's home, Harold accepted her invitation to visit her on the way back and have dinner with a few of her special friends. I travelled down by train from London to Braintree where Beattie and Lord Shepherd met me. It was a lovely day and both were looking gay and happy, mostly because of the coming evening event I think. They drove me over to Toppesfield, Beattie's home, where we spent some time together before Harold's arrival from Mildenhall. Other guests were Lord Gardiner, Lord and Lady Sainsbury, and the Attorney General and Lady Elwyn Jones. They were Beattie's very special friends. Harold had never visited Beattie's home in the country, only her home in London, because pressure of work and other involvements had always prevented him accepting the invitations he received when Dick Plummer, Beattie's husband, was alive.

So this was a special occasion for Harold – and also for Beattie's cook, Mrs Evans, who is as Welsh and as Labour as her name suggests. She prepared a wonderful dinner for Harold, timed fairly late in order to take account of any delays there might be. But the hour got later and later, and we all grew hungrier and hungrier. The trouble was that no one had the courage to say we ought to start to eat, even though the food was not improving with the hours. It is strange how different is the atmosphere, even among close friends, when one awaits the arrival of a Prime Minister.

Everyone is more reticent and respectful. I have noticed the Christian name is hardly ever used, only the title.

Still, even if Harold was Prime Minister, I was getting ready to suggest that we should start the meal when the Lord Chancellor himself intervened, as only a Lord Chancellor could, to suggest that we should forget protocol. That is one advantage in having a Lord Chancellor to dinner. He can make a protocol decision for you. But just as Lord Gardiner had broken the ice, a telephone call came through from No. 10, a somewhat unusual route, but nevertheless the link-line with us. We were told that the Prime Minister would be with us very shortly. He arrived only a few minutes later, to tell us of some of the events at Mildenhall and to join in a very pleasant evening which went on until very late.

That year Harold had another worrying holiday, twice interrupted for Northern Ireland. Then when Harold made his second attempt to get some rest in the Scillies, we had a number of exchanges by telephone about the Party's new publicity campaign.

Harold's first public appearance after his return to London was also his first confrontation with a Trade Union audience since the troubles over industrial relations had come to a head in June. And the Trade Union audience he faced was the most important of all, the full Trade Union Congress meeting for its annual conference at Portsmouth.

He did not regard this as just another official engagement, but treated it as what it really was, one of the main political occasions of the year. Both Political and Private Offices therefore worked together on the processing of the speech. The speech was prepared with great care but with the realization that it would get an almost silent reception. In fact every TUC that he had attended had been a solemn affair. These Congresses have an atmosphere all their own and are quite unlike Party conferences. There are rarely any great demonstrations of enthusiasm and certainly no standing ovations. Only once did there appear to be more than mild approval at a TUC and that was in 1964, before Harold became Prime Minister and hopes were high.

The reception was not bad at all. In view of all that had happened that year, Harold himself thought that his speech had gone off quite well. There was quietness, certainly, but not hostility, because a TUC does not express hostility to a Labour leader unless he is behaving very oddly indeed.

There was an important change in the atmosphere at No. 10 about this time. Even before the summer holidays we had realized that an election was getting close and was unlikely to be postponed for more than a year. From my experience during the periods before the 1964 and 1966 elections, I knew that from now on the going was likely to get very tough indeed.

What we sensed at the beginning of the autumn was a slight but perceptible change in the country. Even without the opinion polls it was quite probable that the worst of our unpopularity was behind us. Some of the old feeling was starting to come back, the feeling that, despite everything, Labour was the Party that genuinely did try to do something for the majority of our people.

For me the election run-up meant getting the Political Office fully manned and organized so that it was ready for any extra duties that might be imposed. Because of shortage of money we could never be as fully manned as we would have liked. Nor could we equip ourselves in the way one ought to be equipped for a modern election campaign. In the end the campaign of 1970 proved to be our worst campaign of all, and in many ways the least well provided for. But during the run-up period it did not seem that way. We thought we had made all the arrangements that could be made.

By October 1969 we were psychologically on a war footing. We had little doubt that Harold's speech to the Party conference would be his last to a Labour conference before the election. For this reason it had to contain once again the summary of achievements and, in addition, a rallying call for those who had been disillusioned or disaffected, either on domestic or foreign affairs, over the past years.

Naturally, the 1969 conference was planned more carefully than any previous one. Its importance was apparent, and we took even more care than usual about even the smallest details.

Long before it was to take place I went down to Brighton with David Candler and Bert Williams, the conference officer at Transport House, to meet the manager of the Grand Hotel. Already we had discussed most arrangements with the manager.

One of the usual points raised was where was Harold to sit in the dining room? The security people, remembering 1966, did not want him to be placed where he could be seen by anybody outside the windows. He was given a discreet table in a corner and this was surrounded by tables occupied by his staff. This prevented him from being seen by anybody outside, but unfortunately it prevented him being seen by anybody in the dining room either. However, this state of affairs did not last for long because he soon transferred himself to a larger table and gathered his friends round him. So much for security!

However, we got splendid co-operation from the hotel manager, who was probably the most efficient I encountered at any conference. He even equipped us with 'bleepers' so that we could always be contacted at short notice wherever we were in the hotel. Our rooms were also better than they had been at the 1966 conference. The flat, where we had to sleep, was used only for offices this time, and so we escaped the nightly tramp-ings of feet in the other flat overhead. I was delighted to be given a beautiful room at the other end of the corridor con-taining the suite occupied by Harold and Mary. It overlooked the sea and even the weather was good for this conference.

But the advance preparations were only a small part of the move to Brighton. We had to pack boxes full of stationery, literature, typewriters and reference books. The Rank Organiza-tion in Brighton installed a Xerox copying machine in the office and we also had an electric duplicating machine. We had to do all this because we were not just concerned with the speech, which was the centre-piece of our week. We were also a mobile Political Office mobilized to deal also with the normal post (which never stops coming, even during Con-ference), the Prime Minister's political engagements, his future plans, his present queries and any references which he might want us to check at short notice.

The moment we got to Brighton on the Friday evening we got down to the speech. Friends and advisers dropped in with suggestions. This was the time that I became conscious of the American phrase about political conferences taking place in 'smoke-filled rooms' behind the scenes. Everybody seemed to be smoking that year, and each of the meetings about the speech, which took place during the evenings on Friday, Saturday,

Sunday and Monday, was held in a haze of tobacco. There was Harold's pipe, of course, but one could hardly complain about that, and anyway I had got used to it. But Michael Halls was a pipe-smoker, and so were Tony Wedgwood Benn and Peter Shore, and Joe Haines, our new Press Secretary, smoked small cigars. Gerald Kaufman, David Candler and I were the only ones not blowing out great clouds of smoke into the room, and after a few half-hour sessions on the speech, I would stagger into the comparatively fresh air of the corridor outside the Prime Minister's suite.

Then there would be dashes to the flat next door to make sure that the mechanical processing of the speech was going all right, the typing, the checking and the photo-copying. These also provided some relief in the clearer atmosphere where one could have a cup of tea or coffee or an iced lager. Sometimes, of course, Bill Housden was there with his pipe, or one of the detectives would be at it too. What I did not know was that I had already caught a cold and that I was to have a mild attack of bronchitis later. Clearly the smoke-filled atmosphere was doing little to help. By the time the speech had been completed, delivered and everyone was happy, I was well on my way to feeling pretty groggy. Ever since I have had an inhibition about smoke-filled rooms at parties. I want to turn tail as soon as I see people lighting up. Yet I make the atmosphere even worse by sometimes smoking myself. But I must say those evenings in Brighton in 1969 cured me of ever becoming a real smoker.

We took a short time off during the preparation of the speech to attend the Party's big rally on the eve of Conference. That year it was addressed by Jim Callaghan. We wanted to hear just how Jim would handle things in view of all that had happened in the Party throughout the year, including the attacks on Harold's personal position and the industrial relations problem.

What happened was that Jim delivered in a concentrated and shortened form more or less everything that Harold intended to say on Tuesday. This remarkable coincidence was not a disaster, however, for it remained for Harold to spell out things in much more detail, and this is what he did.

Everyone concluded it had been a good conference. For us at

No. 10 we felt that it had set the right pattern for the immediate run-up period to the election.

The members of the Political Office who go to a Party conference are limited in numbers. Those left out were invited down to Brighton for the day of the Prime Minister's speech and for the final day as well.

A newcomer to our staff attending her first conference was Lynette Knorr, an enormously attractive Australian. She joined us after we had lost two of our best people, Mavis Blackwell, who had come to us in 1965, and Ann MacFarlane, a Scottish girl from Transport House. They decided to exchange the excitements of No. 10 for the even greater excitements of an overland trip to Australia.

Lynette was remarkable not just for her appearance – she had long thick auburn hair, a beautiful complexion and a magnetic personality – but also for her political views. Her Australian Labour background had given her very strong convictions and she was never slow to express them. On one occasion when Harold dictated a speech on foreign affairs, the photo-copy of the passage taken down by her was found to have a mysterious 'hear hear' typed in the margin. Apparently one piece about Tory east of Suez policies had so roused her that she put in her own comment, not in our favour either!

She played her part together with a friendly and efficient team of girls in the months leading to the election. The actual date was now in the process of being settled. Way back in 1966 Harold had asked Gerald to give him a list of all the important local election dates in 1970. This slip of paper, which is reproduced in this book, was taken out soon after Conference, and from then on it was to prove a very important document indeed. We consulted it frequently, for on its dates depended exactly when Harold would announce the election date. Discussions about the 1970 date were held originally in 1966 and a decision was taken then. All that remained in the last months of 1969 and the beginning of 1970, was to decide on the actual Thursday when the election would be held.

Like other members of the political staff, I was looking forward to the usual brief rest to recover from conference exhaustion. But there was little rest that year. On the Saturday immediately following Conference, I received an urgent call to go over to

Chequers for tea. The reason was not the election, however, but a massive reorganization and reshuffle of the Government.

PRIME MINISTER

Here are the 1970 dates you asked for:

March 27	Good Friday
March 30	Easter Monday
April 6–11	English and Welsh County Council elections
April 9	GLC election
May 4–9	English and Welsh District Council elections
May 5	Scottish Burgh elections
May 7	English and Welsh municipal elections
May 12	Scottish County and District elections
May 17	Religious Whit Sunday
May 25	Spring Bank Holiday
August 31	August Bank Holiday

List submitted to P.M. by Gerald Kaufman 1966

I shall always associate the changes that were made with that afternoon in early October. It was so warm that everyone there, and Harold in shirtsleeves, was sitting in the garden. Harold had been doing his red boxes. I was just about to ring the doorbell when he appeared from the side door leading to the rose garden. We all spent the rest of the afternoon on the terrace talking and sitting in deck-chairs like no others I had seen. They looked like deck-chairs, true; they were extremely comfortable and quite different from the deck-chairs you see at Brighton or Blackpool. I am sure they had begun their life on some ocean liner. They were so old, I felt sure that Neville Chamberlain and Stanley Baldwin had sat in them years before.

For me the most striking result of the reorganization that Harold was planning that weekend was the end of the Department of Economic Affairs, which had been established with such high hopes in 1964. The lesson of the DEA was that it should have been given the backing possessed by Labour's Ministry of Technology or Mr Heath's Department of Trade and Industry.

Certainly the new Department could expect to have support from vast areas of British industry. It also gave Tony Wedgwood Benn a very powerful base politically as well as governmentally. He got too some very able men to help him. They notably included Harold Lever, who got a seat in the Cabinet as well through Harold's backing.

When Parliament resumed it was not the Queen's Speech that provided the main theme but the continually deteriorating situation in Ulster.

Shocking though this was in terms of avoidable human misery, in political terms it provided reinforcement for the view that this was Jim Callaghan's year. He had started off by creating for himself a popular posture on industrial relations, and now he was to dominate the Northern Ireland problem and the treatment of it in the House of Commons. Nobody doubted that he had become a success as Home Secretary. His predecessor, Roy Jenkins, had made a name for himself for his style. Jim's style was totally different, but it was equally effective.

In October there was a reception at No. 10 for the first men who had walked on the moon. When the Apollo astronauts came in, and we realized that here were the people who had actually carried out such a feat, it was like something from H.G. Wells come to life. Life at No. 10 is so hectic, and contains so many crises of its own, that sometimes it is difficult to register properly the events that take place outside. We were impressed not only with their courage, but also with their level-headedness and their sheer charm and personality. Of all the many dinners and receptions while we were at No. 10, this was the most exciting of all.

But there were not many receptions that autumn. The coming election campaign was the only thing that mattered. By now everyone was thinking hard about Harold's campaign and we were in contact with Transport House about this. The study at No. 10 saw more meetings with Percy Clark bringing along a small group of advisers including David Kingsley, Denis Lyon and Peter Davis.

One trouble was that Harold could not let them into his thinking as much as he would have liked. For obvious reasons he had to keep the election date to himself, and the group could not be told that the time in which they had to work must be much shorter than they imagined. One consequence of this was that their propaganda scheme was more in line with a longer-term campaign than we would have wished.

Harold's task therefore was to get them to do things which would help a short campaign while they were looking towards the long term. This proved to be easier than one might think. For, curiously, they came up by coincidence with quite a lot of things which were of considerable assistance even within Harold's timetable.

Percy Clark understood these difficulties though we never exchanged a single word about it. We did not need to do this with Percy. He was too old a hand at the game and he knew Harold too well for us to have to give him a clue.

In November he came over to No. 10 with projector and films to show us clips of election films taken during the Nixon campaign in America. They were fascinating. One of the most impressive slogans urging people to go to the polls was: 'The risks are too great for you to stay home.' Joe Haines, who looked in briefly on another matter, saw the film and produced a funny but sick joke, that it sounded more like an appeal to the tenants of high tower blocks of flats, than an appeal to the voters.

The Prime Minister also went along to the BBC's television studio at Lime Grove for a colour test. This was essential now with the arrival of colour television. Everyone had to see how the party leaders would look. Both the Conservative and Labour leaders had the advantage of having grey hair and blue eyes, ideal for colour television purposes. Britain's first colour TV election gave them both a bonus.

By now the gradual up-turn in Labour's fortunes was being confirmed. The Parliamentary Party was recovering from the shocks of the previous year, the economy was going well, and the trade returns were getting better all the time. In that autumn's by-elections we lost Swindon, for special reasons, but we held the other two seats, though with reduced majorities. This in itself was progress compared with the long run of actual disasters.

It had been a year when we had taken an awful lot of beating. Amazingly, however, we had at last begun to see a light showing now at the end of the tunnel. There was a strong possibility that, with extra effort on everyone's part, we could move very strongly forward to another election victory.

This was one of the reasons why Christmas in 1969 was a particularly happy one for all of us.

On 22 December, after a meeting with Peter Shore, Gerald Kaufman and Thomas Balogh in the study, to discuss the next six months, Harold had a dinner at Chequers for the Political Office staff and some of his closest friends. It was a gathering of old associates and of new friends too, like Lynette Knorr from Australia, Esther Lastick, Lucille Jones and her husband, and Cathy Andrews, another most dedicated party worker from the Political Office. Other guests included Harold's favourite photographer Ann Ward and her husband, and Alfred Richman and his wife. 'Rich' had been a hard-working and devoted friend of Harold's and ever since he became Leader, Rich had accompanied him on all his outside visits in the country. He did the jobs few would have liked to do. Rich always did them with great enthusiasm and gusto and while often running into trouble, nevertheless took everything that happened in his stride. Without him around to bully us, and without him around to shout at, we would very easily have floundered on many of our outside political visits, our conferences and our election tours. Dr Stone was there with Mrs Stone, Beattie Plummer, and another old friend, Felicity Bolton.

In the evening of 23 December, Harold gave a party for all the staff at No. 10. They were not joined by the staff from Transport House who were to come separately in the New Year.

Harold felt that the two staffs should have their own parties this time. One reason was that in the run-up to an election, it was easier for us to be with our own people in a more relaxed atmosphere if civil servants were not around.

Even the preparations of the Christmas cards seemed easier that year. For the first time the photograph of Mary and Harold on the card was taken at Chequers, with Paddy, their Labrador dog. While Ann Ward said it was not the best photograph in the world, because it had been taken in bad weather conditions without all her equipment available, it was nevertheless one of the most popular photographs we had used for a Christmas card.

The buying of the presents for all the staff and distributing them around No. 10, the bottles of whisky and sherry to the messengers and to the custodians and policemen on the front door, the chocolates to the ladies on the switchboard, and the presents to the Private Office and the Political staff, all seemed to be organized more smoothly than before. Perhaps it was the irony of the situation that the last Christmas at No. 10 should prove to be the most easily managed and the most enjoyable of them.

Once the holiday began, Mary and Harold spent the time at Chequers and on Boxing Day they turned around the practice they had undertaken before, of visiting the Stoke Mandeville Hospital. This year they invited the patients and staff at Stoke Mandeville to Chequers. I went over with my brother and sister to help and the afternoon and evening were really memorable.

Peter Murray turned up with Kenny Lynch and Harry and Catherine Fowler. All gave unsparingly of their time to help entertain the visitors from the Hospital. The visitors seemed to enjoy the change from previous years, and were particularly pleased, I think, to have the opportunity of seeing inside Chequers for the first time. There were songs around the piano and Pete Murray presented them all with a collection of records.

After the Stoke Mandeville friends had left, the family, the visitors and other friends had dinner. After that, much to everyone's amusement we were taken off to the Hawtrey Room by Kenny Lynch, to watch a television programme in which he was appearing. In that particular broadcast, he had something slightly hostile to say about Harold which made everyone laugh – some nervously and some uninhibitedly.

We were now going into 1970 very keyed up. But we had one great advantage. We had Peter Shore as co-ordinator of government policy and information. In the October reshuffle which ended the DEA, Peter had taken over the role previously held by Judith Hart. Harold felt this was the one key job needing to be filled by someone who knew him well, who knew exactly how he operated politically and could, therefore, think his thoughts for him over the months that lay ahead, both with regard to his own personal handling of an election campaign and also the more general handling of it by the Government and by Transport House. Peter, who was himself an old Transport House hand, now had the experience behind him of a large government department. He was exactly the right person to do the liaison work with Transport House and to act as Harold's closest adviser during the months ahead. The Political Office were particularly reassured to know he was going to be so closely linked with Harold. We could now depend on him ourselves for advice.

Harold knew Gerald was to fight the election as a candidate, and that he therefore would be largely out of action at No. 10 during the election. But the preliminary work could now be done, for the team was assembled.

12

The Chequerboard

It was not just the structure of the Government that changed during the two Labour Parliaments. The personalities changed as well. This happens in most Parliaments as some big figures inevitably wane in importance and even disappear while new ones emerge, sometimes gradually, occasionally dramatically.

I must say, though, that the number of really exciting figures thrown up in politics has tended to decrease in recent years. More and more the trend is for the emergence of grey men. In our time at No. 10 the most colourful and exuberant figure who gained Cabinet rank was Dick Marsh, but even he has now gone off to work in a nationalized industry.

Still, his promotion to the top rank was a long way off when we took office. The early years were dominated for us quite naturally by Jim Callaghan and George Brown. These were the other two contenders for the leadership in 1963. They were the anti-popes and they had their own legions. To some extent these can still be identified, though the allegiances have long since gone.

But in 1964 they were the men who felt that, but for the grace of God, one of them would have been sitting in No. 10. Psychologically they never really conceded the defeat of 1963, and this was one of the most powerful factors in my view subconsciously motivating their actions throughout their ministerial careers.

George Brown was the runner-up to Harold in 1963. He had polled a considerable figure against Harold, despite difficulties, and this was quite an achievement. In the long run his comparative success did great harm for during this period George seemed to feel that he was not so much a Deputy Prime Minister as the alternative Prime Minister, and often seemed to act as such.

He certainly established himself as the Deputy Prime Minister. No such role exists constitutionally unless a Prime Minister actually makes the statement to the effect that one of his colleagues is acting in that capacity. Nobody queried whether Harold had ever made such an announcement about George and in fact he never did make this announcement, but George was powerful enough to get his own conception of his office accepted, and even Transport House would refer to him in this capacity in communications with No. 10.

This whole psychological attitude of George's was the cause of both his enormous successes and his final failure. He has such tremendous assets; an acute mind, more acute than that of most lawyers one meets, and in many ways his mind was more like a lawyer's than a politician's. He had an abundance of enthusiasm for the jobs he undertook (which cannot be said of all our Ministers). Above all he had an aggressive, questioning attitude to the Civil Service. Of all our Ministers he was one of the men to show real signs of being in charge, even if at times he verged on the brink of rudeness in order to achieve his purposes.

Tony Crosland in 1971 raised the question of Ministers having to get the measure of their Principal Private Secretaries in their Private Offices, so that they can finally establish whether the Principal Private Secretary will tell more to the Minister about the Permanent Secretary than to the Permanent Secretary about the Minister. Of course, the fact is that all good civil servants learn the art right from the start of convincing their Minister of their primary loyalty while doing the same job with their Permanent Secretary, and then performing an equal hatchet job on both, since there is little danger of being found out, and even if this ambivalence is discovered the only penalty normally is promotion.

For George Brown to be unkind to people who operate a system where this technique is accepted is hardly something to be condemned. George was never frightened to take on the establishment. He felt the instinctive working-class, ordinary man's tiredness of being dictated to by these languid fellows.

His technique with civil servants was to chastise them openly and honestly when he felt they had done wrong, rather than to conceal the criticism and attack them behind their backs, which was, I fear, the approach often used by the more sophisticated politicians.

Harold and he had spells of great friendship, punctuated by less enthusiastic periods and sometimes, as in most relationships, by arguments. George wanted, I think, to dislike Harold – or, rather, he felt he should dislike him – but often found this extremely difficult, particularly when Harold was being his ordinary self. Harold essentially is kind, even if he sometimes lacks understanding. The kindness he expressed could stop a stampede, but it never solved the innate problems that George had.

George once said, much to the amusement of some, that he wanted to be loved. This was true and I think that it was both true and touching in a politician, since most know the cruel realities of their profession. However, Harold is a very un-demonstrative man, and the two never became really friendly because of the incompatibility of their personalities. One is very demonstrative, the other the reverse, but both have many basic things in common. They are from similar family back-grounds where love was more obtainable, and in greater abundance, than money. They both are clever – despite George's constant railing against 'university people'.

He was very wilful to keep on with this line since he knows perfectly well that he is infinitely superior to most of the university-trained people that he has had the good fortune or the misfortune to meet. What was curious about him was the constant political schizophrenia in his mind. He was continually accusing Harold of not consulting his colleagues enough, while as a Minister himself he was pursuing a very independent and robust course with only the occasional reference back to the Prime Minister from time to time to see if Harold agreed – very often after the event. But this again was probably part of the old feeling of rivalry asserting itself. As a man who might have been elected Leader, and nearly was, and as the man who felt he should have won in 1963, he was never able to accept fully that Harold was there in possession.

George is extremely fascinating to people because he has great swings of temperament, from being extremely jolly to something rather less. Of course, it is much easier to work with the equable character, the man with the even temper, and to work in an atmosphere where the psychological temperature is known in advance. But there is a fascination about a big figure who has these violent swings in temperament.

George remains a big figure, and I suppose he always will, because of his personality. When he was around, people knew it. He has an aura and a charisma, to use a popular word, of his own. And these are peculiar and valuable assets to the successful politician.

He resigned a number of times, not just on the occasions which became public. This was the result of his temperamental side – the swings from great excitement and elation to depression and frustration, which prompted him to want to leave the Government and not continue with his work. His numerous resignations became after a time amusing, but they were at least human. The final going has been much written about, and everyone has a different version of what happened on the night. Mine is that a search was made for George but was called off, on the advice of his civil servants. Later in the night the situation had changed, but by then events too had moved on. But many looked for him. I did myself at the beginning and then, like everyone else, gave up when the advice filtered through.

George had great confidence in his assessment of Harold's character and of Harold's reactions, and this was the cause of the fatal error he made in that last resignation. He genuinely thought that Harold would not accept it, and failed to realize that Harold had to. Indeed it was essential to the Prime Minister's authority, particularly after the scene in the House of Commons when George held his small meeting of Cabinet Ministers, which produced the telephone call requesting Harold's presence among them.

I don't think George Brown would have allowed himself as Prime Minister to be placed in such a position for a very good reason. I cannot believe George Brown would have tolerated for one moment in a Cabinet he might have headed, a member who had the self-confidence to hold a separate meeting of that kind behind his back. I am convinced too, that George, faced with the situation existing that night, with action needed urgently, would not have felt he had done anything unseemly by getting the job done and relying on senior colleagues who could not be brought in for various reasons to understand and to accept the need for swift decisions.

How would George have treated Harold if George had become Leader and then Prime Minister? Would he have been a great consulter of colleagues? Harold in fact seemed to many to delegate too much and held too many discussions with colleagues. He did exactly what George accused him of not doing when he left. George resigned over a non-existent style of government, but his bluff having been called, he had to go on some issue. Even his resignation letter was not quite a resignation, and it left open the possibility of snatching him back from the brink. But this Harold could not then do. It was already too late for another rescue operation.

For me, George Brown remains a person who, while holding a high position, managed to remain himself. He was always very kind to me, very friendly and warm-hearted, and I don't think that throughout the whole time I knew him we exchanged any cross words. He was someone who was always a solid Labour politician, with his feet firmly on the ground.

What about the third member of the triumvirate – Harold, George and Jim?

Well, Jim Callaghan was the great survivor, and I think he always will be.

As far as I am concerned he is the best political operator we have had in this country for a very long time. Like Harold he has an enormous knowledge of the Party and how it works, and he knows exactly how to operate in a political set-up. I have known him longer than I have known Harold.

When I was at university, I was secretary of the Labour Society in my College. Because of this I inevitably came to meet the secretaries and officers of the opposing political societies in the college. I eventually married the chairman of the college Conservative Association. But well before that the two of us put on a joint debate. I invited Jim Callaghan to address it on behalf of the Labour Party, though for the life of me I cannot remember who it was who came to debate against him for the Tories. We entertained the speakers to lunch in the college dining room before the meeting and I was terrifically impressed by Jim. When I left college I did a crash secretarial course, at St Godric's College, since I had always been determined to work for the Labour Party and for a Member of Parliament if possible. First, I had to find out something about the real Labour Party existing outside the rarefied intellectual politics I had been exposed to in a university atmosphere. For this reason I was glad to have the opportunity of working in Transport House, and of obtaining valuable knowledge about the real centre and heart of the Party, how it works and its organization.

The nice thing about Jim Callaghan was that when he heard I had got married, when I first went to Transport House, he very kindly sent me some table linen as a wedding present. I have kept it to this day unopened and unused. At the time I felt a present from such a distinguished Labour leader was something that really could not be used for everyday living.

I would often run into him when I was working at Transport House, and on one occasion Jim told me that his own secretary had gone off to Geneva temporarily, and he had no one to do his work. This gave me the chance to work for him for a very brief period, and also to get my first taste of the more sophisticated atmosphere of the House of Commons.

Jim Callaghan has always been very charming to me, though I won't say that once I began to work for Harold I was not often ribbed and left with the odd, slightly acid remark ringing in my ears, but it was done in a good-humoured way. I always thought of Jim as a left-winger though I was, of course, to be proved wrong on that later.

In the 1963 leadership contest he had been the middleman set up to stop the other two, or at least to keep their respective votes down. Jim never really conceded the 1963 defeat to Harold either. That's fair game I suppose. It is, after all, what politics is largely all about at a certain level.

Sections of the Party were often to believe Jim Callaghan supported some of the things they held dear, when in fact he was actually trying to get the opposite. As the Chancellor of the Exchequer, he was not as free as he could have been. As Chancellor he consulted Harold, of course, very closely at times of crisis, when he was under heavy pressures. But he confided less during the rest of the time except as the result of inquiries from Harold's office, or from Harold himself. There were no real continuous political and economic discussions between the two, as there were to be later when Roy Jenkins was Chancellor.

George Brown might well have made a better Chancellor for the Labour Government in 1964, and, if the roles of the two men had been reversed, a very different picture indeed might have emerged. The Treasury nearly finished Jim off, despite the political judgement and political antennae which kept him alive even during the worst periods of the stay at No. 11.

But, ironically, devaluation which had seemed such an overwhelming blow for him turned to his advantage. For immediately afterwards he had the good sense to allow himself to be moved to the Home Office. At one point he seemed to hesitate, and the information coming to us from his department was that he was planning to go to the back benches and act as a senior statesman there. But Jim, with his perfect judgement in these matters, finally chose the Home Office and it was the Home Office that built him up again.

There are a number of reasons for this, including his incomparable gift for survival. Another was his long connection with the Police Federation which is a vital body in the world of the Home Office. The Police Federation had employed him as their spokesman and always had kept a great admiration for him.

After the wind of liberation which had swept through the Home Office Department, I think that not only the department, but people in the country as well, were glad to shrink back into a slightly more reactionary world. They wanted, I think, the period of retrenchment that must take place after so many bracing reforms. People at large can only absorb so much.

Of course, the history of Jim's career, and its effect on Harold's is far more complicated than that of George Brown. By comparison George's story is simpler. His complications are obvious and well known.

One of the complications in Jim's life arose during the troubles in the Party in the early sixties when there was a great deal of manoeuvring, for or against Hugh Gaitskell. It was a highly personalized period. During the fifties most members of the Labour movement would have supposed Jim Callaghan to be more to the left than the right of the Party. But at the 1960 Scarborough Conference, when the unilateral disarmers made such a display of strength and when Hugh Gaitskell was fighting for his own political career, Jim Callaghan finally decided to join Mr Gaitskell, and so make almost total his support for the top people within the Party and certainly those in the Shadow Cabinet. There was a great deal of speculation about why Jim Callaghan took the line he did. What is a matter of record is that once everyone was back in London and the defence argument had calmed down, and the leadership election in which Harold took part was over, it was Jim Callaghan who strangely enough was offered the job as Shadow Chancellor when Harold was moved to Foreign Affairs.

From then until our election victory in 1964 Jim did an awful lot of hard work, literally homework, to equip himself for his new job. It must have been very tough going to have to acquire so much detail and technical knowledge on such intricate subjects in such a short time. But nobody can ever fault Jim for lack of effort.

So Harold, finding Jim Shadow Chancellor in 1964, confirmed him as Chancellor after the victory. This was part of the general pattern of appointments, for it should be realized that there never was a Wilson Government as such; a Government, that is, which was chosen by Harold purely on the basis of appointing from scratch the people considered by him to be those he wanted for the job. In forming both Governments, and in making his reshuffles, there was always a sizeable section of people inherited from Mr Gaitskell. And in the early stages at least, the inheritance principle applied to the allocation of jobs as well as the actual people.

There were some surprises certainly – as when Charles Pannell was sent to the Ministry of Works because of the solid work he had done in the House to try to improve the facilities for Members and his dedication to the Parliamentary system and his desire to bring it up to date – but in the main he followed Mr Gaitskell's plan, particularly where Jim Callaghan and George Brown were concerned.

What will these two widely differing characters be remembered for? In the case of Jim there was the work within the Treasury of such outside people as Nicholas Kaldor and the very novel, but highly contentious taxes which Jim introduced in his Budgets, particularly the well-known Selective Employment Tax.

And, of course, Jim Callaghan will have a place in the history books because of the second devaluation. By the time that sort of history is written I hope that devaluation will at last have assumed its right role and be regarded not as a bogy, but as just another weapon to be used uninhibitedly if and when it is necessary.

And George Brown? He will, of course, always be well known for his 'Declaration of Intent' and for the long nights he spent keeping industrialists in line on prices, as well as for the more tempestuous months he spent at the Foreign Office.

But the fortunes of Jim Callaghan and George Brown and the ever continuing pressures they had upon Harold in his work, both politically and governmentally, were losing momentum by 1968. The later years saw the emergence of other figures of equal stature.

Barbara Castle had the disadvantage of being, I suppose a 'Wilsonite'. She had, therefore, not been in the Establishment of the Parliamentary Labour Party, though she was entrenched in the Party in the country which meant she was also a major figure on the National Executive Committee. While she was well known as a formidable political speaker, nobody had quite realized her potential nor how she would measure up in a top job and its demands upon her.

But Harold knew her abilities extremely well because she had been his Parliamentary Private Secretary in the Attlee Government. They had also seen a great deal of each other as Bevanites and as members of the left wing of the Party in the earlier years. He was never in any doubt that she was a very remarkable person indeed.

When he formed the 1964 Government there was a problem of too many people for too few jobs. All the top jobs had already been allocated by Hugh Gaitskell, so many of the colleagues that Harold valued most and wanted to put into key positions could not be fitted in. However, he found a solution to this in the case of Barbara by appointing her to the new Ministry for Overseas Development, which was something he was very keen on, and particularly anxious should succeed because of the Labour Party's special links with what has now become known as the 'third world'. She also came into the Cabinet in that post.

It was soon very clear that she not only had enormous political ability but extraordinary administrative competence as well. She was also very able in handling her civil servants and was totally in charge of her departments. Around her in the Overseas Development Ministry she gathered together people with whom she built up an extraordinarily good relationship, and a great deal of hard work and enthusiasm went into all they did. It was therefore a great wrench for her to be asked to move from there. In fact the funny thing about her is that she was always reluctant to move from any job she held and wanted to stay on to continue with all the projects on which she was engaged. I think this must be one measure of the enthusiastic successful Minister. In spite of this Barbara was never reluctant to take on a different job as a challenge; in fact it was the knowledge that it was a challenge that often persuaded her into acceptance.

While the ODM was an admirable and adequate job, it never got the sort of news coverage which other government departments had unless it was coming under criticism for spending too much of the taxpayers' money. In that sense it was not a department in which you could build yourself up as a big figure.

Once Barbara took up the challenge of the move to the Ministry of Transport, an unusual job for a woman Minister, the speed with which she emerged as an even more powerful governmental figure was amazing. Few people expected her to be the success she was as Minister of Transport, but Harold knew that she could not fail. As a woman in that job she would automatically make news, and newspapers and television would want to cover everything she was doing. Very often their motives would be to criticize, or to prove that the decision to put a woman into what was regarded as a man's job was wrong. But Harold's judgement proved correct because Barbara was quite equal to this sort of pressure and could turn it very adequately and successfully to her advantage and, therefore, to the advantage of the Labour Government.

Despite some of the controversies that surrounded certain acts for which she has become famous, it was an era of modernization and activity within her department. Once again she gathered around her a group of people, not only junior Ministers, but advisers as well, who were devoted to her and had the same enthusiasm as her own for the work they were doing. She was very lucky to have with her Stephen Swingler, later to die tragically, since he was one of the few young men in the Labour Government who, while still on the second ministerial tier, clearly had all the qualifications for promotion to a top job. He did great work in helping Barbara to steer her Transport Bill through the House of Commons.

But the time came once again for Barbara to move and she was offered the Department of Employment and Productivity. She expressed the same regret and reluctance to leave the team she had built up and the work on which she was engaged as when she was asked to leave the Department for Overseas development. She was also quite rightly a little nervous about the trouble-fraught area into which Harold was about to pitch her. But Harold had complete confidence in her total abilities on all fronts and felt she really was the one person who could carry the burden and convince the Trade Union movement of the Labour Government's sincerity and loyalty to the objectives they themselves were pledged to. After all she was a left-winger who was now to operate in an increasingly left-wing dominated world.

She took it on reluctantly although aware of the fact that with this job as First Secretary of State she had now emerged as a top figure in the Labour Government, and that the old triumvirate of Jim Callaghan, George Brown and Harold Wilson had given way to something new. From that point on, there was a quite different situation, with Barbara Castle playing a leading role. Indeed the Press were soon speculating about the future of this formidable woman who could possibly become Britain's first woman Prime Minister.

People clearly have different views about Barbara, as a personality, but I think one of her main achievements has been to convince people at last that she is both a major political public figure, but also still very much a woman too. I have known her for some years now and always I have been aware of the extremely feminine side of her character, particularly in her reactions to the everyday things of life. She has always behaved quite naturally without self-consciously thinking about her position, unique as it has been, as a woman in a predominantly man's world. She is, too, very amusing and extremely friendly without those traces of condescension present with so many public figures.

In the early days, when I first worked for Harold, we always had the enjoyable chore on the last Wednesday of every month of collecting Barbara from her home in Highgate and taking her into the House of Commons, so that she and Harold could go on together to the monthly meeting of the National Executive Committee. Sometimes she would be so late in coming out that she would wave from the window or dash out of the door clutching in her hands her clothes, or with a piece of toast from the breakfast she hadn't quite finished, and throw herself into the front seat next to Harold and immediately launch into a long conversation, or an attack on a particular subject, while fitting in a grumble about being late or warning Harold not to complain about having to wait for her. It was always a typically feminine entrance.

Barbara's sense of humour is not well known to the general public since she has so obviously been involved throughout her political life in serious matters. But her friends know very well that she is a very amusing and enjoyable person.

For women who want to get on in politics she is an example of what one should aim to be and the sort of balance one should try to achieve and maintain. She has always taken a very careful interest in her appearance, particularly in her hair, and in her clothes. She likes to be up to date and loves gay and pretty clothes. She very rarely looks anything but extremely attractive. At every meeting I have seen her attend she has always bounced in looking every inch a woman, and it was fascinating to watch such an essentially feminine person sitting down with a group of men, whose equal she was indeed, and hammering away at them in the most extraordinarily powerful way. Barbara emerged like a butterfly from a chrysalis, and her climb to the top coincided with the climb of the man who was to become the party's Deputy Leader and be regarded as being the most likely successor to Harold.

There is no doubt that Roy Jenkins was Labour's lucky Minister! His first appointment as Minister of Aviation was only short-lived, though he was so able during that period that he established himself as a very solid ministerial figure. Then the resignation of Frank Soskice from the Home Office presented him with the greatest opportunity of his career.

Sir Frank, the first Labour Home Secretary, was not well in health and Roy was his obvious successor. Roy had for many years been associated with groups which believed in liberalizing measures in our social life which would free society from many of the more ugly and repressive restrictions on personal liberty. At the Home Office, Roy was able to preside over one of the greatest periods in progressive social legislation the country has seen. Of course, there has been controversy about it, and a great mass of public opinion that is basically conservative in these matters is very critical of what the Labour Government achieved. They resent the reforms carried out on abortion, homosexuality, capital punishment, divorce and the whole refashioning of much of our legal system. With Gerald Gardiner, the Lord Chancellor, the Labour Government presided over the most extraordinary revolution in our legal system and the whole attitude of the law to society.

Roy Jenkins was lucky because he was the right Home Secretary at the right time. He was lucky that the outburst of young opinion within our society and its desire to be freed from some of the restrictions of what it saw as outworn and outmoded social conventions, had manifested itself then and was making such an impact.

He was lucky later to be able to take over the Treasury after devaluation had occurred. He was also lucky in that the choice of Chancellor fell on him and not on the other major candidate, Tony Crosland. Their qualifications for the job were equal, but Harold felt for a number of reasons that Roy was the person who should go to the Treasury.

Jim Callaghan had had to see us through the hard years of battling to maintain the pound's parity. Then came devaluation, the one thing that was supposed to liberate us and get the economy moving again – and Jim Callaghan went and Roy Jenkins took over.

Roy had the easy spell in comparison, though he carried out

this job with superb panache. He was very much the elegant leisured Chancellor, but he was also the man with the economic background and training who knew very well the workings of the Treasury and the people who staff it.

While very much in tune with much of Treasury thinking he was nevertheless expert enough to be able to maintain a certain control over those who advised him. Yet even so, he allowed much to develop in Treasury advice that could have been avoided.

Roy and Harold had a closer relationship than Harold had with Jim. But, again, the reason why may well be rooted in those days of 1963. Roy, though a close friend of Hugh Gaitskell's, had not in practice been as near to Hugh Gaitskell as Tony Crosland for instance. Although Roy clearly had preconceived ideas about Harold – not necessarily flattering – I am sure that some at least were changed during the course of their partnership together at Nos 10 and 11.

Roy's principal personal adviser, John Harris, was someone we knew very well and with whom we had had a very good working relationship before and during 1964. This was a hidden asset. It helped to establish an underlying political understanding. Roy's personal meetings with Harold were frequent and his consultations on the Budget and strategy were most detailed. Like all Chancellors, Roy kept a great deal of it to himself. All Chancellors want to present the most unusual and startling Budget to the country, but despite this Roy nevertheless consulted Harold a great deal on both the economic and political strategy involved in the Budget-making process.

The 1968 gold crisis was a testing time in their relationship. They came then to know very well indeed their respective strengths and weaknesses. That was a most difficult period politically, overshadowed as it was by George Brown's final resignation. Like many crises within a government, the political repercussions caused greater headaches and greater wear and tear on the individual than did the actual crisis itself.

On a personal level, Harold was particularly pleased by one gesture of friendship Roy made towards him. Roy generously gave Harold a recording of one of Asquith's political speeches, a gift whose clear historical value seemed to symbolize the thought behind it.

Harold naturally realized Roy's ambitions and that his ultimate one was the desire to be Prime Minister. This was one of the realities of politics. One of the fascinations about working in No. 10 is being able to watch the various figures in the Party working out their political careers.

To many people, and certainly to a great many young and progressive people, Roy Jenkins has always had a particular appeal because of his very pronounced and firm views on what he described once rather dangerously as the 'permissive society' when what he was describing was a 'civilized society' within his own definition.

Of all the leading members of the Party, Roy is the man who seems to stand most for these beliefs.

Harold knew of the wide body of supporters Roy had and also of their actions on Roy's behalf. Sometimes these were over-enthusiastic activities, but certainly they were very dedicated to Roy and to his political advancement. I am sure that he often wished that they would be less energetic on his behalf since they sometimes did his cause harm.

Certainly Harold has a preoccupation about the intrigues which necessarily go on within a political party. What is extraordinary is that the Press often comment about the intrigues as if they were some figment of Harold's imagination. What nonsense this is about someone who has been involved in so much intra-party strife and ridden it always with calm and determination. However fierce the intra-party battles may have been, and they certainly became very fierce indeed on occasions, Harold never felt persecuted or felt that some great misdeed was being done to him. Sometimes he suspected plots against him. And quite right he was – there were. There always are against every party leader. But to deduce from all this that Harold Wilson developed some dreadful complex which made him look under his bed every night to find out whether he would discover Denis Healey, Tony Crosland, Barbara Castle, Jim Callaghan or Roy Jenkins waiting there to leap into bed and take his place is fanciful nonsense.

What he felt strongly was that it is a leader's duty to make sure that, while there is a healthy acceptance of this sort of activity, and the freedom to indulge in it, it should never be allowed to get out of hand. At the end of the day it is unlikely any would-be contender for the 'Crown' will succeed in making the operation a total success and what he will succeed in doing is crippling the Party and, therefore, the vehicle through which he wishes to make his bid for power. It is the experience of years that few party leaders are ousted from their posts easily. It is much more difficult in fact to oust a Labour leader than a Tory leader. Conservative Prime Ministers are particularly vulnerable to campaigns against them, while Conservative Leaders of the Opposition tend to be safer.

Another major figure in our life at No. 10 is the man I called the 'Minister for All Seasons' – Dick Crossman. In many ways a maverick figure, a 'rogue elephant' in politics, he was nevertheless the most colourful, thought-provoking and superior individual of all.

In many ways Dick too was Harold's political father figure. They have a curious relationship. They are both close friends and old rivals. In the inner recesses of Dick's mind must lurk the thought that he himself might have been the leader of the Labour Party. Many of the gifts which Harold possessed, Dick possessed in even greater abundance. Indeed they might well have been put to infinitely better use under Dick's sterner control. With Dick one never knows exactly how he will be on any subject on any occasion. He is a great intellectual gymnast, a man who ceaselessly and untiringly argues away with himself about every political and social question of the day. He is forever seeking answers to questions and questions to answers, and his thorough examination of himself and his own approach to problems has a curious parallel in Enoch Powell.

He qualifies on occasions for George Orwell's definition of the man who has the accomplishment of 'double think'. 'Double think,' George Orwell says, 'means the power of holding two contradictory beliefs in one's mind simultaneously and accepting both.'

For me, Dick Crossman was a frightening figure because he was so intellectual. I am instinctively at a loss with someone who applies a seminar technique in trying to draw people out in an argument. I am never quite sure whether it is to find out what they are really thinking, or merely to make them argue a subject out for the sake of the argument.

But while you can be frightened of him, one can never be anything but attracted and fascinated by him.

His mind is so clear and lucid, and his arguments are always so powerful and compelling, that when he is with you and talking to you, he carries you along on an enthusiastic sea of thought which clears away all the doubts and misgivings you may have had.

He has always been close to Harold. This relationship has rarely been broken, though there have been periods when it has had its tensions. They have a great deal in common in that they understand the other's personality extremely well. Dick is always amused by Harold's optimism about so many problems and situations, and Harold is amused by Dick's mental gymnastics.

Dick Crossman has always been good for Harold Wilson and always bad for him too. These contradictory threads, two incompatible influences, existed side by side the whole time.

Commentators argue about what happened over Harold's devaluation statement and Dick's attitude to it. Dick did advise a different and softer approach for the devaluation broadcast. But I am quite sure that once Dick had seen the broadcast being made he became convinced intellectually that the opposite approach was needed and then in turn convinced himself that he had wanted this and advised it.

Dick was always the conciliator within the Government; the conciliator between factions and over arguments, particularly during the sale of arms to South Africa argument. On all these things he became sometimes so obsessed with finding a way round that he forgot the fundamental issue at stake. He is the arch-exponent of the very art of which Harold Wilson is so often accused. In 1968 he worked hard in the post-devaluation period to bring, as he saw it, the Wilson faction and the Jenkins faction together. There emerged, therefore, the triumvirate of Dick Crossman, Barbara Castle and Roy Jenkins acting as a senior advisory group to Harold. What Dick never realized was that there was no real need for a conciliator or middleman. Circumstances themselves would keep the groups in line and developments continued to do so even during the periodic bids for power. But the fact that Dick was there, actively explaining each group to the other, acted as an invigorator even though the advantages of such a service were often overbalanced by the disadvantages. But Dick has an insatiable appetite for influencing, motivated, I am sure, by that deeply buried frustration.

In any job he would have been an excellent Minister, exciting, innovating and tremendously successful, even though in any job he would have made outrageous errors as well. To look at him is to see the outstanding Chancellor of the Exchequer; to see him is to see the progressive Foreign Secretary. But there is a contradiction about him – the extraordinary, outstanding ability and yet the never-ending possibility of the 'rogue elephant' breaking loose. Yet of all Harold's colleagues one wants to write most about him and still feels it is impertinent to write anything. Except that one can hear his laughter ringing in your ears at compliments and criticism alike.

He is the only Minister I have known or read of who could achieve the impossible of gearing a government's Parliamentary timetable to his family arrangements!

His impact on our public life has been enormous, but as yet not evaluated. He has probably achieved more than he would have done if he had reached the job which he so clearly would have loved to hold. Together with John Silkin he brought into Parliamentary life a clear fresh approach which could in time have revitalized our political lives and involved our young people again in the excitement of government. As it was, the work was halted and Dick went on to what was for him the greatest job of all, his post as Secretary of State for the Social Services.

Only those who heard him speak in 1962 on this subject at Brighton at the Party's conference, overshadowed as he was then by the Common Market controversy and Hugh Gaitskell's speech, can recall the mastery, the knowledge, the feeling that Dick Crossman has about the whole subject of Britain's social services and the future of our social security system.

These policies, views and feelings he developed and advocated over the Labour Government's lifetime, even when he was not the responsible Minister. But once he had been appointed Secretary of State, he did a tremendous job in the large, amalgamated department which was formed on his appointment. He was quite naturally bitterly disappointed when we lost the 1970 election and the scheme he had for a complete state system of earnings-related pensions benefits was lost. He was not part of the Gaitskell inheritance.

But many of those who were, continued through the two Parliaments in leading jobs. They served loyally and faithfully under the new Leader and included one of Harold's most stalwart Ministers in the first Government with the tiny majority, Herbert Bowden, our first Lord President and Leader of the House.

There was Michael Stewart too. He was twice Foreign Secretary, and Secretary of State for Economic Affairs in between. To many he seems the epitome of the dull grey man with a colourless approach to politics. Few realize how very amusing and funny he can be. On social occasions he can tell the most extraordinarily funny jokes in a deadpan way, astonishing many who regard him rather differently.

Outstanding figures inherited from Mr Gaitskell were Tony Crosland and Denis Healey, both of whom are considerable Parliamentarians and politicians. They now stand well to the fore in the struggle for the Party leadership when it is next an issue. Denis, with his sharp, crystal-clear, analytical Marxist mind, is the most single-minded of the front runners for this job and possibly the most dedicated and ruthless. Consequently he is the most likely to succeed eventually. Tony Crosland on the other hand, while equally ambitious, and popular with the rank and file of the Parliamentary Labour Party, has without doubt one of the best economic minds in the Labour Party.

There are, too, the Ministers in the Government with whom Harold had a very close personal relationship. These I suppose can be regarded as the Wilsonites.

One was Peter Shore, of course, who has now dramatically established himself during the long debate on Britain's entry into Europe.

Together with Ministers like George Wigg, Edward Short, Herbert Bowden and Judith Hart, were those who came and went in 10 Downing Street as friends as well as colleagues. One of the most frequent perhaps, during his term of office as Chief Whip, was John Silkin. This was not only because of his office. He had a good personal relationship with Harold, based on mutual respect and indeed affection. Harold recognized the enormous contribution John and Dick Crossman were making to the Parliamentary Labour Party in the liberal reforms they brought in. These were in keeping with so much that Harold Wilson believed in himself. He welcomed this partnership.

An awful lot has been written about John Silkin and the deduction made that he was an unsuccessful and weak Chief Whip. The contrary is true. He was a very single-minded, determined one. He did not exercise such a tight control over the Party as Ted Short had done – and needed to do – during the years of the three majority; but he certainly exercised a strict discipline after 1966. After all he had been trained as Edward Short's pairing whip during the early difficult years.

These were the close friends as well as the senior Ministers too. There were, as well, Ministers whom Harold consulted frequently, like Alun Chalfont. Harold knew him well because of Lord Chalfont's friendship with George Wigg.

An outstanding political personality who grew enormously in stature during the Wilson years was Tony Wedgwood Benn. Tony Benn, of course, was regarded by most as a Wilsonite. He was the 'whizz kid' of the Labour Party for many years. He was the hero who renounced a title and fought for progress in Parliamentary politics with his refusal to take up his father's peerage and sit in the House of Lords. He was the first politician to challenge the tradition, and he won.

He is a man of fantastic imagination and inventiveness – what would be called in the business world an 'ideas man'. He is one of the most hard-working people I've met, rising at an early hour and entering his office at the crack of dawn, much to the astonishment of his civil servants. This quickly instilled in them the idea that they were perpetually late for work. For Tony it was not an act of pretence or a demonstration, it was how he operates. He has a ceaseless wave of tireless energy running through him which he must expend throughout the day. It even runs over into the night. Very often, at times of political crisis, he would ring me up at home, sometimes at 3.30 a.m. He was a little surprised at first to find that I answered the telephone very quickly. The reason often was that I had only been in my own home for about an hour when he rang, having been working late at No. 10. Also, of course, the telephone was beside my bed so that I could be contacted quickly and at short notice. He would joke and say we were probably the only two people operating in the small hours of the morning. He told me that he did much of his best work then.

His first job as Postmaster General was one in which he acquitted himself with great drive and imagination. He was able to give expression to those who wanted a more imaginative approach to the whole visual technique in Post Office management – not just on the question of postage stamps, though that was an achievement to get for the first time the pictorials we wanted. But he was also able to update lots of what would be called, I suppose, the technical furniture within the Post Office, to establish a much better working relationship with the Trade Unions who operate within the Post Office services, and to try to put some sense into the ultimate question of whether it was a public service or a commercial enterprise, or both, or neither.

He did have the good fortune of getting Joe Slater as his Parliamentary Secretary. Mr Slater, now Lord Slater, Harold's former Parliamentary Private Secretary in Opposition days before 1964, had a wide Trade Union experience and was able to ease away many of the difficulties which Tony might have encountered in working with trade unionists who were not used to this semi-American driving force.

By the time he got his big promotion to the Ministry of Technology, and became overlord of the empire created in the last period of the Labour Government, Tony Benn, as visionary *extraordinaire* of the technological revolution, was in his element.

Not all of what he did and said was as understandable to me as it doubtless was to those around him. I also confess sometimes to finding his approach a little startling.

We lunched together on occasions, though not as often as I would have liked, nor as often indeed as he generously invited me. When the opportunity arose however, it was always one of the more unusual experiences of my time at No. 10.

Tony did not believe in the elaborate ministerial lunch indulged in by some of his colleagues. He issued no invitations to Soho restaurants, or even to the House of Commons dining room. He believed in sandwiches and a large mug of tea in his room in his Ministry. I like tea myself, and having no particular love for fine food, found sandwiches perfectly satisfactory. We would be served there by a messenger, with large mugs and a plate of assorted sandwiches.

There was the occasion at a major policy meeting when, in the middle of summing up what technology could do to change the face of Britain, he suddenly went off at a tangent and tried to enthuse us with the idea of the electric car. We might, he said, find ourselves commuting in electrically powered vehicles and parking them at meters. There we would plug them into the electricity generating system and while we were working away in our offices, our cars would be recharged, and when we leapt out again into our vehicles they would be fully powered, ready to shoot off to either our urban-renewed home or our dwelling in the commuter belt.

He has this almost childlike gift for seeing the excitement and the possibility of the science-fiction future we have so often been invited to look at. His contribution to the more mundane and earth-bound vision of his colleagues has been enormous, since he has given the uplift needed to make them see the possibilities of technology.

He has been named as the future leader of the Labour Party by many people. Clearly he is the right age, and he has great ability. Whether or not the Labour movement or the British people would be willing to repose their confidence in someone so visionary and way out we shall see.

These were some of the people who dominated and influenced our lives. They were the pieces on the chess-board that Harold looked after and watched, too, so carefully. The fascination lay in watching the pieces being shifted around by the Prime Minister and in watching, too, their attempts at moving themselves from one place to another, often making it necessary for the Prime Minister to place them elsewhere.

The job of those who work for the Prime Minister demands that they be as ever watchful as he is in taking note of all that is said to them both inside and outside Parliament, and telling him of it. Harold had very few political advisers who were not Ministers.

There were people who might have been given the title of 'confidants'. They were very few.

Thomas Balogh is perhaps best known as one half of the Hungarian twins. He was one of Harold's most loyal and devoted friends and supporters. I have often jokingly told him he is a 'professional foreigner', a man of Hungarian origin who longs to be more Establishment in some ways than the English Establishment. He wanted to be in the House of Lords and have a platform from which to speak. Yet at the same time he had – and still has – a deep inbuilt antagonism for the way the Establishment operates and the grip the Tory Party has over it.

He approaches all the problems he handles in a slightly melodramatic, overdrawn manner which sometimes leads to misunderstandings. Yet consistently throughout the years at No. 10 his analyses of the economic situation were generally correct and the advice he gave soundly based. He was, as were all those brought in from outside the Civil Service, obsessed with the personalities who often deliberately organized life in such a way as to make it difficult to survive.

Thomas was the greatest sufferer of all. He was an outsider operating at an extremely high level, who needed to have the complete co-operation of the civil servants to make the work he was doing worth while and meaningful. Yet throughout this period he had an uphill fight against the System. He retained throughout the period the same healthy disregard for conventional institutions and the same loyal and devoted service to Harold. Whenever a crisis occurred Thomas was around, and even when he was ill and feeling very tired, he gave his time and his energies to helping and advising and giving the support which was needed. He did it willingly and unstintingly and, although he received recognition in due course for his work, the real reward he wanted, the co-operation and facilities he needed to enable him to do his job in the best possible way, were denied him. This would have been his ultimate satisfaction; but it was the one thing he was never to enjoy. This was a great loss, not only to Harold personally but to the Labour Government as well.

Despite the fact that Harold found his colourful versions of what was happening around him sometimes amusing and sometimes irritating, they remained, and remain, close to each other. In the first Labour Government there was not easy access for Thomas to Harold for two reasons – his physical

location in the Cabinet Office, and lack of co-operation from
No. 10. But once 1966 had come, and Thomas was located in
No. 10 itself, his access was greater and the contribution
greater too.

In those days there were often gatherings in Thomas's
room on the second floor facing the Prime Minister's flat.
Harold would often look in there on his way to the flat for
lunch, and have a glass of sherry with Thomas before going
their separate ways to lunch. Very often when there Thomas
would have his innumerable visitors like Nicky Kaldor and
Robert Neild and other distinguished economists, historians and
industrialists.

It was a sad day for all of us when Thomas was given a life
peerage and left. But Harold had made it absolutely clear that if
Thomas was going to speak on political matters in the House of
Lords, then he could not remain in government service as a
paid adviser at No. 10. Thomas knew all this, but still made his
choice. I only wish extra pressure had been put on him to make
him stay on.

But there is no disguising that losing him to the Lords was a
blow. And at about the same time Harold lost another loyal
friend, George Wigg, when he went to the Upper Chamber after
being appointed head of the Horserace Betting Levy Board.

George is another fascinating figure. He is tall and dignified
and yet gives an oddly ambling impression. He is not easy to
understand but those who know him well invariably admire
him.

The sphere in which he had a real influence on the Prime
Minister was security. He had been a close friend of Harold's
over a period of years. During that time he had become more
and more preoccupied with security matters, particularly as a
result of his experience over the Profumo Affair. I think
security tended to dominate his thinking and even became at
times an obsession with him. One result was that he would
sometimes persuade Harold of security dangers which, though
they might exist, were still remote. Of course, it is necessary to
be ever alert about security, but it is also possible to be over-
sensitive too.

The contribution George made about security has been
fairly well publicized. What is not so well known is the other

contribution that George made – the generosity, the warmth and the personal friendship. Harold drew on this well of goodwill as freely as he drew on his advice on other questions.

Harold was unhappy when George finally made it clear that he wanted to make another career for himself in the world of racing he loved so much. But Harold accepted his decision, even against advice.

Life with George Wigg was not all sunshine for others though. I recall the times he was censorious with us about security and times when he treated us like the latest members of an awkward squad in a rookie army. We did not like this, particularly when his criticism occurred just as we thought we were doing a splendid job, but most people like to delude themselves they are. So George sometimes affronted us, but those moments are overshadowed now by the genuinely happy moments we had with him – the times we spent joking about racing, talking about his long association with the Party, listening to his anecdotes about Mr Shinwell (to whom George was truly devoted) and hearing his enormous store of information about defence in general and the Army in particular.

He was the one among us who at first, but less later, got on extremely well with the civil servants in No. 10 and elsewhere. This seemed to me to be because he was a military man and thus respected the Civil Service system which is so similar. There was therefore a great affinity between George and the officials, who were disciplined, organized beings while we on the political side were the undisciplined, 'wild', unorthodox, unconventional and uncontrollable elements, as he saw it.

Though many were his friends and comrades, he nevertheless felt that he ought somehow to be bringing everyone into line, to marshal and discipline us, rather than leave people to go their own undirected ways.

Our association with George Wigg was chequered, though our recollections are still warm and the sense of loss when he went was real. It was particularly hard for Harold who had relied on him for a very long time for advice on such a wide range of subjects and for help with so many personal questions.

George Wigg was the man who really introduced into Harold's life in a big way the now famous figure of Arnold Goodman. The future Prime Minister and the future Lord

Goodman got to know each other well first during the ITV strike that broke out not long before the 1964 election. They did not have frequent meetings, however, until much later – certainly not until George Wigg had left No. 10. In a curious way Arnold Goodman seemed to replace George Wigg as the close personal confidant. He visited No. 10 regularly and frequently, particularly during the second Labour Government. As well as being Harold's solicitor, he was also a friend and an adviser to him on a wide range of subjects. Many people find it surprising that subsequently he has remained equally close to the succeeding Conservative administration, but perhaps the links are different from those he has with Harold Wilson, both when he was at No. 10 and later as Leader of the Opposition again. There is no doubt that of all the figures in our public life, Lord Goodman is the most formidable, though until recently he was the least well known.

Then, of course, there were the advisers in a different sense, men like Sir Solly Zuckerman, now Lord Zuckerman, who held the title of the Government's Scientific Adviser, but who seemed to be consulted not only on scientific matters but on many other questions as well.

He is a man with numerous contacts, assiduous in his application to knowing as many people as possible in all walks of life, and in particular to understanding those in the corridors of power – indeed, in the corridors outside power too, since he knew the Opposition equally well. This has brought him fame and achievement, even though perhaps not in the field of scientific expertise, over the last ten years.

Whenever there was a crisis where scientific advice was required, the first name to be heard was the name of Solly Zuckerman. It always sounded something like a court of law. You felt any minute some flunkey would throw open the Cabinet Room door and shout down the long corridor of Downing Street, 'Call for Solly Zuckerman'. Yet at the end of the incident, whatever it might be, and whether it was successful or not, very curiously Solly Zuckerman seemed not to have been involved.

While I was at No. 10 he often wanted to see Harold but did not want the Private Office at No. 10 to know. Then he would telephone me to fix an appointment during political hours. Or else he would see Harold in the evening after the day's work had been done and the official diary had been worked through.

Then there was Gerald Kaufman, to whom I have referred so much. He was a confidant, true, but he was more. He was essentially a close friend. Harold and he understood each other very well indeed. They had an instinctive knowledge of, and an acceptance of, each other's character. Though Gerald is much younger than Harold, the two had a rapport which in the political world is very rare – and, therefore, correspondingly valuable.

Then there was Joseph Stone, of all Harold Wilson's friends the closest. Outside the Whitehall scene, but not outside politics. He has, of course, known the Wilson family for very many years. He was their family doctor long before Harold Wilson became Leader of the Labour Party and then Prime Minister. Harold always took him on his overseas travels and there is probably nobody who has been on more top-level visits with a British Prime Minister. And there can be few people who have sat in on so many conversations which, while unofficial and informal, have been so confidential and revealing. But I suppose being a family doctor is good training for keeping secrets.

He has not just given his services to the Wilsons. He has afforded help just as generously to Harold's friends. This has resulted in those near to Harold being welded into a very close group indeed. Harold has a very small circle of friends, but those he has are warmly attached one to the other, and all in their turn deeply attached to the central figure of all. I am sure that this is the case with all people who reach such a high position of power.

For a close group we certainly were. A lot of the closeness remains, though inevitably there have been changes. But the central fact is that the Wilson years had a dramatic effect on all our lives. Those who are close to the present Prime Minister must be going through some of the same experiences, and I often wonder what it is like for them.

13

Bitter Perfume

The New Year began with a bang – Harold's major speech at Swansea. He had not returned from the Scillies until 2 January and even then he went to spend the next few days at Chequers. But by that time the pattern for the next few weeks had been set. The Swansea speech, a great blast at the Tories and a recital again of our achievements, was to be followed by a further series of declarations which would help to transform the Party into a united movement ready to win the election.

The team, as I have said, had been assembled. Peter Shore was the main political adviser, and there were other members including Thomas Balogh, Gerald Kaufman and David Candler. John Allen from Transport House, who had been with us in 1964, was also a full-time member. And Michael Halls and Joe Haines, both civil servants, would look in on some of the meetings so that the official side should be aware of the workings of the political side.

But one of Harold's problems was that he would lose Gerald to his Manchester constituency as soon as the election started. David Candler therefore now became used to accompanying Harold on his trips in the country. We still had to find a senior Press Adviser for the duration of the campaign, and after some difficulties Will Camp came to join us at a fairly late stage.

There was one event outside the election pattern – a visit of European journalists to Chequers, invited at the request of Hugh Cudlipp of IPC for a function which the Prime Minister enjoyed very much – but Harold's diary generally was devoted to the coming campaign. Percy Clark and his publicity group were now visiting No. 10 regularly, and a meeting of the Party's full campaign committee which Harold attended at Transport House on 6 January provided a clue to his intentions.

We were not the only people thinking of elections. At the end of January the Conservative Party staged a highly publicized conference at Selsdon Park in Surrey to launch the policies that they were going to sell to the electorate to help win the election. Some of these were the very policies which they were to pursue eventually in office with great avidity at first, but with diminished enthusiasm later. The conference itself was counted a success in that it was carefully publicized and its message was put over. Harold Macmillan, however, is alleged to have commented that it would have been better if it had not taken place, since it provided the Government with perfect ammunition. It seems possible that he did say this since this is in fact what Selsdon Park did do for Labour. Harold was able to go on blasting away at Selsdon policies right through the election. 'Selsdon Man' too was born – and how that caught on in speech after speech throughout the country.

We were only defeated in the end by the blatant promises on prices, taxes and unemployment during the campaign itself. But these promises were far removed from the harsher doctrines the Tories put out in January. From then until the dissolution of Parliament, Selsdon provided Harold with a series of propaganda field days. His major rallies included Nottingham in February, a London Labour Party meeting in Camden Town and a May Day rally in Bristol, and at all of these he explained to enthusiastic audiences how the reactionary backward-looking policies expounded at Selsdon Park would do no good for the working man.

Also projected from the Selsdon Park conference was the argument about law and order. The Conservatives alleged that it had totally broken down in this country, largely because of the Labour Government. In line with the American campaign for the Presidency in 1968 they asserted that what was needed was a tougher approach and a return to much firmer attitudes on law and order. This was good stuff for the Alf Garnetts but it was, of course, a nonsense. They never pursued these policies after the election and they had no real facts or statistics to back them up.

The whole atmosphere was changing dramatically. Although there was no recorded swing to Labour we ourselves were so keyed up with the thought of the proximity of an election campaign that we generated our own enthusiasm within the building. Slowly, of course, the tide began to turn in the country as well, and a pro-Labour figure started to emerge in the polls. Even Harold's meetings became more exciting and the speeches became more urgent in tone and consequently more interesting to prepare.

The visit he paid to Birmingham in March was mainly an official visit, though there were visits to Labour Clubs on the schedule as well, and it included a particularly worthwhile engagement with a housing project jointly sponsored by Shelter. It gave Harold his first opportunity of seeing Des Wilson, the man who had caused such a shake-up in housing thinking in this country. Severely critical though Des Wilson was of the Labour Government's policies, Harold found him fascinating and impressive, and hoped very much that, if a Labour Government were re-elected, Des Wilson might find it possible, despite all the reservations he had about the Government, to work closely with it.

It was not all dedication to work and the political campaign ahead, however. On 11 March, Harold's birthday, a large party went off to the cinema to see the film version of *Hello Dolly*. The whole family went, including Mrs Pollard, the housekeeper.

Another apparently non-political event was the Prime Minister's extensive tour of the Lancashire police organization. He spent all day there on 20 March seeing at first hand the work of one of the most up-to-date police forces in the country. Chief Superintendent Cairns, who started off the project, was an old friend. He suggested the tour to Harold when he was in his constituency. But the now famous Chief Constable, Bill Palfrey, was the outstanding police figure there. Although a great deal still remained to be done, particularly about staffing and police pay, here was an example of how a first-class force was operating under a Labour Government. When Harold tackled the Tory case particularly about crime and violence during the election, he was able to refer not only to the Government's record but also to what he had actually seen that day.

Two events struck Harold very hard at this time. One was his visit to Bessie Braddock in the Rathbone Hospital in Liverpool. She had had a very severe illness and was indeed to die soon after the election. Her serious condition was obvious when Harold saw her. Here was a great socialist fighter, a woman who had become part of the history of Merseyside, now looking so defenceless and vulnerable. Bessie and her husband had been dominant figures in Liverpool politics, and though she had switched from the extreme Left to the extreme Right, and had fought many battles with Harold in later years, he had a special feeling for her that their public quarrels did not reveal. Now, with the end near, he was appalled at the change he found in her. He kept in close touch with the Rathbone Hospital, and as an expression of gratitude he felt for what the staff did for Bessie he later invited the Matron of the hospital to one of the No. 10 parties.

The other event that took a great deal out of Harold was the tragic death of Michael Halls on 3 April. Harold was overwhelmed by this.

He had known Michael for so long and they had a relationship quite unlike the usual one between Prime Minister and civil servant. He was a friend as well as an official. Already Harold had lost Dick Plummer through death, even before he became Prime Minister. Thomas Balogh and George Wigg had moved away as a result of their appointments. He knew that Gerald would soon be MP for Ardwick and would also have a different relationship. But Michael Halls' death was unexpected and therefore even more crushing. We had not known previously that he suffered with heart trouble, so that when he had a coronary it was a complete shock. So many people had relied on him for so long – not just for his advice and help, but also for his essential cheerfulness and inherent niceness.

He had experienced his own difficulties in becoming part of the No. 10 system, and there had been tensions inside the Private Office, and with the System. But he had surmounted them all as a result of three qualities – dignity, wisdom and patience. Of all those round Harold he alone possessed all these things in such measure.

I have made it clear that he worked closely with the Political Office and to some it may have occurred that he had shown partisanship. That is not so. He was always completely impartial and meticulous in not stepping over the line that divides politicians from civil servants. But what he did do was to demonstrate how the system worked and what it did allow. Above all, he gave to his political colleagues genuine friendship and warmth, which is surely permissible even in a civil servant.

Looking back now, his death seems almost an omen of what lay ahead. He had died and only then did we realize how much we needed him. Harold was stunned for a long time afterwards. And though the No. 10 machinery ticked over in the highly competent hands of Derek Andrews, it was not the same for the rest of us without Michael's special presence.

The problem of finding a replacement for Michael as Head of the Private Office was not easy. It would have been invidious and difficult to have promoted one of the Private Secretaries within the Private Office itself to the job. Others who were there might have felt they should have had it. An outsider had to be found, but someone who was in tune with Harold and who could get on well with him. This also had to be done very quickly. Harold had to discover someone, too, who could be integrated quickly because of the time factor on the election front.

Sandy Isserlis was suggested. He had served under Quintin Hogg and Duncan Sandys, and had a fairly high reputation in the Civil Service. He was a man with a highly developed, wry sense of humour, but very efficient with it, and, after Harold had met him once, it seemed clear that he would fit in very well. He was to get the appointment and to come to No. 10 even though it was to be for such a brief period. None of the others who were suggested for the job would have been right in that particular context in an election year. Clearly, some had outstanding qualifications, and the man who became Mr Heath's Principal Private Secretary, who was also suggested as a candidate, would have been excellent. But, as I have said, Harold needed someone he could get on well with immediately, and who knew exactly what sort of person he was and how he operated.

There were to be difficulties about the appointment from the Civil Service side, but these were overcome. The Civil Service always likes to keep a check on the health of those members reaching high positions. They add to the file of all the senior people, and possibly the junior ones as well, a record of any illness reported to them. Sandy Isserlis had himself suffered from high blood pressure. This had been reported to the Civil Service by his wife, and this, of course, was on his file. This now became one of the reasons advanced by the Civil Service against his appointment. Harold, however, had a full investigation made by a senior medical expert in London and Sandy underwent a very thorough examination. It proved successful and showed that Sandy was in good health and quite able to carry out the job to which he had been appointed. The examination was good for him in another way since it cleared his mind of any worries he might have had about his health.

In the Political Office we never got the chance to know Sandy really well. Right up to the election he was so busy getting to know the building and the job, that we merely passed him in the corridors or exchanged a few words with him in the Prime Minister's study or in the Private Office.

At these brief encounters he would say smilingly that we must all get together to have a talk. We always promised we would try to arrange this as quickly as possible. But we could not let him into all our thinking, and neither he nor we had the time from then until 18 June.

Within the Wilson family there was a visit from Australian relatives of Harold's, who came to stay at Chequers and were regular visitors at No. 10 from April right through to the election campaign itself. Everyone was delighted to meet them since they were so charming though some felt particularly sorry not to be able to do more to help with the arrangements for them because of all the work connected with the campaign.

Lunches in the private flat became more and more concentrated as we started the final run-up to Dissolution. Although no one was allowed to mention dates in the Political Office, I think everybody was perfectly aware that October was unlikely and June very likely. Indeed, they were all keyed up for it. Our Political Office team suddenly lost Lynette Knorr, but we gained the services of Mary Turk, a left-wing, unconventional girl who had attended Sussex University. She was exceedingly good at the job we wanted her to do during the election period.

At the end of April, Harold had a meeting with the National Agent and the Meetings Officer of the Party when, on a 'need to know' basis, he as good as spelled out to them what was in his mind. They had been doing some thinking on the same lines and discussed with him his election tour.

At that point the decision was made that it would not be just the usual election tour with speeches in the main cities but that Harold would get around to as many Committee Rooms as possible to give heart and encouragement to our workers.

We had a problem here. Many workers in the constituencies had drifted away during the troubles during the previous years and particularly during the industrial relations argument. They were now returning in increasing numbers and felt there was a good possibility of an election victory. But they needed a little extra encouragement to get them started and launched into a really vigorous campaign. Harold felt that if he visited the major Committee Rooms this might help to keep them working full out throughout the campaign rather than just the last few days.

The May Day rally which Harold addressed in Bristol on 3 May was now a major election speech. It hit very hard at the Selsdon Park philosophies which the Conservatives had been propagating. It set out again the record of the Labour Government, including the now very major economic success, all of which would be put seriously at risk by returning a party to office which was clearly dedicated to reactionary and backward-looking policies.

The young people, considering all they had felt over the past years, were rallying round marvellously, organized by Hugh Anderson of Cambridge University. Harold addressed a very large student rally in Manchester for 'Students for a Labour Victory', a group run by Hugh Anderson. It was the first large student meeting that Harold had addressed where there was not rioting or at least large demonstrations against government policy. He was enormously impressed by Hugh Anderson's competence and political acumen. Here was a young man who seemed destined to go a long way in the Party, and his tragic death not long afterwards was a tremendous blow for all who knew him. It was a blow not only for his own family but for the whole Labour Party. When people die in middle age it is often said – and rightly – that their death has left a gap in the Party. I can think of nobody else except Hugh Anderson whose death at such an early age has left a gap still not filled.

How Harold kept up the pace during that period it is difficult to know. In the office we had only the political side to deal with. That in itself was non-stop hard pressure. But he had all the duties of a Prime Minister to carry out as well, all the visitors to see from overseas, and the committee meetings to attend, and all the details of government to superintend. He even managed to fit in personal visitors. Captain Thomas who had been the master of the *Scillonia*, which took Harold across to the Scillies for his holidays each year, came to London and the Prime Minister made a point of receiving him at No. 10.

Harold also took time off to present the *Sun* Television Awards, at the Royal Lancaster Hotel on 14 May. Much to the astonishment of many of us – and a little to our dismay as well – he joined in a song with 'Ena Sharples'. It came over well on television and was widely reported the following day. We feared it would have come into the category of a gimmick though it was an impromptu response on stage to what was said to him. Still this was mild beer compared with some of the things Britain has had to put up with since 1970.

Will Camp, who was to join us for the campaign, had worked in a large nationalized organization, but had never been at the centre of an election campaign. He did not know how Harold worked nor the form. John Allen, who came over from Transport House to help us, had been with us in 1964, and Peter Shore, who had his own constituency to look after, came in and out the whole time and was Harold's main political adviser. But his time, like Gerald's, was limited because of his constituency duties. We were entering a difficult phase with a new, untried team, and only hindsight reveals now just what a gamble it was.

So there we were, with the opinion polls swinging almost wildly towards us, but with Harold committed to a four-week campaign. His strongest argument for having one week more than the statutory period was that the Party would already be surprised by a snap election and unprepared to some extent for it, and that therefore the longer we gave them in the constituencies the more work they would be able to do in getting the vote out. But there was still strong feeling about a shorter campaign and an earlier June date. Quite apart from the Tory machine's superiority, the shorter the time that our people had, then the more enthusiastic and energetic they would be to make absolutely sure that they did get the vote out. If they were given extra time it might make them relax just a little bit more than they would have done with a short sharp period to handle. But Harold, thinking of the Labour movement and how it would react to the demands being made upon it, and bearing in mind anyway that he could not announce a dissolution during the local election period, plumped for the 18th. This meant he had to see the Queen on 18 May.

A special Cabinet was held on 17 May and, with this out of the way, the decision was more or less final, though Harold could conceivably have gone back on it the following day. During lunch on 18 May Harold walked up and down, and as he did, I joked that he could, of course, change his mind. He was thinking exactly the same. Then we all laughed nervously.

18 May was one of the longest days ever. We all tended to watch the minutes ticking away. Harold had a number of other commitments to fulfil in his Prime Ministerial capacity, including a visit at 3.30 p.m. from the Mayor of West Berlin, Herr Schultz. Then, at 5.00 p.m., we saw him off to Buckingham Palace to seek the Queen's approval to a dissolution of Parliament. When he had gone, everyone knew there was no going back. While we had nervously and a little ruefully regarded the previous hours as offering some opportunity of escape, once 5.00 p.m. had arrived we adjusted ourselves very quickly to what we knew now was the inevitable pressure of winning an election.

It was valuable that we had a great deal of the work done before the date came. There had been a long discussion as to where Harold would make his broadcast telling the country of the election, and the interviews he would have to do for BBC and ITV. Since it was a political occasion it could not really be done, we felt, from No. 10 itself. The garden seemed a possibility, particularly since by then the weather was very hot. So the garden was decided upon and the old-fashioned chairs from the 1930s were set out and the television cameras were brought in. Gerald and I went out to watch the Prime Minister perform and he was superb. He was very relaxed, confident, and everything seemed, like the weather, to be sunny and optimistic. Even the television interviewers, who in years before had not been over-enthusiastic, caught the atmosphere, and were more than outgoing in the way they interviewed him. As always with these occasions drinks were served to them all by the official Housekeeper at No. 10, Mr May. After a quick drink, Harold thanked everyone for what they had done. He was always most meticulous about this after every broadcast for he was conscious of the time spent by the technicians, however short the interview that was actually transmitted.

We then all piled into cars to go over to Transport House to a reception being given there by the General Secretary for the Israeli Labour Party. All our friends and comrades were there, excited by the prospect of an election. Our overseas friends were confident of our victory. They presented Harold and Mary with a most beautiful copy of the Jewish Bible and we returned to No. 10 in good spirits.

From now on we were out on our own. Official work was reduced to a minimum. Political work took over almost totally. We had the job of making sure that the organization of the team within No. 10 would be exactly right throughout the campaign and that the links with Transport House would be maintained. We proceeded to make our dispositions and to let all the staff know exactly how everything would be run.

That deceptive weather, like a Greek Circe, lured us on into a feeling of false optimism.

There were so many factors about the 1970 campaign that made it seem unreal at the time and even now, long afterwards, give it an atmosphere quite unlike any other election I have experienced. The weather seemed to dominate everything. It remained continuously hot and bright so that there was almost a holiday atmosphere throughout the month, something very un-British.

During the first week the Prime Minister spent a fair amount of time at Chequers. He was planning tactics, of course, but the main object was for him to get enough rest and sleep to get him into top physical form for the campaign.

The Political Office took over entirely the small office used by Mrs Wilson's secretary. We thought we would use it from time to time for informal staff meetings. It had one advantage for it was opposite Mrs Pollard's room, so we could easily ask her for sandwiches or drinks if we were working late. But it was cramped and had a rather dreary outlook. What we never envisaged was that as the campaign developed we should use it more and more until it became our operational headquarters. But it is a fact that from this small room the Prime Minister eventually ran the whole of his campaign.

There were several comic by-products as a result of this development. We installed an electric coffee percolator on a trolley to avoid bothering Mrs Pollard too much. This would have been a good idea if either had worked properly. But the trolley periodically came to pieces and the percolator showed signs of election strain and started making sinister gurgling noises. There never seemed time to get either piece of equipment repaired, so high-level discussions on tactics were punctuated by the intervention of the wretched percolator or one more piece coming adrift from the trolley. The Prime Minister would occasionally give the percolator a stern or puzzled look but there was always something more urgent to do than getting it serviced.

Even more farcical was the affair of Thomas Balogh and the ice. We had a good supply of ice – and we needed it, because the temperature in the tiny, crowded room often made it like a Turkish bath – and Thomas, who took part in every meeting when specialist economic advice was needed, took to crunching lumps of ice. This was refreshing for Thomas, but disturbing for the Prime Minister. Harold never realized that it was ice that was causing the noise and assumed that Thomas was helping himself from a dish of potato crisps. Throughout one long, tense meeting he kept on looking at Thomas and demanding that people should stop munching crisps. Of course, this passed over Thomas's head. He continued to crunch away at his ice-cubes and seemed as irritated as Harold that anybody should disturb the discussions by eating potato crisps.

George Caunt swiftly joined us at No. 10 and worked hard with David Candler and the rest of the team in answering queries from the public and helping Marian Craythorne to organize the Prime Minister's tour. In previous elections George had gone on tour with Harold, but this time he stayed in London.

For this time it was electioneering with a difference. Instead of great sweeps through the country with frequent absences from London, Harold this time made briefer journeys. They were still numerous but the aim was for him to return to No. 10 every night, or at least to get back to London by overnight transport, so he needed a much smaller staff to accompany him.

The first days of the campaign were arduous for us, but not back breaking. It was mostly planning, broken on 22 May by Harold's visit to Huyton for his adoption meeting. He returned to London overnight, and spent the weekend in Chequers immediately afterwards when he was able to play quite a lot of golf on both the Saturday and Sunday. He was able, too, to work on government papers.

Tuesday 26 May was a day I remember only too well. I went over to the House in the afternoon – apparently only for my usual routine visit, but really to say goodbye to the Prime Minister's room. Now with the benefit of hindsight I know the significance of that visit, but even then I realized it was probably my last look at it all. When I spoke my fears to Harold he was quick to counter them and said that anyway I would have a last chance to look at it all on Prorogation Day. But I didn't go over then, so I didn't have another chance. I only saw those rooms once again – when I looked in on them very briefly indeed after the defeat.

The Thursday of that week was a fateful day. It was then that Dick Crossman had his famous meeting with the doctors, and made the famous remarks, thinking they were in confidence, about their pay claim and the burden on the economy. These words were to be blown up out of all proportion, distorted, taken out of context and, of course, seized upon by the Conservative Opposition. It was also the day when Harold took part in the BBC *Forum* broadcast. I took a tape recording of it so that we could know exactly what had been said in reply to all the questions. Even now when I listen to it I am horrified by the sheer hostility of the questioning he received before the cameras of this impartial Corporation.

The following Friday we left London in the afternoon to

start everything off at Cardiff. The 1966 campaign had been launched in Scotland, but this time we felt that perhaps it might be a good thing to change the routine and start it off in Wales. We were sure that we should receive an enormously enthusiastic reception – and we certainly did. We took with us Stanley Baker, famous film actor, director and loyal Party supporter. He shared the platform with Harold and made a typically Welsh and eloquent appeal for Labour votes. Harold's speech set the pattern for the others which followed, and was used as the 'master speech' throughout.

Now that the campaign was on, Harold's days were clearly defined. He had decided that the main theme should be the same as that in 1966, the Government's record. And, as in 1966, we should fight it from No. 10. This had worked well at the previous election. We had then been less than two years away from Opposition, and still had comparatively close links with Transport House. But now, after much longer in office, we needed closer integration. I believe our physical distance from Smith Square and the absence of firmer contact with some of the senior staff there was to prove a positive disadvantage.

Harold worked to the programme devised by Transport House and this included daily meetings with the Party's campaign committee and Press conferences each morning he was in London.

These news conferences were held at the Trevelyan Hall, near Party headquarters. This was a new development. In previous campaigns they had been held in a large meeting hall in Transport House. This time it was decided to hold them at a hall next to a local primary school. It was hardly a change for the better. The photographs and TV shots of the Press conferences showed Harold and his colleagues seated in low chairs, looking to me remarkably ill at ease.

Harold's tours were successful, popular and well publicized. What were not so successful were his set speeches in the evenings. Enormous pains were taken by Transport House to get regional organizers to co-operate and to make sure that the platform was indoors, that the background was clear and well defined and that it would come across well for television. But what was arranged beforehand frequently failed to work out as we had envisaged. One example was a visit to the East Midlands Region of the Party. That night the television showed pictures of the Prime Minister leaning out of a sash window, supporting the lower half of it with his shoulders, and trying to address a rather bewildered crowd below. It gave the worst possible image of him looking desperately uncomfortable.

Meanwhile the Tories were carrying around the country an impressive set background, which had been carefully prepared for Mr Heath in a most efficient public relations way. We were told that they also had a make-up expert, lighting experts, film experts, the lot, to advise and make sure that on every occasion he spoke, the setting was exactly right. Their finances enabled them to do this. Ours did not. All we could do was to hope all went well at the other end, but very often communications were inadequate.

When Harold went in the middle of the campaign to Birmingham, John Harris was there with Roy Jenkins, so Harold asked John if he would help out with the dual Press arrangements for that meeting. All should have gone well, but for the fact that Harold unknowingly took to Birmingham not a speech he had meant to deliver but what we called 'discards'. These were papers containing parts of the speech which he had originally drafted, but which he had decided not to use. When he rose to his feet, therefore, in Birmingham on Wednesday 3 June, before a battery of photographers and television cameras, he suddenly found himself without the speech he had imagined he was about to make on the all-important question of prices, but with the 'discards' which should have been left behind in London. He was superb. He remembered the original text and even added to it. Few people realized the error, except, of course, those of us watching television reports back in London. We registered horror and amazement and great shame too. This had never happened to him before. It was a sad and depressing fact that it should have happened during that election. It seemed another bad omen.

That last week during the run-up to election day was dominated, as one could never have anticipated, by a newspaper strike.

There had been murmurings that the Press would come out

on strike and it received a very mixed reception in Labour Party circles. Some were not as convinced as others that it would have been so devastating for the Labour Party if the Press had been left totally out of action for the rest of the campaign. Looking back and seeing how biased they were, I think that is probably correct. But Harold, ever optimistic and ever trusting that the Press would play fair, wanted to see the papers back in production. He also liked to see democracy work and wanted to see if he could help to bring the disputants to an agreement. He was able to do just this. The final agreement was achieved by others, but the groundwork was his, and he did this during one of the most vital campaigns in Labour's history.

That was not the only unusual feature of the run-up period. Two other events took place at No. 10, one while Harold was out of London and the other when he was advised he had to be present. On Thursday 11 June, the day many wanted as Polling Day, the Beating the Retreat ceremony took place on Horse Guards Parade. The Prime Minister's stand was filled as usual with people he felt would like to be present, principally friends and colleagues who had helped him in the past. We also took the opportunity of inviting colleagues from Transport House to come along, so that over drinks after the ceremony we were able to talk about how things were going. Everyone was enormously optimistic and felt everything was going well. I was a little surprised to learn on that occasion that David Candler had been looking for a constituency for himself and that we had been in danger of losing him as well.

The most peculiar function of all was on Saturday 13 June when the Trooping the Colour ceremony took place. It was rather like the fiddling that took place in Nero's Rome. None of us wanted to be involved, but were advised that it would be taken unkindly by the Palace and by others if the ceremony was cancelled. Harold was also advised that he should be present. So the ceremony went on and Harold attended. The National Agent went to great pains to slot this function into the election tour.

But it was the most grotesque occasion I ever attended there. There was optimism, but by now it did begin to seem a little false. It was the unreality of it all; the holding of a ceremony so unrelated not just to the campaign in which we were engaged, but to our whole national life in the 1970s. Friends and colleagues who turned up seemed curiously out of touch with reality too. They were very confident and happy to treat it as a social occasion and reluctant to allow those of us who had work to do to return to our offices. Yet here was a time when it was really urgent that we concentrated on what we were doing.

But by that engagement everything seemed under control. The National Opinion Poll had published the fantastic lead of twelve per cent for Labour and everyone felt we were home and dry. Yet it really did seem too good to be true. I was assured that with a margin as large as this it would be impossible for the Tories to catch up in the last few days left to them. No one was to know that this was just what the Tories could do and that while we were celebrating that twelve per cent lead, the erosion was already well advanced. It was to be clinched that weekend with that decision taken by Edward Heath and his colleagues to concentrate not only on prices, taxation and unemployment, but to play too on the fear of a further devaluation. They were to poison people's minds with this on the following Tuesday, hinting that this was what the electorate could expect. They got it – from the Tories.

After the Trooping the Colour ceremony, Mary and Harold then had a genuinely unpleasant experience the following day. They had to go down to Bristol by the quickest possible route, so they chose a helicopter. It proved disastrous. Mary, not a good traveller at the best of times, was violently sick and had to return by train. Harold managed to weather it all and returned by helicopter in time to attend meetings on his speeches and be ready for Monday 15 June in London for his Campaign Committee and Press conference, but he was tired by it all.

That Monday he addressed a large meeting at Hammersmith Town Hall, the only London meeting I attended during the campaign. It was the last big meeting in London and was the one where most of our celebrity supporters were with him on the platform. I could see in the audience members, too, of the Press who had come along specially to hear the Prime Minister and to see what form he was in. They included Lady Hartwell of the *Telegraph*, an avid election follower. By then, many of the Press must have felt the situation was changing. It seemed a very rowdy meeting with a hostile articulate minority at the back of the hall. I was puzzled to be told it was our best meeting yet. I shuddered to think what all the others had been like.

By the Tuesday, the tide had really turned. Harold dashed off to Lime Grove to record his last television broadcast. We felt it had been a good broadcast and ought to come over well. Gerald had come down specially from Manchester to work hard on it all with us. It was at the Lime Grove Studios that we received the jolting news by telephone of what had happened at the Tory Press conference that morning. As the Press corps left they had been handed a statement hinting that a further Labour Government would mean a further devaluation. This was not announced directly by Edward Heath, the man of courage and integrity, but was contained in a duplicated hand-out.

Harold realized the seriousness of this situation. The clarity of their pledge about bringing prices down, reducing taxation and lowering unemployment, together with the suggestion of another devaluation, was obvious dynamite. On the way back to No. 10 Harold dictated a short Press release to me in the car. That was an ordeal in itself. As we careered round the new roadworks at Shepherds Bush, still not completed, I was desperately trying to get it down in my notebook. Immediately we got back to No. 10 I dashed through the front door, shot past everyone, stole the lift away from them, and rushed to the second floor to type out the release so that he could go off with a copy in his file.

It was his last journey from No. 10 as Prime Minister with power. The fact that it was the last journey before Polling Day prompted the staff to go down to the entrance hall to say goodbye as he left for Manchester at 3.30 p.m. We gathered in the hall hoping that it was not to be the last time we should be gathered together in that way and that we would soon be celebrating his return. Many of us by then were fearful that this was a sadder occasion than was obvious and that we would remember it for that reason.

I joined the Prime Minister in Liverpool the following day after he had done his tour of Manchester. I stayed there for the rest of the campaign until the return to London.

Polling Day on 18 June was the usual waiting game, with the Prime Minister visiting the Huyton constituency to see how things were at the polling stations and to greet the workers.

I spent most of Polling Day in Liverpool itself, apart from the odd visit to Huyton. It was not just hot in Liverpool, it was extremely hot. There was no breeze and it was still and oppressive. I felt it was unlikely in these conditions that many people would feel like going out during the day to make the effort to vote or to do it after a hard day's work under hot conditions. This worried me enormously. Marian Craythorne, our former Women's Officer in the Yorkshire Region, who was with us in Liverpool, felt as I did. It was not a very good outlook. I think we would have been happier if it had been raining. Rain is traditionally difficult for getting the vote out, but that unnatural torrid heat seemed even more ominous to us.

Harold decided to hold his party for the Press before the results started to come through. This would then leave him clear apart from the Huyton declaration. As I have said he did this because he had decided long before to return to London by car. Once he left the Adelphi Hotel for the count in Huyton, he would not be returning there again as he had done during other elections. There was no other reason for holding the Press party early, despite other explanations that have been given.

It was a rushed but good-humoured party. Everyone seemed to be optimistic for the Party. Indeed all day I had been told they were. At lunch I was told a story that Nora Beloff, the *Observer*'s political correspondent, had already written her piece explaining why Labour had won. She certainly had the quiet confidence of one who had completed her tasks as she sat eating a solitary lunch.

That, really, was the end of the campaign for me. There was the inevitable ritual ahead – the first results, the hurried calculations of swings and possibilities, the formal declarations at Huyton. But at that moment in the dining room of the hotel I remember feeling that one phase had ended, and the next one was about to begin.

When I look back at the campaign, I remember most of all the nightly returns of the Prime Minister. Each evening as Harold and Mary returned from any event near London, we knew when the car was approaching by a quick signal on the horn that Bill Housden gave whenever he approached the house. Sometimes we would take the lift from the second floor to the ground to be there ready as two weary and sometimes dishevelled figures entered the building. Sometimes they were covered by flour, tomato ketchup and almost always by egg. It was a rough campaign that the gentlemen's party waged.

Once Harold had a hard-boiled (though it may have been china) egg thrown at him. It hit his temple and bruised him badly. Dr Stone had to be sent for because it was near a place from which Harold had once had a cyst removed and serious damage was feared.

We all often felt we were fielding them rather than welcoming them back home. But the two always kept their dignity, their campaigning spirit – and, amazingly, their sense of humour.

Throughout all this deliberate and vicious activity the Wilsons never flinched. They not only kept their spirit. They kept their popularity. Wherever they went they got great crowds and warm, affectionate receptions, except from the more lunatic of their opponents. They had acceptability. This Mr Heath did not have then and does not have today.

So why did we lose when we had a leader whose popularity remained unchallenged despite the harsh events of the years before? Possibly there was a reaction against the pollsters, a desire to prove the computers wrong. But primarily it was surely a matter of people switching or abstaining as a result of the actions of the final week, particularly that bold, crude, uncompromising promise to reduce taxation, to halt the rise in prices and to bring unemployment down. Nothing, not even the asset of a popular leader and his wife, was sufficient to counter this beguiling prospect.

14

The Inevitability of
Gradualness

Nobody in the Labour Government can delude himself that all the hopes of 1964 were fulfilled. We did not succeed in doing what we set out to achieve. We took over power at a time when the odds were against us, and the handicaps that we inherited proved too great. We experienced dramatic failures, but we can also claim credit for some successes which, though not so well publicized, were still of permanent and outstanding value.

I believe that what failures we had can be attributed largely to our defeats on two separate fronts. One battle was against the Civil Service. This was a struggle which we never fought with much heart or conviction. The other was the effort to produce a prices and incomes policy. Here we did struggle hard, even though we did not win. What we needed, however, was a prior agreement with the Trade Union movement. We still need this, and unless we get it no future Labour Government can go forward with confidence.

But the struggle with the System – or, to be more precise, the Civil Service – was lost from the start. Looking back now one can realize that this was inevitable. Thirteen years away from the corridors of power had caused most Labour politicians to forget how essential it is to take firm control in this area. Too many of our leaders were overconfident of their ability to handle the civil servants and come out on top.

In the offices of Whitehall and in the clubs of Pall Mall lies immense power. The electorate believes that on Polling Day it is getting a chance to change history. The reality is that in many cases the power remains with the civil servants who are permanently ensconced in Whitehall, rather than with the politicians who come and go at elections. Of course, there are exceptions. Some Ministers are capable of taking on the Civil Service at its own power-game and winning. But they are far too few.

The System is in the hands of the upper grades of the Service. They are the only civil servants with which a Government deals. Politicians have day-to-day encounters with the lower ranks who service the System and look after its buildings, but when a Government thinks of the Civil Service it thinks of the Administrative Class. Of course, politicians are aware of other important civil servants, such as the scientific, legal and other specialist classes, but their encounters even with these highly-qualified men and women are rare since their advice and information is usually transmitted through the Administrative Class.

The Fulton Report summed up the situation when it described the Administrative Class as the people 'who control and co-ordinate the work of other departments. They formulate the policy and give direct advice to Ministers. They occupy virtually all the top posts in the Service.'

At the very top of the Administrative Class are the Permanent Secretaries, the heads of big departments. The general public knows vaguely about these departments, since they are aware there is a Minister in charge of each one. If the Minister is a particularly colourful personality, the work of his department will become as well known as he is. However, while the general public will know the names of the political heads of the more newsworthy ministries, there is rarely any knowledge of the names of the permanent features of the departments, the Civil Service heads. Yet some of them have far more influence than their Ministers.

These Civil Service heads of departments, the Permanent Secretaries, are the so-called 'Mandarins', as they have been christened in years. They in their turn have a sort of head-master and deputy headmaster in the Cabinet Secretary, Sir Burke Trend, and the head of the Civil Service, Sir William Armstrong. Whether you regard Sir Burke or Sir William as the

Head depends on whether you are a politician or a civil servant.

When Labour took office in 1964 the Civil Service was not then separately administered as a department in its own right. At that time it was merely a sub-section of the Treasury. There were two Permanent Secretaries in the Treasury, Sir William Armstrong, who headed the financial and economic side, and Sir Laurence Helsby, who headed the 'Pay and Management side', which dealt with the Civil Service. While Sir Laurence Helsby was directly responsible to the Prime Minister on certain Civil Service matters, the Chancellor of the Exchequer nominally controlled both Permanent Secretaries. In this way the Treasury and the Civil Service were intertwined. In this way, too, it was a limiting feature because the Chancellor, the man who controlled the nation's purse-strings at the Treasury, was also the man who controlled the Civil Service. Only later was the Civil Service to be hived-off into a separate department with a senior Permanent Secretary in charge and designated Head of the Civil Service.

This was a move which one can hope was in the right direction and one which will lead increasingly towards a speeding up of the aims of the Fulton Committee. The only drawback to this improvement was that the new Civil Service Department, headed by Sir William Armstrong, now consists in the main of the old 'Pay and Rations' section of the Treasury, as it was called, hived-off and put into a separate building. It would have been far more reassuring if the new Civil Service Department had been a completely new Department in Whitehall, with new staff and different arrangements within it, rather than this hiving-off process of a section already existing in the Treasury. Though it was independent of the Treasury it did not bring in the new men the Fulton Committee believed were needed if the reforms they recommended were to be implemented.

I make no apologies for the feelings I have in the main about the Civil Service. I feel it is undemocratic, particularly at the top; exclusive; and with a strange personality of its own, half reminiscent of the Army, half of a masonic society. Certainly many of the members of the Administrative Class seem unrelated to the outside world.

One of the criticisms which the Fulton Committee made of

346

the Administrative Class was that the geographical origins, past experiences and backgrounds of its members were much less representative of the community at large even than those of other groups within the Service. Most of the Administrative Class came from the south-east and metropolitan area, with only a small proportion from areas 'north of Luton'. Even in the universities, where many imagine that there is a fair degree of remoteness, there is more relation to the community as a whole. Selection there for posts and places is far more representative than in the Administrative Class of the Civil Service, which contains the exclusive two and a half thousand people who virtually run the country.

They have their own language, their own way of communicating with each other. Anthony Sampson, in his book *The Anatomy of Britain* states that, 'Permanent Secretaries are very Oxbridge and communicate easily in that special vernacular'. One must assume, therefore, that the peculiar language to which the Service is addicted is a result in the main of their Oxbridge backgrounds.

Their grapevine is the most efficient secret intelligence service this country possesses. A half-sentence spoken, a thought articulated out loud in front of a Private Secretary, either dangerous or potentially dangerous to them, or even slightly newsworthy, can be round Whitehall on the grapevine before the person concerned has returned to his office. Private Secretaries will ring Private Secretaries in other Private Offices to inform them of whatever piece of information they want passed down. And so it goes round the small Whitehall circle. The Private Secretaries at No. 10, certainly when we first went there, were not averse to using this particular method frequently and effectively.

Permanent Secretaries, the heads of the big departments, keep exceptionally close links with each other, socially as well as in working hours. They eat together during the day, they meet together in the evening at social functions, and they attend committee meetings together during the course of a week. Their contact with each other is continuous and total, and because of this it is far more effective and powerful than any communications that exist between politicians within a government. The same sort of social and working intercourse goes on between all those in the Administrative Class. Private Secretaries keep in touch with the other Private Secretaries in all the other Private Offices in Whitehall. The process is a never-ending one. Indeed, the application given to this mutual information network is phenomenal. If half the time spent was put into more positive work far more would be achieved.

However, despite its many serious and irritating deficiencies, it is one of the most efficient and best-oiled administrative machines in the world. One could in fact take a charitable view of it if it were accountable to anyone for what it does. But often it acts as if it is a sovereign power responsible only to itself.

Very few outsiders come in to upset the civil servants' equilibrium or to disrupt their neat set-up. They make mistakes and the politicians carry the can. If civil servants are inefficient or personally unsuitable, the only way to remove them from their posts is by promotion, putting them on a higher grade with a better salary or greater status.

One might ask if one of the reasons why change and progress in Great Britain is so slow is related in any respect to the way in which the Civil Service is organized.

Many questions are raised by the operation of the System. Do the Civil Services perpetuate too many things that are wrong in the United Kingdom? Social inequality, class consciousness, elitism? Are they really neutral as they so often claim with such sanctimonious self-satisfaction – satisfaction either in the belief that it is true, or worse that the claim it isn't cannot be discovered to be more accurate? But what is neutrality anyway within a body with such immense power over so many lives?

The Civil Service, and those particularly at the top, are the men who are called to carry out the policies handed to them by their political masters. But more significant these men also have the responsibility of advising their political masters on what policies should be followed. Since, as it is well known, Departments generally have favourite courses of action which they are anxious to sell to Ministers irrespective of the political complexion of that Minister, this in its turn can create enormous problems too, particularly for an inexperienced incoming Government. If neutrality is to mean anything in such an area, it really has to be something clear-cut and identifiable. But a glance at the Service, and particularly recruitment at higher levels, makes it quite impossible to accept the neutrality argument.

Unfortunately, too few ordinary people know how the chosen few who dominate the Civil Service are chosen for their jobs. It is odd the general public have so little curiosity about it. They make jokes about the Civil Service, call them the makers and drinkers of endless cups of tea, the wearers of a peculiar form of dress, but almost nobody wants to have a serious debate and thoroughgoing inquiry into the Civil Service.

The Civil Service is, nevertheless, as much an estate of the realm with all the influence that implies, as Parliament, the City of London, the Trade Union movement, the Press or Industry. All the others can be and are criticized and put under a microscope. But not apparently, the Civil Service. Why? The very fact they seem above criticism is bad.

Any thoroughgoing reform of the Civil Service will be difficult and almost certainly abortive. Recommendations and inquiries when they emerge, are all too often placed in the hands of the civil servants themselves to carry out. It is just as if a Government decided to legislate on the monopolistic tendencies of British industry, reached a final view on it, set out a series of proposals in a White Paper, and then handed these over to the CBI, the representatives of industry, to implement. Yet this is exactly what happened to the Fulton Report.

The Committee produced volumes of evidence and material, some of its recommendations were accepted, and then the matter was handed over to the civil servants themselves for implementation. Indeed it was handed over to the very people who had in the past proved conclusively that all the recommendations that the Fulton Committee were making were necessary.

We are told that now the Civil Service is run by the new head, Sir William Armstrong, a man who does not shun publicity, all will be different. He is the new broom in Whitehall which is going to sweep everything clean. This may well be so.

The Fulton Committee in its Report recommended the abolition of two sorts of class barriers within the Civil Service, the class barriers to vertical movement within the Service, between Clerical, Executive and Administrative Classes, on the one hand, and the class barriers to horizontal or diagonal movement within the Service; for example, between someone in the Scientific Officer Class and the Administrative Class, or between the Experimental Officer Class and the Executive Class. The Labour Government accepted this recommendation in the following terms when the Prime Minister reported to the House of Commons. In his announcement he said: 'Thirdly the Government accepts the abolition of Classes within the Civil Service and will enter immediately into consultations with the Staff Associations with a view to carrying out the thoroughgoing study proposed by the Committee, so that a practical system can be prepared for the implementation of the unified grading structure in accordance with the time-table proposed by the Committee.'

Amen. This was a fairly formidable challenge to reformers, yet it is unlikely, I am afraid, that a great deal will be seen of the recommendations unless a Prime Minister, or a Government, or indeed Sir William Armstrong himself, has a mind to make a reality out of them.

Perhaps Sir William does realize that the abolition of classes so far achieved, while allowing movement up from one grade to another, still does not allow complete fluidity with sideways and diagonal moves and a continual flow between all sections with all types of civil servants, specialists and others, crossing and inter-changing within Departments and gaining new experience and taking advantage of promotions available.

What is true is that there has been in the past some fluidity and movement from job to job within the same Class. In fact one of the curious defects of the Civil Service has been that people within an office doing a particular job have only been allowed to stay there for about two years and after this tour of duty have been passed to another post which they have then had to learn.

As of today, however, the Fulton Recommendations on the unified grading structure seem to have ground to a halt. The old Administrative Class seems to have won its battle to thwart the implementations of what the Fulton Committee envisaged. The Civil Service Department itself seems to be suggesting now that it is far more important as a priority to facilitate the increasing vertical movement of individuals in the Service between the different classes from the Executive to the Administrative Class, than the horizontal movement of individuals between Classes which was envisaged by the Fulton Committee. They throw into the argument, too, the question of how pay in a unified grading structure is to be settled, although this would seem to be more a weapon for them in the general argument than a belief in a principle to which they are wedded. Yet it is increasingly clear as modern technological society makes even greater demands upon our administrative services, that one of the greatest priorities is the unified grading structure complete within the Service making it possible for more sideways movement from the Scientific and other specialized grades into adjacent areas of the Administrative and management sections of the Service, giving these specialists valuable experience in administration and management; it is important too for this to happen at lower levels as well in the Service. This is the real meaning of a unified grading structure throughout the Service below the level of Under-Secretary, and it is the only means of equipping these various specialists with the necessary experience they should have to enable them in turn to take full advantage of the open structure which is to be introduced from the Under-Secretary level upwards.

A question mark, therefore, now appears over the whole question of Civil Service reform despite the bright hopes held by so many people during the years of the Labour Government and when the Fulton Committee was at work.

I strongly believe that people should be interested more deeply in these questions, and, too, in the total pattern of recruitment to the Service. Up until 1969 for instance, the Administrative Class in the Civil Service was recruited in two ways. There was Method One and Method Two. The first Method was mainly by way of written examination. The second mainly by interview. It was found by the Fulton Committee that most entrants were coming into the Administrative Class under Method Two. Why? One of the peculiar things the Fulton Committee discovered was that the quality, academically, of entrants was going down, and that coincided with a curious increase in the number of Method Two entrants compared with those coming in on Method One. Recruits with first-class degrees were declining in proportion to those with lower-class degrees. The Civil Service Commissioners set out specifically to seek recruits for the Administrative Class with qualities, therefore, other than purely intellectual ones. This was all very admirable. It may well be, and clearly was, the reason why the first-class degree people went down in numbers. Clearly the others, therefore, with a lower-class degree had something which the first-class degree people did not have. What? No indication was given as to what the qualities were which were being looked for, nor obtained. But, what did emerge from the Fulton inquiries was that a comparison of the two groups recruited under Method One and Method Two showed that since the war the Administrative Class had become 'more socially exclusive' and that the proportion of recruits from LEA maintained schools had not increased. Another of the more alarming aspects of recruitment discovered by the Fulton Committee was that few women seemed to gain entrance to the Administrative Class. After all, how many women have held senior posts in 10 Downing Street?

One other disadvantage which women suffer, too, is that if they gain admission to the Administrative Class, they tend to remain spinsters or leave. This seems to be about the most ludicrous example of short-sightedness in any profession. Surely by now a solution should have been arrived at whereby married women and those with families can do administrative jobs within the Service, leave for a short time if they wish and return later? This is one of the few areas where it should be particularly easy for highly qualified people to become mobile.

For me the most classic criticisms that emerged from all the Fulton inquiries were contained in the following quotations from their Report:

Members of the higher classes in the Service mostly have, as we have shown, 'superior' social and educational backgrounds, and better educational qualifications than members of the intermediate classes; and members of the intermediate classes are similarly mostly superior to members of the subordinate classes. This is much as expected.

So there we had social class divisions within the organization itself, so one can imagine how much 'togetherness' that encouraged. Then, describing the general characteristics of our administrators they said:

Social origins is the most useful summary index of the complex of social forces, which impinge on the upbringing of an individual and which determine, through a chain of opportunities and acquired aspirations, the actual rather than the potential field of applicants, from which the Civil Service must select its recruits.

. . . The same process of social selection, which brings individuals to diverse occupational destinations, also fashions and maintains norms of outlook and shared assumptions amongst the members of the profession. The character of these tacit values and assumptions is surely of crucial importance in a profession such as the administrative class, which plays the vital role in the public management in the lives of all classes of society.

Candidates come then from this small select background, mainly middle class, educated mainly at public, private or direct grant schools. They are mainly middle class and they themselves, as they move up the ladder of promotion, will become the people who later will be performing the task of selecting new candidates for the future. Can it be doubted that the criterion they will use then will be the same criterion used by those selecting them?

It is small wonder, too, that while politically these people are said to have no direct affiliation to a political party, their whole background is so conservative in origin that their inclinations must be more to the Right than to the Left. There are liberal and progressive spirits amongst them, and often they stand out head and shoulders above the rest. But they have also often been side-tracked or promotion-blocked.

Without reform at the roots the vicious social circle will preserve the *status quo*. School, university, and parents' social background will stand for more than ability, while the clever ones from ordinary schools, ordinary universities, and from ordinary backgrounds will be continually put off from applying to become members of this élite group of people.

It was this influence that made it necessary to set up a Political Office at No. 10. This was a creation which was accepted by the succeeding Government. The post of Political Secretary was continued under Mr Heath. Yet the Political Office was an innovation in 1964. It was considered a useless luxury by many people. Even Ministers who had ready access to the Prime Minister, like George Wigg, the Paymaster General, felt it was so. George Wigg wanted the Civil Service to carry on all the work that was necessary and give all the advice needed. Yet what would have happened without the creation of a Political Office? Of course, the Prime Minister would have had regular contact with his senior colleagues. But inside No. 10 the only close advisers he would have had on a day-to-day basis would have been civil servants, mostly very senior men almost completely out of touch with Labour politicians and the Labour Party after thirteen years of uninterrupted Conservative government.

Of course, the Labour Party has a relationship of a sort with the civil servants, but it is a very different relationship from that which the Tory Party enjoys. Socially the Tories meet leading civil servants regularly, just as they meet other members of the Establishment. They encounter each other over luncheons, dinners and at cocktail parties. Sometimes they belong to the same clubs. Only comparatively few members of the Labour Party operate in the same circles, and the majority of Labour MPs have only a theoretical knowledge of this world.

All this means that the Tories don't only get co-operation when they take office. They also get it when they are not in government. Many Tory advisers have known the top civil servants for a long time. Not only do they belong to the same Metropolitan network but in some cases they are old friends from school or, more likely, Oxbridge. They have what the Fulton Committee described as the same 'shared assumptions' and 'tacit values' as the civil servants.

That is why Tory Prime Ministers view the Service so complacently, and this is why they have been happy with the set-up inside No. 10. Here is how Mr Harold Macmillan saw the position when he was Prime Minister:

The staff at the disposal of the Prime Minister has grown from the very meagre allowance enjoyed up to the First War and has considerably increased since then. Nevertheless, it is minute in comparison with that provided for the President of the United States, and doubtless to the heads of administration in other countries. It is still small, and during all my time remained so. Its strength depends upon the Private Office, as it is called, consisting of three or at the most four Private Secretaries of modest rank in the civil service, who can all sit together and understand what each one of them is doing. The Principal Private Secretary held the rank of Under-Secretary, the others of Principals. I was admirably served first by Freddie Bishop and later by Tim Bligh, at the head of this little group. Philip de Zulueta who dealt chiefly, though not exclusively, with Foreign Affairs, was a tower of strength and remained with me throughout. Others, especially Neil Cairncross, Tony Phelps and Philip Woodfield, dealt mainly with Home Affairs and were special masters in the art of answering Parliamentary Questions, including the essential 'Suggestions for Supplementaries'. Serving them were the Duty Clerks and what was called the 'Garden Rooms' – a series of admirable 'young ladies' (we inherited and confirmed Churchill's appellation), who were secretaries and typists of quite remarkable calibre. These were presided over by Miss S. A. Minto, of great experience and unswerving loyalty. To this list must be added the Parliamentary Secretary. I had in my time three – all devoted – Bobby Allen, Tony Barber and Knox Cunningham. This little staff, whether in London or at my own home in Sussex or at Chequers or on tour, gave me continued support and comfort as well as the most efficient service. I should add that I made in May 1957 an addition to the Private Secretaries in the person of John Wyndham (now Lord Egremont), who had served me in the Ministry of Supply, in the Colonial Office through-out the Mediterranean campaign, and in the Foreign Office. On and off he has helped me with his friendship and advice for a period of over twenty years. He acted without remuneration, but shared to the full in all the work.

Last, but by no means least in importance, was the official charged with what are euphemistically called 'public relations'. My Victorian predecessors would indeed have been puzzled and shocked by such an idea. Even in the first years of this century, the post was not officially recognised, whatever methods may have been used to secure the end in view. Today, with the vast extension of news – through the British, Commonwealth and Foreign Press, and through the new media of radio and television – it is important that those employed in these multifarious tasks should at least be given the facts. Propaganda is best left to Party organisations. But a Government has a right, as well as a duty, to secure that accurate information should be constantly available. I was indeed fortunate in obtaining the services of Harold Evans. He came at the start and served me to the end. He built up a remarkable reputation both for wisdom and candour. The 'lobby journalists' had complete confidence in his integrity. He trusted them; in return he earned their trust.

Parallel to the Downing Street staff, but not exclusive to the service of the Prime Minister, is the Cabinet Office. Its head acts as Secretary to the Cabinet, and he and his colleagues serve all Ministers alike. But necessarily, since all Cabinet papers are circulated by permission of the Prime Minister, and since all the various committees of Ministers, permanent and temporary, are set up only with the approval of the Prime Minister, the Secretary to the Cabinet acts in effect both as co-ordinator and friend in a very special degree. It was my good fortune to have from the beginning the outstanding services of Sir Norman Brook. When he retired in 1962 he was succeeded by Sir Burke Trend, who gave me equal support. This little band, with very few changes, were my colleagues and comrades throughout the whole adventure.*

This sort of set-up may well have been satisfactory to Harold Macmillan. But what he does not mention is that John Wyndham came in more as a political and personal adviser than a civil servant, even though he was described as an unpaid temporary civil servant. He had been at Conservative Central Office, and as someone who was not on the payroll of the Civil Service he was therefore not as accountable to them as he was to the man for whom he worked. His job was a personal one.

There was little difference between a 'John Wyndham' in 1963 and a 'Marcia Williams' in 1964. The only difference was that I was not a 'temporary civil servant unpaid', but someone whose salary was paid personally by the Prime Minister; I was called Political and Personal Secretary, even though I owed no accountability to Labour Party head-quarters. The difference was small indeed, yet the queries surrounding my job were to be far greater than any queries which arose from John Wyndham working at No. 10 Downing Street either at the time or afterwards. So much for Women's Lib.

One of our aims – largely unfulfilled – in setting up the Political Office was to produce a continuing political presence in No. 10. For the Conservative Party this need had already been met. They had John Wyndham in the Private Office, sitting in with the official Private Secretaries, fully informed and a party to everything that was done. They also had a young lady from Tory Central Office sitting downstairs in the

*Harold Macmillan: *Riding the Storm* (London 1971).

Garden Rooms, completely integrated with the Garden Girls, working as one of them. This girl was accountable to Central Office and did the political side of Harold Macmillan's work. How different to the outcry that went up when members were recruited for the Political Office after 1964. Queries were raised, questions were asked about the security aspects of enlisting people to do political work within No. 10. But nobody seemed to have queried the young lady's existence in the years of the Tory Government. She had been sitting in a highly sensitive area in the Garden Rooms. Our Political Office was situated in the Prime Minister's private quarters well away from any sensitive areas.

Harold Wilson thought in terms of improving the lower grades rather than the upper grades. He certainly never had it in mind when he first took office in 1964 to set up a small advisory unit within No. 10. That would have converted it into a power house, particularly if it had been incorporated into the Civil Service at a high level, each member holding a high rank in the Service, able to digest the civil servants' work on the policies put to them, and able also to initiate policy themselves.

Thomas Balogh had a Civil Service salary worked out after considerable consultation. This caused difficulties because his status was not clearly defined and he was not given a Civil Service rank, a high-level one, easily identifiable, acknowledged by every other member of the Service.

Knowing the Prime Minister's views and sensitivity about the problem, the civil servants were not slow to realize that if they wanted they could make it very heavy going for those who were brought in.

The outstanding example of this – though there were also examples in other government departments – was Thomas Balogh. To begin with Thomas had to engage in a continual fight with the Civil Service; a fight to establish himself within the set-up and to obtain all the information he needed to give the advice which the Prime Minister needed and which the Prime Minister could then relate to the other advice and information he received from the Service itself. It was often almost impossible for Thomas to receive all the Cabinet papers which he needed to read in order to be fully informed about what was going on. Only by recourse to the Prime Minister, so that instructions could be given and then carried out, was Thomas eventually to receive the papers he needed. But it required arguments, and then a direct approach to the Prime Minister.

All this came at times when the Prime Minister was more than a little occupied with the crises and problems of the day.

It is true, as Harold Wilson has himself said, that the first stages of the D Notice Affair were totally his decision. Many others who worked inside No. 10 are entitled to ask whether or not better advice could have been given to the Prime Minister thereafter. The worst example perhaps was the advice given to the Prime Minister not to be legally represented at the Select Committee's inquiry.

Any modern Prime Minister will realize that the 1970s require a self-contained top grade personal advisory unit within No. 10. This is more necessary for a progressive government than a Conservative government since the Conservatives can rely on the Civil Service being tuned in to what they want to do. But the Labour government must have a small core of highly qualified, highly expert individuals to initiate policy and ideas which can filter down through the machine. This unit should also assess decisions coming up through the machine via the departments for the Prime Minister's approval. This is what a Labour government for the future must have and it should start planning such a unit now.

It is also absolutely essential that the Labour Party should undertake the education of their own political staff at Transport House and elsewhere about the workings of the Civil Service. There must be no gap in the knowledge about this in the future. In 1964 few of our people knew much about it nor how it worked. They were unaware of how much it could obstruct the course of work they were engaged upon. There can be no excuse for such ignorance in future. All who are likely to be involved in the work of a future Labour government must be educated in the workings of the administrative machine, so that they may know immediately just what channels they can use and how they can get their ideas through to the right person or persons.

Let us not again be nervous or embarrassed by the suggestion. What Harold Macmillan could do before 1964, and what

Edward Heath, Sir Alec Douglas-Home and a number of others have done after 1970, should also be done by us. Conservatives have had no qualms about introducing many Tory Central Office people into various departments. Labour should follow their example and start earmarking eager, enthusiastic, able young men and women to be trained in the work they must do when they accompany future Ministers into the departments. Their function must be to ensure that political assessments of policy can be as accurate and as good as the flow of Civil Service advice. The liaison between No. 10, the departments and Transport House must also be perfected.

The other main problem on which the Labour Government failed was the question of how to ensure continuing economic success. Success can only be based, as increasingly large numbers of people now recognize, on an agreement between all sections of the community, the most important being between the Trade Union movement and the government of the day on an incomes policy related also to prices.

It is true that when Labour took office in 1964 its leaders had already formulated policies on every major question that they thought required action. Before 1964 there is no doubt that there was a tacit agreement, or appeared to be one, between certain sections of the Trade Union movement and Labour leaders about the need for certain action – if not an incomes policy, then certainly a declaration of intent which would be meaningful in real terms. The Leader of the Party made a number of speeches on the question outlining such a requirement. It was an agreement with the Trade Union movement which would bring them in return a growing social equality and redistribution of wealth.

What was never formulated, however, was a properly agreed incomes policy; a policy which had been fully thrashed out within individual unions, agreed with the TUC, and confirmed with the Labour Party. It is naïve to expect that this could be brought about easily. However, if it is the case that the Trade Union movement forms a large party of the Labour movement, and is indeed at the very heart of it, the industrial part of the movement will eventually have to face the fact that the survival of a Labour government in this country must depend upon such an agreement. Only a meaningful agreement will make it possible for a Labour government to move forward with its economic policies, with socialist measures and not borrowed or amended Conservative ones, based on the knowledge that they are backed by the Trade Union movement and by a reasoned incomes policy. Such an agreement would make it possible in difficult times to solve the crises which arise and would help to create the conditions and the wealth output and production to produce the other side of the coin, namely the greater social equality and redistribution of wealth which the Trade Union movement rightly expects to see in the years ahead.

But what happened after 1964? The National Plan that emerged in 1965 had all the ingredients of the balanced package that a Trade Union movement would expect from a Labour government, but still missing was the essential which could make a success and sense of all the Labour Government was trying to do.

One handicap was that Labour leaders underestimated the seriousness of the situation existing in 1964. They did not think it was as bad as it was. They were only aware of the reality after they took office. On that fateful day, 16 October, when Harold Wilson entered the Cabinet Room and was told the full facts, there dawned the realization that he was really out on his own. There was no real backing from the one section of the community on which he depended for survival.

Believing that the situation was bad but not frightening, Labour leaders expected that while having to use Tory financial and monetary policies during a short initial phase, they would quickly be able to right the situation, turn the balance of payments deficit into a surplus, and move forward to greater production and output to give the wealth needed for all the other things they wanted to do.

But they found the £800 million deficit far too big a figure to turn so quickly. They also found that the repeated runs on sterling, for whatever reasons they may have occurred, aggravated the situation to such an extent that any headway they might make in one direction was soon lost by the speculation. They moved from crisis to crisis and spent so much time solving the crises as they went along that their minds were totally dominated by this. They became psychologically tuned in to crises rather than tuned in to success. When they formulated their prices and incomes policy, it was not in the right mood. It is small wonder that its reception by the Labour movement, and the body which had to approve it, the Trade Union movement, was greeted with less enthusiasm than might possibly have been the case if there had been homework done before the 1964 election.

Still, the lesson appears to have been learned. I doubt very much whether there are Labour leaders left now who don't realize that the first need for them is to come to an agreement with the Trade Union movement beforehand. Their whole attitude has become one of thrashing the whole problem out with the leaders of the big Trade Unions ahead of Government and trying to find common grounds on which they can agree so that a back-up policy will be there to provide, if necessary, the main thread in stabilizing the economic situation, enabling growth.

What is iniquitous on looking back is that so much mud was flung at the Trade Union movement for strikes, lack of cooperation, and for all the other actions that arose from disappointment and disillusionment. The Tory Press never attacked speculators for being unpatriotic or unreliable. Nor is there any attack on management when our national newspapers discuss quite dispassionately whether or not management is going to invest, even though it is pointed out that our economic future depends on such investment. No one asks the question whether management should not behave in a patriotic fashion and take risks and gambles as part of its national duty? The answer presumably is that it is their money that they are putting at risk. But for organized labour their capital rests in the work they can perform. They have an equal right, surely, to argue about whether or not they should put it at risk or gamble it in ventures of which they disapprove. It is no more illogical for them to use the strike weapon or any other argument based upon the only capital they possess, their labour, than it is to use the argument that investment in Britain can only take place if patriotic businessmen with capital feel that they can take the risk of investing in their country's future.

So there were failures during the Labour Government, failures of policy, failures of tactics, and some failures which were built in, predestined almost, stemming inevitably from the situation in which the Government took office. But what of its achievements which were large enough and important enough and lasting enough to make it an historic Government?

First of all there were the Government's economic achievements – even though its successes were not only in the economic field. Our five and a half years seem to have been dominated by getting the balance of payments right. But the Government did get it right in the end. It was a dramatic achievement; even though it was written down by every Conservative newspaper. The deficit that was discovered in 1964 to be nearing £800 million had been transformed by 1970 into a surplus of £600 million and with this came the prospects of having ever-increasing successes on that front. That was the one great achievement Labour handed over to the British nation. It should have provided the country with a release from the burden of always looking over its shoulder to see whether the balance of payments was all right. But the Heath administration frittered away this priceless inheritance in less than two years.

Today Britain has moved away from the world where these things seemed to be a matter of total concern. The country is moving into an international atmosphere where they are losing their importance or significance. Even devaluation as a weapon is gradually becoming less of an immoral act now everyone does it. It is just another event in international financial life.

But the Labour Government's main achievements for me are those which relate more to the transformation in the quality of British life.

Those thirteeen years of Tory rule from 1951 to 1964 saw a growing distortion in values and priorities in this country. Materialism was the new god. Social capital, upon which a nation's real well-being depends, became increasingly neglected.

Professor Galbraith's famous old quotation about 'public squalor and private affluence' began to apply to Tory Britain as well as the United States. Consumer goods, washing machines, refrigerators, television sets and the rest were more highly regarded than investment in public health, education, houses, roads and all the other things that Britain needs.

Perhaps the worst area of growing concern was housing. It

was not just the shortage of housing, though that was real enough. By 1963 one million families were without homes of their own. There were at least one million slum dwellings awaiting demolition. Over two and a half million houses lacked the basic amenities of hot water supply and bath. The over-all deficiency was between two to three million homes.

But shortage was just one thing. The vicious developments in the housing market added grievously to the problem. After their victory in 1951, the Tories moved towards free market policies in housing, just as they did after the 1970 election win. Their 1957 Rent Act, setting the landlords free, became one of the notorious Acts in our post-war social history. Thousands of families were to suffer as a direct result of its implementation. There were evictions, homelessness and exploitation, but even worse was the disturbing violence and intimidation as Rachmanism flourished in the new free-for-all world created by the Tories in housing. Those years were not quickly forgotten by those who suffered as a result of the 1957 Rent Act. When Harold Wilson referred later to it at meetings throughout the country, and to the Labour Government's abolition of that Act, he was always greeted with a roar of applause.

A free market there may well have been, for house and rent prices soared, often being pushed up beyond the level that an ordinary family could afford. Yet it was not complemented by the necessary development in more house building, particularly by local authorities, where it was most needed. We have been told often enough of the Tory record in their good years. But few quote the bad years as well.

The area where socialists saw the greatest Tory insensitivity and lack of awareness of real priorities was in social security. Old age pensioners were particularly neglected, and incomes for many had been falling well below subsistence levels, mainly because they were too proud to expose themselves to the means test operated by the Tory Government which might have given them additional benefits under the National Assistance scheme. It was the same story for widows, the sick and those on unemployment benefits, the disabled, families with low incomes; all were inadequately provided for, all fell rapidly behind in the rat-race for material affluence.

Yet it was not just the direct benefit or lack of it that affected people. It was the social stigma too, that often accompanied it. Those less fortunate felt like second-class citizens and the Tory Government made no effort to put this right.

This distortion of the priorities by which a community should be organized is the picture of Tory Britain in 1964. Yet my criticism still omits the class divisions of that time. It omits too the great basic need for industrial modernization, for the modernization of our communication links, and the modernization of our ways of thinking, not only as a nation but individually too.

But personal freedom never comes without economic freedom, and the Tory years never produced that kind of economic freedom which would have given the majority the confidence to make the personal choices in life that we are increasingly taking for granted now.

But what did Labour do? Well, Francis Hope, contributor to the left-wing *New Statesman*, dismissed six years of hard effort in the following sharp sentence in the *New York Times*: 'The achievements of the Labour Government were mostly minor acts of decency.' I am amazed both at his confidence and his casualness. I wonder how many journalists bother to ascertain all the facts before they dash off the odd dismissive phrase.

The Labour Government in fact achieved the greatest shift ever in the balance of government expenditure between vital domestic needs and overseas spending. Under a succession of deeply committed reforming Ministers, social services in this country were transformed. As far as national expenditure was concerned, the social services became a priority area. Before Labour took office more was spent on defence than on education. Over the years this changed, with defence claiming less in terms of public expenditure than either the social services or education. Our first priority was to increase the share of resources devoted to health and welfare.

Despite serious economic difficulties the balance slowly altered. The change in priorities came and the distortions in those areas identified in 1964 altered. Of course, it is true that in doing this, and with increasing national prosperity, there came other distortions with minority groups becoming sharply underprivileged as the years went on. But these were problems we were already beginning to plan for and to tackle by the time we lost office.

In the health field the hospital building programme was more than doubled after 1964. Nursing staff received a fairer deal. Greater attention began to be shifted, too, to mental health and to the improvement of health and welfare services.

In housing the first thing was to get rid of the Rent Act of 1957, which we did. Then action was directed towards giving protection to our people. Labour's 1965 Housing Act brought security of tenure, freedom from harassment and a fair rent machinery. Council rents were carefully watched and the Minister responsible had the powers to refuse excessive rent increases.

There was help, too, for householders with low incomes; with our rate rebate scheme. In 1968 over one million people were already beginning to benefit by more than £15 million a year from rate relief.

To help more people to own their own homes we introduced an option mortgage scheme and 100% mortgages to go with it. This helped those who could not afford a deposit on a house, only the repayments.

Our house building record, despite its critics, was impressive when looked at against the background of economic crisis and lack of funds we operated in. Nearly two million new homes were built in Britain after 1964. Public expenditure on housing increased by 70% during the last full year of the Labour Government. We built over 300,000 more houses than the Tories did in their last four years of office. We achieved an increase of 40% in local authority house building and we increased building by private owners by nearly 13%. The 222,000 private houses built in 1968 was the highest figure since the war. Slum clearance also proceeded at record rates compared with the years of the Tory Government.

The shift in priorities and expenditure covered education too. A great scheme to reorganize secondary education on comprehensive lines was set in train, bringing with it expanding educational opportunities for schoolchildren. Gradually we were reducing educational apartheid and getting rid, too, of the detested 11-plus selection system.

School building increased and higher education, particularly on the technological side, was given a greater boost.

The showpiece was perhaps the Open University, Harold's

own invention using television and radio to make it possible for many to obtain qualifications until then only gained at educational institutions. The Open University is now providing degree and diploma courses comparable with those from residential universities. This was one of the most imaginative ways of expanding educational opportunities at higher levels.

The most urgent area needing attention was, needless to say, in the field of social security.

Labour attempted a number of reforms here. There was first the measures to give immediate relief to those living on low incomes. This was done with increased old age pension rates, supplementary benefit rates, widow's pension, unemployment and sickness benefits. The earnings rule was relaxed too, not only for the pensioners, but for the widow as well, enabling them to keep more of the money allowed to them. The period during which the widow was given an allowance to help her resettle after her husband's death was extended from thirteen weeks to six months. Benefits to war widows and industrial injuries widows were also increased to keep in line with other national insurance benefits. Family allowances were increased.

Then the system needed modernizing, both immediately and for the future. Immediately, the most important act was the abolition of the National Assistance Board and its replacement by an integrated Ministry of Social Security with a Supplementary Benefits Commission operating within that department. This saw that people received the benefits to which they were entitled when their incomes dropped below a certain level, or when their needs required additional help from the State, particularly in the case of illness or other special circumstances. The new supplementary benefits scheme was not just a change of name, it was a change in the whole attitude towards State help. The whole image of benefits changed with the introduction of this new system, and the stigma of being on National Assistance was removed. Far more people now felt able to come forward and claim additional benefit where previously pride had prevented them from undergoing all the rigours of a means test and the old stigma which had been attached to being on National Assistance. The same book was now used for claiming either benefit.

To help all those thrown out of work there was the introduction of the Redundancy Payment Act. This gave a lump sum compensation relating to service to those affected by redundancy. This was intended to help the transition for workers from one job to another, but of course in days of high unemployment, particularly under the Heath administration, the Redundancy Payment Act, together with many of the other benefits, including unemployment benefits, introduced by Labour during its years of office, has helped to fashion a cushioning system which prevents the immediate feeling of hardship which otherwise would have been experienced by those thrown out of work in such large numbers, and who would have had to suffer the indignity of not being able to provide for themselves.

These are only a few of the main measures which Labour undertook to correct the trend of priorities which had become so distorted under Tory rule. Only by looking back, however, and recording the sense of priorities the Conservatives set themselves, and the balance they gave between social capital and material capital in the country, can one get any realization at all of what the Labour Government achieved, nor can anyone anticipate without such a backward look what can very well develop now in the years ahead with the present Conservative Government in office.

The Labour Government was proud of the record it had in liberating great areas of Britain's life. One of the greatest areas for reform was in our old-fashioned rules and customs. During the years of the Labour Government more law reform was carried out in four years under the supervision of Gerald Gardiner, one of the greatest Lord Chancellors this country has had, than in any other four years in the century.

The Criminal Justice Bill presented to Parliament during the Labour Government saw the biggest overhaul of our criminal law and procedure we had had for a long time. Young people were given the vote at eighteen, the Honours system and the working of Parliament were reformed, and the office of Parliamentary Commissioner or Ombudsman was created to bring protection to the individual against abuses he might feel he had suffered at the hands of a government department.

There were, too, new and enlightened attitudes about

questions where personal liberty and individualism were concerned. Many Labour MPs, rightly expressing the views of the electorate, were reluctant about some of the changes which came into force; but nevertheless there is no doubt that the abolition of capital punishment, homosexuality law reform, abortion law reform and the abolition of theatre censorship all formed part of the liberating process over which the Labour Government presided.

While the main working architect was, of course, Roy Jenkins at the Home Office, the Prime Minister could either have encouraged the campaign for reform or sided with those who thought we moved too fast. He kept a careful watching brief. However, it is a fascinating fact that a surprisingly large number of people within the Cabinet and within the Government were against the reforms that were carried out.

The election of the Government coincided with the highly-publicized arrival of youth as one of the greatest forces for change in this country. Young people now emerged as a result of economic independence, high employment in the early 1960s, and high wages. This economic independence meant that fashion was largely dictated by them as well as taste and style in music, in films, in the theatre, in literature and in the arts generally. The 'Mersey Sound', which started in Liverpool with the Beatles, erupted in London and spread outwards to become internationally famous. The new sound and its followers were representative of the new revolution amongst youth in Britain.

Young people in the sixties wanted more out of life than the stereotyped restrictive conservative background against which their parents had had to live. It was over this sort of scene that the Wilson Government had to preside. It was to Harold Wilson's credit that as the representative of the ordinary man, understanding the aims and aspirations not only of his own age group, but of the young as well, he tried to change society in Britain, to widen opportunities, and generally to give effect to what was increasingly wanted.

He has been criticized for the style of entertaining he indulged in at No. 10. It was his view that those in our national life who were most representative of it, no matter what walk of life they came from, should be allowed to participate at a national level. It was because of this that the dinners and receptions at No. 10 gradually changed. When the Government took office the style of entertaining was rooted in the past. It was organized mainly by the Foreign Office and was very Establishment and unimaginative. Those present at the dinners, and the few invited to the receptions afterwards, were mostly representatives from the Civil Service, industry and finance, with a few trade unionists thrown in to make it look good.

No one ever bothered to ask a visiting VIP what sort of people he wanted to meet in Britain, or whether he had any particular preferences or which members of the Government or Parliament he would like to meet. The dinners I attended at the beginning were stiff and formal, the conversation was quiet, subdued, desultory and very limited. By the end of the Labour Government the parties, however heavily criticized in the Press, were lively, gay and interesting. It is not true that only 'pop' people were invited along. Each guest list for receptions and dinners given by the Prime Minister was a balanced list. Those representing the popular arts were balanced by those representing the more serious arts. There were scientists, professional people of all kinds, nurses, ambulance men, school-teachers, miners, weavers, farm workers all invited along to 10 Downing Street to meet visiting dignitaries. Harold Wilson tried to include a cross-section of British people so that an overseas statesman might see for himself those who had achieved excellence in their own profession and those who represented the real Britain, not just the hybrid, sophisticated and exclusive Establishment in London.

Herr Willy Brandt met soldiers from the Berlin garrison. The Rumanians met those who had been engaged in selling a large irrigation scheme in Rumania.

Many foreign visitors were particularly keen to meet those who appeared in the BBC's *Forsyte Saga*, because it had been shown all over the world. Small wonder that Eric Porter felt he almost lived at No. 10 because he was asked for so often. All the *Forsyte* stars were enormously popular.

When the first men to set foot on the moon were entertained at Downing Street, great care was taken to invite along those to whom it would have the greatest meaning – children. Although it had to be organized at the last moment, schoolchildren from schools in the London area came to No. 10 to meet the moon-men. They had a marvellous time. Indeed, so carried away were they (and we too, by the sheer excitement on their faces), that we did not have the heart to stop them whisking the odd glass of champagne off a waiter's tray and consuming it behind a large vase of flowers or a door. The children became very high spirited and left the building thrilled to have been given such a unique opportunity. Some of them were disabled, and one was a blind boy whom Harold had met in Liverpool and with whom he has kept in touch, Kevin Carey. Kevin has gone on now to Cambridge University and has become President of the Cambridge Union.

There were, too, the receptions given for the paraplegics, organized through the Stoke Mandeville Hospital. To these parties were invited entertainers who Harold wanted to act as hosts for the occasion and give them all an enjoyable evening. This they did.

One has only to look at a guest list for the early years, and compare it with a guest list for one of the later years, to see what a change Harold Wilson achieved in making functions at No. 10 Downing Street more representative of people to whom the building, after all, really belongs. It is too often the attitude of politicians and people in Whitehall that Parliament, No. 10 and the Departments of State belong to the Establishment, not the people. In fact they belong to those who have to pay for them, namely the taxpayers, the general public. There is no reason why entertainment at No. 10 should not be widened out to include the general public, so that they may, too, have the opportunity of meeting special people invited from overseas and of seeing at first hand the institutions and the buildings which they have to support.

On one occasion the Private Office was a little worried in case the numbers grew so much that the floors of the State Rooms would not be equal to the demands upon them. One of the facts of entertaining is that it is the rule to over-invite, rather than under-invite, since many people will have to decline because of prior commitments. However, after a period, and particularly when a lot of publicity had been given to some of the parties, we found that there were hardly ever any refusals and mostly everyone turned up. We were delighted to see them all, to have the opportuinity of meeting people we had admired for a long time like Iris Murdoch, Dame Barbara Hepworth, Dame Sybil Thorndyke, Daniel Barenboim and Jacqueline du Pré, Colin Davis, Paul Schofield, Laurence Olivier, John Mills, Stanley Baker, Sean Connery, not for 007 roles alone, but as a distinguished, much admired actor, and Morecambe and Wise. Here in the guest lists was some indication of the Labour Government's attitude to the arts, but this support was not confined to invitations to No. 10. The grant to the Arts Council was the highest ever in 1968/9, the last full year of the Labour Government. It was £7.75 millions, representing a 184.% increase over the figure of £2.7 millions given by the Conservative Government in their last full year, 1963/4.

The arts were also recognized in the Honours list which the Prime Minister always helped to compile. Again he tried to include a cross-section of the whole country. He was much criticized for those cases where unfortunate publicity surrounded the recipient. Some of the sports which were considered to be barely acceptable in Establishment circles became increasingly recognized in the Honours lists.

The total style of Harold Wilson was one of involvement with the ordinary people of whom he and his Government were so representative. Everyone in the country, whatever his job or status, was to be involved, as he saw it, in the nation's life. The Wilson style became one of self-identification. Everyone could identify himself with his Government, the ordinary as well as the extraordinary. The relaxed, informal, casual, direct-contact style which was manifested most of all in entertainment and in Harold Wilson's tours of the country, meeting vast numbers of people in industry and in social welfare projects, was combined with great intellectualism and expertise in many other areas where enormous achievements were recorded to our credit.

This contribution, this liberation of so much within our nation, was the greatest contribution Harold Wilson could have made during that period. He opened up vast areas of our social life, liberated vast areas and helped free the country from the inhibiting effects of class consciousness and social segregation. The Wilson years saw an ever-increasing speeding up of this process in which individual expertise became increasingly appreciated.

But it was the era too, when the consensus in British politics reached total acceptance. Now, of course, it has become the fashionable approach to regard consensus politics as something to be disliked. The harsh, abrasive policies being pursued by the present Tory Government are considered to be far better for the community than 'the consensus'.

Despite all the criticisms which have been made, there were achievements in international affairs. Personally I would have liked to have seen the Labour Government dissociate itself from the United States on their Vietnam policy, but I understand and accept the reasons why it was not possible to do this.

On Rhodesia again, while I disagreed with the policy adopted and would have liked to have seen force applied, I admire the way in which Harold Wilson was to gain a consensus agreement in this country on Rhodesia, bearing in mind the very great popularity Ian Smith enjoyed here.

On the Common Market, although I personally am not a pro-European, I supported throughout the policies which Harold Wilson adopted at No. 10. I felt, as he did, that we should at least find out what the Europeans were offering.

The consensus is the only way in which to run a country like Great Britain. Here reasonable compromise is the way in which we have usually conducted our national life. There is no point in causing dissension and hardship unless it is unavoidable, unless it is wrong not to do so. What is certain is that the British public will want to see a return of consensus politics again, away from the hard, unfeeling attitudes which are now becoming widespread.

The pendulum swings, no matter how long it takes to do so. The next Labour Government will be much more aware of the pitfalls awaiting it, and of the preparations it must make before it takes on the task of governing again. The Establishment should be warned that it cannot rely next time on ignorance or seduction to help it fight off change and progress in order to maintain a *status quo* that is the vehicle for its private well-being.

But what sort of a situation will the next Labour Government find? One thing is certain. The political and the industrial arms of the movement will have to reach an agreement before it takes office. Then, with that agreement on how to achieve the aims and ideals to which both sides are dedicated, with both arms making concessions, we should have a formidable socialist government capable of remaining in office for twenty years and producing greater progress and reform, more social equality and a fairer distribution of wealth and income than we have ever experienced before.

Then we should see the emergence of the truly egalitarian society that we have talked about so much but never achieved. Then, perhaps, we should see women released from the confines inherent in the present economic situation.

And the people who can achieve this, and who almost certainly will achieve this, are the young people of today. I base my hopes on them. They are the ones who create fashions and set the pace. It is no good any party trying to tell them what they must think or what they must do. They want to discover first hand what life is all about and what suits them. But – and this is an important political fact – they appear to have a greater sense of community responsibility and a greater sense of feeling for their fellow human beings than any previous generation.

If this sense of community responsibility continues, and if individuals have the opportunity to express themselves fully, liberated from economic and social restrictions, then we have the best chance we have ever had to establish a really just and valuable society. That was the aim of the last Labour Government and I believe it will be the achievement of the next one.

Index

INDEX

5.17